The Tragedy of Optimism

SUNY Series in Contemporary Jewish Thought
Richard A. Cohen, editor

The Tragedy of Optimism

Writings on Hermann Cohen

Steven S. Schwarzschild

Edited by George Y. Kohler

SUNY PRESS

Cover art: Sabine Kahane, "Portrait of the Young Hermann Cohen" (2017)

Published by State University of New York Press, Albany

© 2018 State University of New York

All rights reserved

No part of this book may be used or reproduced in any manner whatsoever without written permission. No part of this book may be stored in a retrieval system or transmitted in any form or by any means including electronic, electrostatic, magnetic tape, mechanical, photocopying, recording, or otherwise without the prior permission in writing of the publisher.

For information, contact State University of New York Press, Albany, NY
www.sunypress.edu

Production, Diane Ganeles
Marketing, Kate R. Seburyamo

Library of Congress Cataloging-in-Publication Data

Names: Schwarzschild, Steven S., author. | Kohler, George Y., editor.
Title: The tragedy of optimism : writings on Hermann Cohen / by Steven S. Schwarzschild ; edited by George Y. Kohler.
Description: Albany, New York : State University of New York Press, [2018] | Series: SUNY series in contemporary Jewish thought | Includes bibliographical references and index.
Identifiers: LCCN 2017011557 (print) | LCCN 2017012797 (ebook) | ISBN 9781438468372 (e-book) | ISBN 9781438468358 (hardcover   ) | 9781438468365 (paperback   )
Subjects: LCSH: Cohen, Hermann, 1842-1918. | Jewish philosophy.
Classification: LCC B5800 (ebook) | LCC B5800 .S35 2017 (print) | DDC 181/.06--dc23
LC record available at https://lccn.loc.gov/2017011557

10 9 8 7 6 5 4 3 2 1

Contents

PREFACE • vii
George Y. Kohler

ACKNOWLEDGMENTS • xi

INTRODUCTION • xiii
George Y. Kohler

CHAPTER 1 • 1
The Democratic Socialism of Hermann Cohen (1956)

CHAPTER 2 • 23
To Recast Rationalism (1962/1970)

CHAPTER 3 • 29
Truth: The Connection between Logic and Ethics (1966)

CHAPTER 4 • 33
The Day of Atonement (1968)

CHAPTER 5 • 35
Franz Rosenzweig's Anecdotes about Hermann Cohen (1970)

CHAPTER 6 • 43
The Torah Radicalizes on Many Levels (1972)

CHAPTER 7 • 49
Historical Excursus: On Cohen's *Infinitesimal-Methode*

CHAPTER 8 • 61
Applications of the Infinitesimalistic Theory in "the System"

CHAPTER 9 • 69
The Tenability of Hermann Cohen's Construction of the Self (1975)

CHAPTER 10 • 93
"Germanism and Judaism"—Hermann Cohen's Normative Paradigm of the German-Jewish Symbiosis (1979)

CHAPTER 11 • 119
Ethics of the Pure Will—Introduction (1981)

CHAPTER 12 • 141
The Title of Hermann Cohen's *Religion of Reason out of the Sources of Judaism* (1986)

CHAPTER 13 • 151
History of the *Religion of Reason*: Part II of the Introduction

CHAPTER 14 • 165
The Theologico-Political Basis of Liberal Christian-Jewish Relations in Modernity (1986)

CHAPTER 15 • 185
The Religious Stake in Modern Philosophy of Infinity (1987)

CHAPTER 16 • 197
Book Reviews

- 197 • Samuel Atlas, *From Critical to Speculative Idealism: The Philosophy of Salomon Maimon* (1966)

- 202 • William Kluback, *Hermann Cohen—The Challenge of a Religion of Reason* (1987)

- 204 • Mechthild Dreyer, *Die Idee Gottes im Werk Hermann Cohens* (1989)

EPILOGUE • 209
Entry on "Cohen, Hermann" in the *Encyclopedia of Religion* (ed. Mircea Eliade) (1987)

NOTES • 215

INDEX OF NAMES • 305

Preface

Almost thirty years ago, when Steven S. Schwarzschild was still alive, Menachem Kellner published with State University of New York Press an important volume, *The Pursuit of the Ideal: Jewish Writings of Steven Schwarzschild*.[1] This collection of articles, however, excluded all essays Schwarzschild had written on the Jewish thinker he himself deemed the most important of all: Hermann Cohen. Of course, Cohen played a significant role in the *Pursuit* volume, but Schwarzschild's numerous writings dedicated *exclusively* to Cohen's philosophical thought did not find a place in this book. I hope it was Steven Schwarzschild's idea to publish those essays in a separate volume, but I am certain that he saw the thought of Cohen as considerably wider than what in general counts as "Jewish Writings." After all, Schwarzschild has written on Cohen's neo-Kantian ethics as well as on Cohen's mathematical theories of the infinite, or on Cohen's conception of human selfhood.

In an extensive 1992 academic review of the Kellner volume, Schwarzschild's friend Norbert M. Samuelson wrote, "In general, Schwarzschild was a disciple and advocate of the philosophy of Immanuel Kant as interpreted and expanded by Hermann Cohen. How original his own interpretation of this tradition is cannot be assessed here. This judgment awaits the publication of his work on Cohen, which must be evaluated in direct relationship to the writings of Kant, Cohen, and their disciples in the so-called 'Marburg' tradition, most notably, Ernst Cassirer and Samuel Atlas."[2]

The present volume, at long last, will attempt to answer at least Samuelson's first request, the publication of Schwarzschild's writings on Cohen; the second, the judgment, will hopefully be based on the reception of this book. Another reason for publishing this collection was probably noticed by all students of Schwarzschild's interpretation of Cohen: many of his essays were originally published at the most inaccessible places, in odd conference volumes of the German Liberal Party, or in an out-of-print Festschrift for the Jewish Community of Berlin, among others. I have therefore collected here, as I hope, all of Schwarzschild's texts that deal either exclusively or to a large extent with Cohen's philosophy: research articles, book reviews, encyclopedia entries, introductions to works by Cohen, and more popular smaller pieces of thought.

The present volume includes two previously unpublished manuscripts by Schwarzschild: one is the extended version of his introduction to Cohen's posthumous *Religion of Reason out of the Sources of Judaism* (1918), of which only the first section was printed with the second edition of the English translation of the book in 1995. Schwarzschild, in fact, wrote three more sections about the philosophical, social, and the reception history of the *Religion of Reason*, which are published here for the first time.[3] In addition, my collection includes two parts of an unfinished manuscript by Schwarzschild on Cohen's early work in the philosophy of mathematics "Das Princip der Inifinitesimal-Methode und seine Geschichte" (1883), as I found them in Schwarzschild's literary remains.[4] Another part of this manuscript is in the hands of Prof. Robert Gibbs in Toronto. It seems, unfortunately, that the full version is lost. Traces of it can be found, however, in an extraordinary chapter on Cohen in Norbert Samuelson's "An introduction to Modern Jewish Philosophy"[5] who used Schwarzschild's manuscript to portray Cohen almost exclusively as a philosopher of mathematics.[6]

The order of the texts is chronological, although the subjects of Cohen's thought discussed here by Schwarzschild range, as mentioned earlier, from mathematics, socialism, neo-Kantian ethics, human selfhood to what might be called more "Jewish ideas" of Cohen and their reception in the Jewish and non-Jewish world. But since Schwarzschild was honest enough to openly point out several changes of his mind regarding his interpretation and appreciation of Cohen, the chronological order was more appropriate for the reader to follow this development in Schwarzschild's thinking—from outright criticism in his youth to an unshakable philosophical love of Cohen in the mature writings of Schwarzschild on his mentor. Intentionally, I refrained from publishing excerpts from Schwarzschild's unpublished dissertation on Cohen (and Nachman Krochmal), assuming this was not in Schwarzschild's interest because he has never published this text himself. Also, from a scholarly point of view, it is my opinion that the dissertation would not add new aspects of Schwarzschild's reading of Cohen.

I have in most cases left Schwarzschild's often extensive notes and references unchanged, even if there was now newer research available on the subject mentioned. At some points I have corrected wrong or insufficient references, however, or added what I thought Schwarzschild intended to refer his reader to, especially in the works of Cohen himself. I have given the titles of Cohen's untranslated German language works in German, where Schwarzschild usually refers to them with his own translation of their titles into English (i.e., *Logic of Pure Cognition*). I have added references to respective volumes of the new academic *Werke* edition of the works of Cohen,[7] where Schwarzschild referred to the original books. In most cases, the *Werke* edition presents reprints—where the page numbers differ (*Kleinere Schriften*, volumes 12–17), I have given the page numbers of the *Werke* edition.

My colleagues Reinier Munk and Robert Gibbs are working on a multivolume edition of Schwarzschild's collected works. My book is aimed at people interested in Hermann Cohen, and their book will be aimed at people interested in Schwarzschild; thus we are reaching for two different audiences. It is likely that the two projects will complement each other, and that each will stimulate interest in the other. Schwarzschild was sometimes criticized for not having published a single monograph during his lifetime. But as we know today, he left behind several highly interesting book manuscripts at his untimely death in 1989: a work on "Heidegger and Rosenzweig," a book on "Jewish Meta-Ethics," and others. Certainly, those manuscripts will soon be published by Munk and Gibbs, as those texts deserve it. Surprisingly, none of Schwarzschild's unpublished books contain longer, substantial material on Hermann Cohen. Therefore, here too, the two book projects do not seem to stand in each other's way.

I would like to thank Menachem Kellner for encouraging me to undertake this project, after I presented him the idea a few years ago. Menachem also brought me in contact with Maimon Schwarzschild of San Diego, Steven's son, who was of immeasurable help for the entire project.

— George Y. Kohler

Acknowledgments

Previously published portions of this book are reprinted with permission of the copyright holders. Every effort has been made to contact the entities that hold copyright. Any copyright holders the editor was unable to reach are encouraged to contact the publisher.

"The Democratic Socialism of Hermann Cohen," in *Hebrew Union College Annual* 27 (1956), 417–438.
"To Recast Rationalism," in *Judaism*, 11 (1962) 205–209, again in: *Arguments and Doctrines, a Reader of Jewish Thinking in the Aftermath of the Holocaust* (ed. Arthur A. Cohen), Philadelphia: Jewish Publication Society of America, (1970) 191–196.
Introduction to Schwarzschild's translation of *Truth: The Connection between Logic and Ethics*, taken from Hermann Cohen's *Ethik des reinen Willens*, in *Judaism* 15 (1966), 466–473.
Introduction to Schwarzschild's translation of *Day of Atonement* taken from Hermann Cohen's *Religion der Vernunft aus den Quellen des Judentums*, in *Judaism* 17 (1968), 352–357.
"Franz Rosenzweig's Anecdotes about Hermann Cohen," in *Gegenwart im Rückblick: Festgabe für die Jüdische Gemeinde zu Berlin 25 Jahre nach dem Neubeginn*, ed. H.A. Strauss and K.R. Grossman, Lothar Stiehm Verlag, Heidelberg (1970), 209–218
"The Torah radicalizes on many Levels," in *Sh'ma - A Journal of Jewish Ideas*, April 31, 1972, 84–87.
"The Tenability of Hermann Cohen's Construction of the Self," in *Journal of the History of Philosophy* 13:3 (1975), 361–384. © 1975 Journal of the History of Philosophy, Inc. Reprinted with permission of Johns Hopkins University Press.
"Germanism and Judaism - Hermann Cohen's Normative Paradigm of the German-Jewish Symbiosis," in *Jews and Germans from 1860–1933* ed. D. Bronsen, Universitäts Verlag Carl Winter, Heidelberg (1979), 142–154.

Introduction to the 1981 reprint of Hermann Cohen's *Ethik des reinen Willens*, in Hermann Cohen, *Werke*, vol. 7, Olms, Hildesheim (1981), VII–XXXV.

"The Title of Hermann Cohen's: *Religion of Reason* out of the Sources of Judaism," in *The Life of Covenant, The Challenge of Contemporary Judaism: Essays in Honor of Herman E. Schaalman*, ed. Joseph A. Edelheit, Spertus College of Judaica Press, Chicago (1986) p. 207–220, reprinted with the 2nd edition of the English translation of Religion der Vernunft: Hermann Cohen, *Religion of Reason out or the Sources of Judaism*, (trans. S. Kaplan), Scholars Press, Atlanta (1995), 7–20.

"The Theologico-Political Basis of Liberal Christian-Jewish Relations in Modernity," in *Das deutsche Judentum und der Liberalismus*, Dokumentation eines internationalen Seminars der Friedrich-Naumann-Stiftung in Zusammenarbeit mit dem Leo Baeck Institute, London Comdok-Verlagsabteilung, Schriften der Friedrich-Naumann-Stiftung, St. Augustin (1986), 70–95.

"The Religious Stake in Modern Philosophy of Infinity," in: *Daat* 22–23 (1987), 63–83.

"From Critical to Speculative Idealism," in *Journal of Bible and Religion* 34:1 (1966), 64–68.

"Hermann Cohen, the Challenge . . . ," in *Idealistic Studies* (January 1987), xvii/1, 83–84.

Dreyer review, in *International Studies in Philosophy* 21:1 (1989), 76–78.

Entry on Cohen, Hermann in *Encyclopedia of Religion*, ed. M. Eliade (1987), 559–560. © 1987 Gale, a part of Cengage Learning, Inc. Reproduced by permission. www.cengage.com/permissions

Unpublished

"History of the *Religion of Reason*: Part II of the Introduction," from the private Archive of Maimon Schwarzschild, San Diego.

"Historical Excursus: On Cohen's Infinitesimal-Methode."

"Applications of the Infinitesimalistic Theory in 'the System.'" From: "The Papers of Steven S. Schwarzschild," bulk 1945–1989, AR 25376, in Leo Baeck Institute, Center for Jewish History, Subseries 2: Teaching and Research Materials, 1932–1989, Box 5, folder 10. (http://digifindingaids.cjh.org/?pID=475354)

Introduction

Hermann Cohen was arguably the most important figure of Jewish philosophy at the turn of the twentieth century. Not only was his philosophical description of historical Judaism as the essential foundation of an ideal *"religion of reason"* in many respects the climax of nineteenth-century liberal German-Jewish theology, Cohen was, significantly, also the authoritative reference for most of those younger twentieth-century thinkers who completely rejected his idealistic approach to Judaism and who viewed their own Jewishness in rather existentialist terms, such as Rosenzweig or Buber. Cohen's work in Jewish philosophy summarized and systematized all that which rationalist Jewish theologians had developed starting from the Middle Ages in Spain to the heyday of Reform thought in mid-nineteenth-century Germany, as reflected in his ethical God-Idea, his collective and future-oriented Messianism, his enthusiasm for the social message of the Hebrew prophets, and his functional understanding of ritual law. All those elements of what he saw as Jewish ethical-rational monotheism he incorporated in his well-ordered system of religious thought, setting them side by side with those features of his theology that were a product of his own, original thinking about Judaism: the emphasis on divine atonement as the actual purpose of all religious activities, and the special place and the "peculiarity" (*Eigenart*) of religion as a "phenomenon of human consciousness" vis-à-vis logic, ethics, and aesthetics, that is, the classical fields of rational philosophy. Moreover, Cohen's original theory of the "I's discovery of the Thou," that is, the individual *Mitmensch* (fellow human) as the foundation and justification of peculiar religious consciousness, has had a lasting influence until this day.

But Cohen, as a person, was also the archetype and, at the same time, the symbol of the self-respecting, bourgeois, highly educated, patriotic German who nonetheless was also a proudly Jewish German Jew—the type of Jew produced in ever-increasing numbers in the second half of the nineteenth century. Cohen was the first openly Jewish *ordinarius* in the humanities at a Prussian university, and he founded and headed there an influential school of German *Kathederphilosophie*, in Germany probably one of the most prestigious of achievements. Before and still also after his turning to the intensive treatment of Jewish subjects in the last twenty years of his life, Cohen published six distinguished volumes of neo-Kantian philosophy, earning him a scholarly reputation even among those German philosophers who remained unaware of his Jewish writings.

From all we know, Cohen was actively practicing Judaism and became a relentless opponent of the new wave of anti-Semitism that hit Germany from the 1880s onward.[1] Cohen was convinced of the towering progressiveness, and thus superiority, of the Jewish religion over even the most modern form of cultured Protestantism, as it represented the commonly professed faith in the German states of his day. Cohen supported at the same time the establishment of chairs for Judaism at German universities and the victory of the German army in World War I. Cohen gave evidence before a German court of law for the overall humanism of the Talmud, and at the same time he excitedly adopted the results of Julius Wellhausen's research concerning the different layers of chronology and authorship of the Pentateuch. His Judaism was one of the future, as a source of new pride for the modern Jew, based on an awareness of what crucial ideas Judaism had to contribute to world civilization.

Probably as good as any demonstration of Cohen's intellectual authority is the fact that he was the subject of extensive contemporary criticism. He was attacked by the leaders of Jewish orthodoxy and by Zionist nationalists alike: he was accused by the orthodox thinker Isaac Breuer[2] of founding a sectarian group of "ethicists" within Judaism through his openly selective reading of the sources, and he was accused by Martin Buber of his failure to understand the notion of nationality as a reality of the ethos and the spirit. Cohen's overwhelming idealistic optimism as to the abilities and eventual victory of human reason over prejudice, his related belief in the unstoppable social progress of modern society, and, most of all, his identification of Germany as the most fertile ground for those developments, Cohen was easy prey for the accusation of naivety and even ignorance, especially after the Holocaust.[3]

But in terms of his stature as a philosopher of Judaism, the most influential and far-reaching effect on Cohen's intellectual legacy was none other than Franz Rosenzweig. It is an irony of history that put Rosenzweig in a position to not only shape the modern view of Cohen's personality and religious positions, but to even steer the majority of the academic research done on Cohen to date, and likely far into the twenty-first century. Rosenzweig, who was disappointed about being excluded from the editing of Cohen's last work, the *"Religion of Reason* out of the Sources of Judaism," was eventually asked in 1924, six years after Cohen's death, to write the introduction to Cohen's collected essays on Judaism, a three-volume project called "Jüdische Schriften." The untimely death of Cohen's most faithful disciple, Benzion Kellermann, who was the designated author of the introduction, cleared the way for Rosenzweig, and the lengthy text that he eventually provided became, for complex reasons, the ultimate reference of what Cohen "really was"—for both the scholarly and the nonscholarly world.[4] Rosenzweig described Cohen here, effectively using a number of anecdotes about Cohen's life, as a rationalist philosopher of religion who was deeply disturbed by and concerned with his own inability to grasp the more intuitive and more traditionalist aspects of Judaism, and was thus eventually drawn to a pious existentialism of Rosenzweig's own preference.

From this point forward—excepting some criticism of Cohen during the Weimar years and an emotional celebration of his 100th birthday by Buber and others in 1942 in Jerusalem that took place in the shadow of the unbelievable horrors unfolding in Europe at the time—Hermann Cohen's Jewish philosophy remained largely untouched by researchers until the early 1990s. However, the interim years were punctuated by some significant contributions. For example, two monographs by Jacob Klatzkin (1919) and Siegfried Ucko (1935) appeared before the Holocaust. Beyond these, Hugo Bergmann included a chapter on Cohen in his "Thinkers of the Generation" (Hebrew 1934) and Julius Guttmann climaxed his *Philosophie des Judentums* from 1933 with a long discussion of Cohen's thought. In 1945, Natan Rotenstreich dedicated a detailed chapter to Cohen's Jewish philosophy in his "Jewish Philosophy in Modern Times" (English 1968), and in the 1960s, Alexander Altmann, Hans Liebeschütz, and Heinz Mosche Graupe wrote learned articles on Cohen as a neo-Kantian Jewish thinker. But all of the aforementioned were historical accounts, portraying Cohen in his time, long past now, and, under the effect of the mass murder of European Jewry, also belonging to a very distinct past. It seemed by then that Cohen's influence and importance for modern Jewish theology was bound almost exclusively to the pre–World War I era, and that for traumatized post–World War II Jewish thought, his now notorious religious optimism and his insistence on Jewish universalism had nothing substantial to say anymore.

There were a few isolated islands of scholarship, however, where Hermann Cohen was always considered highly relevant and, given their actual and eternal philosophical truth, his ideas of Judaism were believed to have the potential for a great impact even on post-Shoah Jewry. Of these islands, by far and away the most significant was Washington University, St. Louis, of all places, and it was the lifetime achievement of the American rabbi and philosopher Steven S. Schwarzschild (1924–1989), working there, to have carefully preserved the intellectual heritage of arguably the most German of all Jewish philosophers, to have intensely studied and jealously defended it against all attacks, and even to have cautiously modernized Cohen's Jewish teachings. Over the course of more than three decades, from his first essay on Cohen in 1956 until his death in 1989, Schwarzschild managed to move the center of Cohen research, at least concerning Jewish subjects, from Europe to America, with the lion's share of this accomplishment being completed long before the first English translation of the *Religion of Reason* appeared in 1972. As a direct consequence of Schwarzschild's efforts, Cohen's thought not only began to influence wider parts of American Judaism,[5] it also entered the discussions within postwar general philosophy—discussions in which, appropriately, Schwarzschild was an active participant.[6] And interestingly, this transatlantic influence went both ways: not only did Schwarzschild present his European take on several selected and self-translated chapters from Cohen's Jewish writings, which he published in his own American-based journal *Judaism* during the 1960s, he also later contributed an introduction to Cohen's neo-Kantian *Ethik des Reinen Willens* from 1904, when this volume was republished in 1981 in Europe, as part of an edition of Cohen's "Collected Works" in the German original.

In Europe, the main island of Cohen scholarship was Zurich. Cohen's neo-Kantian philosophy was intensely studied there by a group of philosophers that had been formed from the 1970s onward around the Cohen expert Helmut Holzhey, concentrating, as just noted, almost exclusively on Cohen's general philosophical writings, without reference to Judaism per se.[7] Here again it was Steven Schwarzschild who provided the transatlantic synthesis in the research of Cohen's thought—especially with his pronounced and singular contention that essentially there is no difference between the two sides of Cohen's works.[8]

Steven Schwarzschild was born in Frankfurt am Main, and lived in Berlin until his family fled the Nazis to America. He returned to Germany in 1948 as a young rabbi, helping to rebuild the Jewish community of Berlin. After his return to the United States, he served as a rabbi for several congregations, until in 1963 he began his professional academic career at Brown University, before moving on to Washington University in 1965, where he taught until his untimely death in 1989.[9] Like Cohen, he was a liberal socialist and severely criticized Zionism. Schwarzschild believed, in the wake of Cohen, that the ethical relatedness of neo-Kantianism to jurisprudence would yet provide the best possible solution for a modern but still halachic understanding of the Jewish religion, and throughout his lifetime declined to associate exclusively with any of the "denominational streams" of modern Judaism.[10]

We owe to Steven Schwarzschild a sustained and clear understanding of Cohen's thinking that, if taken seriously today, could correct several decisive misunderstandings still dominating the Cohen-research of the last twenty years. Unfortunately, Schwarzschild is, if noticed at all, frequently considered to hold "exaggerated" positions in his reading of Cohen.[11] Interestingly, the argument underlying this claim is founded on the same methodology that denies the radicalness of Cohen's own views and resorts to what Schwarzschild himself called (Aristotelean) "middlingness" (in his discussion of Maimonides' ethical philosophy).[12] But philosophical truth, Schwarzschild would argue, is identical with the divine truth of religion—and God's demands are never moderating or conciliatory, but always radical. In the same way, the Platonic-Kantian-Cohenian concept of the ideal is by definition as radical as possible, because it does not describe what *is*, but what ideally *ought* to be. Therefore, Schwarzschild is, at least methodically, much closer to Cohen compared to his critics, for Schwarzschild was radically idealizing even Cohen's thought itself.

There are at least four larger themes where Schwarzschild's radical interpretation of Hermann Cohen essentially clears up widespread misperceptions about Cohen's life and work, regardless of whether one agrees with either thinkers' views. All four themes are closely connected to one another, and are:

1. The philosophical and systematical **unity of all of Cohen's writings**, whether "Jewish" or neo-Kantian, and thus the consequent rejection of an "existentialist turn" in Cohen's last book, as well as the exposure of Rosenzweig's anecdotes as unreliable;

2. The rejection of any reduction ("**de-ontologization**" as Schwarzschild called it) of Cohen's ethical idea of God to a divine realium, emphasizing instead that, in a very real sense, ideas can be said to possess "being" more than the objects of experience;[13]

3. Cohen's overall neo-Kantian method of "**regulative idealization**" of Judaism, especially in his intentionally selective reading of Jewish sources (first and foremost of Maimonides), that was often misunderstood as not reflecting a historical "totality" of Judaism; and finally:

4. Cohen's conspicuous **German patriotism**,[14] being nothing but a special case of a philosophical idealization of a certain culture and its values, and not to be confused with any given historical reality in the Germany of Cohen's time (or later).

All four of these themes appear over and over in Schwarzschild's essays on Cohen, and can thus be explicated with confidence.

Ad 1. Throughout his entire corpus of writings on Cohen, Schwarzschild almost aggressively rejected any attempt to divide Cohen's works into "Jewish" and "philosophical" sections, or, even worse for Schwarzschild, into an earlier neo-Kantian Cohen and "the last Cohen," represented by his posthumously published last book, which is said until today by many to be "post-neo-Kantian and proto-existentialist." This latter claim was, of course, first made very successfully by Franz Rosenzweig in his introduction to Cohen's Jewish Writings, and when Schwarzschild set out to refute it as a merely "dreamt up" and quite intentional misinterpretation by Rosenzweig, he had ipso facto attacked the stated opinion of a united front of an overwhelming majority of well-known scholars, including Hugo Bergmann, Natan Rotenstreich, Julius Guttmann, and Karl Löwith.[15] This attack came in a twofold way: first, as early as 1970, Schwarzschild deconstructed Rosenzweig's famous theological anecdotes about Cohen on a rather personal level, and then sixteen years later, he provided a thorough philosophical refutation of the underlying claim that Cohen had given up religious idealism, at least in part, in the last few years of his life. In the 1970 essay, Schwarzschild showed not only that Rosenzweig had never presented any historical evidence or trustworthy witnesses for the anecdotes, but even more, that the supposedly late baal tshuva version of Cohen, falsely presented by those stories, was very much in accordance with Rosenzweig's own philosophical preferences, especially with regard to the assertion that Cohen had before his death accepted the "reality" (as opposed to ideality) of religious concepts like God and the Messiah. In other words, Rosenzweig had merely projected his philosophy on to Cohen, while ignoring the fact that "the unattainability and imperative approximability" of these concepts was the supreme feature of Cohen's lifelong religious idealism. For Schwarzschild, it was unthinkable that Cohen would compromise on such a basic claim, because if "Cohen and Kant did not stand for this, they stood for nothing." And he added sardonically: "It is philosophically no easier, therefore, to believe Rosenzweig's famous anecdotes about Cohen than to believe that Kant told a friend that yesterday on the street he had run into and said 'hello' to a noumenon."[16] As textual proof for his refutation of Rosenzweig, Schwarzschild referred to a remarkable, longer passage in Cohen's early book *Kants Begründung der Ästhetik* from 1889, where indeed almost the entire alleged "novelty" of 1918, concerning the individual character of religion, as opposed to philosophical ethics, is virtually anticipated.[17]

Only in 1986, when Schwarzschild wrote an essay on the meaningful title of Cohen's *Religion of Reason*, did he devote a longer passage to a philosophical justification of his clear-cut opposition to Rosenzweig's widely accepted theory of an "existentialist turn" in the late Cohen. According to Schwarzschild, Cohen's last book has its tight-fitting place within his overall systematic oeuvre, and does not stand out in any way vis-à-vis novel philosophical or religious ideas. The place that *Religion of Reason* occupies in Cohen's philosophic system, Schwarzschild claims here, is precisely analogous to the place that *Religion Within the Bounds of Reason Alone* occupies in Kant's: the respective titles of the fourth works of both philosophers turn out equally to be conceptually translatable as "Critique of Practical-Religious Reason." Thus, the overarching unity of all of Cohen's works is found precisely in their strictly idealist, transcendental approach, and this philosophical idealism is rather confirmed (and not broken) by the development of a theology built from the transcendent ideas of religion in Cohen's

Religion of Reason: the ideas of creation, revelation, redemption, and most important, the idea of God.[18] Therefore,

Ad 2. No ontological claims whatsoever "about God or man or the world are made in this work," Schwarzschild argued. To the contrary: expounding the "correlation" between God and man, Cohen is even more careful in his last book to avoid the impression that this correlation is held to be a relationship of two empirical terms; it is rather ethical man that stands in relationship with the idea of God.[19] The deity always remains an idea, even in Cohen's *Religion of Reason*. God is never "real," but a "transcendentally necessary presupposition for man's total ethical life." Again and again Schwarzschild stresses Cohen's "epigram" that while traditional religionists and realists usually say that according to his view God was "only an idea," neo-Kantians would say that Cohen's God "was *even* an idea."[20] As opposed to common sense, the whole notion that an idea is somehow less real than an empirical object, than a phenomenal existent, simply makes no sense philosophically. Indeed, it is the opposite of the truth for Plato, Kant, Cohen ("most especially"), and Schwarzschild (and also for Maimonides, as the last two thinkers mentioned claim).[21] Therefore, explains Schwarzschild, for Cohen, God is not and never was a Biblical personality, nor a sensual object, but *more than that*: God is "even" the idea (in the neo-Kantian, regulative sense) of the normative, infinite realization of the good in the world. This same realization is known in religious language as the establishment of the messianic kingdom on earth by means of *the imitation of God*. Schwarzschild's consistent and belligerent resistance to any attempt to de-idealize, that is, to re-ontologize Cohen's concept of God, no matter if made in Cohen's name or against Cohen, is not only a romantic defense of a philosophical role model; an insistence on the purity of Cohen's idealism is seen by Schwarzschild both as ultimately decisive for a correct understanding of Cohen's entire systematic thought (which would not be systematic without it), as well as constituting Cohen's true and most important legacy for contemporary and future philosophical debates—in and outside Judaism.

Ad 3. Inside Jewish circles, one of the main points of criticism, still during Cohen's lifetime but more so after his death in 1918, was his treatment of the rich literary sources of Judaism, which he extensively used to support his theological ideas. Cohen was an enthusiastic reader of the Biblical prophets, and identified strongly with particular messages about ethics and hints to universal moral concepts. And though he possessed but mediocre knowledge of the Talmud, he found support for his ideas therein as well. But he was perhaps most at home studying and indeed rediscovering the religious philosophy of Maimonides, whose *Guide for the Perplexed* became of increasing importance to his own idealistic understanding of the basic concepts of Jewish theology.[22] But Cohen's reading of these sources was intentionally highly selective. He chose those passages that fit his own philosophical agenda: the messianism, the social engagement, humanistic ideal and antimystical tendencies in the Prophets, a proto-Kantian philosophy of self-contained legal duties in the Talmud, and most of all, a proto-idealism of Maimonides' famous "negative theology" from the *Guide*, where nothing absolute could be predicated of the deity, and only His actions are known, which are entirely ethical in nature according to Cohen. This reading of Maimonides seemed strikingly to anticipate Kant again, both regarding the apparently de-ontologized nature of Maimonides' God, and the epistemological nature of the method of Maimonides' argument.

The almost universal outcry of the scholars of Judaism (excluding a small circle of Cohen disciples) against this "idiosyncratic" treatment of his Jewish sources by Cohen is clearly audible until this day:[23] such a "self-serving" approach, say the critics, gives a highly "distorted" picture of the Bible and also of the Rambam, who in many other places held very different opinions from the ones Cohen preferred, and thus Maimonides in particular was presented by Cohen in a biased and lopsided manner, to say the least. Here again, Steven Schwarzschild was of great help in dispelling what he saw as a widespread misunderstanding, by expounding the neo-Kantian methodology underlying Cohen's reading of Maimonides' *Guide* and all other sources. According to this justification, it never was Cohen's intention in the first place to present an all-embracing picture of empiric Judaism, or its intellectual representatives, as it unfolded in history. As a Kantian philosopher, Cohen was interested in precisely those aspects of historical Jewish thought that supported or even confirmed his own view of

Judaism as rational, ethical monotheism, and therefore those same Jewish concepts are not so much historically true as universally true, in the philosophical sense. Other aspects, especially irrational or mystical developments, as much as they belong to empiric Jewish history of thought, can and should be philosophically neglected.[24] Schwarzschild thus claims that Cohen consciously *idealized* empirical reality, but not from ignorance or arrogance, but in order to carve out the rational-ethical essence of Judaism, that is, Judaism's contribution to the development of culture: "In Critical philosophy, 'idealization' not only does not mean what it generally means—glorification, enveloping grimy reality with a nimbus of ideality, etc., but, in fact, it means exactly the opposite."[25] Thus, Cohen himself would happily concede that historical Judaism is far from being the ethical *"Religion of Reason"* that he described and aspired to, but Cohen would insist that Jewish literary sources provided (next to many other theological doctrines) almost all the raw material for the theological components necessary for this *"Religion of Reason."* On the other hand, critical idealizing is also not the attempt "to *dissolve* existing Judaism into an abstract, philosophically-inspired *religion of reason*," as Emil Fackenheim wrote of Cohen's Jewish thought.[26] Here the concept of an arbitrary empirical breadth of phenomena ("Judaism"), by calling it "alive," is confused, according to Schwarzschild, with the potential human ability to act. It is mistaken, at least, for the telos of moral action, founded on the primacy of practical reason. On the contrary, only an abstract *religion of reason* makes moral human action imperative, because it logically requires us to approximate the idea of God.[27] Ultimately, Cohen's method in his approach to empirical reality—with empirical reality including Jewish and other literary sources—is identified by Schwarzschild with the neo-Kantian principle of "regulative idealization," as developed in Marburg.[28] According to Schwarzschild, this method can be outlined, following a Marburg practice, with quite mathematical formulas. He writes:

> "Idealization" is the rational, conceptual construction, the postulation of a morally desirable condition (A), for the purpose of measuring against it any actually given condition (B), so as necessarily to reveal that (B) falls short of (A) [(B) = (A) - x],

and entailing the categorical challenge that the most strenuous efforts must be made to narrow this gap urgently and increasingly [so that (B) = (A) - (x - a)].[29]

Ad 4. Therefore, even the probably strangest views of Cohen, his apparently naive and exaggerated German patriotism, his fervent endorsing of German arms during World War I,[30] can be conveniently explained using the principle of "regulative idealization."[31] Of course, the charge of political naivety is overshadowed by the murderous events that took place in Germany many years after Cohen's death, events that no sane human being could anticipate. But Schwarzschild, working in modern day America, was interested less in saving Cohen's reputation as a prophet as he was in saving Cohen's project of a humanistic, universal idealism, as he understood it from some of the sources of Judaism. During Cohen's era, Schwarzschild writes, "German culture held pride of place in much of the world, and, correlatively, the acculturated German-Jewish community, together with its ideals, dominated worldwide Jewry somewhat similarly to the role of American Jewry in our time."[32] Thus, the question that arises here is far more general: Could it be said that the ashes of the death camps made the very existence of the Jewish people and the vitality of its culture capable of preservation only in separation from other societies, such that, as per Schwarzschild's own formulation, emancipation and acculturation, "the ideals to which Cohen was dedicated, would, therefore, seem to have been massively refuted by the facts of 20th-century history, if by nothing else"? It is against this still prevalent opinion that Schwarzschild argues when he defends Cohen's "Germanism" (*Deutschtum*) and the relationship of it to his Judaism. For if it were true, this opinion would undermine also Schwarzschild's own vision for diaspora Jewry in America and the world.

Yet even setting aside the Nazi horrors, already in Cohen's own time religious anti-Semitism was on the rise, the project of the integration, as Jews, of German Jewry into the majority Protestant German society met more resistance than expected, and, at the latest with the Treitschke-Affair of 1880, anti-Jewish prejudices had reached even into the academic world in which Cohen was at home. But it is precisely Cohen's awareness of these developments, and even more so his lifelong active stand against political and religious anti-Semitism, which render the accusation of naivety baseless in Schwarzschild's view.[33] As much as Cohen was not interested in the "real" Maimonides, his true love was never empirical Germany, neither in history nor in the present. Again, his passion was rather an *idealized* Germany, the country she ought to be and the culture she was to develop, following the greatest of her minds. It is thus another widespread misunderstanding that cultured German Jews, among them Cohen, venerated Goethe and Schiller, and even Kant (whose anti-Jewish remarks the Jewish Kantians were well aware of) because they were eager to imitate those Christian authors' thinking and thus close the "education gap" with their German neighbors.[34] It is yet again rather the opposite that is the case: enlightened German Jewry believed that those famed writers thought essentially like good Jews ought to think. As such, Cohen's emphatic Germanism is a classical "regulative idealization." Germanism was understood by Cohen to be what he often called "the nation of Kant."[35] But this nation is rather cosmopolitan (*weltbürgerlich*, as Kant called it), not Teutonic. In Schwarzschild's words, it is "not the narrow and, as Cohen knew only too well from his own lifelong experiences, historically disastrous reality of Germany, but the intermediate embodiment, as he wished to see it, of the progressive development of humanistic values from Plato through Maimonides to Kant, the French Revolution, and the socialist movement, which had, by that time, achieved greater political successes in Germany than anywhere else."[36]

While those four points may be called Schwarzschild's pioneering contributions to academic Cohen research, there was for him always also a personal level in his relation to the Marburg philosopher. "Yes, I love Cohen," wrote Schwarzschild in 1972, "for his philosophical erudition and perspicacity, for his moral grandeur, and for his Jewish profundity." And in an even more personal note he added, "I have his memorabilia in my study and his portrait, done twice by Max Liebermann, on both sides of my sitting-room, so that no visitor can avoid the look of his searching eye."[37] Cohen cannot be ignored philosophically and thus must not be avoided, in Schwarzschild's view. This was certainly a matter of Jewish pride; Cohen had after all "circumcised, as it were, Plato and the European tradition,"[38] but not only. Whoever avoided him had very explicit reasons, whether religious, moral, or political—with the boundaries between them often blurred. On this score Schwarzschild cited Buber and Rosenzweig as examples of thinkers who, "no less tragically defeated by the history of the twentieth century than Cohen—diverged from Cohen's path to their and our loss."[39] Philosophy, but especially Jewish theology, is clearly also a matter *ad hominem* for Schwarzschild, for as an ethicist he would not accept that one's moral behavior can be divided from one's philosophical assumptions. Therefore, Schwarzschild called himself a lifelong follower of Hermann Cohen also on a direct, almost private stratum, in one of his last texts he wrote: "I started out with Hermann Cohen while I was still in high school, and I am still (indeed more) with him now. He has been very good company and a very good guide—Jewishly, as well as philosophically."[40]

This is an important statement because Schwarzschild is one of the very few philosophers who would ever publicly correct their own earlier views when they became aware of apparent errors. Thus, he stated in 1989 that the only "detour" from this lifelong devotion to Cohen was "to have fallen prey to the temptation of Franz Rosenzweig" during the 1950s and 1960s, but, as he added with a touch of humor, "I recovered."[41] The detour via Rosenzweig is the reason for two "substantive corrections" he later made to his positions, and in both cases it was Hermann Cohen who eventually convinced Schwarzschild that Rosenzweig was misled in his views.[42] The first correction regards the Messiah. While Rosenzweig held that Cohen's Messiah, *who comes only in eternity*, therefore never comes, Schwarzschild eventually returned to the view that the Messiah is an eternally approached ideal.[43] A Messiah who is eternally approaching is *coming* at every moment, while a Messiah that eventually arrives, as per Rosenzweig, actually never comes, because upon his arrival he would no longer be the Messiah.[44] The other correction in favor of Cohen rejects Rosenzweig's notion that divine revelation, or "an ultimate intuition" are called for to provide "a necessary surplus of moral cognition," but that in the sense of Cohen (and Kant) "reason alone suffices for all people to arrive ideally at the truth, and therewith also at the good."[45]

And moral good, in the end, was always practical for Cohen and Schwarzschild. The rational character of all of Cohen's ethical optimism, Schwarzschild claims repeatedly, leads to peace, as opposed to irrationality, pessimism, and value-relativism, which only lead to fascism (as Schwarzschild believed was the case with Heidegger). Moral progress is conterminous with the belief in human rationality, and therefore to philosophize is a religious obligation. For the Kantian thinker Hermann Cohen, "progress is, contrary to all forms of Hegelianism, not asserted because of any natural or actual inevitability, but in spite of historical irrationality. It is an *ought*, the more categorical for its empirical failures." This is what might best be called, as Schwarzschild concluded, Hermann Cohen's *tragic optimism*.[46]

— George Y. Kohler

Chapter 1 | 1956

The Democratic Socialism of Hermann Cohen

In wide circles the term "Democratic Socialism" has fallen into disrepute in our time chiefly because of attacks leveled against it by two opposing factions, factions united only in this common enmity. On the one hand, Marxist communists condemn it as the label of what they call "bourgeois opportunism and treason to the working class," while conservatives proclaim that it designates a political movement, which inevitably develops into the advanced stage of Stalinism with which they, therefore, throw it in the same pot. For reasons of historical and social accuracy alone it is only proper that the ideological sources and the motivations, which may be impelling this trend of thought even today, be correctly understood. When, to this point of interest, are added the philosophical authority, the ethical enthusiasm, and the Jewish devotion of the man who was the greatest Jewish technical philosopher of the closing nineteenth and beginning twentieth centuries, the subject becomes one of intriguing significance.

Historical Background

Offhand one might expect Hermann Cohen to be among the last to join the band of convinced socialists. He was born into the lower middle-class German-Jewish family of a small-town cantor. Having, as a young child, witnessed the liberal revolutions of 1848, which set Europe aflame, he lived his mature and productive years precisely from the Franco-Prussian war of 1870, out of which the German empire of Bismarck was born, to the end of World War I in which this Empire was destroyed. He was at all times a fervent German patriot who, very much like most German Jews

---

First published in *Hebrew Union College Annual* 27 (1956), 417–438.

of that period striving for complete emancipation, identified the progress of his country with his own progress and the essence of his religious faith with "Germanism" at its best, ardently defended the righteousness of the Kaiser's cause in the great war, and even wrote a booklet "Germanism and Judaism" that today makes his most loyal disciples cringe. In his personal career he advanced meteorically, yet respectably and conventionally, from private instructor to full professor at a German university. In his appearance, as in his manner of life, he was an unmistakable member of the middle class, quite stout, and appropriately academic. And, so far as his teachings were concerned, he was the outstanding European spokesman for pure or critical idealism in the tradition of Kant, which, to the layman, often seems ethereal and unpractical; to the dialectical materialist, diversionary and unrealistic.

There existed also historical factors in this period, which may have contributed to the crystallization of Cohen's socialism: the rising German-Jewish middle class felt that it had not yet been completely enfranchised and that only a radical improvement of social conditions would ameliorate this state of affairs. Even those rights that they had already acquired they felt to be endangered by the rise of that progenitor of Nazism, the organized anti-Semitism of nationalist, religious, and academic Germans, which raised its ugly head in the middle of the reign of the "Iron Chancellor." During that same period German political opposition became increasingly concentrated in the Social Democratic Party, which was as yet not split between socialists and communists, which, differing from its later stages, still stood squarely on a platform of complete doctrinal socialism, and which was gaining electoral strength to a surprising degree. Bismarck himself inaugurated the system that became known as "state socialism." Above all, however, it was philosophical, ethical, political, and religious considerations of a very elaborate and technical nature, which led the "father of the Marburg school" of philosophy to a lifelong espousal of socialism.

Attitudes to Socialist Materialism

The first question that must arise in one's mind, when one tries to imagine the exponent of radical philosophical idealism associated with the political party, which has usually stood on a program explicitly based on economic determinism, is how Cohen overcame this obvious contradiction. The answer is that, in the first place, he disagreed with the commonplace refutations of this doctrine even more than he did with socialist materialism itself. Second, he tried to reveal the ethical and idealistic foundations that underlay the materialistic doctrines, though it rarely happened that these were consciously understood by their framers. And, last of all, he powerfully and cogently argued against philosophic materialism not only on theoretical grounds but also on the ground that, for logical as well as historical reasons, philosophic materialism is basically antagonistic to socialism.

Conventional bourgeois idealism frequently accuses socialists of being materialists, but this term is used not in its philosophic implications but rather in its colloquial connotations. Because socialists are primarily interested in the improvement of economic conditions they are supposed to be concerned only with crass matters of physical comforts rather than with such "spiritual" values as freedom, independence, and culture. This, in Cohen's time, was known among political controversialists as the "questions of the stomach" (Magenfrage). This argument Cohen calls "pious hypocrisy."[1] With the invocation of such lofty phrases, conservatives merely wish to cover up their desire to preserve their privileges and advantages under the status quo, and for this purpose they are perfectly willing to rely on ancient prerogatives. When this does not suffice, they seek, in all haste, to preserve their advantages by rewriting the law. This "egotism hostile to ideals" is the real materialism.[2] Furthermore, Cohen quotes Maimonides[3] to the effect that social injustice and economic misery are obstacles that have to be removed before the higher and nobler spiritual aims can be achieved. Therefore, "we must be allowed to begin by concerning ourselves with the questions of the stomach, but, from the very outset, the crux must be the question of the spirit, the question of spiritual, that is to say, of moral freedom."[4]

Because the theoreticians of socialism have seen through this persiflage of conservative idealism, they have usually taken a materialist position in philosophy. "It might well be, therefore, that men are so enraged and outraged by the hypocritical utilization of moral ideas that they point to the immoral conditions of real relations of power in order to unmask in them the driving force of all past history. This would then be anything but materialism. Rather is it a restrained idealism which guides this view of history."[5] Thus, for example, the budding sociology of Cohen's time regarded itself as firmly based on scientific, Darwinian, and materialistic assumptions. It exhausted itself in collecting data about social conditions and treated these as if they dealt with formations of rock. It elicited averages, juggled them mathematically, and sincerely believed that through them constructive conclusions could be reached. Cohen calls this kind of sociology "moral statistics" (Moralstatistik). Yet, at the same time, he recognized and stressed that this type of naive scientism served humanity better than did the pompous idealism, which constantly prattles about human values and dignity; for fundamentally scientism was interested in existing facts only in order to change them and to improve them for the future.[6] Or, to give another illustration, Cohen certainly rejected all forms of eudaemonism and hedonism as antagonistic to the purity of ethics and philosophy and as making of history and morality mere matters of egotism. Still, he pointed out that the historical functions of eudaemonism and hedonism have usually been progressive and healthy. When they were superseded by Roman stoicism, which foreswore the pleasure of the senses, there was symptomized a state of political lethargy, which withdrew from the world and left its conduct in the hands of a few political conspirers, and, when Schopenhauer's "exotically dressed-up apathy of political pessimism" succeeded the optimism of the Enlightenment, there was reached a nadir in democratic progress.[7] Cohen climaxes this entire line of thought when, in a central place of his major work in which he worked out his radical philosophic idealism, he eulogizes Karl Marx, the grand-daddy of modern socialist materialism. "When the socialism of a Marx, from its high historical perspective, wants to stigmatize the compelling power of material conditions, it unwittingly becomes satire. A fiery ethical spirit motivates all his great work, theoretical as well as practical. It were pedantry to offer, to such an emissary of the God of history, little maxims of spiritualistic morality."[8]

But, when all this has been said, it must be added that "the materialism of history is the most direct contradiction of the ethical idealism in which socialism has its roots conceptually as well as historically."[9] True, it only replaces the atheism of the rationalist enlightenment, which saw in religion the malicious handiwork of priests and kings, by its own atheism, which makes of God "the scarecrow of the agricultural economics that produce all culture."[10] True also that, as we have seen and as we shall see further, socialist materialism is an intellectual error, not a moral one. But this intellectual error, when carried to its logical end, will cancel all socialist aspirations and convictions. It is based on the belief that history is ruled by the law of theoretical reason or logic, which thinks in categories of cause and effect rather than of aim and will, that is, the laws of ethical reason or morality. The result is that history, as the story of man, his ideas and goals, becomes part of natural history, the inevitable sequence of effects following inevitably upon inevitable causes without regard to moral ideas like freedom and justice. This not only destroys history as such but also implies approval of all historical realities because they are necessary and can, therefore, not be morally reprehensible.[11] Indeed, except by philosophic sleights of hand, Marxist dialectics have never been able to get around this dilemma of historical necessity which they posit versus social betterment to which they aspire. The father of this original sin of modern socialism is Hegel.[12]

Attitude Toward Hegel

Indeed, nothing could have been more regrettable and injurious from the point of view of the socialist movement than that its modern founders traced their intellectual ancestry back to Hegel. Hegel's basic error consists of having assumed that theoretical reason, rather than volitional ethics, governs history. The result is that history is conceived of as a pantheistic system in which an absolute essence, Spirit, in the course of time and by absolutely necessary stages, reveals itself inherently through its own laws of manifestation, that is, through dialectics. History thus becomes part of nature since both obey the same causal evolutionary laws of the absolute Spirit. This is Hegel's version of *Deus sive natura*.[13] This in turn leads to the logical conclusion, which neither Spinoza nor Hegel shirked, that everything that *is* is necessary and rational and, therefore, in its time and place, is also good. And that, of course, constitutes intellectual and ethical acquiescence to every historical reality, be it good or bad, just or unjust. It requires submission to every reality, however abhorrent it may appear to be from the social and socialist point of view, and pulls out the moral ground from under the feet of any ethical protest and revolt. Cohen exclaims: "Perhaps nothing has contributed so much to making philosophy contemptible in the pre-revolutionary age than the reactionary motto of Hegel: The real is reasonable, and the reasonable is real."[14] Conventional conservative religionists invoke this god who is the author and approves of everything as it is when it is, in order to justify their egotistical greed.[15] Politicians of a reactionary stripe wallow in the romanticism and mythology, which glorify the past and its products to assert that history teaches the limits of what can be and what can be done, that "there can be nothing new under the sun" and that, therefore, all striving for reform is a vain chasing after the wind.[16] And, in the course of time, Hegelian philosophers were able to refer to their teacher in order to defend the most diverse and mutually contradictory political programs. The Hegelian school was split between those who looked forward to the most radical social revolution and those who regarded the existing Prussian state as the acme of perfection, between those who proclaimed a consistent atheism and those who endorsed orthodox religion—all of them presenting the seal of their master's approval by relying on the dictum that whatever is or whatever will necessarily be is rational.[17] Ethical idealism, Judaism as well as Kant, must and does answer this pernicious doctrine with the counterproposition that the rational is never real and that it is man's task on earth to realize it ever more.

Apart from the faulty philosophic bases from which Hegel starts, erroneous concepts regarding the operation of history also contribute to the irreconcilability of all forms of Hegelianism with socialism, despite the intertwining of the two in the standard ideology of what Cohen calls "party-socialism." In the first place, belief in development presupposes knowledge of the aim of the development. Development means purposive movement but, without knowing what the purpose is, one cannot know whether movement is development or simply meaningless chaos and turbulence. On the basis of belief in the causal, Darwinian, nature of history, it is impossible to conclude as to the existence of a purpose, because, since purpose is an ideal, hypothetical, definition that acts as an ethical norm, it cannot be deduced from empirical observation. The empirical facts of history may point to any number of varying purposes, or they may point to no purpose at all, depending on future occurrences that cannot be presaged. Therefore, since Hegelians are unable to know whether there is a purpose to history, and since, if they were to know that there is a purpose, they would not know what it is, they also cannot dogmatically stipulate that history is development. This destroys the very bases of Hegel's and Marx's belief in progress.[18] The invariable result is that metaphysicians—and that is what they both were, because they both assumed the reality of forces, which reason cannot deduce—posit all sorts of finite purposes for history, such as the Prussian state, in the case of the former, whose effect is to stifle the infinite search of man for perfection and to lull him into satisfaction with lesser realities.[19] Again, the idealism of socialism is outraged by such an imposition.

So far as the dialectical laws are concerned, that history proceeds according to the scheme of thesis, antithesis, and synthesis, into which Marx squeezed the functions of the determining economics, instead of into Hegel's absolute spirit, Cohen admits that by means of their manipulation a certain deepening, flexibility, and appreciativeness were introduced into historiography, which had previously been quite narrow-minded and mechanical. And yet, by denying in effect the basic logical law of identity, those dialectical laws also annihilated the rational security on which all thinking is premised, and therefore endangered rationality as such. Furthermore, "one or a very few" continuous and not contradictory motives are sufficient to explain the progress of history, which is, consequently, much smoother, surer, and less cataclysmic than might otherwise be supposed.[20] What, indeed, is the materialist rationale for assuming the existence of dialectical laws and the bloody conflicts, which they are supposed to bring about in history? Is it, as we have already seen it would have to be, to be movement for its own sake, without rhyme or reason? And if, as Hegel declares, human pain and suffering testify to the existence of conflict and to the dialectic that explains it, then the simultaneous existence of pleasure and joy should also testify to the validity of the law of identity and the resulting continuity of historical progress. At this point, it is evident, Cohen expounds a doctrine of socialism that involves his own basic optimism and that has more in common with Fabian gradualism than with Marxist eschatological speculations. Indeed, he often asserts that progress in history comes about through the reform of one small institution after another, and that each new institution remains in continuity with its predecessor through the revamped remnants taken over by the one from the other.

Rejection of Existing Realities as Ideas

The principle underlying Cohen's rejection of Hegelianism in its original form as well as in its transformed state of socialist materialism is the refutation of the pantheistic doctrine that "everything that is is rational, and that everything rational is," on the grounds that, philosophically speaking, this constitutes a confusion of the ideal with the real, of the hypothetical with the empirical and that, ethically speaking, it amounts to a vicious justification of any given status qua in history and society. Hegelianism and socialist materialism, in short, are the denial of voluntarism in favor of quietism. Cohen is amazingly radical and consistent in the application of this criterion to all cultural and historical realities.

He even judges art by this standard. Art grows out of a political and social soil. By showing existing facts in an idealized form, transforming the palaces of the aristocracy into temples of religion, tracing present monarchs back to an idealized patriarchal and even divine origin,[21] and by beautifying empirical man in his social environment, art internalizes, and justifies social cleavages.[22] By contrast, the art of "the new age," which was born out of Shakespeare's transformation of the tragedy into the historical drama, where human life becomes subject to the direction of its own will and is, therefore, guided to the basic motif of history, to wit, freedom; and out of Goethe's establishment of the aim of man as "the free man working on his own soil,"—that art was begun and foreshadowed by modern French painting, which places the worker into the center of attention and shows him in his real condition.[23] (One is somewhat uncomfortably reminded of the "new realism" of Nazi Germany and Soviet Russia.) And Cohen concludes his lengthy philosophic study of esthetics with this eulogy and accolade to the new age: "France has led up to a new world of states, a new nature of the state—not without the hard, horrible contradictions that make the spirit of nations and of their leading individuals ambiguous and the spirit of world-history ambivalent, and yet with the clear-cut self-evidence of a world-shaping principle. Beyond the contradictions that afflict revolutionary politics, cosmopolitan humanity, as a latent principle, became the highest axiom of the life of states and nations. Out of this basic direction, the new politics of socialism grew and, whether the artist admits it or not, modern painting reaches its climax in the human rights of the workers."[24]

This same criterion annihilates the hero-cult as historiography. For in it the natural, empirical man, man as he is, becomes the ideal, and whether this hero be the sage of stoicism or the Jesus of Christianity or the "leader" of the corrupt forms of modern socialism, the hero-cult inevitably leads to "the materialism of the worship of power," and in politics it is, after all, never the poor and miserable but the strong and the mighty that become heroes. Thus the basis is laid for an aristocracy and for inequality.[25]

Most important, the rejection of given realities as ideal and history-forming forces results in the refusal to accept the "people" (Volk) as genuine historical units. Hegel himself and the historical school of the philosophy of law (Savigny) as well as the former's Jewish disciples, most eminently among them Nachman Krochmal, traced national cultures back to the genius of each people, or the spirit of each people (*Volksgeist*). This theory, Cohen replies, not only accepts biological realities as God-given ideals, not only does it induce Savigny to deny the contractual, democratic basis of the state in favor of a natural explanation, but it also inevitably leads to the chauvinism of racial nationalism.[26] To the contrary, peoples are only the natural raw material, the problematic given facts of history, which correspond to the problematic given facts of the senses in critical epistemology, out of which the ideal structure of the state makes an historic force tending, as its aim, toward the life of humanity.[27] And we shall see that, consequently, socialism likewise will have to work through the state, more in accordance with Lassalle's national socialism than with Marx's internationalism, for the state is a legal, contractual product of ethical, ideal wills and can, hence, be teleologically oriented.

Philosophical Foundations of Socialism

Having, on the whole, rejected the commonly accepted philosophical bases of socialism, as well as a number of the operative details built on them, we must next ask what, positively, the conceptual foundation is on which Cohen erects his own socialist ideology. For that purpose we must first understand, at least in outline, his view of history as such.

History, if it is to give us reliable knowledge, must be a rational science. Like every science, it will have to comprise two elements, the element of the materials with which it works and the element of the method that it uses to work on them. Now the materials of history—though, also regarding them, some vagueness of definition may exist that can be overcome only by the most scrupulous attention to the best and most original sources of information—are generally agreed to consist of the historical information deposited in the records of the past and present life of humanity. As for the methods, however, a great deal of confusion prevails. It is, therefore, imperative to realize that the method of historical science, like that of every other science, is basically hypothetical; that is to say, the aim of this science, as of every other, is to unify the available multitudinous and chaotically meaningless material by means of as few principles as possible into an organized and rational whole. This can be done only by formulating a reasonable idea, not empirically derived from the so-called facts—since these, after all, constitute the problem—which will have the two functions of every idea or hypothesis: first, to be used experimentally as a criterion for the selection, classification, and comprehension of all relevant facts, and second, to represent the norm or goal for the complete attainment of which existing facts should be modified and improved. We have already seen that history, as human development, is inconceivable without an end or aim, and that such an end cannot be defined by means of empirical observation of past events.[28] Therefore, it must, to the contrary, be an end that is not empirical but pure or ideal; which is only another way of saying that it must be perfect and can, consequently, be realized only in infinity. Otherwise, if the end were not infinite, though not fulfilled in reality now, it might be at some future time and would therefore be in principle, if not in actuality, of an empirical character. The operative effects of such an ideal end, by means of which the facts of history are serialized are that, in the first place, these facts, which have hitherto lain about at random and without meaning like stray pieces of iron, are now directed toward a significant purpose, as if straightened out by a gigantic magnet; and, in the second place, the course of history, never completed in time, continues into infinity toward ever greater perfection brought about by man's action in history.

Idealistic historiography, in short, rationally defines ideal aims, which are to be accomplished and are, therefore, ethical in nature. By means of these ethical concepts, it orders and explains the facts of history, economic as well as cultural.[29] It is interesting to note to which three causes Cohen attributed, even in his time, a skepticism about such idealistic historiography in terms of preferring a so-called "realistic," "empirical," or "objective" method. Since, as we shall see shortly, the God of history is for him an ideal in the sense in which we have just defined it, (though that is the highest degree of reality itself) he suspects, in the first place, that dissatisfaction with such an ideal God stems from the Protestant desire and necessity to prove the historical and empirical existence of Jesus as a deity. He attributes it, in the second place, to a general cynicism about the reality of ideas as such and, in the third place, to the recrudescence, in Jewish circles, of a biological naturalism which, in line with the Hegelian and Krochmalian "pantheism" with which we have already dealt, glorifies the people in a burst of nationalism, which is regarded as the source of cultural values.[30]

The hypothesis according to which history functions and toward which it strives must, hence, be perfect, infinite, and universal. Now history, being the history of men, must strive, therefore, toward the perfect unity of all mankind living together, in accordance with ethical precepts, in perfect peace and in the fullest knowledge of truth. Indeed man, being the empirical fact of the historical science of man and becoming an object of that science only through the hypothesis of that science, actually exists only insofar as he orients himself toward that unified humanity.[31] And this end, of perfected mankind, living in the ethical society, has been called "the messianic age" by the Biblical prophets who first envisaged it. The prophets may, therefore, rightly be called "the inventors of history."[32]

The messianic belief is primarily the belief in the ethical norm of a united humanity created by the moral endeavors and history-shaping actions of men.[33] It involves the fundamental religious virtue of "sympathy" (*Mitleid*) through which the suffering and misery of fellow humans is deeply felt as an evil. This evil is recognized not in the inevitability of biological death, out of which rather resignation and mythology arise, but in the wickedness of societal and, therefore, remediable poverty.[34] The misery of poverty, as the original evil of society, is furthermore not viewed as punishment for sin but as the symptom of a profoundly unjust and unstable condition of humanity, a condition conquered in the triumph of the righteousness and justice of messianism.[35] Messianism is thus only the religious term for socialism. "The politics of the prophets are nothing but what we today call socialism. Their faith is to have justice done to the poor, and their religion is morality."[36] The universal priesthood of all men is the religious term for the socialist concept of the dignity of all workers. And the motto of all future history beginning with "this new age" must be: "It is a matter of literally and truly realizing the basic faith in God: the love of neighbor, which is to say: the regeneration of the nations out of the ethical ideal of socialism."[37]

This hypothesis is, by definition, one that cannot be transformed into reality except in infinity. The objection must, therefore, lie close at hand that it is an unreachable ideal, and men, in despair of ever being able to attain it, will easily give it up as a useless and hallucinative castle in Spain. For that reason Marxist socialists constantly indict those who find the rationale of their socialism in a philosophy other than theirs as "sentimentalists and utopians," for they believe that all who do not share their faith in the prognosis made by Marx of the inevitable, objectively necessary and invincible progress of history toward communism can give neither themselves nor others the assurance of eventual victory—which is a premise of effective action. That such an assurance is required is admitted also by Cohen but, that it cannot be given on the Darwinian, Hegelian, grounds cited by Marx, he has already demonstrated. It can be given only through a rational faith in God. God is understood to be the creator of nature in a manner and through reasoning not directly pertinent to our considerations here; messianism, on the other hand, is the belief in the ethical norm of a just, universal, society reached in infinity. Now society can exist only on the backdrop, as it were, nature. Nature is the stage on which the play of history takes place, and if this play lasts into infinity, then, in order to make it possible to play it through to its end, nature must exist into infinity. Faith in God then means the belief that God guarantees the eternity of nature so that the infinite tasks of ethical history may be performed.[38] Faith in God is thus the idealist's answer to the Marxist accusation of utopianism, and Cohen grandiosely even returns the accusation in terms of his own philosophy: "Through its atheism socialism deprives itself of its pinnacle, its roof; through its materialism it deprives itself of its basis, its foundation. Through its atheism it indeed becomes utopianism."[39]

Cohen's socialist ideology also differs from that of orthodox Marxist socialists in its evaluation of the state. We have previously noted, and must here mention it again, that the state, compared to the natural, biological unit of the people, is an ideal structure, arising out of a democratic contract of all the people that it comprises.[40] Its ideality is testified to by the fact that it allows no discrimination between its citizens, that it deals in universals and not in majorities—the latter concept being the excuse that politicians use to except certain cases from democratic, social rights. "Necessity, universality, is the logical means which ethics uses to guard against the possibility of exceptional cases. By the latter, politics is wont to confirm the general rule of the love of neighbor. The Negro, too, is a man, even before he has become a Christian."[41] On the other hand, it must be clearly understood that this ideal state of which Cohen speaks is not the empirical state of history which he himself characterizes as "the power state of the ruling classes"?[42]

If, with regard to the people, the state is an ideal, it must also be kept in mind that it is less than ideal with regard to the eventual aim of history, namely, a united humanity. It is thus a transitional stage between the natural fact of peoplehood and the messianic aim of humanity.[43] Since it is such a transitional stage, socialism must work through it, and not apart from or in opposition to it, as orthodox Marxist internationalism maintains. Here Lassalle, according to Cohen, was closer to the truth than was the greater man, his antagonist.⁴⁴ Also, due to this character of the state as a relative ideal, it is a constituent part of the eventual messianic society, and thus the unity of humanity must not be conceived of as a unification of biological peoples but rather as a federation of ideal states.⁴⁵ Indeed, the fact, that the individual state can be conceived of as leading to and eventually integrating itself into a federation of states, is the best proof of its transitional ideal nature; for, if it should be claimed that religion is more conducive to the unification of mankind, it must be pointed out not only that religion has historically always been divisive but that, due to its necessary claim of possessing the only truth and the whole truth, must always remain divisive. While a unity of religions is a contradiction in terms—unless the "principle of toleration and similar bromides" be called upon—the state naturally points beyond itself to the unity of states.⁴⁶

In view of this position, which so strongly upholds the legitimacy of the state, Cohen is entirely justified—as he would perhaps be even without the details of his personal political ideology—in saying: "Compared to anarchism, socialism unwittingly assumes the role of defender of state and law. Therefore, instead of disrupting the party in this necessary police work by suspicions and accusations, this fact should rather be gratefully acknowledged."⁴⁷

Despite the earlier reservation that the state he is talking about is, of course, not the actual, empirical state, there is nonetheless obvious danger in Cohen's apology for it. This danger is counteracted by the concept of society. Society is the concept of the true and genuine, ethical as well as universal, association of men. This concept, therefore, acts as a corrective to the state by holding in front of it the picture of what it should be, and thus pulls it out of any possible smugness, self-satisfaction, petrification, and narrowness. It represents the infinite perfection in comparison with which the particular and actual state always becomes aware of its limitations.⁴⁸ Economic determinists do the concept of society and its effectiveness a great deal of harm when they use it as the designation of the actual economic and cultural entity, contrasted with the legal entity of the state, rather than as this ideal norm. "In the term society echoes the sound of reform and the heartbeat of revolution."⁴⁹ Finally, what the philosophers and sociologists call "society" religion calls "the kingdom of God." The kingdom of God is the concept that corrects the existing realities by confronting them with ideality, and it has the advantage over the concept "society" in that it refers, through its religious connotations, to the guarantor of its own eventual victory and thus of being divine where "society" is merely human.[50]

Reactionary Philosophical Obstacles to Socialism

The two most malicious doctrines expounded by thinkers to retard the progress and realization of this philosophical, idealistic socialism, which Cohen expounds, derive from Greek philosophical sources, on the one hand, and from religious obscurantists on the other. Even the father of all idealism, of the hypothetical method and of ethics as a science, "the divine Plato," could not rid himself of the aristocratic prejudices with which the society in which he lived was suffused. Nowhere in his political utopia of the "Republic" does he indicate any moral abhorrence of the institution of slavery, which so profoundly disfigured the social landscape of ancient Greece. To the contrary, slaves are treated as an eternal and natural class. The philosophical basis of this social reactionism is the intellectual snobbery, which believes that not all men are capable of understanding, cognizing, and acting in accordance with the truth; therefore, science must always remain the prerogative of a privileged few. There will always be a hard distinction between the rulers and the ruled and, consequently, even the loftiest motto of the philosophical politics of Plato still retains the dichotomy between the two: "Let philosophers become kings and kings philosophers!" Will there always be kings, Cohen plaintively asks, or will not one day the ruled also be the rulers? Wherever the doctrine is expounded that some men are more capable of intelligent and rational thinking than others, there political reaction prevails.[51]

The other roadblock to the socialist society among thinkers is the tendency to explain social institutions and historical facts in terms of divine revelations or ordinances. When, for example, the Sabbath is explained as the result of a heavenly fiat rather than as the social institution, which it was intended to be and is,[52] "the rest day of the working classes," which, on the seventh day of the week, foreshadows the seventh year in which the slave will be completely liberated, then social obscurantism is being engaged in which, by disguising the humane purposes of the origin, makes impossible the humane improvement of the future. "The belief that something comes from God or the gods is the expression of scientific bafflement and means nothing but the confession: we cannot, or we will not explain it in terms of man." After all, not only good things but also evil ones have always been explained and justified as divine institutions and, furthermore, does not everything ultimately come from God? Why then isolate one thing?[53]

Specifics of Socialist Policy

Cohen, being a philosopher, pursued the business of elaborating a technical epistemology, a generalized theory of ethics and esthetics and even wrote a theology. It cannot be expected of him that he should also devise the details of a political program. His ideology of socialism remains, therefore, necessarily broad in outline. Nevertheless, with the sense for reality that he possessed and with his ethical and social enthusiasm, which he also demonstrated in his active participation in Jewish community affairs, references are strewn throughout his writings, which indicate some of the specific social alterations, which he subsumed under the name of socialism.

We have already seen that socialism meant for him that eventually the distinction between ruler and ruled will be obliterated, that the people will rule themselves in a complete democracy.

It was a dictum with him that, "all values are created by labor,"[54] (a phrase not unreminiscent of Marx). Quite apart from the truth of this proposition, if only on the grounds of Kant's categorical imperative, the worker must never be used, as is too easily the case in capitalist society, merely as a means of economic production and for the enrichment of his employer. The worker also is an end in himself.[55] Therefore, "a person has not value but dignity. Is the concept of the market value of labor compatible with the dignity of man? This is the great question of modern politics and of modern ethics."[56] The trouble is that, in advanced capitalism, the laborer is actually degraded beneath the level of the earlier laborer. While the worker used to be at least definable as a person who produces economic value by working on the land or in the factory, in all cases actually creating new economic objects, the modern proletarian does not even produce. He is only a cog in the wheels of communication, which has assumed such central importance in our society. He merely transports.[57] And Cohen comes even closer than this to Marx's germinal concept of the degradation of the worker through the system of surplus-value. As Kinkel put it, "Is it really true that the worker's product is his property as is the case with the capitalist's product? This question, repeated from Marx (by Cohen), destroys the entire mythology of capital."[58] And, as Atlas repeats, Cohen declares that the surplus-value theory is based on ethical assumptions, for what other reasons than ethical ones exist to protest the appropriation of a man's product by another?[59] Only two structures can lessen the severities of such private profit and property: the state[60] in its ideal functionings, and labor unions, which, even on juridico-philosophical grounds, Cohen regards as the ideal of ethical, because legal, persons.[61] Compared to these monstrous extremes of capitalist society, even militarism is a lesser, though by no means inconsiderable, evil, which may sometimes be used as a bogey-man to divert the people's attention from the real forces that manipulate it.[62] It must be remembered that Cohen wrote this sentence during World War I in which he fervently supported the cause of German arms.

Needless to say Cohen opposed capital punishment. It is worth retracing the philosophical argumentation, which caused him to take this position: execution is the most evil of all legal actions, for it cannot have any conceivable moral or constructive purpose. It constitutes not betterment but "the annihilation of the moral personality," for without life there can be no ethical person. Furthermore, law is moral only so long as the person subject to it shares in its legislation and responsibilities; but a dead person is outside the law.[63]

Finally, socialism meant to Cohen something that his temporal and geographical conditions required, namely, the demand for schools of universal, public, and compulsory education. These did not as yet exist in the Germany of the Kaiser, and universal education is, of course, the necessary corollary of the previously indicated plank which makes universal human rationality the basis of democracy.[64]

The Place of Israel

We have already noted that, at several crucial points, Cohen's socialism is based on religious premises that he obtains from the Bible. Thus, God is the guarantor of the eternity of nature required to make possible the infinity of the ethical, socialist tasks. Thus also prophetism and its messianism are for Cohen the inventors, discoverers, and synonyms for socialism. Since Christianity and Judaism, as well as all religions, which Cohen would regard as genuinely rational and ethical, have these factors largely in common, the only advantage of Judaism—to which Cohen, of course, throughout his life passionately and actively adhered—is that it possessed them first in time. For a rationalist like Cohen, such a temporal difference would at first appear to be incidental and unessential, even if it be granted that Judaism continues to possess them in a purer and less adulterated form than do the others. But the fact is, in Cohen's view, that this temporal difference is also an essential one; for, in accordance with his "philosophy of origin," originality denotes purity, and on the purity of the rational, messianic faith depends, of course, the desired purity of the messianic society.[65]

That Biblical Judaism, together with its natural continuation through the Talmud, represents this pure, rational, messianic, and therefore socialist faith is proved by the fact that it never sinks into the morass of mysticism or unworldly escapism. Rather, it always takes religion out of the theological and speculative realm into the historical world of humanity by concretizing itself in social, moral, and even political statutes.[66] Indeed, Cohen's admiration for and adherence to this concept of ethical and political religion in the form of Judaism goes so far that, even though, on modern and national grounds, he is a strong advocate of the separation of state and church, he nevertheless maintains that the peculiar Jewish mixture of religion and civil legislation, which characterizes Bible and Talmud, is also typical of the messianic society, correctly understood, and that, therefore, whatever its dangers, theocracy is the term describing the laudable permeation of politics with ethics in historical as well as in the messianic society.[67]

So far as the Jewish people is concerned, it exists exclusively in order to perpetuate the teachings of the prophets and to carry them to all mankind. And, if it should be argued that an ideology does not require the continued existence of one particular social unit for its perpetuation, as Achad Ha'am did in his famous essay "Slavery in the Midst of Freedom," Cohen argues, in rebuttal, that this is generally true of other aspects of culture but not of monotheism. The latter, due to the necessity of a purity, which can be fulfilled only by the originators, could not be maintained for the benefit of mankind at large by any but its creators: "One mankind could come to be under only one God. This One God was found only by one people. . . . This one people must perpetuate it."[68] Along with this insistence on the necessity for the survival of Israel goes, in Cohen's ideology, a severe anti-Zionism. The people must survive but not its state. In fact, "the destruction of the Jewish state is for us the model of historical theodicy. It is our proud belief that we live among the nations as a divine dew and remain productive among them and for them."[69] The homelessness of the Jewish people—a term that Cohen, incidentally, rejected because he insisted that we are at home and want to be more at home wherever we are—is the great historic symbol through which the Jewish people in its actual life foreshadows the future federation of states and the universal reign of God. "The One God deprived us of our fatherland in order to give it back to us in the form of humanity. . . . To induce the whole world truly to acknowledge this one God—that is our task in world-history."[70]

It is true that Jewish history, as a result of this messianic dispersion, is a history of martyrdom and suffering. But, then, such is the fate of the Messiah, who vicariously takes the injustices and cruelties of an imperfect world ever upon his shoulders. The prophets already predicted this in the figure of the "suffering servant of God," who suffered precisely because he was the carrier of salvation to all other men, and also in order to indicate his social mission, which is primarily concerned with the poor and the miserable. It is for this very reason that his identity was changed from the royal "son of David" to the poor and unknown sufferer.[71]

Conclusion

There are a number of serious problems that suggest themselves as we consider Cohen's philosophy of socialism. These have reference both to the philosophical underpinnings as well as to the political ideology itself.

In the first place, Cohen's concept of God, crucial and basic as it is to his entire system, is the result, admittedly, of this simple line of thought: psychologically men need the assurance that the things in which they profoundly believe and to which they are to devote themselves wholeheartedly must eventually come to pass. This assurance can only be given by God; therefore, there must be and is God. Now to derive objective, even if not ontological but ideal reality, from need is always a bad argument; it is worse when it is based on psychological need; and it seems worst of all when it comes from a philosopher who explicitly abjures psychologizing logic! But, even if the argument should be accepted as valid, Guttmann's objection then becomes the more cogent: "In this connection the further question arises, which can be fully answered only after Cohen's concept of reality will have been completely clarified, whether this function does not go beyond the character and capability of a God defined as an ideal—whether God must not be conceived as a highest reality (in the ontological sense) in order to be able, as the determining power, to guarantee the realization of the ethical ideal in the processes of nature."[72]

This very convincing objection of Guttmann's can legitimately be carried yet a step further. It can be applied also to Cohen's conception of messianism. Cohen regarded the concept of a personal, individual, Messiah rather contemptuously as a naive and mythological formulation for the rational idea of the messianic age. But he did so not for the reason current among the nineteenth-century Jewish liberals, namely, that the belief in the personal Messiah is a belief in miracles and that miracles conflict with the scientific spirit of the age. To him messianism meant the infinite approximation to the infinitely ideal society in history. Now, exactly what is the approximation to infinity supposed to mean? Cohen always compares it with the mathematical curve of an asymptote, which approximates an axis into infinity without ever reaching it. But the very point of the concept of infinity would seem to be that, however far you go toward it, you are in the end—or rather not at the end—just as far away from it as you were in the beginning! Progress thus becomes an illusion, indispensable though it was to Cohen's view of history. Therefore, if there is to be any guarantee that the socialist ideal will be reached, this guarantee cannot be given by the concept of infinity, and the Marxist accusation of utopianism stands unrefuted. The fact is that the guarantee can be given only if, in the first place, one believes that the infinite and infinitely small distance between asymptote and axis will eventually be bridged, and if, in the second place, one is ready to believe that, for this purpose, the rational, mathematical infinite distance will be irrationally and unscientifically overcome. But such a belief is a belief in miracle; consequently, there would exist no further justification for frowning upon the unscientific concept of a personal Messiah. In other words, as Guttmann wonders whether the ideal character of Cohen's God satisfies his own requirement of guaranteeing the infinity of nature, so we must wonder whether the impersonal character of the Messiah satisfies his own requirement that the eventual reality of the messianic, socialist society be guaranteed.

Actually, when one centers one's attention for a while not so much on Cohen's method, which is admirable and enduring, but on the specific content of his thought, it becomes painfully obvious that this content consists exclusively, or at least overwhelmingly, of the commonplaces marking nineteenth-century optimistic liberal religion and liberal philosophy of history: the concept of God as an idea and ideal, the Messiah as an age rather than a person, the overpowering stress on the prophetic rather than on the legal aspects of the Bible, the belief in the mission of Israel, which consists of nought but the spreading of universal, rational, and ethical tenets, the opposition to Zionism on messianic grounds, the belief in inevitable progress, gradualistic socialism, and the like.

On the political level, this optimistic rationalism expressed itself, in the case of Cohen, not only in a reliance on the German state—which history since his time has tragically disposed of and about which it is more merciful to keep silent—but also in an excessive dependence on the concept of the state as such. One may venture to suggest that, even in his time, there were indications of the tempting pitfalls created by this ideology of the state. It is hard to read Cohen's repeated statement that, while the people only constitutes the natural, biological unity, the state constitutes the ideal unity of a particular society, without thinking of Heine's bitter quip about the Prussia in which censorship was justified and glorified as bringing about that "ideal unity." Furthermore, any praise of socialism—such as Cohen uttered—on the grounds that it helps the empirical state to defend law and order, should make us suspicious; one would think that, from a socialist point of view, it is dubious praise indeed! The fact is that, though he believed he recognized ideality in it, Cohen lived in a Germany that had just attained its national unity; understandably he fell prey to the assumption that the state is a necessary human institution—an assumption that neither history nor philosophy warrants. If Cohen could say that "the state makes it clear beyond all doubt, particularly in our time, that man puts his higher metabolism into circulation in the organism of his state,"[73] then we, with our experience of the state, may retort that, in our time, we have come to know this organism in an entirely different, yes, in a threatening light. Still, it must be held to his credit that Cohen, at the very climax of his most Germanistic, anti-Zionist, state-intoxicated broadsheet, *Germanism and Judaism*, leaves himself an opening out of his assimilationist impasse—though he can hardly even conceive of the theoretical necessity for it: "A Germanism which would demand from me that I divest myself of my religion and my religious inheritance—such a Germanism I would not acknowledge as an ideal peoplehood with the right to the power and dignity of statehood.... Were I born into such a peoplehood or such a statehood, I would then regard myself as entitled to claim 'a publicly and legally insured home'" (the phrase in the Basle platform of the Zionist Congress formulating its aspirations in Palestine).[74]

Kant, at one point, said that the occurrence of the glorious French revolution in his time constituted an irrefutable proof of the basic goodness of man, for it was to his generation a *signum rememorativum, demonstrativum, prognosticum*.[75] Cohen also recognized such signa all over the landscape of his generation. One marvels what the *signa rememorativa, demonstrativa et prognastica* for humanity in our age are to be—our wars, the H-bomb, the annihilation of European Jewry or the advancing degeneration of libertarian democracy throughout the world?

All this is not to deny the effectiveness of Cohen's methodology in the philosophy of history, which resulted in his concept of social democracy. But it may cause one to pause and rethink the details of his ideology and to consider whether the rejection of eschatology by the nineteenth century, in favor of rationalistic messianism, satisfies the requirements of human reason.

Chapter 2 | 1962/1970

To Recast Rationalism

The most influential thinkers in contemporary Jewish philosophical theology are unquestionably Martin Buber and Franz Rosenzweig. Both give expression to the "postidealistic temper" of our age. Both start out with certain "data," *Gegebenheiten*, of human experience. Thus Buber begins his fundamental work *I and Thou* with the famous words: "To man the world is twofold"—and then proceeds to offer what might be called a phenomenology of human relations, describing the I-Thou and the I-It relationships. Rosenzweig starts out with the reality of death but quickly arrives at the stipulation of the three elements of reality-God, man, and the world. From these respective experienced bases both then proceed to construct their theoretical systems. As they go along they always continue to analyze real life rather than to manipulate terms, concepts, or definitions.

This practical approach to the tasks of philosophy accounts to a considerable extent for their persuasiveness with modern man. In the writings of Buber and Rosenzweig he recognizes his own situations and feelings and, therefore, trusts their extrapolations and conclusions. It is philosophy in a key very different from that of the classic rationalists, who begin their considerations in such theoretical phrases as Spinoza's: "By that which is self-caused I mean that of which the essence involves existence ..."; or Kant's: "In whatever way and by whatever means cognition is related to objects, the instrument by means of which it is immediately related to them and the goal toward which thought as a tool always aims is intuition." Indeed, it was precisely in rebellion against this kind of preoccupation with ideas at the expense of human existence, an attitude that the postidealists identify with Hegel, that Kierkegaard and the contemporary religious as well as atheistic thinkers began their new philosophic search.

First published in *Judaism* 11 (1962), 205–209.

But this is also the ultimate weakness of such a stance. Suppose one has not had the experience that Buber and Rosenzweig simply assert? For this reason, perhaps, there is so little, if any, discussion between the so-called existentialists on the one hand and the naturalists and positivists of all stripes on the other: they do not inhabit the same universe of experience. All the peremptory statements in the world, such as the one Hugo Bergman recently made again, that "all great men of faith, in effect, testify in similar words that God can be found and faith be achieved by every person,"[1] will not convince an honest person who must simply stick to his admission that, as for him, he has not found it to be so.

There is, furthermore, a fundamental philosophical objection to be raised against this method, apart from the practical one just mentioned. What criterion is to be used in determining what the basic types of human experience are from which all thought must presumably start out? And who is to make such a determination? No one has, for example, answered Nathan Rotenstreich's perfectly valid question[2] of why Rosenzweig picks just God, man, and the world to be the three constituent elements of reality and why not others, or at least additional elements. And as regards Buber, Moshe Maisels' book, *Thought and Truth*[3] powerfully illustrates the danger of such dogmatism. He starts out with precisely the basic direction, which Buber makes but, unlike Buber, does not manage to keep the two orientations to life connected with one another and, therefore, his universe breaks completely into two thoroughly dichotomous parts; lack of original rational derivation leads to the destruction of the unity of reality. Indeed, much of contemporary "existentialist" and religious philosophy is afflicted with this kind of dogmatism. Thinkers do not reason any longer; they narrate, much as did Rosenzweig, who insisted that modern philosophy must be autobiographical, and as has Rabbi J.B. Soloveitchik, who recently began a lecture by saying that he would merely tell about his own personal experiences and the listener could either accept them or not. This leads to a paralysis of reason and to an individualized atomization of truth. We must, therefore, again ask Solomon Maimon's question: Quid juris? How do we get to the facts, to the data? And we must resume the Cartesian search for a universally acceptable basis of rational thinking.

I suggest that we can find our way out of this dead end by going back to Hermann Cohen. Cohen was the last great rationalist in Jewish philosophy. Cohen was also the teacher of both Rosenzweig and Buber. Of Rosenzweig this is known, for he himself eagerly proclaimed it. Of Buber it is not generally known, for the first great and well-known encounter between them was one in which they stood not in a relationship of teacher and disciple but of antagonists on the question of Zionism. But it is, nonetheless, true. In the *Religion der Vernunft* the following passage occurs:

> By the side of the I arises, different from the It, the He. Is this He nought but another occurrence of the I which would, therefore, already be implied in the I? Language itself guards against this error: before we get to He we come to Thou. But is the Thou only another occurrence of the I, or does the Thou require a separate discovery even after I have become aware of my I? Perhaps it is the other way around—that only the Thou, the discovery of the Thou, can bring about my awareness of my I, the ethical cognition of my I. . . . [4]

Need more be said?

In contemporary Jewish theology the great breakthrough from rationalistic, idealistic thinking to "the new thinking" is supposed to have taken place when, according to Rosenzweig's interpretation of Cohen in his "Introduction" to the latter's *Jüdische Schriften*, Cohen advanced a new concept of the correlation (in his posthumously published *Religion der Vernunft*), which Rosenzweig claimed left the charmed circle of idealism behind and penetrated into ontology. Most subsequent students have followed this interpretation. Guttmann never did,[5] and in an essay, "*Hermann Cohens Begriff der Korrelation*," Alexander Altmann documents the untenability of Rosenzweig's thesis. Cohen, in fact, never did break out of "the system"—though it is, of course, true that his last writings taught a concept of religion considerably deeper than had previously been the case. The great breakthrough actually occurred when Rosenzweig argued with Cohen[6] that the recognition of truth begins with "irrational realities" rather than without any preconceptions, with the "nothing" of the "philosophy of origin." We have seen where this deviation led. We must go back to Cohen's "nothing" so that reason and human discourse may begin again.

I am not, of course, suggesting that we revert to Cohen's liberalism, optimism, or even to his own definition of rationalism. This is neither possible nor desirable. We must, indeed, go forward to a more wholehearted resubmission to the historical realities of Jewish history and established law and doctrine, and to the theological realities of God and

Revelation. This we have learned from Buber and Rosenzweig, and from our experience. But this must be done on the basis and with the means of Cohen's rational canons. It can, I believe be done.

I have in the past suggested where the *Ansatzpunkt* for such an extension of Cohen beyond himself lies,[7] even as Cohen extended Kant beyond himself; and again Guttmann supplies the stimulus:

> The further question arises, which can be fully answered only after Cohen's concept of reality will have been completely clarified, whether this function does not go beyond the character and capability of a God defined as an ideal—whether God must not be conceived as a highest reality (in the ontological sense) in order to be able, as the determining power, to guarantee the realization of the ethical ideal in the processes of nature.[8]

The same can be said of Cohen's concept of the Messiah. If it should turn out, as I believe it will, that God and the Messiah must be understood in "realistic" terms in order to satisfy Cohen's own rationalistic demands upon these concepts, then we shall have broken through the solipsism of idealism; but we shall have done it not by abandoning the rationalistic footing of scientific, critical philosophy but by pursuing this very philosophy to its own logical conclusions. Thus a rationalistically corrected doctrine of Jewish "existentialism" may be formulated.

Such a recast rationalism will also make it possible to explore anew and fully the complete range of the historic Jewish search for truth. It is well-known, indeed notoriously so, how rabidly and vitriolically the rationalists of the nineteenth century, for example, Heinrich Graetz (but also Maimon, Krochmal, and Cohen), rejected what they called the obscurantism and superstition of the Kabbalah. But as we observe the intellectual situation today, such a neat and simple-minded differentiation between "rationalism" and "mysticism" is utterly outmoded. We can and must find truth in Kant and the Baal Shem Tov at the same time. And this is not as inconsistent or eclectic as it would have seemed a generation ago. From Buber and Rosenzweig we work our way backward to Hasidism and from Hasidism to Kabbalah and forward to Lubavitch and Rabbi Aharon Rote and from them to Roman Catholic mystics like Thomas Merton and even Hindu mysticism; at the same time we work our way back from Buber and Rosenzweig to Hermann Cohen and Kant and forward even to Jamesian pragmatism.[9]

The notion that everything from Kant to Kabbalah and from Cohen to Merton should be relevant to a proper understanding of rationalism must initially appear absurd; but it is not really absurd. Study a compendium of Kabbalah, like the *Shelah Ha-kodesh*, and it is inconceivable how anyone not thoroughly versed in scholastic Platonism and neo-Aristotelianism, and, therefore, in Plato and Aristotle, can even begin to appreciate it. Rabbi Isaiah Hurwitz and Hermann Cohen both descend from the same parents, the Bible and Plato. But then, what in Western philosophy, religion, and culture does not? There is, on the other hand, I believe, a very clear criterion for distinguishing rational, that is, meaningful discourse from the irrational (as different from the outworn distinction between rationalism and mysticism)—and this criterion is whether any form of thought may be subsumed under the principle "truth is reality, and reality is truth," or under the opposite principle that "truth is above reality—truth is an Ought, not an Is." The outstanding philosophical exemplars of the latter are, of course, Judaism on the one hand, which awaits the Messiah and teaches that "God is the place of the world; the world is not the place of God"; and Kant—Cohen, on the other, who have demonstrated that even the cognition of reality is an ethical imperative. The outstanding exemplars of the former are Spinoza, who exclaimed *deus sive natura*, and Hegel, of whom Cohen wrote: "Perhaps nothing has contributed so much to making philosophy contemptible in the prerevolutionary age than the reactionary motto of Hegel: 'The real is reasonable, and the reasonable is real.'"[10] Thus, to identify the truth with the real—God with nature—inevitably leads to theoretical mysticism in the pejorative sense of the word, to moral and political reaction, and to religious atheism, for it deprives nature of its pedestrian, scientific character, ethics of its need for progress, and religion of its supernatural anchorage.

On the broader Jewish philosophical front, three tasks, it would seem, thus confront us: (1) a deepening of contemporary *existenz*-philosophy by retracing its development from its rationalistic sources; (2) a renewed exploration of—and strengthening of loyalty to—all of the classic and legitimate texts of Jewish revelation, from the outermost "left" boundary of scientific rationalism to the outermost "right" boundary of unreconstructed mysticism; and (3) a strengthened and aggressive reconquest of all forms of pantheism, to reestablish the Most High God whose seal is truth.

Chapter 3 | 1966

Truth

The Connection between Logic and Ethics

It is scandalous how little literature is available that deals with Hermann Cohen (1842–1918), the founder of the vastly influential school of neo-Kantianism that is also known as critical idealism or Marburg-Kantianism. As far as I have been able to discover, not a single one of his many shorter writings, much less any of his substantial works, has been translated. Of the very little amount of secondary literature that exists in this area virtually none concerns itself with his basic philosophic system, but it rather concentrates—quite superficially at that—on his Jewish religious philosophy.

Franz Rosenzweig, in his introduction to the three German volumes of Cohen's *Jewish Essays*, put forward the claim that the posthumous *Religion of Reason out of the Sources of Judaism*, Cohen's last work, constituted essentially a break with his earlier philosophic system. This claim has been largely accepted by later writers. But one may take leave to have one's doubts about it for a number of reasons.[1] In any case, Rosenzweig's thesis can be tested only against a thorough knowledge and understanding of the system itself. The latter is impossible for the student who does not master German.

I have translated a section of the first and important chapter of Cohen's *Ethics of the Pure Will* (Berlin, 1904, 82–92) as a first fulfillment of the desideratum. The Ethics is the second member of the systematic trilogy, of which the first is the *Logic of Pure Cognition*, and the last, the two-volume *Esthetic of Pure Feeling*. The present chapter is important because, apart from its own concern, it also, among other things, adumbrates the total structure of the *Ethics* and establishes the connection with

---

First published in *Judaism* 15 (1966), 466–473.

the *Logic*. This, however, also makes it a difficult chapter to read: Cohen is always a technical philosopher who assumes a great deal of knowledge in science and literature; here, in addition, he often presupposes a thorough acquaintance with the results of his *Logic*.

A running commentary to the chapter would, therefore, require a complete exposition of his philosophic system. Even to crystallize some of the more significant doctrines contained within it would lead to a substantial presentation of Cohen's ethics. In this introduction I want to limit myself, therefore, to pointing up one single important implication which the chapter contains.

In the first place, it must be noticed that the *Ethics* was written as and remained the pinnacle of the philosophic system—long before what Rosenzweig claimed was Cohen's turn to theology. Yet the conclusions for philosophic religion and even specifically for Judaism are perfectly clear and sometimes explicit in the chapter. In the second place, the question forcefully arises what Cohen meant when, in his philosophic as well as in his Jewish writings, he speaks of the realization of ethics in nature. The historians and interpreters invariably explain that this thesis states that, according to Cohen, the "fundamental law of truth" guarantees that nature will exist into infinity so that the infinite tasks of ethics can be carried out in it and so that they can be carried out successfully. The successful fulfillment of the ethical tasks means the total rationalization and ethicization of nonrational and nonethical nature.

Now, it is true that in a number of places Cohen sounds as if he were primarily saying just that. But this raises serious philosophic and even ethical problems. As I have tried to point out elsewhere,[2] the stipulation of an infinite nature is a dogmatic prediction about the future course of science and society, which fundamentally contradicts the strongly antidogmatic *Tendenz* of Cohen's entire philosophic work. Even ethically it appears to turn morality into a sort of sophisticated eudemonism, by guaranteeing the success of the ethical enterprise—than which Cohen rejected nothing more vehemently.

This chapter, now, makes it perfectly clear what Cohen essentially means when he speaks of the unification of nature and ethics. The law of truth not so much guarantees the ultimate, though infinite, historical realization of ethics in nature but their methodological unification in principle. It is not primarily concerned with history but with epistemology. In other words, this "law" does not speak chiefly of the total historical effectiveness in infinity of the ethical enterprise, which would be dogmatic prophecy, but of the possibility in principle of enacting the ethical imperative in the real, natural world right here and now. Unless nature and ethics share a common origin, Cohen is saying, it might be that nature takes its own course—ethics has its own laws—but possibly "never the twain shall meet," that is, the latter might never be actionable in the former. A man might know that he ought to do good, but the world might be such that he could in no way act accordingly. (The philosophical, ethical, and theological implications and allusions of such a doctrine are obvious.) To put it yet another way, the unification of nature and ethics is primarily a matter of origin and of the present, not so much of an historical future. The fundamental law of truth, as Cohen sees it, proclaims the practicability of ethics.

In the ninth chapter of the *Ethics*, which is the precise complement to our first and in which the infinite historical fulfillment seems most explicitly and repeatedly to be stated, on the very last climactic page (440) Cohen restates our meaning of his proposition in so many words: "What methodological sense would there be in an ethical system of concepts unless there be assurance of their applicability? Doubt of such applicability would not only be a matter *ad calendas graecas*, but it would be able to interrupt every step of ethical progress. The suspicion would always intervene that reality might block itself off from the *élan* of the pure will."

Chapter 4 | 1968

The Day of Atonement

In presenting this chapter, a number of characteristic features may be pointed out. (It might be noted, too, that, apart from its general and philosophico-theological interest, the material in question can also serve as a preparation for the imminent fall season of the Jewish calendar.) There is, first, the unexpressed personal, Jewish passion of Hermann Cohen. He likes to quote the prophet Ezekiel, not only because he regarded him as a path setting mark in the development of Jewish religion, but also because he was especially proud of the fact that Ezekiel was his own Jewish name. Cohen's father had been a cantor in Dessau, and, for that reason as well as others, like his dissenting and admiring disciple, Franz Rosenzweig, he saw much significance in Jewish liturgy. Contrary to the general impression, Cohen will here be seen to pay loyal attention to the Rabbinic shaping of Judaism, despite his indisputable "liberalism."

Further, many of the major themes of Cohen's philosophy and theology are adumbrated in this chapter: sin as *shegagah*, unwitting sin, in the spirit of Socratic evil as ignorance; the "correlation" of God and man as the major contribution of religion, which Rosenzweig and others have used to reinterpret Cohen; the centrality of the concept of repentance; his ethical optimism profoundly qualified by his deep sympathy for human suffering in general and by his understanding of Israel's paradigmatic suffering in history as part of his socio-ethical theodicy; his Kantian "asymptotism," in which perfect human identity and redemption are ideal, regulative norms, only to be approximated in history, his equal Kantian requisite of punishment for sins, so that human moral dignity can be preserved; and, finally, his passionate protests against pantheism and Christianity.

The reader will notice that, contrary to common English usage, pronouns referring to the Deity are not capitalized in the text. This follows

---

First published in *Judaism* 17 (1968), 352–357.

Cohen's practice in the German original. It is the more remarkable as, of course, German capitalizes as words much more than does English, and, indeed, Cohen italicized words and phrases that he thought were most significant even more than is common German practice. There can be little doubt, though, that the lower-case usage, with reference to the Deity, symbolized for Cohen his understanding of the ontological status of the God-concept. As all the textbooks do not tire pointing out, God was, for him, an "idea," not an "empiric reality."

Franz Rosenzweig, and others following him, claimed that this was true of Cohen's earlier philosophic works but no longer of the posthumous *Religion of Reason*. The present practice alone should make us wary of this claim. In any case, these re-interpreters miss the main point. For Cohen, as for Kant himself, "actuality," empiric, experienceable reality is a lower level of reality than ideas. Ideas are, in one sense—but in a most significant sense—more "real" than reality. (In this spirit Cohen pitted the Jewish God-idea against the Christian doctrine of the incarnation.) Kant's own classic words on this point (*Critique of Pure Reason*, Part I, Division II, Book I, chapter 2, "About the transcendental Ideas") were often echoed by his disciple Cohen: "Thus someone might say: the absolute totality of all phenomena is only an idea.... But the practical idea is always most fruitful and, with respect to real actions, indispensably necessary. In the idea pure reason even possesses causal power to produce that which its concept contains. One may not, therefore, say of wisdom, deprecatingly, as it were: it is *only an idea*. Rather, just because it is the idea of the necessary unity of all possible purposes, it must serve as the original, at least limiting condition of the rule of everything in the realm of the moral."

One must, underneath the technical language, feel the passionate commitment to the work of reason and of ethics that speaks out of these words—and out of the lives—of Kant and of Cohen if one wishes to understand this modern philosophical tradition at all. And who can gainsay that Judaism and the contemporary world stand in sore need of commitment to the works of reason and ethics?

Chapter 5 | 1970

Franz Rosenzweig's Anecdotes about Hermann Cohen

My associations with the Berlin Jewish Community are close. I was raised there between 1931 and 1939 and attended its schools; my late father was a member of the leadership echelon of Berlin and German Jewry during those years; after it was reconstituted in 1945 I came from America to be its rabbi between 1948 and 1950. The latter two years were full and agitated, the political partition of the city and blockade, the establishment of Israel and relative normalization of the Berlin Jewish Community, and so on, not to speak of the fact that I met my wife there, working for the (British) Jewish Relief Unit.

On the occasion of the twenty-fifth anniversary of the reconstitution of the Community it would be appropriate and useful to go back into my files and to make an historical record of some of the Jewish, political, and human experiences, which we underwent in the years 1948–1950. But to do this I would have to switch to a completely different set of interests from the ones that in fact preoccupy me these days. As my offering of concern for this occasion I, therefore, beg leave to submit the excerpt under the stated title. It is taken from a monograph, *Franz Rosenzweig's Methodology in the Historiography of Philosophy*, which, almost completed, I laid aside a few years ago because, again, other tasks pressed upon me.[1] Its suitability to the purpose at hand is clear: it deals with two of the greatest men in the history of twentieth-century German Jewry—the personal encounter between them took place precisely in the setting of the Berlin Jewish Community of two unbelievably long generations ago—and the issue between them is, I believe, of the most urgent Jewish, philosophical, and ideological relevancy today.

First published in *Gegenwart im Rückblick: Festgabe für die Jüdische Gemeinde zu Berlin 25 Jahre nach dem Neubeginn*, ed. H.A. Strauss and K.R. Grossman, Lothar Stiehm Verlag, Heidelberg, 1970, 209–218.

I want to examine the credibility of some of the anecdotes about Hermann Cohen, which Franz Rosenzweig weaves into his writings and which—partly, no doubt, because of their quasilyrical character, partly because they are easier to understand than subtle theological and philosophical arguments, and finally because they appeal to a neo-orthodox mood in the second third of the twentieth century—have become standard fare and "indubitable evidence" among virtually all later writers. Rosenzweig had—it is generally conceded by those who knew him—a sharp, witty, and inventive tongue. Furthermore, it is not unusual among bright people to "drop names," embellish tales, and make one's point in a somewhat hyperbolical fashion.[2] The Cohen anecdotes, which Rosenzweig relates, derive almost invariably from private conversations that are alleged to have taken place—and thus there is nary a third party to testify to them.[3] If, under such circumstances, the upshot of a story flies in the face of what we know about the subject of the story but fits in very neatly with the purpose of its narrator we may be allowed to doubt, putting it mildly—the historical accuracy of the story (which does not necessarily detract from our admiration of its possible poetic truth in another context).

Probably the most frequently retold tale in this group is the one when, speaking about messianism, a subject that was always central to Cohen's concerns, the old gentleman turned to his young disciple and asked: "When do you think the Messiah will come?" Embarrassed by the naively profound nature of the question, Rosenzweig muttered something under his breath about "hundreds of years," whereupon Cohen, misunderstanding him as having said "a hundred years," is seized by the passionate urgency of the apocalyptic mood in wartime Germany, by his liberalistic optimism, and by the expectancy of old age, and pleads with him: "Oh please, make it fifty!"[4]

Now, this makes a great story. It has been cited by innumerable "postliberals" to show up the self-delusions of "nineteenth-century optimism" and even the Jewish treason of assimilated German Jews. (It is then often put together with Cohen's notorious and misinterpreted wartime broadside about *Germanism and Judaism*.[5]) Furthermore, it fits perfectly into Rosenzweig's scheme of things: thus, he said, for example, that "anything that happens in eternity never happens"[6] and he insisted on the "reality," rather than "ideality," of religious and other subjects (although in fact the statement here attributed to Cohen would rather go in just this direction). When he tells the story in his "Introduction" to Cohen's *Jewish Writings* he himself contrasts it with the chapter on "the ideal" in the *Ethics of the Pure Will* and thus mutedly guards Cohen against the accusation of "vulgar developmental progressivism"; still, the anecdote makes Rosenzweig's chief two points: (1) that Cohen was much more convincing as a Jewish man than as a philosopher,[7] and (2) that theologoumena must be "de-idealisticized" and "re-realisticized."[8]

It must be said bluntly that anyone who knows and understands Cohen's philosophy and his philosophical theology as he understood and believed them passionately himself simply cannot believe that the event could have happened the way it is described. Not only the chapter in the *Ethics* to which Rosenzweig refers but literally everything that Cohen wrote, said, and did during his lifetime, including preeminently the chapters on messianism in the posthumous work on which he was presumably working at that time, testify to his unbounded commitment to the Kantian proposition that "the ideal," that is, ultimately the "messianic" reconciliation of all nature with all ethics is a purely "regulative," "normative," not "constitutive," infinite goal, which can never, in all eternity of time, be reached but only "asymptotically" approached. Its unattainability and imperative approximability are the supreme significance of the ideal. If Cohen and Kant did not stand for this they stood for nothing. It is philosophically no easier, therefore, to believe Rosenzweig's famous anecdote about Cohen than to believe that Kant told a friend that yesterday on the street he had run into and said "hello" to a noumenon. To Rosenzweig, on the other hand, the story is entirely applicable: when he tells it in his *Yehuda Halevy* he adduces it as an example of the propaedeutic value of pseudo-messianism, that, as Ernst Simon put it,[9] false messiahs are wrong instantiations of a true doctrine. For Cohen, however, anyone who believes in a false messiah has not understood the messianic doctrine in the first place.

The other best-known such story is the one of the old Jewish gentleman who is supposed to have come up to Cohen after a public lecture in Marburg and said to him: "Professor, your philosophical concept of God is very interesting. But where in it is the *boray olam* ("Creator of the world," i.e., the 'real' God")?[10] And, says Rosenzweig, Cohen turned away with tears in his eyes.

Now, again, no one can gainsay the effectiveness of the tale. It subtly alludes to Pascal's famous distinction between "the God of the philosophers" and "the God of Abraham, Isaac, and Jacob."[11] It also triggers off a reminiscence of Napoleon's famous question to Laplace: "Where,

Sir, is God in your system?" and of the genuine connection between Laplace's reply and Cohen's explication of hypothesis. It pits deep, if naive, faith against the lostness of the sophisticated intellectual. Again it displays Cohen's native reactions to have been more authentic than his philosophical constructs. Above all, it serves Rosenzweig's main philosophical point, that "the God of Cohen's system" who was only an "idea," a "concept," did not ultimately satisfy Cohen and that he, therefore, "broke through" to "the real God" in the postsystemic *Religion of Reason*, in whose behalf Rosenzweig also raises his voice.

For all that, this story is also simply incredible. Historically it may be noted that Rosenzweig does not cite a source for it, although he cannot himself have been present if only because he did not know Cohen in Marburg. Leo Strauss, in *Philosophie und Gesetz*,[12] claims to have told it to him. But, of course, also Strauss cannot have been present when it allegedly happened, since Cohen was no longer alive when Strauss came to Marburg.[13] Where then does the whole story originate? Indeed, on the face of it, who could have reported it—Cohen, the old gentleman, a bystander? In the second place, whatever Cohen's views may have been when he wrote the *Religion of Reason*, everyone concedes that during his Marburg period at least he was theologically committed to "the idea of God" as a postulate in the Kantian sense. Furthermore, the whole notion that an idea is somehow less real than an empirical object, a phenomenal existent, simply makes no sense—indeed, is the opposite of the truth of the matter—to Kant,[14] or a neo-Kantian, and to Hermann Cohen most especially. We will content ourselves here with only two quotations from Cohen to this effect—one from his earliest writings, where, in *Kants Begründung der Ästhetik*,[15] he coins the epigram that one ought not to speak of "only ideas but even ideas," and the other from his posthumous book, where, among similar statements, he says: "God is not real, and He also is not alive in the sense of living beings. Maimonides put a clear halt to this notion. Only the truth is the valid value which corresponds to the being of God."[16] Finally, even the chief thesis of Rosenzweig's "Introduction," that the *Religion of Reason* is philosophically and theologically discontinuous with Cohen's "system," can be and has been shown to be incorrect.[17] In short, if the event in Marburg happened at all, Cohen may have had tears in his eyes because he was sorry that he had not got across to the old gentleman, because he was sorry for him, or for some other extraneous reason; that his tears betokened philosophico-religious scruples simply does not square with the facts as we know them.

By now it must be clear from our analysis of these personal anecdotes that there is an underlying philosophico-theological issue, which is in fact being embattled between Cohen and Rosenzweig. This basic issue is whether, as Rosenzweig claims, after Cohen had finished his *Esthetics of Pure Feeling* and had gone to Berlin, he took "a Jewish turn" and entered into a new, postsystemic, post-Kantian, proto-"dialogical," theological "last phase." This question must, of course, be decided on the philosophical evidence.[18] Still, Rosenzweig raises it in *ad hominem* terms, and it is, therefore, legitimate to look *en passant* at the personal, anecdotal evidence bearing on the question as well. By the criteria of both methods it can be answered only through a comparison of Cohen's putatively "Jewish" Berlin period with the previous, putatively "philosophical" Marburg period.

As for the latter, the historical evidence is quite unambiguous (although usually overlooked). Another one of Rosenzweig's well-known stories relates that when Cohen was praised as a "ba'al teshuvah" (a "returnee" to Judaism) on the occasion of the much-applauded visit he paid to Russian Jewry immediately before the outbreak of World War I, he protested that he had returned almost forty years earlier.[19] This, as Rosenzweig points out, would date his re-commitment to Judaism during the famous "Treitschke affair" of ca. 1879–1880.[20]

That Cohen never ceased to occupy himself with intensely Jewish intellectual and even political matters after his involvement in the Treitschke affair his biography, letters, and the contents of the three volumes of his *Jewish Writings* make abundantly clear. What, then, is left in his life as a possible period of alienation from Judaism? At most the few years are left between 1864, when he left the Rabbinical Seminary in Breslau, and 1879.

But also for this short period the historical evidence is to the contrary—even if (and for once we resort to Rosenzweig's ploy of possibly understanding the man better than he understood himself) he thought otherwise himself. The *Briefe*, selective as they are, tell the following story: in 1865, already in Berlin, he maintains his Jewish commitment and, for example, at one point asks his father to send him a copy of David Friedrich Strauss' biography of Ulrich von Hutten "and my *tallis*"(!)[21] A little later he requests Munk's famous edition of Maimonides' *Guide for the Perplexed*—manifesting his concern with Maimonides, which he was to retain, and, indeed, deepen throughout the rest of his life. He dates his letters according to the Jewish calendar.[22] Once he gets to Marburg this line of action and attitude is not altered. Even the famous exchange with Friedrich Albert Lange, his predecessor in the chair of philosophy and his patron, in which he identifies what Lange calls "Christianity" with what he himself calls "prophetic Judaism," after all assimilates Christianity to Judaism at least as much as it does the reverse. He officiates as an assistant cantor with his father after he has become professor at the German university.[23] He continues to worry about Talmud studies.[24] He enters into close relations with the Marburg rabbinate, takes a leading part in the determining its personnel,[25] and engages in what today would generally be regarded as rather obscure pietistic liturgical practices.[26] On April 16, 1878, he writes the following letter:[27]

> My beloved father:
>
> This letter will presumably reach you on the first Seder evening. I need not tell you how dearly I would love to be with you all—for our covenant is not only based on nature, which is sacred enough, but as much on spiritual communality. Therefore, no words are needed to tell you that as long as I live I shall think—and, in the natural necessity of the case, think with the greatest devotion—of the manner in which, conversationally, you have practiced *marbeh lessaper bitzi'at mitzrayim* [a phrase from the Mishnah and the Passover liturgy: "the injunction to discuss the Exodus from Egypt as much as possible"] toward me. I do now and will always take satisfaction in the thought that I have striven diligently to bring nearer the fulfillment of *Ieshanah haba'ah birushalayim* [a prayer from the Passover liturgy; "next year in Jerusalem!"], in our interpretation. I will not slacken in this striving, and I hope devoutly that you may continue to witness this and its possible fruit This time I cannot be with you—you understand and approve of this. Especially since I entertain the justified hope that you will be able to take the greatest pleasure that can crown old age in the happiness of our home and our marriage. [Cohen was about to marry—and shortly did—Martha Lewandowski, daughter of the chief cantor of the Berlin Jewish Community and one of the handful of famous Jewish liturgical composers.] Today we applied for the license at the marriage-bureau, and the wedding has been set for Thursday, June 6, at 10 a. m. It will doubtless give you

pleasure to learn of this at the Seder. . . . With a hearty wish for simchat y't ["the joy of the holydays"] and with a devoted Kiss—your son Hermann.

By now we have covered, albeit cursorily, Cohen's life in the period at issue. (There is no debate about the succeeding years.) The biographical evidence would certainly appear to speak for itself.

The philosophical evidence for his Jewish commitment during the Marburg period is in fact no less unambiguous. To summarize it as it appears in "the system" one could put it like this: it is true, "God" is for Cohen no "*realium*" but an "idea" in the fullest Kantian sense of that word. On this he always insists most emphatically, even aggressively. But, in the first place and as we have had previous occasion to demonstrate, this is no derogation of God as either Kant or Cohen saw it; to the contrary, an idea is a "noumenon," a thing-in-itself, rather than mere appearance, a "phenomenon." If anything it is God conceived as a *realium* that is inferior, in terms of the best sense of "reality," to the idea of God. Never in his life did Cohen cease to polemicize militantly against the Christian doctrine of the incarnation for precisely this reason. Furthermore, he identified this idea of God with the classic Jewish doctrine of God's spirituality, unpicturability, incomparability, and especially with Maimonides' "negative theology" and that of the mediaeval Jewish mainstream tradition. He went further: he also identified the Kantian doctrine (especially as propounded in the *Critique of Judgment*) of the ultimate, infinite identity of nature and ethics—and the socialist goal of the classless, just society[28]—with the equally classic Jewish doctrine of messianism. These were the two supreme peaks—actually one philosophical doctrine of Cohen's system.[29] (One would have to cite virtually all of Cohen's works, especially his *Ethics*, chapters 8 and 9, etc. etc.[30])

Cohen held that this is ultimately what rationalist, idealist, Kantian philosophy is all about—and that it was Judaism that always continued to supply it! Far, therefore, from dissolving Judaism into philosophy, he in fact made all philosophy Jewish! He was saying that one cannot be a true philosopher without being (at least conceptually) a Jew! As Rosenzweig himself points out, unlike even the greatest Jewish philosophers other than himself, all of whom worked at "reconciling" Judaism with whatever philosophical system they happened to subscribe to (thus leaving the two side-by-side, at best not enemies or even friends, but throwing whatever they regarded as "the truth" open to all philosophers, Jews and non-Jews), Cohen did not philosophize Judaism away but Judaized philosophy. The academic German patriots of his time, and Heidegger later, who denigrated him as an un-German thinker, were on to something, after all.[31] And Cohen himself saw it precisely this way. In a well-known letter to a B'nai B'rith lodge he said in 1904:[32]

> It is a fact that the duty of truthfulness demanded a proper appreciation of Judaism in my systematic ethics. My enthusiasm for Judaism is rooted in my conviction of the ethical value of our idea of God; my Judaism is part of my scientific beliefs... I allowed not the instinct of loyalty to religion or descent but philosophical methodology to guide my Jewish consciousness.

Chapter 6 | 1972

The Torah Radicalizes on Many Levels

What are some of the philosophical issues—and, indeed, some of the most pressing social issues—that decisively concern us today?

In philosophy it is asked, for example, what is the rationale for and the proper procedure of scientific method. Hermann Cohen dealt with this problematic extensively, most usefully, and even now unexhaustedly, in his *Logic of Pure Cognition*, his *Principle and History of the Infinitesimal Method*, and so on. In ethics it is asked whether there are any ultimate criteria of "the moral thing to do," and if so—what they are. Cohen analyzed these problems creatively in his *Ethics of the Pure Will*. In esthetics it is asked what the nature and function of art are, and Cohen gave productive answers to this question in his two-volume *Esthetics of Pure Feeling* (whose very title, by the way, gives the lie to the shallow, if not illiterate, criticism often leveled at him that he did not pay sufficient, if any, attention to the emotional life of man). In politics we search for the relationship between ethics and power and for "the good society." Cohen unpacked this problematic in his democratic, humanist socialism. In religion God is sought, and—so far as Judaism in particular is concerned—we ask: What is the Jew to do? Cohen comes to grips with these questions in his magisterial *Religion of Reason—Out of the Sources of Judaism*. While addressing himself to any and all of these questions Cohen always, *en passant* but systematically, sums up not only the facts but also the dynamics and the upshot of the historical developments leading to the contemporary situation.

Exemplifying the Necessity for Jewish Truth

This neither is nor means to be anywhere near a bibliography of Hermann Cohen's writings. Also his ongoing, though very insufficient, influence

---

First published in *Sh'ma - A Journal of Jewish Ideas* 31, April 1972, 84–87.

in later philosophical work, in Europe, among Jews, and elsewhere, is not indicated. (Not a single one of his major works has been translated—partly, probably, because the cultural and philosophical contexts are missing, and partly, no doubt, because they are really very demanding—not so much linguistically as substantively. *The Religion* is now, finally, about to appear in Hebrew.) Nothing has been said either about his "practical" life and its achievements—in the university, in politics, and in the Jewish community. It was only intended to show that virtually all of the decisive problems with which the world grapples in the last third of the twentieth century cannot be properly handled without the most serious attention to the work that Cohen did as much as a century ago. What is particularly important for the Jew in this—and unique in modern times—is that Cohen demonstrated, and exemplified, that all of these problematics, however universal and abstract, require for their elucidation and progressive resolution, Jewish truth, and Jewish truth-bearers.

The Real Cohen Is Lost

The place of Cohen in history is deeply troubled by, among other things, the fact that the real Cohen completely disappears between the complementary distortions that German anti-Semites and Jews have respectively superimposed on him. Anti-Semitic academic ideologists accused him of destroying the German "soul" through his insistence on the critical, rational, scientific, universalistic intellect. Some Jews, like Buber, early in the game, accused him, on the one hand, of betrayal of the Jewish "folk-spirit." (Note should be taken, to the contrary, that many of the finest spirits of prerevolutionary Eastern European Jewry flocked to his lectures—men like Aron Steinberg, Leo Rosenzweig, Klatzkin, Gawronski, Pasternak.) Other Jews, at the same time, have seen him as a philosophical assimilationist, who handed Rabbi Akiba over to Immanuel Kant—whereas the opposite is the case: in the best tradition of the medieval synthesis, Cohen circumcised, as it were, Plato and the European tradition. The Jews most sympathetic to him tend to limit their interest to his "Jewish writings" and pay virtually no attention to his systematic philosophical work. (Jacob Agus' early book is a laudable exception.) As a result they lose sight of his towering greatness. More importantly, thus they also bar access to him for many especially valuable potential students: not everybody is turned on by what a man a hundred years ago had to say about Jewish ethnicity; such people may, however, very well be grabbed by, for example, the apparently outlandish propositions that "The Magic Flute" is a footstep of the Messiah in history and that the infinitesimal calculus is an explication of how the "Infinite" God of the Kabbalah creates the universe through His *sephirot*.

Meeting the Objections

Without going into specifics—which is the only thing that really ought to be done—some of the major Jewish objections that are commonly leveled at Cohen, usually in terms of some contemporary *Zeitgeist*, can be invalidated by a simple but cogent comparison with Maimonides. Cohen was no more devoted to Kant than Maimonides was to Aristotle, and Kant's fundamental commitment to "the primacy of practical reason"—ethics and pragmatics—can easily stand the Jewish comparison with Aristotle's aristocratic, esthetic positivism. (Be it remembered that Maimonides' *Mishneh Torah* is just as Aristotelian as his *Guide For The Perplexed*.) Guttmann argued then rightly, for this and similar reasons, that the modern Jewish philosophers generally were Jewishly more "authentic" than the medieval authorities. Maimonides held no less firmly than Cohen (as, indeed, do the central Jewish classical texts) that, in principle, all of Judaism—God, the 613 Commandments—was ultimately of ethical character. If God does not want truth and righteousness—that is, humanistic reason—what does He want? Surely none of the pagan mystifications of Heidegger or the biologico-"ethnic" power-drives of "blood-communities."

The Moral from a Story

The present situation is strikingly reminiscent of a story that Shai Agnon told (*Bishnay Olamot*, Tel Aviv, 1962, Hebrew, 17—it is hard to make out why), literally like this:

> Dr. Me'ir Weiss told me that when Hermann Cohen was in Poland he prayed in a Chassidic synagogue on the night of the Day of Atonement. When they came to the verses "Hear our voice . . . !" there was much emotion. And when they came to the

verse "For My house shall be called a house of prayer for all the nations" the cantor recited this verse in a voice of weeping. Hermann Cohen said to himself: How receptive and sensitive this Polish Jew is to the great vision which the prophet envisioned for the world, when all the nations will cognize and know that they are one nation and that they will all pray as one in one house of prayer!—After the service Hermann Cohen went up to the cantor, blessed him, and said: Why did you weep on the verse "For My house shall be called a house of prayer for all the nations"? He replied: How can I help but weep when the House of our holiness and glory will be filled with *goyim*!

The attacks on Cohen's tragic German patriotism are facile, ironic, and self-refuting. He fought a long, losing, and sacrificial battle for humanism, Jewish ethics, and universal civilization. The life of reason internationally as well as nationally was his categorical imperative. He identified these values heuristically with German culture. The German chauvinists defeated him, on a world-catastrophic scale. Let no Jew now come and, with Jewish "ethnic" weapons, kill him a second time! And if Cohen had a tragic love affair with Germany, what do we have with America? Are we going to give up on America before the last strike of the last half of the last inning of this game is completed, when there is no other game in town?

"Idealists" are always accused of being unrealistic, not "at home in the world." Thus Hegel and all his disciples in the nineteenth and twentieth centuries set about to locate Kant's "ought-to-be," the true and the good, somewhere in "actuality"—be this metaphysical Being, the state, the laws of history, or the *Volksgeist*. When Cohen gave precedence back to Kant over Hegel he did so for the ethical reason, which he expressed eloquently, that to identify the ideal with any part of the real, or with all of it, is idolatry (whether in the form of the incarnation, pantheism, Hegelian or Heideggerian phenomenology, positivism, Marxism, political nationalism, or racism). This has not saved him from once again being attacked, on the Jewish side, by Franz Rosenzweig, Buber, and now Emil Fackenheim on the ground of his "abstractness." Fackenheim, as is his wont, even makes use of (abuses) the Holocaust toward this end: he argues that Cohen's "abstract" God produced Cohen's "unrealistic" politics, whereas our concrete Jewish experiences require an "existing God," who, then, sets his seal upon our survival by any means, folkism, chauvinism, and war. Judaism, the Jewish people in its authentic embodiments, and Hermann Cohen have always known better: God "is" not—He commands laws (which Cohen's critics sometimes conspicuously set aside), because only the ideal can make demands upon the real, and life is guaranteed only by living for values higher than life. And our Sages were clearly right when they taught that idolatry is the theological form of immorality.

Speaking from the Heart

I want to add a personal word. Yes, I love Cohen—for his philosophical erudition and perspicacity, for his moral grandeur, and for his Jewish profundity. I have his memorabilia in my study and his portrait, done twice by Max Liebermann, on both sides of my sitting room, so that no visitor can avoid the look of his searching eye. I appreciate Eva Jospe's half-hearted vindication and Michael Wyschogrod's nostalgic respect for him. But both are—to my mind—condescending to him. One has to be awfully tall to condescend to Hermann Cohen. Whatever we are contemporaneously as Jews we are by virtue of what Cohen did—whether we receive it through Rabbi J.B. Soloveitchik, through Martin Buber or Franz Rosenzweig, through Ernst Cassirer or Erich Fromm. (As the years and their problems pass I am more and more convinced that Buber and Rosenzweig—no less tragically defeated by the history of the twentieth century than Cohen—diverged from Cohen's path to their and our loss.) If these be the chords from the past of Frankfurt and Berlin, as well as Brisk and Cordoba, of Trier and Jerusalem, that Wyschogrod hears in our voices—voices in the cacophonous wilderness of the Black Forest and Forest Hills, Moscow and Washington, Sharm-el-Sheik and Saigon, then I and—I imagine—also Arnold Wolf are content to have it that way. Just let him not suggest that the grammatical or actual antonym of Hermann Cohen's alleged "German humanism" is "generalized radicalism." Cohen's and—*lehavdil*—our striving is to imitate the acts of Israel's Ruler of all worlds—that is, if you please, generalized, radical, Jewish humanism.

Chapter 7 | 1976

Historical Excursus

On Cohen's *Infinitesimal-Methode*

A. Prehistory

The philosophical concepts that have gone into the making of Cohen's theory of the infinitesimal have a very long and broad history. In breadth it includes much more than the history of the development of the infinitesimal calculus, which it is generally allowed the *Infinitesimalmethode*[1] itself surveys excellently; notions such as infinity, "the nothing," productivity–creativity–creation, "reality," thought and matter, and many others devolve upon it. In length, too, it, therefore, really comprises the entire history of philosophy. Cohen was a roundly erudite and very literate man, and there can be no doubt that his thinking on this subject, as on many others, received significant influences from many different quarters in this vast history. Furthermore, much that has happened since his time, especially in modern science, is also importantly relevant to a proper understanding of the main point that he wants to make: a number of serious mistakes in philosophy and science could and should be uncovered, and on some scores better comprehension of what we know could and should be attained, by measuring Cohen's theory of scientific and infinitesimalistic epistemology and his developing positive scientific theory against one another. It cannot be our task here to write such a history. For one thing, this is not a historical but a philosophical study. For another, the task set by the previous paragraph is obviously too big for any one single enterprise. For a third, happily there exists a considerable body of literature that already covers various parts of this large area of subject-matter. All we want to do in this excursus is to direct attention to some important corners that have not, perhaps, been sufficiently looked into in extant treatments and highlight some others because of their inherent interest and value.

One question that should be raised about the prehistory of Cohen's doctrine is its place, if any, in specifically Jewish intellectual history. Offhand this is likely to raise eyebrows. What can be Jewish or non-Jewish about a theory of the infinitesimal calculus? Cohen himself certainly makes no such explicit claim. On the other hand, there has been a very unfortunate tendency to split Cohen's work, and, indeed, his person, into Cohen-the-Jew and Cohen-the-philosopher. Only the vehement anti-Semitism to which he, his associates, and his theories were exposed in his own time and afterward seems to imply some unitariness—a negative one, to be sure—in which Marburg neo-Kantianism was perceived. He himself made no such distinction. This expressed itself in many different ways—by what he said about the nature of his Jewish, and his philosophical commitment, by the manner in which his Jewish and his general philosophical work were interwoven, by the sources that he often explicitly adduced and by the doctrines, which he expounded (without necessarily emphasizing their Jewishness) in his major books,[2] and so on. Some such adumbrations can also be found in the *Infinitesimalmethode*.

Cohen incorporates, for example, Lazarus Bendavid's thesis that unmeasurable quantity is the "intensive" origin of quality in his own, historically derived theory.[3] Bendavid was a Jewish disciple and close associate of Kant's. In general, Jews are extremely prominent and numerically highly represented in Kant's circle, from Moses Mendelssohn, through Bendavid, Marcus Herz,[4] to Salomon Maimon,[5] and so on. This is, as far as Kant is concerned, the more noteworthy when one considers the historical and cultural conditions that prevailed at the time. In any case, their names invariably occur in Cohen's work, and their books were assiduously collected on his shelves. The reader endowed with some imagination may sense a degree of personal identification on the part of Cohen with such people: they prefigure his own spiritual constitution—philosophers, Jews, profoundly devoted to an intellectual orientation for which they are indebted to Immanuel Kant and to the intellectual and cultural inheritance of Judaism at the same time, Germans in language, education, political enthusiasm, and yet somehow strangers in their native setting, invariably political liberals and yet, though "enlightened" and suspected by their coreligionists, men in whose minds and hearts religion played a very important, albeit never simplistic role.

Mendelssohn is, of course, a special case in this group. He, too, finds passing mention in the *Infinitesimalmethode*. His relationship to Kant was clearly very different from that of other people here mentioned.

He was really a philosophical competitor to Kant, though a friendly and mutually respectful one, and not a disciple. More than one edition of his publications and collected works and a lot of secondary literature revolving around him are to be found in Cohen's surviving personal library. Cohen clearly regarded him, as did all of modern German Jewry, as the personal embodiment of the ideal of German-Jewish symbiosis at its very beginning.[6] At the same time, very much the very intellectual and philosophical distance that separated Mendelssohn from Kant was bound to separate Cohen—identified as he was with Kant—from Mendelssohn. It is characteristic that under the circumstances Cohen refers to him on one of the points where he can agree with him: a polemic against Mendelssohn's Jesuit contemporary Ruggiero Guiseppe Boscovich, who, in discussing the "law of continuity" raised what Cohen must regard as a bad question—whether points are extended or not.[7]

Actually a closer look at Mendelssohn's work throughout his lifetime, such as Cohen clearly took, makes it very likely that Cohen—consciously or semiconsciously—derived much more benefit from Mendelssohn also for his infinitesimal theory than this one direct reference would seem to imply. A thorough perusal of Altmann's biographical study reveals many points of contact. Mathematical questions in general and questions relevant to the infinitesimal occupy Mendelssohn in one way and degree or another from his early prize-essay about "Evidence in Metaphysics and in Mathematics" (in a competition in which also Kant and others participated) until his last work, *Morgenstunden* (especially chapter 13).[8] In the prize-essay the infinitesimal calculus is characterized as knowledge that is certain but without what Altmann renders as "perspicuity" (Fasslichkeit: "graspability," intuitability). Between the mathematical realm of quantity and the philosophical realm of quality an intermediate realm is stipulated that comprises unextended or intensive magnitudes and forms the basis for "degrees of quality." Into this conception Leibniz's monadology and Baumgarten's *mathesis intensorum* have, of course, entered.[9]

In Mendelssohn's *Phaedon* at least two relevant discussions occur. A doctrine of the asymptote is expounded here, which Cohen might have adopted almost literally. "By imitating God one may gradually come nearer to his perfections, and the happiness of the spirits consists in this approximation; yet the road to it is infinite. . . ."[10] Connected with this, he argues further that there can be no transition of the soul from existence to nonexistence, because of "the law of continuity"; Kant replies to this in the "Refutation of Mendelssohn's Proof for the Endurance of the Soul" in the *first Critique* with an argument based precisely on the doctrine of intensive degrees of reality.[11] In what amounts to a running commentary and interpretation of Leibniz's essay of the identical title, *Causa Dei*, or *Providence Defended* (1784), Altmann admits that Mendelssohn virtually conceded the cogency of Kant's argument, though earlier[12] he had denied it: "Thus Mendelssohn who once had warned against the application of the infinitesimal calculus (Newton's *methodus fluxionum*) to 'un-extended quantities' now declares it also to be very fruitful in philosophy...."[13] Finally in *Morgenstunden* he holds that God must be not only "extensively infinite" but also intensively so[14]—a question that had come up between them in their first contact through Mordecai ben Hirz Levi: Marcus Herz.[15]

It is not only persons who were themselves Jews at the end of the age of the Enlightenment through whom one may discern some specifically Jewish involvement in the history of the developing infinitesimal calculus on Cohen's part. He regarded himself, as did all of emancipated German Jewry, very much the child not only of the Enlightenment but also of the French Revolution. The ideals of liberty, equality, and fraternity under the goddess of reason had made them what they were. This plays so large a part in Cohen's entire outlook that his two-volume *Aesthetics*, for example, ends with an apostrophe to the effect of the Revolution on modern art. When he then calls upon Carnot as a witness[16] one might remind oneself that Carnot was not only a mathematician and engineer but also one of the most outstanding "ideologues" under the French Revolution and beyond Napoleon—a "liberal" of very much the same stamp as Cohen. Carnot furthermore moved in circles in which Kant had rapidly become an influence, as, for example, through Mme. De Stael.[17]

The "Jewish" aspects of the matter hitherto appealed to are really only trivially Jewish, in the sense that we ran across people that were Jews and that were distantly connected with Jewish historical developments who, for the rest, worked in one way or another on the conceptual underpinnings of the purely mathematical infinitesimal calculus. There has been nothing doctrinally Jewish about the facts so far considered. Is there, though, something like this, too?

We ought to take at least a brief look at the Kabbalistic doctrine of "the creation," the "origin" of the universe. So-called negative theology, the *via negativa*, had reached its Jewish scholastic peak in Maimonides, for whom God could be described essentially (disregarding the "attributes of action") only by negative attributes: He is "not so-and-so"—he is infinite, and so on. Cohen paid a great deal of attention to Maimonides in his historical studies, most especially proffering an interpretation of his "negative judgments" as Kantian "infinite judgments." The Kabbalah, now, fed by this tradition of negative theology as well as by general neo-Platonic ideas about "the nothing"[18] and "the one," which is beyond number, developed a doctrine of the God beyond God who is no-thing, nothing, *ayin*, of the kind that also developed in Christian mysticism. Meister Eckhart was to declare, for example: "Man cannot know what God is. One thing he does know: what God is not."[19] Within these parameters the doctrine of *creatio ex nihilo, yesh me'ayin* in Hebrew, thus came to mean that something and everything was produced by and "originated" in the nothing. What the precise nature of this process of coming-into-being from non-being (and from the Non-being) is was a matter of much dispute among the theologians and philosophers. It was rather common ground to them, however—neo-Platonists as they tended to be and, therefore, committed to a model of a hierarchical, graded universe (*pace* "the chain of being" and "the law of continuity")—that the process was one of almost infinitesimal degrees of increasing materialization out of spirit.

Hermann Cohen cannot very well have sipped at this cup. Little was known of Kabbalah in his time and in his militantly rationalist circles. The little that was known was held in ferocious contempt. (His teacher Heinrich Graetz, the famous Jewish historian, wrote his strong anti-Kabbalistic views into his standard history, and, although Cohen disagreed with him about many other issues, on this they were at one.)[20] But there are at least as many ways of receiving historical influences as there are of skinning a cat. Like several other important originally Jewish strains, Kabbalistic notions came down to modern culture through European and Germanized channels.

Kabbalah entered the mainstream of modern European culture, as is well-known, no later than in the Renaissance, not only in the denominationally very eclectic circles of esoterics, millenarians, magicians, and mystics but also through acknowledged philosophical writers like Bruno, Leone Hebreo, Pico della Mirandola, Reuchlin, Agricola.[21] In this limited context we neither can nor need to trace how these connections came about, how they developed, and how they then branched out through many different and later disciplines and cultures. Suffice it to remember that to people of such religious, theological, mystic, and millenarian interests particularly Kabbalistic notions concerned with infinity and their various ramifications, with numerological combinations, and with immaterial "forces" were especially appealing. Once such notions were entrenched in general European culture it is not very difficult to watch how they trickled down to so thoroughly Europeanized a Jewish intellectual as Cohen.[22]

In a direct way the mystical, Kabbalistic inheritance of the German Reformation, particularly its "Left wing," was absorbed, transmuted, and disseminated especially by pietistic proletarian poets like Angelus Silesius and Jacob Boehme.[23] Leibniz' monad, as the infinitesimal-infinite, metaphysical "point," which, standing between, as it were, God and matter and, though "nothing," producing the latter, is traceable precisely to such theses in Kabbalistic, particularly Lurianic literature even in a direct historical manner.[24] The rampant millenarianism and religious, Bible-exegetical speculativeness of Isaac Newton, hidden behind his facade of cool calculations, have been uncovered only in recent years.[25] In the intervening centuries Newton's mysticism was as carefully guarded from the tender eyes of his rationalist and scientific admirers as the nineteenth-century guarded enlightened Jews from the seductions of Kabbalah. It is, therefore, the more noteworthy that Cohen, who could not have known of these aspects of the man whom Kant and he regarded as the greatest scientist of them all, somehow managed to focus his personal attention on just those passages in Newton's then-known writings, which give a hint of his ultimate religious concerns.[26] In his copy of *Sir Isaac Newtons Mathematische Prinzipien in der Naturlehre*,[27] for example, with his characteristic reading marks and fragments of a personal index on the back inside cover, Cohen underlines for his own attention Paragraph 61 of Book III, section V, "General Remarks," where Newton, to begin with, asserts a transcendent rather than immanent God.[28] Newton goes on to assert the immaterial, spiritual nature not only of God but, by analogy, of human personality.[29] Cohen then checks the sentence: "This is what I have to say about God, whose works to investigate is the task of natural doctrine. . . . I have not yet achieved deriving the cause of these characteristics of gravity from appearances, and hypotheses I do not devise."[30] (Cohen double-marks the last phrase.)[31] And Newton goes on to speak of spiritual substance that pervades bodies—attraction, warmth, and so on, but laments that not sufficient experiments have been possible so as to define their laws.[32]

The mystical stream in the transmission of this body of Kabbalistic ideas was revived and supplemented further directly from late mediaeval and early modern German literature by the Romantic writers and thinkers in Germany in the later eighteenth and earlier part of the nineteenth centuries. Thus, it is that we find explicitly acknowledged Kabbalistic and even Hebrew snatches in the early Hegel as well as, more covertly, in his maturer writings and certainly in Schelling. (The story is, of course, extremely complicated. Among these "absolute idealists" one must also recognize the influence of Giambattista Vico, who, in turn, made no bones about his concern with the Hebrew spirit and about his friendship with Joseph Athias.) What Hegel has to say, for example, in paragraphs 258ff. of his *Philosophy of Nature* about the point, time, space, motion, the nothing, and being requires no significant changes to reflect the essence of Cohen's philosophy of the infinitesimal.[33]

The entire famous "Pantheism controversy" around the turn of the eighteenth and nineteenth centuries infused a new strong dose of Spinozism into the mainstream of European thought, including its own well-known Jewish and Kabbalistic components.[34] And the Kabbalistic influences that Gershom Scholem has begun to reveal in the French Revolution and in early nineteenth-century German rationalism only fortified further the lines of influence that we have observed.[35]

One must not regard these things simplistically, of course. The transmission of ideas that we have sketched out here is, after all, only one—though a very important, interesting, and historiographically much neglected—factor in the total picture. We have rather artificially abstracted this one factor from the complete context. Obviously Reuchlin and Pico, Newton and Leibniz, Kant and Hegel derived their intellectual sustenance from many other and even more potent sources than these usually highly attenuated and mediated Jewish ones. Furthermore, it must not be forgot that Maimonides, for example, was himself a devote of Aristotle and that the Kabbalah is distinctly a Jewish acculturated form of neo-Platonic and general mysticism. The question is, therefore, not whether Jewish religious doctrines are the sufficient cause but whether they are *sine-qua-non* for, and again retrospectively, whether they are reconcilable with, their philosophical views.

B. Subsequent Developments

In the body of our exposition of Cohen's theory of the infinitesimal we have stressed the close mutual relationship that was prerequisite to and stipulated by the philosophical theory on the one hand and positive scientific practice on the other. This relationship was itself not a merely theoretical, abstract one in Cohen's own work, nor has it remained so since his time.

In a not merely anecdotal way it is noteworthy how much of Cohen's personal library was devoted to contemporary science and mathematics: Husserl, Bolzano, Brentano, Boole, and Cantor, and so forth on mathematics—and all sorts of things in science: the first translation, in German, of Darwin's *Origin of Species*,[36] Avenarius and Mach, all the way down, when Cohen was already a very old man and presumably set in his ways, to the first edition of Einstein's 1913 *Entwurf einer verallgemeinerten Relativitätstheorie und einer Theorie der Gravitation*.[37]

To possess and even to read books is one thing. Of course, philosophical utilization of scientific results and scientific utilization of philosophical concepts are another. Here, too, though, Cohen is as good as his word. He uses Helmholtz and Planck to illustrate the productivity of his theory in physics.[38] Indeed, Helmholtz's *Die Lehre von den Tonempfindungen als physiologische Grundlage für die Theorie der Musik*[39] is in his library, well read. And this has important ramifications in Cohen's philosophical psychology[40] and aesthetics. With respect to Max Planck one might refer to his famous essay "Das Prinzip der kleinsten Wirkung" ("The Principle of Minimum Effect"),[41] whose "Introduction" begins with the demand for one and only one ultimate principle for all nature. He calls this demand an "ideal problem" and an "asymptote," which "(is) not utopian but rather eminently fertile . . . and practical. . . ." "The principle of the smallest (minimum) effect (action)" comes nearest, at this stage of the development of science, to this universal principle, not the principle of the conservation of energy, since the latter can be derived from the former. Indeed, Cohen himself outlines how the infinitesimal can be made to work in the reduction of descriptive physics to genetic, chemical physics.[42]

Of particular importance is the fact that the *Infinitesimalmethode* ends[43] with an outline of how his infinitesimal method can and should be put to use in scientific psychology. Cohen had begun his philosophic life, during the brief period before he wrote his dissertation on Kant, as a philosophical psychologist. Throughout his subsequent teaching career philosophic psychology—in a strictly Kantian vein, to be sure, after his "habilitation"—occupied an inordinately large place in his curriculum. A look at his officially announced courses at the University of Marburg[44] makes this very clear: from 1877 on he regularly offered courses and tutorials in psychology, philosophical pedagogy, and even experimental psychology; as the years passed this practice intensified, so that some semesters were entirely preempted by such subjects; from 1905 on the most formal courses were, characteristically, entitled "Psychology as the Encyclopedia of Philosophy." (He still taught this when, in 1916, during the war, he came out of his Berlin retirement to substitute for teachers called to arms.) Indeed, we know that he intended to round out his "System of Philosophy," consisting of his *Logic*, *Ethics*, and *Aesthetics*, with a transcendental *Psychology*, which was to show how, in the interaction between reason and the works of culture, the human mind normatively constituted itself. It was thus to be not an individualistic but a *Kulturpsychologie*. (Parallel to the other titles in the "System," it could then well have been called "Psychology of Pure Culture.") Why no notes or manuscripts of this projected work have been found, and what, if any, the relationship is between this projected psychology and the executed but posthumous *Religion of Reason*, must be discussed in another connection. (Again, it is worth pointing out that in his personal library Cohen collected psychological literature and professional journals assiduously.)

The first dissertation written under Cohen's sponsorship was by Ferdinand August Müller, "The Axiom of Psychophysics," 1881.[45] The very title indicates the direction of Cohen's concern—to ground psychology in quantitative science. Gustav Fechner's technical work at that time gave the lead to his efforts. If psychology was to be quantitatively scientific, "mentalistic mythology" would have to be eliminated, and instead physical data would have to be its basis. On the other hand, these physical data would themselves have to be rationally, mathematically deductible, and this brings us back to an infinitesimal calculus. When Kant spread psychic experience on a scale from 0 to 1, and when Mendelssohn, in the journal *Know Thyself, or Magazine of Experiential Psychology . . .*,[46] explicitly used the infinitesimal calculus in order to stipulate psychic experience even in sleep, not only the basic Freudian notion of the subconscious and, indeed, of the unconscious (= 0-consciousness) but occasionally even Freud's operative concepts and vocabulary were presaged. As Cohen then puts it: "Thus the psychological problem is resolved by means of the epistomologico-critical determination of reality."[47]

In terms of the central contemporary discussion about psychology the issued could, perhaps, be put as follows. In Kant's *Third Critique*, in the context of an analysis of psychology, it is particularly important to remember that its proper title is *Critique of the Capacity of Judgement*, not the customary one of *Critique of Judgement*—a priori teleological concepts are applied to living organisms in an heuristic manner, that is, for the purpose of chopping out sections of observed phenomena so that they can then be subjected to asymptotically increasing causal, mechanistic explanation. In our time Noam Chomsky wants to do the former job without doing the latter, and B.F. Skinner wants to do the latter job without the former. Thus Chomsky turns into a Cartesian ("dogmatic") idealist and Skinner into a naive empiricist. One could wish that they might read the *Third Critique* together and reconstitute the dialectical unity of "critical, empirically oriented idealism." This is precisely the position that Cohen takes: living, particularly conscious entities are ideal concepts, nonempirical, rational derivatives of the dy/dx (psyche) = (0+), which serve as the ideal goals for the increasingly causal, empirical quantitative explanation of phenomena that, for one practical reason or another, we want to classify as "organic" and especially as "human." It is not incidental that Cohen indexes for his own use the epigram of Georg Christoph Lichtenberg: "Materialism is the asymptote of psychology."[48]

Many other and recent examples could be cited of how the—usually unknown—Cohennian theory of rational concepts infinitesimally produced in order to make possible the scientific structuring of empirica serves positive science both to make progress and to correct its errors. It cannot be our task here to survey general scientific developments in the twentieth century; a couple of examples will have to suffice.

There are many current examples of how scientists can mislead themselves into terrible self-contradictions and falsehoods because they are ignorant of such theory and, therefore, consciously or semiconsciously wedded to antiquated substantivist notions about the nature of reality. The constantly renewed claims to have "discovered" the ultimate subatomic indivisibles of matter, "primeval matter," only to be outbid very soon on behalf of new smaller components, evokes the wry reaction that one would wish they all took Kant's antimonies in the *First Critique* to heart. Another example of this kind of substantivist thinking was the announcement in the *Physical Review Letters* of the American Physical Society of August 25, 1975, that magnetic monopoles, that is, particles that embody only one pole of a magnetic field, had actually been observed. The underlying premise clearly was that at least two discrete bodies must not only logically but also physically be prior so that they can establish a relationship. No bones were made, in any case, at the time of the much-touted "discovery" that what were referred to as earlier mathematical calculations, especially by Paul A.M. Dirac, but what were in fact the mathematical inferences from physical (quantum) mechanics, had long motivated physicists to expect to find such monopoles. Some conceptual training in Cassirer's functionalism and Cohen's infinitesimalistic relationalism would have prepared students of the field to receive such claims with extreme skepticism. It was not long, then, before the newspapers reported, under headlines such as "Reported Find in Magnetism Partly Based on Inaccuracy,"[49] that the evidence that had been adduced turned out to be entirely diversionist.

It is not only in the natural sciences that such hypostatizing mistakes are made, against which the concept of the infinitesimal as an heuristic, "ideal" construct would guard. The Jewish Hegelian theologian Franz Rosenzweig, a late but deviant disciple of Hermann Cohen's, tried to reinterpret his teacher by turning Kantian normative concepts into Hegelian ontological ones, and he has impressed much of the later literature with his thesis. He performed this distorting operation on a number of scores, the concept of God, for example, and the infinitesimal. Where zero, infinitesimal, and number had been ideal, rational constructs that do not describe but produce and structure *realia* in Cohen, these turn, in the First Part of Rosenzweig's *Star of Redemption*, into descriptive and even ontic terms. Infinity can thus become descriptive even of historical and metaphysical entities, and completed infinities at that.[50]

If these are examples of science and philosophy insufficiently informed, indeed annihilatingly uninformed of critico—infinitesimalistic theory, then Sir Bernard Lovell's presidential address to the 137th annual meeting of the British Association for the Advancement of Science[51] is an (albeit unconscious) example of its positive employment. Lovell's excursions into philosophy, ethics, and even religion on this occasion are unfortunately not on a par with his scientific sophistication. In cosmology he adheres to "the big-bang theory." This he explicates in indubitably "Marburgian" terms. It is clearly Marburg critical idealism to declare: "Maybe, the problem of understanding (the 'basic mechanism of big-bang') arose because, at the deepest levels, it was not possible to separate man from the object of his investigations. We cannot evade this deepest problem of our existence by an escape into philosophical idealism or realism. We are forced to recognize that, although in our daily lives we can investigate problems as though the object of our investigation existed independently of us, this is not possible when we search for answers in the depths of the natural world.... Physically and intellectually, we stand at the centre of immensities." And the big-bang is defined by Bernard

Lovell in the precise language of Cohen's infinitesimalistic theory: "At time zero, the universe was infinitely small and of infinite density.... (O)nly one second [sic] after the impossible [!] transformation from zero size and infinite density to understandable primeval concentrate, the precise nature of these sub-atomic interactions determined the proportion of hydrogen to helium...."

Chapter 8

Applications of the Infinitesimalistic Theory in "the System"

Some of the logical and methodological questions that have arisen in our discussion of Cohen's infinitesimalistic theory may be helped along if we take a brief glance at how he practically puts them to use in his concrete philosophical work. In order to follow this fully we would have to go into the details of the entire "system," since the infinitesimal is methodologically so central to all of it—and this would, of course, be premature at this point. We will, therefore, restrict ourselves here to one characteristic and important example out of each of the three/four "parts" of "the system"—the *Logic*, the *Ethics*, the *Aesthetics*, and the *Religion*. (The word "pure" in the title of each part of the system is really only a transcription of the infinitesimal notion. It does not occur in quite the same way in the *Religion*; to what extent the phrase "out of the sources . . ." is to be taken as synonymous with "from the origins . . ." and thus refers back to the notion of rational, infinitesimal purity must be left to an analysis *in locu*.) A welcome by-product of this procedure will be that something that we have previously claimed as a theory can now be illustrated in practice, namely that, though it is true that the infinitesimal is always = 0, this 0, nonetheless, differs, as it were, in value depending on what it is the infinitesimal of—what we have symbolized as (0+)a, (0+)b. . . . Thus we shall here run into the dy/dx = 0 (scientific object), dy/dx = 0 (moral person,) dy/dx = 0 (aesthetic feeling) and dy/dx = 0 (God)/(compassion).

The title of the work that lays the first foundations to Cohen's "system of philosophy" expresses its prime concern: *Logic of Pure Cognition*[1]— that is, the scientific, human activity of coming to know ("cognition") what there is (in other words, the real universe) is determined by certain laws ("logic") such that these laws, by themselves, without the intermixture of anything else, alleged prior "experience," desires, prejudices, and so on ("pure"), account adequately and meaningfully for, validate, what we claim to find there. As we found in the *Infinitesimalmethode* that mathematics was ultimately and necessarily oriented toward science so here logic itself is oriented toward the epistemology of science. Surely no philosophy could emphasize the final criterion of experience and science more than this, and nothing could be more misleading than to accuse it, as has often been done, of "idealism" in some pejorative, metaphysical, or even mystical sense!

Science is concerned with determining the nature of objects in the universe and the causal conditions ("origin") that make them behave as they do. Any such scientific object must, logically, start out as a "problem," that is as something not yet known, for otherwise it would be a prejudice, a prejudgment, and science would be left without a task. The object is a preliminary hypothetical x, as yet undetermined but in principle determinable, a no-thing that bears the potentiality of turning out to be not only some-thing but a specific thing A. The path of knowledge progresses from $x(A)$ to A, from no-thing to object.

The entire procedure sketched in the previous paragraph is chockfull of "judgments"—not in the sense of subjective, emotive reactions but in the sense of rational mental activities.[2] There is, in the first place, what Cohen—following but also somewhat varying Kant—calls an "in-finite judgment," that is, the judgment that there is an object $x(A)$, which has not yet been defined except as $x(\text{non-B})$. At the end of the scientific analysis there is the judgment that object A exists in such-and-such a place. And these two judgments must be brought together by a "judgment of origin"—that is, the formulation of a rule how, rationally, the A has arisen from the x.[3]

These judgments are made according to extremely complex and subtle criteria. To explicate them fully would require the entire technical apparatus of a philosophy of science, and this is clearly not the place to supply this. Suffice it now to say that a sense-datum or a set of sense-data are tentatively accepted as a cognitive problem (x). A rational concept is then formulated, derived nonempirically—from "no-thing," "purely," infinitesimalistically—$x(A)$ as a tentative explanation ("hypothesis") of what constitutes the unity of the data in the object (A). This hypothesis—or concept or idea—is, of course, connected in all sorts of complicated ways with the total language in which it is couched, the culture within which it arises, the history and contemporaneous condition of science as a whole of which it is a part, and so on (pace the Kuhn-Popper debate). Above all, the "fit" between the problematic "givens" of the data and the concept that is constructed in order to account for them is the criterion

Applications of the Infinitesimalistic Theory in "the System" | 63

of the validity of both. In other words, a constant dialectical mutual check goes on between them: data are or are not accepted as evidence, in varying forms and degrees, dependent on whether they can or cannot be integrated into the conceptual theory (and thus they are literally "produced" qua scientific evidence by the theory), and the theory in turn is or is not accepted, again in varying forms and to varying extents, depending on whether it appears to explain the data stipulated in an adequate fashion. New relevant data, can, of course, always emerge, but even with a given set of data this dialectical process is infinite: whether a given piece of wood is, indeed, the leg of a chair depends in some measure on every new occasion on which someone tries to sit in that object. The concept is thus an infinite judgment in several ways. It is infinite, in the first place, inasmuch as the process of mutual verification between itself and the data which it organizes goes on without end. It is infinite, in the second place, in the sense of being an infinitesimal. That is to say, a chair, for example, is explained as the empirical integral of a rational infinitesimal which is a "nonchair." It might be thought that a nonchair is the same thing as literally an infinity of other concepts, such as, for example, a "nonelephant" and a "nonbook," but it is in fact a nonchair rather than any other such "non-thing" by virtue of the fact that if all its infinite negative predicates with which we qualify it were removed, by what Cohen calls a negative infinite judgment, a chair rather than an elephant or a book would remain.[4] And it is infinite finally in that the hypothetical A will be derived from an x, which starts out as an $x(A) = x(\text{non-B})$, and, of course $B = C/D \ldots \infty$.

There are then no fewer than two fundamental nonempirical operators involved as indispensable prerequisites for the performance of a scientific activity. One is infinity—indeed, various orders of infinity. The other is the notion of "origin." Origin, or first cause, as cause of causes, is also obviously never "given" in experience, not only in the Humean sense that we never experience causes but only inductive associations, but also in the sense that chronological as well as logical priority cannot, by definition, be sensuous representations. Origin is thus a logical notion, and Cohen says: "Only thought can originate being."[5] The "judgment of origin" is, therefore, a purely "operational concept"—that is, $x(A)$ is defined as that which permits a rational, scientific law to be formulated according to which A can be validated.

An undeniable element of circularity is involved in this analysis. The sense-data determine in some measure the hypothesis, and yet the hypothesis also determines the sense-data that are acceptable as scientific evidence. No amount of locutions about dialectical, mutual verification can or should disguise this element. It is inevitably rooted in the solipsistic nature of human knowledge of the universe. Any number of different scientific theories can, therefore, in principle be maintained indefinitely—the Ptolemaic cosmology no less today than a thousand years ago. "Elegance," simplicity, and so on, as criteria of acceptability, which are then called upon to make final decisions, are not, after all, even claimed to be descriptions of a noumenal universe but characterizations of human rationalization. Also, that scientific theories, once accepted, produce their own evidence is an almost daily experience of science: "Freudian symptoms" have multiplied, if not begun, in psychology only since the Freudian theory has been put forward. "Black holes" have presumably existed in the sky ever since men have looked at the sky, if they exist at all, and yet they seem never to have been "seen" until scientific theory had reached the point where black holes fill a void, if one may put it so paradoxically, in the picture of the sky as science paints it.

If a hypothesis produces its own evidence, as Cohen quite literally argues, it would seem to follow that no hypothesis can ever be falsified. In a very limited sense this is true. The Ptolemaic or the astrological hypothesis cannot so much be proved false as it is the case that in the context of all the other hypotheses that are scientifically accepted at this time its maintenance becomes so much more difficult and complex than another that it is in fact, and rightly, replaced. (The place of what Kant calls "the primacy of practical reason" in this scheme must be discussed elsewhere.) The entire procedure so far exposited may not yet have displayed its mathematical character. Even the uses of such notions as infinity and infinitesimal may still have appeared to be more metaphorical than technical. But in fact it is easy to realize the mathematical operations of which it consists. The sense-data with which (but not—to use Kant's famous phrase—from which) it began, are, for a start, to be determined on a scale from, say, 0 to 1 as proposed in "the principle of anticipation."[6] Furthermore, in the mathematico-physical sciences the object constituted by these quantified data is itself, of course, described and used mathematically. It follows, therefore, that the scientific law, which describes the manner in which tentative *sensa* and accepted object are related, must also be a mathematical formula. And finally the heuristic infinitesimal from which all of these later consequences may be derived must in turn be a concept that is in principle, though not necessarily in fact, mathematizable. And thus Cohen introduces the chapter on "Judgments of the Laws of Thought" with an exposition, based on the history of earliest philosophy, of the mathematical character of the notions of "purity," oneness and wholeness, that underlie the very possibility of perceiving unitariness in and of nature.[7]

The examples of the application of the infinitesimalistic theory in the other parts of "the system" can be kept within shorter and easier bounds.

The conceptual center of his *Ethics* is Cohen's theory of human personhood.[8] Its essence resides in the recognition that a human being, as a naturalistic fact, is blatantly not an "individual," inasmuch as its physical as well as its psychic components are not only obviously infinitely divisible but also change infinitely as well as infinitesimally. For this reason the notion of the individual, or moral personality, has never been successfully derived, nor can it be, by empirical methods. It is, to the contrary, a normative rational concept according to which a human being can and should form itself. As Eckstein[9] then put it early and well: the moral person is an ethical reality—that is, an "ought," constructed by reason alone in such a fashion that from a nonreal concept of selfhood, with an empirical value, which is literally infinitesimal = (0+), the person forms itself, "practically" as Kant called it, as the first integer in a series that lawfully ends only with the infinity of "humanity."[10]

This, too, can in principle be translated into a properly mathematical function, not one merely similar to mathematics, once the physical data that we unify as "a person" are stipulated in the mathematical terms of physics, chemistry, the psychic data and actions in quantificatory psychology, and so on.

In the *Critique of Practical Reason* Kant had developed the foundation for a theory of "pure," that is, reason-produced, not empirically caused, feeling in the instance of "respect for the law," or "awe"—that is, a feeling (!) that arises in man's psyche ("Gemüt") when he considers the fact that a rationally constructed maxim can confront him with the force of absolute obligatoriness. In the *Third Critique* pure feeling then extended beyond the limited field of moral respect to aesthetics. The feeling of "sublimity," for example, is not empirically produced by the object in the use of which it arises but rather rationally produced by the incongruity between and in favor of the power of the human mind, on the one hand, and its greatest possible object, on the other.

The empirical fact is that human beings experience feelings (!) produced by purely rational causes quite frequently; only the prejudice entrenched in language, that "feeling" arises, like "a feel," only from nerve ends, and in culture, that feelings are qualitatively different from thoughts, hide this fact from us. For example, an editorial in the (London) *Guardian* of June 23, 1975, begins with the words: "Mathematicians, it is said, are sometimes to be found in tears over the austere beauty of an equation. In much the same way, there are some cricket-lovers whose most cherished recollection may be of 17 runs scored in two hours on a malevolent wicket against skillful flight and turn...." Indeed, talk about "elegance," "simplicity," and "beauty" is rife not only in mathematical circles but also among philosophers of science—surely aesthetic terms. I once had a teacher who stopped in the middle of a complicated casuistic Talmudic argument—leaned back, closed his eyes, and, to the complete incomprehension of the students, sighed: "How lovely!" Leonhard Euler's *Tentamen novae theoriae musicae* (Petersburg, 1739) was directly related to his contribution to the theory of the infinitesimal calculus. As we have previously had occasion to note, in Mendelssohn's time the notion of a calculus, indeed an infinitesimal calculus, of feelings was widely and seriously entertained. And, as again we have seen, Helmholtz's *Die Lehre von den Tonempfindungen* was a formative scientific influence in Cohen's early years.[11]

Cohen's *Aesthetic of Pure Feeling*, apart from the large-scale and broad historical survey of the historical arts that it brushes, elaborates Kant's germinal notion of "logos—produced feeling" into an entire system of applied *a priori* feeling. Thus, the title of this two-volume work formulates, as did the title of his *Logic*, the quintessentially infinitesimalistic theory on which it is built. The different arts are, indeed, shown to be the "expressions" of various feelings—quite in consonance with the essentially Romantic, irrationalist aesthetics which have constituted the main-stream of the history of this discipline—but these feelings are shown, in considerable technical detail, to be the psychic products of various ways of producing and organizing universes of discourse, that is, universes of symbolic[12] articulation, on a level of "ideal" rational perfection. What an art-object accomplishes is the utilization of the components of the empirico-scientific world, themselves rationally produced, as we have earlier noted, and, therefore, susceptible to such utilization, in the sensuous representation of ideal concepts.[13] It thus shares with ethical ideas the normative character of displaying the gap between the real and the ideal and implying the imperative to overcome this gap; but, unlike ethical norms, it also achieves a partial, symbolic *realization* of the ideal, and this is its exemplary moral value. As in Kant so in Cohen, art is the third part of "the system," which anticipatorily *real*-izes the coincidence of the scientific actual with the ethical ideal. It accomplishes this by extrapolating the mathematically, infinitesimalistically produced *sensa* to their fullest possible, approximately and approximatingly ideal mathematical extensions (as, for instance, in Mondrian's geometric figures, in Calder's kinetics, in Schönberg's tonal constructions)[14] And the art-objects so produced then in turn produce the aesthetic feelings that correspond to them. Kant and Cohen both complete and round out their critical systems in their respective aesthetics, and then they overarch their completed systems with their philosophies of religion. In this Cohennian capstone infinitesimalistic theory plays no less a decisive role than in the constitutive parts. One way in which this shows up is the transference of the theory of pure feeling from the *Aesthetic* to the *Religion of Reason*. Whereas in the former feeling is that which, produced by reason, determines the value and materializes the aesthetic cognition of the art-object, in the latter it actually extrapolates rational ethics into the creation of new moral entities. Without here anticipating what will have to be done in a more appropriate setting, we can say that the feeling of compassion that a person extends to another person transforms the second person from a "neighbor," an adjacent man ("der Nächste," *Nebenmensch*) into a fellow-man or "co-man" (*Mitmensch*)—and compassionate co-men act toward one another in a much more intense, helpful, and even sacrificial manner than mere neighbors would. This compassion, now, is a product of the pure will, inasmuch as it consists of the mixture of the moral imperative and of the affect of love. The imperative is, of course, a rational *a priori*,—but so, too, is the affect: a feeling produced by rational, universal considerations, for the purpose of what Kant called a trigger (*Triebfeder*) for moral action.[15]

Infinitesimalistic theory is even more central in the *Religion of Reason*, however, than this overlap of aesthetics and ethics. The very concept of God itself is based on it. God is a correlative concept to the concept of man.[16] That is to say, the notion of a moral individual is formulated on the model of the notion of God as an uniquely (and perfectly) moral being, even while the reverse is equally true, that the notion of God is extrapolated into infinity ("the infinite being") from selected moral obligations imputed to man. Both concepts are formulated as teleological ideas, that is, as rational, practical norms, whose validity is tested by their effects on moral life. "Reciprocity enters man's knowledge of God in accordance with correlation. It is as if God's being were actual in man's knowledge only, so tremendous is the effect of the correlation.[17] Man is no longer merely God's creature, but his reason, by virtue of his knowledge and also for the sake of it, makes him at least subjectively, as it were, the discoverer of God."[18] God, in other words, is also and decisively a rational construct, an "idea,"(but, then, what isn't?) for the logically necessary and compelling purpose of rationalizing both reality and morality. And since man is the centerpiece of this construction, both as the practitioner of reason and as its beneficiary, the infinitesimalistic mathematical construction of man which was earlier performed in science and ethics also determines the "pure" concept of God.

Let us then restate briefly what the philosophical upshot and importance of Cohen's infinitesimalistic theory are. The theory claims to be able to show how man, by the lawful use of his reason alone, constructs a full mathematical system *ex nihilo* and that this system in turn then produces, equally *ex nihilo*, entirely *a priori*, a real scientific universe for his use. If this claim can be supported, as has here again been argued, it follows that all of what Kantians call "human interests"—science, ethics, aesthetics, and even religion—can be rationally satisfied only by the fullest application of idealistic rationalism oriented toward mathematical science and aiming for a society structured by an universal ethic.

Chapter 9 | 1975

The Tenability of Hermann Cohen's Construction of the Self

The philosophical search for the self (personal identity, human individuality, personhood, or whatever else it may be called) has generally been pursued in one of three standard directions: "the self" has either been taken as some kind of somatic term, or as some kind of mental term, or finally as some kind of combination of the previous two.[1] All such enterprises have, however, succeeded inadequately at best; it might even be said that they have failed. All one needs to do is look at the contemporary philosophical disputes revolving around this question—the mutual refutations and counter-refutations—to draw such a conclusion.[2]

Still, the need of a philosophical conception of human selfhood is obviously imperative. It should, therefore, be extremely useful to look at an approach to this problem, which differs not merely in one detail or another, but in principle, from the three previously mentioned procedures. Here it is argued that the self designates neither a physical nor a mental phenomenon, nor even a psychosomatic one; that all attempts at justifying this notion along such lines are, therefore, foredoomed to failure; and that in fact the self is an idea in the Kantian sense—a concept, a normative or regulative notion. I shall present this argument and critically compare it with other relevant and current views of the matter, chiefly by summarizing three chapters in Hermann Cohen's *Ethik des reinen Willens*[3] that deal directly with the self, together with some correlative texts: chapter 4, "The Self-Consciousness of the Pure Will"; chapter 5, "The Law of Self-Consciousness"; and chapter 7, "The Autonomy of Self-Consciousness: (1) Self-Legislation; (2) Self-Determination; (3) Self-Responsibility; and (4) Self Preservation."[4]

First published in *Journal of the History of Philosophy* 13:3 (1975), 361–384. © 1975 Journal of the History of Philosophy, Inc. Reprinted with permission of Johns Hopkins University Press.

Hermann Cohen

Cohen begins by distinguishing, along established Kantian lines, between desire and will (or "pure will"). Desire is caused by and directed toward any empirical object or state of affairs, and such object or state of affairs is, of course, found through cognition (or "thinking"). Thus, for example, when I see an apple and want to eat it, or when I feel hungry and want to sate that hunger, it is the cognized apple or the sensed hunger, which produces desire in me. In both cases we are dealing with "hypothetical imperatives": if I want to eat that apple, of if I want to sate my hunger, I ought to do what it takes to bring about the desired consummation. We would be dealing with hypothetical imperatives also in any case in which another person (human or divine) commands us to do something, because it is, again, true that if that other person did not command us to act in such a wise we would, presumably, not do so. In short, desire is heteronomous.

Will, on the other hand, as distinguished from desire, is commanded by reason, not conditioned by any empirical considerations. Thus, for example, the precept always to tell the truth is presumably derived from rational considerations, regardless of any and all psychological or historical conditions that prevail. Any imperative so produced is, then, as the use of the word "always" indicates, not hypothetical but "categorical." And the reason that produces it cannot, by definition, be found in the empirical world, in the world of objects. (It may, of course, use objects in enacting itself.) That which is not an object we call a subject. Thus will is autonomous—that is, it is produced by its subject. A subject is then that which emerges from enactments of will. It is a consciousness of self in the making. Indeed, it is the unity of its willed actions (pp. 191–196). Another way of saying it would be: the self is the pragmatic referent of the prefix "auto-" in the word "autonomy," the "law of the self."

The next step in the argument begins with an attack on Fichte. Fichte affirms the reality of the 'I' and distinguishes it from everything else as the non-I, the world of objects in which the I enacts itself. This is, however, a fundamental mistake, says Cohen. A non-x must be an "infinite judgment,"[5] from which the x is produced, not a y or any other arbitrary entity. We can, perhaps, illustrate this point of Cohen's with a current locution such as "nonbook": a nonbook is presumably also a nonelephant, but we call it a nonbook rather than a nonelephant because if we could eliminate those of its predicates that we subsume under "non" it would turn out to be not an elephant but a book. In our case, then, the non-I is another self, not anything in (nor all of) the inanimate world[6]; it is the *Nebenmensch* (199), a fellow-self.

Now, an x or a non-x is an ideal construct, an hypothesis—in this case, "man as an idea" (200). The *Nebenmensch* thus cannot be experienced, as also the bulk of the contemporary discussions of the problem of "other minds" illustrates. But this ideal non-I is "the other." The I comes to be in "correlation" with the other.[7] "The other, the *alter ego*, is the source [*Ursprung*[8]] of the I." Self-consciousness is conditional upon the consciousness of the other (201f., 260). And therefore, the self, which emerges in a relationship to an ideal, hypothetical other, must, of course, itself be an ideal construct.[9] It is a normative concept, a task to be achieved, not "the ghost of a soul"[10] to be experienced.

The usefulness of the distinction between an empirical and an ideal self can be illustrated with a concrete example taken from an entirely unphilosophical source—a literary book review of J. Calder, *Chronicles of Conscience: A Study of G. Orwell and A. Koestler*:[11]

> Orwell's narrator, his I who may make a major political assertion or toss off a throwaway remark about a chamber pot in Wigan or a militiaman dead in Catalonia—this I was not just the voice of a reporter, but a literary creation, the voice of a solitary artist. In Koestler's writing, by contrast, the I seems always to be Koestler himself, presenting himself in sharp daylight; that is, we are listening to an intellectual who is European, Jewish, a writer of enormous vitality and the widest interests, who has been through upheaval and the Communist Party and so presents his experience to enlighten the reader. Often he presents this so intently that, as Mrs. Calder says of *Scum of the Earth*, the other characters come to seem like an enlargement of Koestler's own many-sided experience.

The concept of the correlation of two ideal selves is explicitly and emphatically modeled by Cohen on legal notions.[12] Action of the will corresponds to a legal *actio*, and a legal *actio* requires two parties. These parties must be clearly demarcated from and yet bound to one another by a contract (202, 213ff). Furthermore, the parties to a legal action are juristic, not empirical, persons. And a juristic person is not, of course, primarily a man, even insofar as he has legal standing, but what we, too, call "a legal person"—*a persona*, not an *homo*. Cohen's model of a legal person is, interestingly, not a corporation but a labor union or cooperative (*Genossenschaft*).[13] Unions act as unified selves, and as such they own property. They act by a unified will, a Rousseauean *volonté de tous* (217–229).

The *volonté générale* of Rousseau's Social Contract, in which the individual seems overwhelmed by the group, is justly feared by many as one source of modem state totalitarianism. Cohen, however, in the tradition of Kant places another, provocative interpretation upon this notion.[14] The *volonté générale*, as a component in an ideal construction, is itself not a real will but an ideal one. Translated into functional language this is to say that it is the state's task to see to it that its will become the will of all, not merely that of a majority that may run roughshod over a minority. In other words, the "general will" (or the state) must increasingly act in such a fashion that the will of literally every single individual be properly taken into account and merged with it. The *volonté générale* must become the *volonté de tous*. This is, of course, an inexhaustible task. But then, such is always the nature of ideal tasks: they serve as ultimate norms, to be reached only asymptotically (221, 229–232).

We have spoken of the self as an hypothesis, as a possibility. The self is the possibility of the will. To transform this possibility into reality is the task. We are thus speaking "not of the will of the self but of the will to a self" (321, and 245, 252). The self enacts itself in actions, not in any and all actions, of course, but only in those that tend to constitute a unified whole. This whole we call "character" (251). In other words, the actions that go to make a self follow a law—or better, a lawfulness—toward the set task. The law, like the self, never speaks in the indicative, but only in the imperative mood; that is, it consists not of descriptive but of hortatory and in this sense futuristic propositions (264, 266).[15] "Only to the future, and always only to the future, does that reality belong which is to be striven for and attained as the self-consciousness of the pure will" (267). And the future, ideal self realizes itself in stages of relative selves, which are themselves determined by lawfully produced actions (332).

The lawfulness according to which willed actions go to constitute a self is actually derived from the positive law of the state. The individual will confronts the positive law as the "thou," "the other," of its own lawfulness: if the two coincide then the I has found its definition in a given reality; if, like Socrates in jail, the two diverge, the I defines itself in simultaneous acknowledgement of and protest against a given reality (250f.). The positive law in turn is defined by, among others, the ethical category of universality: it must be applied to all men and to all suitable cases.[16] Indeed, ethics generally and the law are dialectically related: ethics crystallizes the principles of the law, criticizes the law in terms of these principles, and impels the law in the direction of these ethical principles (256–263).

Here, then, the will (if enacted lawfully) is identical with the "ought." And its lawfulness is derived from the positive law. "It is the juristic person of the state by means of and through which the consciousness of self becomes a moral, ethical person. No fiction can be verified so precisely as this" (268).[17]

We can summarize what Cohen has to say about the relationship between the human individual as so defined and society or the state, by citing the manner in which Friedrich Schiller states it (with suitably greater literary felicity, but still based on their common Kantian heritage) in the "Fourth Letter" of *On the Aesthetic Education of Man*:

> One may say that every individual man carries within himself the potentiality and purpose of a purely ideal man. It is the great task of his life to have all his permutations coincide with the unchangeable unity of this ideal man. This pure man, who is more or less clearly discernible in every subject, is represented by the state—the objective and, as it were, canonical form in which the multiplicity of subjects seek to become unified. Now, two different ways can be conceived of how a man in time can come to coincide with man in the idea—and the same is true of how the state affirms itself in the individuals: either the pure man suppresses the empirical, the state surplants the individuals—or the individual becomes the state, the man in time ennobles himself into the man in idea.[18]

Up to now we have dealt in very general concepts. In chapter 7 Cohen turns to spell out what they specifically mean and how they function. He does this by defining in great detail the term about which also Kant's ethics revolve, "autonomy."

Obviously, this term covers both concerns with which we have been dealing, the self ("auto-") and the law ("-nomy"). In line with our earlier description of the self as a thesis or hypothesis, that is, according to the Greek meaning of this term as a "setting up" or "positing," Cohen proposes to think of autonomy not so much as self-legislation, but rather as self-setting (*Selbstgesetztheit* rather than *Selbstgesetz*). And it must be reason that sets up the autonomous self, for the "affects" (i.e., emotions), as the term indicates, are the effects of outside, heteronomous actions, and, therefore, of pathology (i.e., passions, rather than actions).

Autonomy also always means self-determination: "autonomy is autotely."[19] Here Cohen becomes most specific and technical in defining what constitutes an autonomous, that is, "free" action through which the self determines itself. An action, in this sense, begins with an intent (*Vorsatz*), again a form of hypothesizing.[20] "Intent is pre-choice, anticipation, pre-determination of the definite content of an action. Intention is not reflection but decision—decision in reality, among the specific facts. Therefore, there can be no will and no action without intention. In an intention task and reality seem to converge. This is not objectionable but right and necessary. The concept of 'task' requires that it pass into solution—and then return to being a task."[21]

On the other hand, it could not, of course, be meant literally that there are no actions without intent; we all perform many actions all the time without consciously intending them. The kind of actions Cohen has in mind comprises "free," "autonomous" actions, which go to determine the self. How are we to conceive of free actions, however? Here Cohen again uses the reality of legal practice to provide an answer. So that a judge may be able to hold a person responsible for an action which he has performed, it must be determined that this person had the intent (the *mens rea*, the psychological state of willing) to perform that action, and the event submitted to the law must be shown to be the end-result of a causal chain stretching from the intent to the event.[22] "Free" in the sentence "this was a free action" is thus not a descriptive but a value term.[23] The object of a verdict in such a situation is a self (333–340). So that it may be an autonomous self it must accept, or rather impose upon itself, this verdict.[24] If one were to shift the responsibility for the action committed to some other agent—for example, to laws of physical, psychic, or social determination, or to God—one would be denying one's own self. Responsibility, therefore, and self-responsibility, are the foundations of the self (347–352, 357).

Finally, we may adduce two aspects of the penological doctrine, which Cohen derives in this connection. Responsibility for an action having been assigned to a person by the law and having been accepted by him, and this person thus having been established as a "self," the legal view is that once the penalty imposed for the crime has been paid the person's "guilt" has been annihilated; he is no longer a criminal, but he is still, and continues to be, a self (357f.).[25] Capital punishment, on the other hand, is obviously ruled out, because (apart from other reasons) it would destroy the self, which it is the purpose of the law to establish (359f.). Thus the preservation of the self[26] for the purpose of the continuous making of the self turns out to be the ultimate principle of ethics and law (361–364).

This is as far as Cohen goes in his "construction" of the personal individual in his *Ethik*. He has repeatedly said that he is eliminating from consideration questions which, in his view, go beyond philosophy, that is, beyond epistemology and ethics—especially "guilt" as distinguished from juridical culpability. Guilt is a profoundly personal matter, not "objective" in the philosophical sense, and where a consideration of such guilt may lead Cohen reserves for separate treatment. This treatment—and with it a final step in the construction of the self is found only in Cohen's posthumous "theology," *Religion of Reason: Out of the Sources of Judaism*. Here he first restates the essential argument in a series of chapters as central as their equivalents in the *Ethik*: chapter 5, "The Creation of Man in Reason"; chapter 6, "The Attributes of Action"; chapter 8, "The Discovery of Man as the Fellow-Man." Though, under the circumstances, the restatement is formulated in a more theological vocabulary, not only its contents but also explicit cross-references to the *Ethik*[27] make it perfectly clear that we are dealing with a reiteration.[28] In chapter 10, "The Individual as I," and in chapter 11, "Atonement," the supplementation is then provided.

Briefly to summarize the reformulation: if in the *Ethik* the philosophic derivation of the concept of man began with the assumption that this enterprise must be conducted by means of reason, then this assumption is here undergirded with the theological proposition that man is "created in reason" by a God of reason (what Cohen calls "spirit") (chapter 5). "Reason" is ethical reason, that is, reason as it manifests itself in social deeds; and thus, both the God of reason and the man created in reason are moral entities (chapter 6). The *Nebenmensch*, that is, the phenomenon similar to ourselves that we encounter (132) and that we construe as a fellow-person, is transformed into the *Mitmensch*, co-man, when we construct the latter out of reason.[29] But now, of course, unlike what happened in the *Ethik*, "reason" is identified with the idea of God,[30] and thus we are "constructing" the *Mitmensch* as being, like ourselves, the *imago Dei* (147, 150ff., 185ff.).

This theological formulation must not mislead us, however, into some kind of metaphysics. Cohen reemphasizes the rational, philosophic move that is being made: "God has, it is true, created man, but the co-man has to be created by man himself" (170). It ought to be added that we are impelled to perform this transformation of the empirical *Nebenmensch* into the ethical *Mitmensch* because we witness his social suffering, primarily poverty, and thus relate ourselves to him out of *Mitleid*, "sympathy," "compassion," "co-suffering." In short, *Mitleid* creates the *Mitmensch*, cosuffering produces the co-man (157f., 160f, 165, 170). And, remembering that the I, in turn, was produced out of the correlation of a thou and an I, it follows that our own selfhoods are likewise produced out of social, moral compassion (166; chapter 7).

It is at this point that the step beyond the self of the *Ethik* is taken. In the latter work we have seen that, for example, the criminal acquired his selfhood only in relationship to society; his guilt was not at issue, only his culpability. Thus, were there no society he could not be a person. Also in the *Religion of Reason* up to this point even the *Mitmensch* created in God's image is still defined in terms of his relationship to other men. He is a self even now, not as a person with absolute ultimacy, but only as a member of a class: "Also the *Mitmensch* is not yet an individual which could be determined as an I" (192f.). It is not yet an "absolute individual," or what Cohen also calls an "I-individual" (193; cf. also 160, 209, 214f.). Beyond being the *Mitmensch*, therefore, the individual rises to stand in a correlation with God. Before Him he is not only culpable but also guilty, and here he assumes "self-responsibility" in the fullest sense (194f., 207ff.). And even as the criminal emerges from his self-imposed penalty before the judge as a social person, so also the sinner emerges from his atonement before God as a "freeman" (219f., 225). Before God the self, "the soul," is, of course, abstracted from all social relationships—though on another level he always retains these connections—and he is, therefore, finally the "absolute person."[31] The absolute human person comes to be in correlation with the absolute divine personality.[32]

By way of illustration it is again possible to give a concrete example of the conflict between "the social person" and "the absolute self," or a parallel thereof, from an entirely nonphilosophical context. In a speech at the end of his trial in Bolivia Regis Debray made this statement:[33]

> Revolutionary war is not a question of individuals facing individuals—everyone has a family, parents, sons, loved ones, a childhood. They are but mere representatives of two irreconcilable orders. These acts of war are the fruits of the social, economic and moral antagonisms existing independently of the will of the actors and preceding them. No one has created these

antagonisms, and no one can take them away, but they should indeed be surmounted and settled. Naturally, the tragedy is that we do not kill objects, numbers, instruments, but, precisely, on both sides, irreplaceable individuals, essentially innocent, unique for those who have loved, bred, esteemed them. This is the tragedy of history, of any history of any revolution. It is not individuals who are placed face to face in these battles, but class interests and ideas; but those who fail in them, those who die, are persons, are men.[34]

A number of features of the absolute self must still be noted. It, too, makes itself. It is not made by God; it merely makes itself in correlation with, or "before," God.[35] That is to say, even as it was the fact that the criminal accepted responsibility for his act—or better yet, imposed it upon himself before the judge, rather than having the judge impose it upon him, that constituted him a moral person, so here it is the "repentance," the "turning" (*teshuvah*) of the sinner before God, not the forgiveness bestowed by God, which constitutes him an absolute person (225f.). In the process a man unifies, integrates himself; he overcomes his inner self-fragmentation and self-contradictions, that is, the contradictions that contradict the self and "prevent the individual from achieving the unity of the I" (220, 222). This, too, is of course an "infinite task," a norm to be achieved rather than a state of affairs attained at any given empirical point (238, 241). Thus, even the absolute person is an ideal construct. Finally, while an aggregation of ethical persons constitutes society, an aggregation of absolute persons constitutes a community (230; chapters 10f.).[36]

To the exposition of Cohen's construction of the self I want to add an historical consideration about the relationship between Kant and Cohen.

The "Marburgers," disciples of Cohen, have often been attacked for "idolizing Kant." In fact, in Cohen's conception of the self we have an instance of the founder of the Marburg school criticizing Kant, I believe unnecessarily and wrongly. Cohen repeatedly claims that his conception of the self is different from and better than Kant's. I shall try to show that it is, in fact, identical—with one minor exception, in which he usefully supplements but does not contradict Kant.

Cohen offers three strictures of Kant on the self: (1) Kant regards the self as a noumenon rather than as a "task" (321–324);[37] (2) Kant limits the functions of the self in "the transcendental unity of apperception" to cognitive reason, instead of having it unify "pure" and "practical reason"

(195ff.); (3) Kant makes an invidious distinction between law and ethics by defining law as that which compels the will heteronomously, while morality determines the will autonomously (216f.).[38]

(1) It is very difficult to understand on what grounds Cohen makes the first claim. For one thing, in his own *Kants Begründung der Ethik* he had stated the opposite (109–113).[39] In fact, the whole Kantian doctrine of the transcendental unity of apperception has for its thrust precisely the conception which Cohen proffers: it is "transcendental" because it is related to and involved with experience;[40] therefore, an external world in which experience can take place is necessary so that the self can be constituted; and the self can be found only in its activities, that is, in its cognitions.[41]

We are here using the self as it emerges out of Kant's *Critiques*. Presumably, Cohen could not have known Kant's *Opus Posthumum* as we know it. From our vantage point, however, it can be said that, difficult though the *Opus Posthumum* is to put together, the self that is there argued for by Kant at the end of his life, especially in "convolute 7" and in convolutes 10 and 11,[42] is an extrapolation of his earlier doctrine, which comes out about where Cohen's extrapolation comes out a hundred years later. "The subject is not a discrete thing but an idea."[43] It posits itself through acts of the power of its imagination in order to be able to experience the world, even as it posits the world in order to be able to realize itself.[44] In other words, the world and the I are dialectical creations of one another.[45] The acts of the imaginative capacity occur in two forms: cognitive, in which the self affects and effects itself transcendentally in space and time,[46] and ethical, in which the self turns itself into "person."[47]

(2) The self is a noumenon as all noumena are noumena, namely as a normative concept;[48] it is the self as something to be achieved. The self is "not an *ens* nor a *non-ens* but a principle of possibility."[49] Kant even derives his doctrine of immortality from this consideration: to wit, the self is to be approximated through moral self-determination *ad infinitum*, and for this infinity finite life is, of course, too limited.[50] (Again, Cohen himself had made all this perfectly clear in *Kants Begründung der Ethik*, 87, 100, 103, 160f., 197). Indeed, from whom can one have learned better than from Cohen how "the primacy of practical reason" is required by the *First Critique* and, through the "ideas" of the "Dialectic,"

leads into the *Second Critique*? That is, the ideal noumena of the *First Critique* in and of themselves are the ethical noumena of the Second, the self prominently among them. In any case, strictures (1) and (2) are mutually exclusive on Cohen's own view: if something is noumenal it is related normatively to phenomena and is thus ultimately ethical.[51]

(3) The third stricture remains. Here Cohen would seem to be right. As Lisser makes clear,[52] the self, which Kant constitutes out of the moral experience is in danger of being either a psychological or (to avoid this) a metaphysically noumenal self. Cohen overcomes this danger by deriving it not from some "sense of duty" but from the law. It is, as a matter of fact, interesting to watch the Jew Cohen put his finger on Kant's Protestant, Pauline abhorrence of the law (253ff.):[53] he points out that all law, positive as well as ethical, has for its purpose the compelling of the will, and that "compulsion" is, therefore, not sufficient reason for regarding a law as heteronomous (258). But Cohen's insertion of the law into this argument is surely no opposition to, but is rather an extrapolation and strengthening of, Kant's derivation of the self.

Erik Erikson

The total philosophical conception of the human self, which Hermann Cohen has thus offered might appear at first glance to be a highly abstract, unreal construction. A brief comparison with Erik Erikson's psychological description of the development of personal identity will, however, demonstrate its empirical validity.[54]

Erikson can be said to distinguish four stages of the self:

(1) What Freud called the "id" Erikson sometimes calls the "unconscious ego," which he identifies with Heinz Hartmann's "self" as the empirical object of the linguistic "I" (217f.). Cohen does not have and cannot be expected to have an equivalent for this; since he is a philosopher, he will concern himself only with the human self that is thought about, that is, the self as conscious.

(2) What Freud called the "super-ego" Erikson sometimes calls the "self" (ibid.), but he explains that he means a "pre-rational ego-ideal"

(209f.), that is, a conscious but presystematic notion of what a person would like himself to be.

(3) The Freudian prerational superego Erikson wants to connect with but distinguish from what he calls the "ego-ideal" (210) or the "I" (218), which he identifies with Hartmann's "ideal self," that is, a person's rational notion of what he would like himself to be. This corresponds to Cohen's self as a normative concept. It comprises three equivalent components in Erikson and Cohen. (a) As Cohen stipulates, so also Erikson has the normative self evolve from the actions that it performs, not from any ideal substance nor from any theoretical form with which it is endowed. Erikson says that an "identity crisis" can be "overcome only by a sense of identity won in action. Only he who 'knows where he is going and who is going with him' demonstrates an unmistakable if not always easily definable unity and radiance of appearance and being" (300). "The pertinent question, if it can be put into the first person at all, would be, 'What do I want to make of myself, and what do I have to work with?'" (314). (b) As the last two quoted statements have already made clear, Erikson's view, that the normative self is produced through action, implies that it comes to be only in social contexts. Cohen's insistence that the I is produced in correlation with a thou stressed the same point. Erikson is particularly concerned with emphasizing the environmental determinants in the formation of the self and its inevitable as well as desirable integration into the "group ego" (p. 218).[55] This corresponds to the function of the state and the role of the *Nebenmensch* in Cohen's analysis of the formation of the self. (c) Erikson is at one with Cohen in regarding every empirical self as a stage in the process of striving toward a literally infinite, normative self: "While the imagery of the ego ideal could be said to represent a set of to-be-striven for but forever not-quite-attainable goals for the Self, ego identity could be said to be characterized by the actually attained but forever-to-be-revised sense of the reality of the Self within social reality" (210f.).

(4) Finally, in Erikson as in Cohen the individual has to be ultimately anchored in "God." As we have seen, Cohen holds that the human person becomes "absolute," rather than "related to" history and society, only in the correlation to "the absolute person" of God, and only on this level is the *Nebenmensch* transmuted into the

Mitmensch. Even so, Erikson claims, "How did man's need for individual identity evolve? Before Darwin, the answer was clear: because God created Adam in His own image, as a counterplayer of His identity, and thus bequeathed to all men the glory and the despair of individuation and faith. I admit to not having come up with any better explanation. The Garden of Eden, of course, has had many utopian transformations since that expulsion from the unity of creation—an expulsion which tied man's identity to the manner of his toil and of his cooperation with others, and with technical and communal pride" (40). "The counterplayer of the I, therefore, can be, strictly speaking, only the deity who has lent this halo to a mortal and is Himself endowed with an eternal numinousness certified by all 'I's' who acknowledge this gift. That is why God, when Moses asked Him who should he say had called him, answered: 'I am that I am.' He then ordered Moses to tell the multitude: 'I am has sent me unto you.' And, indeed, only a multitude held together by a common faith shares to that extent a common I, wherefore 'brothers and sisters in God' can appoint each other true 'You's' in mutual compassion and joint veneration" (210).

The philosophical and psychological coordination between Cohen and Erikson can, then, be clarified in this table:

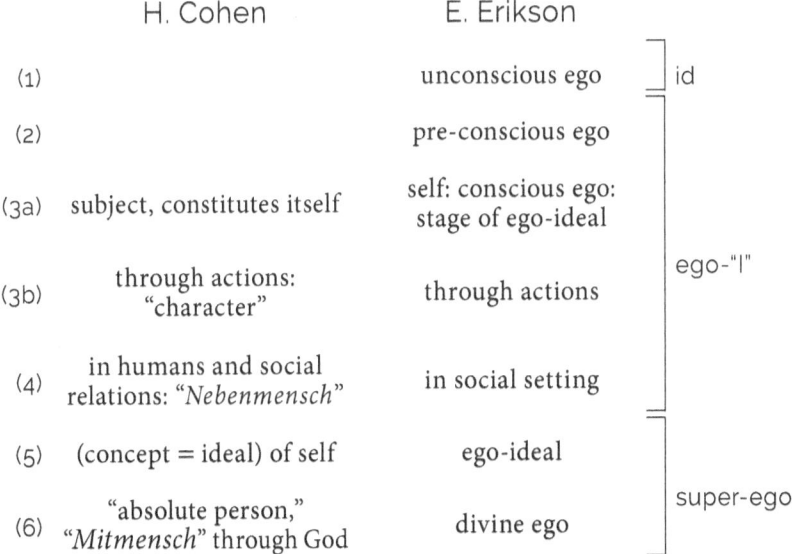

I think it will be profitable to compare Cohen's neo-Kantian construction of selfhood with some related though very different and, I believe, much less satisfactory ones.

Ernst Cassirer

Ernst Cassirer was also a neo-Kantian and a "Marburger," himself a close disciple of Hermann Cohen.[56] When he published his Leibniz book in 1902,[57] not only was it dedicated to his teacher Cohen, but it also treated Leibniz as a precursor of Kant[58] and expounded a theory of the self, which in every way coincides with Cohen's.[59] But by the time he published his *Philosophy of Symbolic Forms* (3 volumes, 1923–1929)[60] a certain ambiguity had crept into Cassirer's view. In some part this may be due to his increasing kinship with his fellow Cohen-disciple and later dissident Paul Natorp, whom he had already thanked in the preface to the Leibniz book;[61] in larger part, however, it is due to what may be called his "anthropological turn" away from a philosophy of science to a philosophy of historical culture.

Despite the extended and somewhat diffuse treatment, which Cassirer bestows upon the notion of selfhood in *The Philosophy of Symbolic Forms* (II, Part III, chapters 1–2; III, Part I and into Part II), it can be summarized rather concisely. He begins by accepting Natorp's premise that selfhood is not rationally constructed, but is the primordial pre-assumption of all experience and knowledge, mythical as well as rational. Indeed, both claim that, phylogenetically as well as ontogenetically, we first experience the world as a whole as being selfhood, that is, animistically or anthropomorphically (III, 51–56). In fact, it is this that is called "myth." "There is a kind of *experience* of reality which is situated wholly outside [the] form of scientific explanation and interpretation. It is present wherever the being that is apprehended in perception confronts us not as a reality of things, of mere objects, but as a kind of presence of living subjects" (III, 62). Only in the course of time and with the use of symbols (language) do we extrude certain phenomena from the world of selves and come to regard them as objects (III, 65–78). In one area, however, we always retain the mythical view—the area of what we call persons, ourselves, and others (III, 79–103).

This analysis displays some peculiarities and inconsistencies. (E. Gadol rightly calls them "bizarre I-Thou polarizations."[62]) In the first place, is it not strange to apply the notion of anthropomorphism (or its equivalent) to people? What should be in the "form of humans" if not humans? More importantly, this thesis seems to say in effect that to regard selves as selves is mythical thinking. If so, the conclusion would no doubt have to be that scientifically we ought to cease doing this, but this is a conclusion that Cassirer himself clearly repudiates.

He extricates himself from the fix by first distinguishing intelligent beings (animals and men) from nonintelligent ones, and by then differentiating men from animals by virtue of the former's use of "symbolic intelligence," that is, language.[63] This, in turn, however, might compel the further logical step of imputing a "symbolic language" of their own to, say, trees among themselves; or, alternatively, one would have to deny to men's symbolic language any veridical value beyond that of any hypothetical other such language—unless one persisted in a special veridical claim on ethical grounds. In the numerically as well as chronologically earlier volume II Cassirer had in fact said precisely this (II, 166f., 200, 206); but now, in the first place he does not seem to say it in so many words, and in the second place if he were to do so he would be right back where Cohen had been initially. The only advantage that accrues to the argument from his detour through historical anthropology is that it accounts—very persuasively, incidentally—for the notions of selfhood widely held in prescientific cultures and minds. This is of historical but not of philosophical value; as Nelson Goodman puts it: "Personification may thus echo an aboriginal animism. The reapplication is nevertheless metaphorical; for what is literal is set by present practice rather than by ancient history."[64]

Anglo-American Metaphysics

If the British empiricist tradition from Hume through Ryle comes functionally to the same effect as Kant's and Cohen's dissolution of a substantive self in favor of one that, to use Wittgenstein's phrase, cannot be "found in the world,"[65] then there is also—if only to confound all facile dichotomies between "the British" and "the Continental traditions"—a recurrent temptation in English speaking philosophical circles to revert to metaphysical conceptions of the self.

F.H. Bradley

Cohen's "construction" and his British contemporary F.H. Bradley's ontological conception of the self seem to parallel one another in many ways, yet they go in radically different directions. Their resemblances and dissimilarities are due to their respective direct descents from Kant and Hegel.

The nub of their difference is the Hegelian-Bradleyan insistence that "the actual is the rational" (or something awfully close to this), that God and man are one.[66] Applied to our problem, this results in the view that the moral self is identical with the empirical self (or almost so),[67] contrary to the permanent and wide disparity between the two that we find in Kant and Cohen. What results from the Bradleyan insistence is, as in Hegel, the glorification of every status quo, that epitome of all "reaction" (14); moral selves are defined by "our station and its duties" (163–180),[68] which, in turn are, or may be defined "despotically" (187) by the positive state (165–199). When Bradley does realize that there is nonetheless a gap between the highest conception of a moral self and the empirical self, either he brings the former so close to the latter that the gap virtually disappears again, by insisting once again that "the ideal" is defined by "social reality"("Ideal Morality," 227–334); or when even this move does not achieve its purpose, he goes off into an "other-worldly" ("Concluding Remarks," 327ff.), Protestant "religion of faith" (313–331). Here, since God is man, man in turn is indeed his own highest self in reality.[69]

The very "abstractness" of Kantian "ideas," which Bradley, like Hegel, denounces (see his chapter against Kant and 175, 248, 323), makes it impossible for a Kant or a Cohen ever to identify the real with the rational and, therefore, to be seduced into the Spinozistic proclamation that the state is "the real identity of might and right" (183f.).[70] or the Nietzschean "sacred Yes."[71] In short, Bradley first sublimates, or sublates, the ethical self into the empirical self, then sublimates the empirical self into the political self, and then finally sublimates the political self into the religious self. (All but the first are construed as real, ontological entities rather than as "ideal constructs.") Man is thus "at peace with reality" (183),[72] whereas for Cohen, on the contrary, there is always the ethical tension between the empirical self, on the one hand, and the "ideas" of ethics, society, and God, on the other.

P.F. Strawson

Currently it is P.F. Strawson who dogmatically stipulates personal selves. His is a quite Cartesian substance-notion of persons, and he simply posits "the logical primitiveness of the concept," defined as possessing physical and mental predicates.[73] Surely, however, the proper philosophical task is to justify such use, not simply by an unnecessary or premature resort to "primitivity" to accept extant linguistic or conceptual practice.[74] Strawson himself seems to have an intimation of his failure when he says (but merely lets it go at the statement): "We may still want to ask what it is in the natural facts that makes it intelligible that we should have this concept.... I do not pretend to be able to satisfy this demand at all fully" (108).[75]

Strawson's chief argument to support his claim for the primitivity of "person" is a piece of logical legerdemain. He says, "The main point here is a purely logical one: the idea of a predicate is correlative with that of a *range* of distinguishable individuals of which the predicate can be significantly, though not necessarily truly, affirmed" (95n). The trouble with this argument is twofold. In the first place, it calls a metaphysical supposition a logical implication, to wit that in order to be able to speak of something as a predicate there must be ("is correlative" [?]) a subject of which this predicate can be predicated. The present study can serve as an example of why this supposition is by no means necessary, and that in fact it is false. And, of course, "no-ownership" theories have been put forward long since.[76] An "individual," in this case a "person," is precisely the conceptual construction of a number of "free-floating" predicates into an unity for some purpose or other. The second trouble with Strawson's argument is that it offers—as he is wont to do—precisely what the problem is, as a solution. We want to know why we may regard ourselves as justified in operating conceptually with items that we call "individuals" or "persons," and all that Strawson replies is that we commonly do!

Strawson's thrust is brought out more pungently when one takes it together with his critique of "Wittgenstein's *Philosophical Investigation*."[77] I take it that what Wittgenstein's argument comes to is that the "I," like everything else, is a function of the social context and of behavior. This position, though couched in very different language and arrived at in a very different way, is, as far as it goes, entirely in accord with what Cohen is driving at. Wittgenstein, like Ryle,[78] is performing a Humean destruction of metaphysics, which has to precede whatever a Kant or a Cohen will do, to arouse us out of our dogmatics lumber. It follows, then, that Strawson feels compelled to argue against Wittgenstein, however ineffectively (21–28, 41f.).[79]

After having proposed his theory of human selfhood in *Individuals*, Strawson presented a reading of Kant's *First Critique*,[80] a goodly portion of which is also concerned with personal identity. His explication of Kant's "transcendental unity of apperception" would appear to be entirely correct. Thereafter, however, a couple of interesting things happen. (1) He reads Kant virtually as if no one else had ever read him before; certainly the kind of interpretation here summarized in behalf of Hermann Cohen is completely ignored. As a result he is not prevented from giving a willful, indeed false reading. (2) He counters Kant's thesis with his own, taken over from his *Individuals*.

(1) Strawson interprets the Kantian noumena in general as ontological claims (236ff.). Therefore, the noumenal self is also interpreted in this way (173, 238, 245). These noumena are then taken to have been proposed by Kant as "quasi-causes" of "their" phenomena, and consequently the noumenal self is taken to have been proposed as "a source, not merely an outcome, of the conditions of experience" (174). Now, this is a reading of Kant as "orthodox" as it is self-contradictory, as easily refuted by Strawson as it has been refuted by Cohen and others in the past. From this result Strawson draws the conclusion that when one subtracts from Kant's view the notion of ontological noumena, what he identifies with the "transcendental" part of Kant's idealism, one is merely left with the truisms of idealistic phenomenalism. But this is false. Indeed, ontological noumena do not make sense, but then Kant never proposed them. Noumena are, however, normative constructs; they are the reasons for, not the causes of, their phenomena;[81] and so also the noumenal self is the definition of the self as an ethical task.[82] Without this no adequate conception of the self can be arrived at, as we have seen: it is the case that we put together, "organize," our life-experiences such that, when we are rational and "healthy," the result is some consistent entity that we call "personal identity", but philosophically we must be prepared to answer the questions of what it is that does this organizing and of the nature of the ground rules according to which we do the organizing.

Strawson himself is uncomfortably aware of the dubiousness of his Kant interpretation. As he fudged the issue in *Individuals*[83] by blithely admitting that he has no answer to a fundamental question that must be put to his thesis, so here he blithely concedes the evidence against himself, only to proceed as if nothing had happened: "I do not deny that all this, too [Kant's talk of a noumenal self], might be construed as a mere manner of speaking about the structural characteristics of phenomenal fact. So to construe it would be to treat the model *as* a model, an expository framework to be discarded when its purposes are served. But it seems, to say the least, unlikely that this is how Kant viewed the matter" (174). (What he calls "unlikely" is in fact precisely the case.) With the last quoted sentence Strawson concludes his chapter on "Soul," but he refers the reader to his later treatment of the subject. Yet there, too (246; cf. also 249) he is forced to admit that his "crude model" of a "timeless self.... does not feature prominently in any of the detailed structures of the argument in [the *First Critique*]." In short what he says is that his interpretation is neither necessitated by Kant's reasoning nor justified by his actual statements.

A single sentence from Kant's *Opus Posthumum*, which could be duplicated many times in the same work and which has been shown to be in entire accord with the *First Critique*, should suffice to lay the ghost of Strawson's and others' explication of Kant's noumena as metaphysical hypostatizations:

> The difference between the concept of a thing in itself and the concept of a phenomenon is not objective but merely subjective. The thing in itself (*ens per se*) is not another object but another relation (*respectus*) of the representation to the same object [; it is] to think that object not analytically but synthetically as the ideal conception [*Inbegriff*] (*complexus*) of the intuitive representation [in the form] of phenomena, i.e. as representations which have their merely subjective ground of determination in the unity of intuition. It is *ens rationis* = x.[84]

(2) Of course, Strawson does try to answer the questions about the nature and the *modus operandi* of the "organizing self." In his Kant-book he makes it perfectly clear that the answer he proposes is the theory of identity in *Individuals*: "The topic of personal identity has been well discussed in recent philosophy. I shall take the matter as understood" (164n). "A man is something perceptibly (if only relatively) permanent...." (164). He speaks of "criterionless self-ascription and empirical criteria of subject identity [which] are not *in practice* severed" (165; cf. 242).

"Criterionless self-ascription" presumably refers to the notion of personal identity as a primitive, and "empirical criteria of subject identity" presumably refers to the "P-predicates" of that primitive. The entire thesis cannot stand up to relatively simple analysis, as we have previously begun to show. After all, we deal in material predicates all the time, and when we do we require the fulfillment of certain clearly stipulated criteria. Thus, at least the P-predicates that go into Strawson's definition of personal identity cannot be regarded as a primitive.[85]

Furthermore, everything applies to them that Hume said in criticizing the notion of a "substantive" self. Again, realizing this difficulty, Strawson follows his practice of fudging the issue by inserting into his thesis its refutation and proceeding undeterred—this time inserting the innocent-looking but deadly concession, "if only relatively," into his definition of "a man" as "perceptibly permanent" (164). To add personal predicates to the material ones surely cannot solve the problem, since it is precisely these personal predicates that constitute the problem, not the answer. It is hard to imagine how the addition of an unsolved conundrum to a refuted theory can solve a philosophical problem.

Shoemaker and Sellars

If one way of copping out of the philosophical business of ratiocinating is to resort to primitivity before it is needful and fight to do so, or when it is entirely supererogatory, then another way of copping out is to designate a concept as "unverifiable and true," as Sidney Shoemaker ends up doing with the "self"-concept.[86] Shoemaker traces himself back to the tradition of Thomas Reid and Bishop Butler in dealing with the self as undefinable, and he explicitly opposes any "construction" of such concepts (256f.). The danger of such an approach is perhaps best brought out by the fact that in the end, and consistently so, everything turns out to be "unanalyzable" (ibid.). At this point surely reason and philosophy have in fact committed suicide![87]

Shoemaker will also argue against Wittgenstein, but reasonably enough in agreement with Strawson.[88] He insists that, since we cannot find the self by perception, "as object," and since I cannot perceive objects without an "I," *ergo* there must be, albeit unverifiably, an "I." And then we go on to complexify Strawson's schema to the new heights of "P*"-predicates! But, of course, all this would be true only if there were such a thing as "the self" in the first place. To put the same thing somewhat differently, all the problems that Strawson and Shoemaker grapple with so extensively, and in the end so unsatisfactorily to rationality, turn out to be pseudo-problems once the self is seen, as it was, for example, by Cohen, as a slice out of the ongoing process of cognition and action. Wilfred Sellars constitutes a special case in this discussion. On the one hand, he arrives at a Kant-interpretation and a philosophical conception of human selfhood that coincide entirely with the views defended in this study in the name of Hermann Cohen (of whom, for the rest, he too seems to be unaware). Categories and concepts are "functions"[89] by means of which "men," not "minds," that is, psychosomatic entities, cognize the world. Things-in-themselves are properly "things as ideal science would find them to be";[90] the "I" is then "a system of capacities pertaining to the various modes of thinking";[91] and on his interpretation of Kant it only may be what we have shown it in fact to be, "a system of scientific objects."[92] And these scientific objects are ultimately determined by the human purposes and interests unpacked in the *Second and Third Critiques*.[93]

On the other hand, Sellars simultaneously holds a philosophical view of his own on the nature of human selfhood and an historical view of Kant's thesis which directly contradict the position just outlined. For one thing, he still wants to maintain that substances logically precede their functions,[94] and that human substances have, after all, "innate abilities."[95] If, however, categories are functions—and "substance" is presumably a category—how can it precede itself? Worst of all, Sellars falls away from his understanding of noumena as "ideal scientific objects" and deals with them after all as quasi-"real," ontological, analogically conceived entities.[96] This is, as he recognizes, Strawson's (mis)-understanding of Kant. Yet at the same time he reproaches Kant for holding it and calls it a "neo-Platonic alternative."[97]

The issue between Sellars and ourselves, on the historical as well as on the philosophical score, can perhaps be focused on his claim that Kant "therefore takes refuge in the claim that, equally, we cannot *know*, on philosophical grounds, that as noumena we are *not* autonomous."[98] He would be right if he inverted the last phrase: Kant argues (rather than taking refuge in an obscurantist claim) that as, and only as, we are autonomous are we noumenal. This is to say, (a) we are not dealing with ontological noumena; (b) noumena are values, cognitive as well as ethical, that serve as "ideals," that is, as human normative goals; and (c) persons are "substances," that is, ostensible units, in precisely the degree to which they approximate such norms.

Finally, it will be worthwhile to compare Cohen's construction of the self, and especially his thesis of "self-determination,"[99] with J.-P. Sartre's argument about the *ego* and self-making. The two have much in common: they both begin on the basis of German idealism, and they end with results that are close kin. By this very token, in the end there are also significant, albeit marginal, differences between them. I think, however, that these differences can be resolved by philosophical argument.

Husserl

Edmund Husserl had begun by replying specifically to Natorp,[100] using almost the very words of Hume on this point: "Now, I am utterly unable to find this primitive ego as a necessary center of conscious reference."[101] By the time of the second edition of *Ideas*, however, he had completely reversed his position.[102] And from then on the notion of an ultimate substantive self increasingly became so important to him and to the very foundation of his philosophical enterprise that, on his understanding of Kant, he wanted to call himself a "transcendental idealist."

On the Kantian score one can do no better by way of criticism than to quote Paul Ricœur:

> The transcendental experience which opens up to the phenomenologist beyond the threshold of the phenomenological reduction at first glance seems totally foreign to the Kantian spirit. Is not the very notion of an "experience" of the cogito some sort of monster for a Kantian? To examine and describe the cogito, is this not to treat it as a phenomenon, hence as an object in nature and no longer as the condition for the possibility of phenomena? Does not the combination of the transcendental and the eidetic reductions remove us still further and more decisively from Kant by the use of a suspect mixture of psychologism (the subjective process) and Platonism (the eidos ego)? Is this not the place to recall that the "I-think" of originary apperception is in no way the ego grasped in its eidos and reduced to the unifying function that supports the synthetic work of cognition? So then, how will the "transcendental experience" escape from

this dilemma: either I am "conscious" of the "I-think" but it is not knowledge, or I "know" the ego but it is a phenomenon in nature? It is on just these grounds that the neo-Kantian criticisms of Husserl are founded.[103]

Husserl's desire to derive himself from Kant is thus surely unjustified. It made better sense to base himself on Descartes' ego-substance; and indeed in the *Cartesian Meditations*, most especially in Meditation IV, all of phenomenology is then reduced to "egology."[104] And it is at just about this point that Sartre's critique of Husserl's "transcendental ego" sets in.[105]

Sartre

Sartre's entire early polemic against Husserl's "transcendental ego" makes precisely Cohen's essential point, including even the perhaps most controversial notion, that the *data* of experience are the products of rational *Ursprung*.[106] Sartre designates a very similar process as *anéantisation*. In general, in *The Transcendence of the Ego: An Existentialist Theory of Consciousness*,[107] the following parallels with Cohen can be cited: the ego is constituted by its states, actions, and qualities (38, 61). It is the "ideal and indirect (noematic) unity of the infinite series of our reflected consciousnesses" and "transcendent" (60; cf. 61, 87).[108] It is subject to correction in the light of its ongoing growth through activities (75). And it is not the source but the result of activities (97f.). The last two pages of the essay anticipate the basic thrust of the *Critique of Dialectical Reason* in insisting that neither objects nor selves but their interrelationships are the "absolute" from which all other realities stem (105f.).[109]

In view of the striking coincidence of this Sartrean notion of the self with Cohen's, it is very difficult to understand why Sartre nonetheless insists on some kind of ultimately "realistic" view of the *ego*: he reiterates that the "I" is "real" (64) and that it is an "actualization" of a "real" potentiality, whatever that may mean (70, 77). In the first place, this claim contravenes the basic direction of his thought. In the second place, it causes him all sorts of philosophical difficulties from which he can scarcely extricate himself (pp. 80ff). In the third place, his only real argument against the *ego* as an "hypothesis" is that we are not prepared to say "I may perhaps be an 'I' " (76). But to begin with, this may not be true. Furthermore, even if true, we may well be wrong in not being prepared to say this. Most importantly, he misunderstands what an hypothesis is: of course, while we are working with the hypothesis of the law of gravity we do not say, "There may perhaps be a law of gravity" but withal it is an hypothesis, since among other considerations we are, if compelled by evidence, prepared to revise or even to scratch it, just as in his case of the ego.

In *The Transcendence of the Ego* (32, 51), as later in *Being and Nothingness*, Sartre takes repeated cracks at "neo-Kantianism" and "Criticism." Our argument shows how unwarranted this is. It is, in any case, not quite clear to what he refers with these denigrations. He may have Paul Natorp in mind,[110] but he certainly does not hit the target of Cohen.[111]

As has been noted, our argument with Sartre is not one of opposition but, as it were, of friendly rectification. It is also in this spirit that Ulrich Sonnemann offers an additional critique of Sartre's notion of the self, which ought to be particularly persuasive to the latter since both thinkers are in the contemporary vanguard of revisionist Marxism. In an unusually opaque but trenchant essay, "The Cartesian Inheritance: Tractate about Freedom and the World,"[112] Sonnemann argues rightly that Sartre, with his vestigial notion of a real, self-subsisting *ego*, lines himself up in the modern tradition from Descartes through Husserl; the Cartesian dichotomy between the *ego* and externality has, in the logic of such a perspective, led to modem sociocultural solipsism, paranoia, and manipulated submission to the status quo.[113] To the contrary, argues Sonnemann, the self is itself incarnate; it is therefore in the external world and subject to historical change. Both world and self are dialectically dependent on one another. And this is, of course, one other way of saying what Cohen had argued—that the self is the creative construct of its inter-relationships with other selves and with the perceptual world.

Pindar's famous dictum ought to be inverted: Be what you become.

Chapter 10 | 1979

"Germanism and Judaism"— Hermann Cohen's Normative Paradigm of the German-Jewish Symbiosis

Hermann Cohen was certainly the most significant and the most characteristic Jewish academic intellectual of the Second German Reich. Throughout his long life and in his complex works he was committed to two ethicosocial values, which he cherished equally; he called them "Germanism and Judaism" (*Deutschtum und Judentum*)[1] and he tried to fuse them into one such value: "German Judaism."[2]

In Cohen's historical period and cultural universe almost all Jews embraced the same commitment, for the Western ideology of Jewish emancipation and acculturation reigned virtually undisputed in the second half of the nineteenth century. During this era German culture held pride of place in much of the world, and, correlatively, the acculturated German-Jewish community, together with its ideals, dominated worldwide Jewry somewhat similarly to the role of American Jewry in our time. This German-Jewish hegemony extended as far as America, if only through emigration, and Eastern-European Jewry through the "Haskalah" (Enlightenment) movement and as a political model of emancipation.[3] Also Orthodox religious Jewry throughout the Occident was deeply influenced by these values of acculturation: Samson Raphael Hirsch's "Neo-Orthodoxy," for example, had just some such symbiosis in mind when it wrote on its banner the punning motto *torah im derekh-eretz* ("The Torah together with worldly civilization"),[4] and, for that matter, the traditional Orthodoxy had always tended, in Western as well as in Eastern Europe, to strive for a modus vivendi with whatever were prevailing conditions.

First published in *Jews and Germans from 1860–1933*, (ed. David Bronsen), Universitätsverlag Carl Winter, Heidelberg, 1979, 142–154.

There were really only two quarters from which significant opposition to the Cohennian or a similar program of German-Jewish symbiosis emanated in Cohen's lifetime and within his purview. One was a large and constantly growing sector of German society itself. We shall note many symptoms of this reaction as we go along. The second developed only in the last decade or so of Cohen's life and comprised a new Jewish ethnic nationalism that began to catch up with the European folk-ideologies. This, too, we shall have occasion to look at from closer range.

The history of Germany, of Europe, and of the Jewish people since that time (which needs no rehearsal) has been such that, on the face of it, it is extremely easy—indeed, facile—to assert, as is done almost universally, that Cohen's program was clearly wrongheaded. The conventional view is that Germany and Jewry have proved to be far from identical or even closely kin and, to the contrary, to be positively, murderously incompatible. The very existence of the Jewish people and the vitality of its culture are, on this view, held to be capable of preservation only in separation from the societies with which they had previously been intermixed. The German anti-Semites and the early Zionists of the turn of the century appear to have understood the nature of the two cultures better than Cohen and his fellow emancipationists. And the ideals to which Cohen was dedicated would, therefore, seem to have been massively refuted by the facts of twentieth-century history, if by nothing else.[5]

I want to take a new look, both wider and closer, at Cohen's ideology of the German-Jewish symbiosis. Hermann Cohen's father Gerson was the cantor, the effective rabbi, of the small Jewish community of Coswig, Anhalt. The son was born there. When Gerson Cohen died the son buried him in the Jewish cemetery of Marburg, where by then he was a university professor. On the tombstone, unimpaired by intervening events, the inscription reveals, among other things, that Gerson Cohen was born on April 15, 1797 and died July 26, 1879.[6] A year earlier, on June 6, 1878, the son had married Martha Lewandowski.[7] She was born on June 20, 1860, daughter of the chief cantor of the Berlin Jewish Community (and perhaps the most important synagogue composer of modern times). Hermann Cohen died on April 4, 1918, and lies buried in "the honor-row" of the great cemetery of the Berlin Jewish Community in Weißensee, under a tombstone, which, too, has been preserved undamaged.[8] His wife long survived him—to be deported to the concentration camp of Theresienstadt on September 1, 1942. Here she died and was cremated eleven days later. Her ashes were cast into the Eger River.[9]

If the life of Hermann Cohen's father can be regarded as one generation and the life span of his wife the next, then it can be said that no more than two generations of German and European Jewry covered the period from 1797 to 1942—that is, from the time of the French Revolution, well prior to even limited legal emancipation for all but a few stray U.S. and French Jewish individuals, to the Nazi holocaust, the catastrophic end of any pretense at an European-Jewish symbiosis. It is true that in making such a calculation we are using the term "generation" somewhat differently from that of historical statisticians. On the other hand, emancipation took really no less than the rest of the nineteenth century to be legally instituted in Central Europe—not to speak of social emancipation; and the era of acculturation was, in the nature of the case, even briefer. Thus, it can fairly be said that, in a general sort of way, two generations exhausted the emancipationist and acculturationist capacities of Europe and its Jewry.

I want to stipulate two more periodizations, which I think will be useful in this context.

Immanuel Kant, Cohen's great *spiritus rector*, died in 1804. By that time the "Zeitgeist" had moved from his Enlightenment, rationalist, cosmopolitan ethicism (which proclaimed "the primacy of practical reason" and hailed the French Revolution as the dawn of a new age) to a new Romantic, increasingly ethnicist German nationalism. The course of the French Revolution and its expansion under Napoleon were certainly one important cause for this shift. Internal German socioeconomic and ideological causes also contributed to it. In any case, from ca. 1800 on the philosophical aegis under which German culture and politics carried on was no longer that of Kant but rather that of Fichte, Schelling, and especially Hegel. Historicism rather than rationalism, nationalism rather than what Kant liked to call "Weltbürgertum" (cosmopolitanism), and revived Romantic religiosity rather than republican secularism dominated the rest of the nineteenth century in Germany and beyond. From no later than 1815 onward German philosophy ("Absolute Idealism") tended strongly to identify the moral ideal with the empirical German polity, as is best illustrated in Hegel's magisterial *Philosophy of Right* and in his proclamation of his own philosophy as the end of history. After no later than 1848 then, having erroneously and injuriously identified itself with the state in the previous generation, philosophy tended to withdraw from politics altogether in favor of either scientific positivism or quasi-religious metaphysics. In short, it can fairly be said that the great spiritual watershed of modern German history, and with that also much of the rest of the world, was the evisceration of the Kantian spirit after ca. 1800.

In the 1860s Otto Liebmann and some others raised the cry: "Back to Kant!"[10] This implied above all a backward transcendence, though not necessarily a rejection, of Hegel. Consequently, the second half of the nineteenth century, well into the twentieth, spawned a multiplicity of so-called neo-Kantian philosophical schools.[11] Several features of this development ought to be noted. For one thing, it may be questioned to what extent, if at all, most of these neo-Kantian trends really rid themselves of the quintessential Hegelian incubus. As one example, Kuno Fischer attempted some sort of synthesis of Kant and Hegel. (I shall return to this point later.) Certainly, none of them rejoined the sociopolitical fray—but for, in the words of Hermann Luebbe,[12] "the exception of Marburg neo-Kantianism," that is, Hermann Cohen and his associates. Of Marburg neo-Kantianism it must, furthermore, be noted that practically all its exponents were Jews (with the exception of Paul Natorp, who was a sort of Carl Jung to Cohen's Freud), and it remained, of course, an extremely small trend, with extremely little effective influence in its own time and virtually none afterward.[13]

Luebbe ascribes the general depoliticization of philosophy in the German nineteenth century to several factors: the real or perceived incompatibility of Hegelianism with the actual progress of the positive sciences—the conflict of what he, too, regards as Hegelian liberalism with the actual political development of Germany after 1848 and 1871—and the backlash to the radicalism of the French Revolution.[14] This explanation cannot be fully argued here. I think it is, in any case, truly wrong to ascribe any basic, genuine liberalism to any sector of Hegelian philosophy, even its so-called Left Wing—and Luebbe's own examples of Trendelenburg and David Friedrich Strauss substantiate my view. Instead, I want to suggest another explanation.

The most fundamental philosophical disagreement between Kantianism and Hegelianism concerns the nature of the "ideal" and "noumenon."[15] For Kant these and connected notions are purely heuristic, regulative, normative, nonempirical, and nonontological. For his troubles he has been accused ever since of being "abstract," "unrealistic," transcendental in a pejorative sense, irrelevant, and so on, by Hegel and all his followers, including the Marxists. They undertook instead to "bring the noumenon back into the world," as a so-called concrete universal, as reason incarnate in empirica, and above all as "the rational that is real (actual)." About this Cohen exclaimed:[16] "Perhaps nothing contributed so much to making philosophy contemptible in the period before the 1848 Revolution as the reactionary motto of Hegel: 'The real is the rational, and the rational is the real.'"

We cannot here enter into the subtle and complex technicalities of this philosophical question. Suffice it to say that the specific phenomena in which the ideal was then proclaimed to have been actualized ranged from and beyond the Prussian state to the Germanic Volk and to various other historico-empirical entities.[17] Also in various neo-Kantian, though non-Marburgian, schools of thought it consequently was no longer a question of constructing new rational regulative ideals toward which to rectify the given actualities but of *verstehen*, empathizing with ultimate metaphysical realities—be these the *self* or *national essences*, and so on. Thus, Dilthey followed Treitschke in his nationalistic anti-Semitism,[18] and Meinecke followed Dilthey; Stewart Houston Chamberlain combined his Wagnerian-Hitlerite-Christian racism with a form of Kantianism;[19] and in 1916 Bruno Bauch, a very sophisticated Kantian, manipulated Cohen and Ernst Cassirer out of the *Kant Gesellschaft*, of which he was then president, by means of his philosophical racism.[20] All in all, in this manner the Kantian/neo-Kantian infinite tension between always unsatisfactory reality and the categorically imperative "ought" was shrunk to zero in the universe, and Marx's famous motto reverted to its original Hegelian, "inverted" form ("standing on its head")—that the philosopher's task was not to change the world but to understand and make his peace with it. This posture makes politics impossible in the end, of course. One leans back and grooves on what is actually happening—brought about by others, to be sure. The cultural, then the economic, and finally the military and politico-social rise of the Germany of the nineteenth century provided immense self-satisfaction to the German bourgeois who felt justified in believing that not only were their selfish interests being sewed but that these selfish interests of their *völkisch* essence turn out to be the realization of ideal, universal values. "Am deutschen Wesen soll die Welt genesen."[21]

The defeat of World War I cast doubt on this proposition. It was also responsible for the establishment of the Weimar Republic. But to many the old quasi-Hegelian *hybris* could be maintained by conspiratorial theories about "the stab in the back" and by regarding the republic as a Western, liberalistic imposition at the hands of "criticistic Jews"[22]—Thomas Mann's "republic of the (mere) understanding." One might (just to complete this bird's-eye view of recent German history) give expression to the hope that the Federal Republic after World War II and its "Scandinavian turn" have finally brought Germany back in touch with the stream of Enlightenment rationalism and ethical, cosmopolitan republicanism.

Jewish emancipation from birth to death and the rise of reactionary antirationalism thus wholly coincide, between ca. 1800 and 1945. Jewish emancipation was an ideal developed originally not by Jews but by seventeenth- and eighteenth-century rationalists (deists, secularists, skeptics, materialists and empiricists, and moralists). By most of the Jewish masses and their established leadership it was usually resisted as long as possible. Where the push for emancipation had succeeded by the end of the eighteenth century, in the U.S. and France, it was more or less firmly entrenched by the time the rationalist spirit began to recede during the nineteenth century.[23] In Germany (and other European countries) it had to be established during a century which was fundamentally inimical to it, and consequently it progressed only very slowly, grudgingly, and fragmentarily. Where universalist reason was pushed back—as by the defeat of Napoleon, the blocking-out of Thomas Paine, and the end of Bismarck's liberal honeymoon—it was curtly countermanded.[24]

Hermann Cohen's career, now, fits precisely in the chronological and geographical middle of this modem European ambience. Born on July 4, 1842, he was fortuitously ready and eager for an academic appointment (which is a government function in Germany) after his first philosophical work—*Kants Theorie der Erfahrung*[25]—was published in 1871, that is, simultaneous with Bismarck's establishment of the all-German monarchy. The German liberals had long striven for this political consolidation, and also Bismarck thought that these liberals, and perhaps even Lassalle's trade unions, could team up to create the new empire and to fight the "Kulturkampf" against the Roman Church in the Western and Southern German regions. Thus the Bismarckian "honeymoon with the liberals" came to pass. Even so, Cohen had a great deal of trouble in obtaining an appointment, because not only did he bear the name "Cohen"[26] but he also was a professing Jew. Had it not been for the fact that Friedrich Albert Lange, an old and courageous 1848-liberal, took him under his wing at the University of Marburg[27] and Bismarck's minister of culture was the liberal Adalbert Falk, Cohen might well have had to act on his serious qualms about aspiring to a scholarly career.[28]

The liberal honeymoon ended very quickly. When the full impact of the first great economic crisis overtook the German state by 1879/1880 the tenor of the times precipitously declined. The "Kulturkampf" against the Roman Church was replaced by the new anti-Semitism, which combined old religious bigotry with new biologico-ethnicist and historicist-political programs. The very term "anti-Semitism" was coined at this time by Wilhelm Marr, with its racist connotation. Cohen reluctantly felt constrained to take up the cudgels against Heinrich v. Treitschke, then the most influential academic figure in Prussian politics.[29] And for the rest of his life he could never put them out of his hands again. In sum, before 1873 Cohen could not yet have attained his position, and after 1879 he could no longer have attained it; he slipped in luckily during an extremely short interval. He is thus also a good symbol for all of the rising middle and professional class among German and other European Jews when he identified his own social advancement with the values of what has remained known in Germany as its classical cultural age, from, say, approximately Kant's birth to Goethe's death.

Anti-Semitism became an increasingly potent and public political force in Germany until and beyond the Revolution of 1918. According to S. Lehr,[30] for example, there were no fewer than sixty public ritual-murder affairs in Germany and Austro-Hungary between 1873 and 1900. Cohen was often involved in "antidefamation" activities. Also in philosophy this spirit manifested itself. Nachum Goldmann claims[31] that it was Rickert, and Jakob Klatzkin claims[32] that it was Kuno Fischer who went so far as to make the famous statement that Cohen's thought was not really a matter of philosophy but of race.[33] And in the Bauch-episode during the war this was flagrantly thrown into his face.[34]

What was meant by this kind of anti-Semitic claim was, in the first and most obvious place, that the Marburg School consisted almost entirely of Jews. (It turned out ultimately that even Natorp would not preserve his philosophical loyalty.)[35] That many of the younger Jews came from Eastern Europe also did not ingratiate the school in such circles. What was meant in the second place was that Cohen himself and virtually all other "Marburgers" publicly proclaimed not only their political liberalism but even their active socialist enthusiasm—and this was always suspected as at best dubiously patriotic. Most broadly what was meant was that Marburg neo-Kantianism was perceived, only in part justly, as an enactment of what the Nazis later were to call "the corrupting, criticistic, negative, rationalistic Jewish spirit," and what this referred to was the centrality of concern with the positive and mathematical sciences and the unrelenting rationalism, analyticism, and methodologism that ruled here.[36]

Even, and particularly, in his own university, and most especially in his own faculty, Cohen had to confront this phenomenon. He obtained his full appointment only after undue difficulties. Starting no later than in the middle 1880s Cohen's and Natorp's scholarly values, projects, and students were increasingly combatted and constricted. Thus he writes in 1894 about "our miserable faculty conditions."[37] The anti-Semitic wave of 1880 was resumed, as is well known, in the 1890s with full force.[38] In 1892 Cohen wrote of "(D)ie Zeit der Sorgen und des Kummers, die so lange schon über uns lagert."[39] In 1899 he wrote:[40] "Unfortunately one must admit that we had overestimated the maturity of the times. We are unfortunately not yet on the eve of the messianic age." Intra-departmental hostilities repeatedly reached the point of governmental involvement and possible resignations. Cohen always felt painfully encircled by enmity. He was occasionally accused by his closest associates of paranoia about anti-Semitism.[41] And at least behind his back he was teased about his love for travel; one suspects that this was motivated by his malaise in the small, provincial town of Marburg that was—and is—dominated by ecclesiastical and dynastic forces[42] and of which Otto Hahn wrote recently[43] "Marburg does not have a university; it is a university." Certainly Cohen must have been the only famous German professor throughout the Second Reich—founder of an important intellectual school at that—who was never offered another university chair during his career.[44] His disciples, too, could not obtain academic appointments, and the ironic aspect of this state of affairs was that Ernst Cassirer, for instance—not to speak of Dimitri Gawronsky—was rejected by the general establishment for being too Jewish (which was far from true), while Benzion Kellermann, for another, was rejected by the Jewish establishment for being too radically philosophical.[45]

On August 1, 1912, Cohen finally resigned from the university in an act of ideological protest against the reactionary German forces arrayed against the social and religious liberalism he represented.[46] Though then seventy years old, he did not yet need to retire. He took this step in order in this manner to object to his untraditional exclusion from the process of selecting his eventual successor, which, in turn, was motivated by the desire to keep, not only any Jew but also any adherent of "Critical idealism" and socialism, out of the chair which he had occupied for forty years.[47] It was no less a polemical act on his part to move to the big and relatively liberal city of Berlin and there to spend the rest of his life teaching at the liberal rabbinical seminary, concentrating on religious questions. It was thus inescapably clear to everyone that at the end of an illustrious and influential career, in which most of the major intellectual and social concerns of the world had been treated, conditions in Germany—cultural, political, and ideological—had so far eroded that, because of anti-Semitism and philosophical irrationalism, what Lange and Falk had done for Cohen in 1873, Cohen could no longer even hope to effect for someone else in 1912. An incidental by-product of this timetable is that Cohen's quasi-professional Jewish life precisely preceded and followed the peace-time existence of the Second German Empire, while his professional philosophical career coincided completely with the delimited historical duration of that state. (Simon Dubnow called it "the age of the second reaction [1880–1914]" in the subtitle of Vol. X of his *Weltgeschichte des jüdischen Volkes.*)

Several valuable, indeed decisive, inferences can be drawn from this synchronism, which we have now established. The standard procedure in the last few decades has been to identify Hermann Cohen with the motto and ideology of "Germanism and Judaism"—to take it for granted that by the term "Germanism" he meant to refer to empirical Germany, or at least to actual, historical German culture—and then to refute his thesis of an identity or symbiosis by simply pointing to the blatant discordancy between his irenic conceptual fusion and the real conflict between the two entities. But this presupposes that Cohen was blind and insensitive to the historical realities that surrounded and even impinged so painfully on his own life. He would have had to be stupid for this claim to be valid. The facts overwhelmingly refute it. While he was still looking for any kind of job, he wrote with some bitterness to Professor Lange: "If this (anti-Semitic proscription) is possible in the new Reich, I'd have to learn something with which I can earn a livelihood. Kantian philosophy won't make it in Palestine."[48] The material collected in Helmut Holzhey's *Cohen und Natorp—Ein Beitrag zur Geschichte des Neukantianismus—Texte, Briefe, Interpretation*[49] more than suffices to show how Cohen throughout his life suffered from, lamented, and tried to fight against the constantly growing political and cultural conservatism of Germany during the existence of the Prusso-German state. In the second edition of his *Ethik des reinen Willens*—perhaps his central work and certainly the one closest to ethico-social concerns—he adds to the preface an emphatic proclamation of the fundamental divergence between his own sociopolitical program and the real development of German history all around him:[50] "While I must take a principled posture of opposition to this modern style of Germanism, I feel fortified by the knowledge that I am harking back to the original power of the essence of the German spirit, contrary to its ephemeral distortions." And Luebbe rightly observes[51] "Cohen was vividly conscious of his uncontemporaneity, this impossibility of being in philosophical accord with the fullness of rational reality." (Notice Luebbe's Hegelian vocabulary: even he assumes—and this is important for the thesis that he, and many others, put forward—that Marburg theory was unfortunately practically irrelevant due to its ivory-tower abstractness.)

And then, toward the very end of his life, during World War I, all the strains and pains of the postulated German-Jewish symbiosis erupt once more—this time mainly over the issue of the official census of Jews in the German army. Even the cherished lifelong, intimate friendship of Cohen and Natorp threatens to break up. Cohen is profoundly shocked by the bitter fruit of German anti-Semitism in the midst of the war, which he has been endorsing so fervently qua Jew. At the very time that he speaks publicly with the voice of *Deutschtum and Judentum* he writes privately to Natorp that his "optimism is only historical (i.e., only for the longest run), not current,"[52] and so is his patriotism.[53] In reply Natorp comes dangerously close to accusing him of disloyalty.

Cohen is often accused of some sort of fatuous historical as well as philosophical optimism.[54] This accusation displays real psychological and conceptual insensitivity. On the subjective score Natorp writes on September 24, 1904, for example?[55] "The younger people who have helped him proofreading and compiling the index (to his *Ethik*) are quite overwhelmed by his gay optimism, which contrasts strangely for those who are close to him with his often torturous pessimism and with his almost unqualified distrust of all non-Jews or fellow-travelers of Jews." In terms of objective historiography Cohen says at the very end of his farewell lecture in Marburg[56] "World history is no proud victory parade, no steep, open path to the peak. It has its retarding moments; it has its descending curves; occasionally it is even retrogression. We have to reconcile ourselves to this. We may not proudly disregard it. It must make us think and challenge us the more to serious work."[57] The purely regulative character of this Kantian/neo-Kantian belief in "steady progress" is strongly adumbrated in the last phrase.[58] Progress is, contrary to all forms of Hegelianism, not asserted because of any natural or actual inevitability but in despite of historical irrationality. It is an ought, the more categorical for its empirical failures. This might be called a tragic optimism, or in Gramsci's phrase[59] "a pessimism of the intellect and optimism of the will." Perhaps heroism is the best description of it altogether.[60]

The spirit of Marburg neo-Kantianism was in fact largely determined by the Jewishness of its adherents. These Jews had good reason to know that the real Germany of which they were (or, in some cases, were not) citizens was very far, indeed, from any ideal state. They were the products of the rising German-Jewish middle class, still in the process of embourgeoisement, still knocking on the doors of German and European society. Their personal experiences and those of their fellow Jews sensitized them so that they also identified their own cause with that of other exploited, excluded, and expropriated social groups. And together they resisted every Hegelian temptation to identify the real Germany with their ideal.[61] The Gentile German middle class was sociologically placed in such a way that the Hegelian identity of the rational with the actual could be increasingly embraced by them; the rising Jewish middle class in Germany, on the other hand, was sociologically so much situated as outsiders, and, indeed, increasingly as endangered outsiders, to this society that they understandably fell back on the infinite gap between the real and the ideal that Kant had presented as a moral challenge to his world in the period of earliest capitalist development.[62] Cohen put it in philosophical language:[63] "Here the world-wide difference between Hegel and Kant shows up; for Kant would say: what is rational is not actual but ought to become so." Aphoristically one could say that middle-class Gentile Germans adapted to their *Gegebenheiten* ("givens") by means of Hegelian *Aufhebungen* ("sublations"), while Jews had to try to conquer the *Gegebenheiten* by means of Kantian *Aufgaben* ("tasks"). Hannah Arendt put it well:[64] "It is obvious that no matter how far distant or how close at hand the realization of mankind ("weltbürgerliche Absicht") may be, one can be a world-citizen only within the framework of Kant's categories. The best that can happen to any individual in the Hegelian system of historical revelation of the world-spirit is to have the good fortune to be born among the right people at the right historical moment . . ." "Deutschtum" ("Germanism"), sometimes even "Deutschheit" ("Germanhood"),[65] is then in these Jewish mouths a rational, ideal, normative construction, which, far from being identical with, in fact constantly opposes and challenges "Deutschland" ("Germany") to moralize, "idealize" itself radically and infinitely.

The most obvious manner in which the actual thrust of the Marburg School gave expression to its dissatisfaction with the current state of affairs (and affairs of state) and, for that matter, with the potentialities that seemed to inhere in the conditions that then prevailed in Germany was its commitment to socialism. Critical idealism was not only the sole philosophical movement that so daringly advocated socialism (and for its troubles continues to be patronized as among the "Katheder-Sozialisten") but, as Luebbe has rightly noted, it was the only one engage in practical politics of any sort. From before its inception until well after the death of its founder Critical idealism and democratic socialism were inextricably intertwined?[66] F.A. Lange presaged it—Cohen articulated it—and D. Gawronsky, leading member of the Second International and of the Russian Left Social Revolutionary Party, wrote what may be the first Left-radical critique of Lenin's dictatorship in 1920.[67] When ideological alliances were contemplated, they had to be sought out not in philosophical or academic circles but in the ranks of the Social Democratic Party. In this way the discussions came about around the turn of the century that are usually referred to as "the revisionist controversy" and, which were, in fact, largely attempts to derive socialism from and reformulate it in accordance with Kantianism rather than (Left) Hegelianism. Eduard Bernstein is the best-known name associated with this episode, but there were also Vorländer, Kurt Eisner.[68] Among many other things that this Marburgian socialism gave expression to is, of course, precisely the affirmation that the ideal Germany, the morally imperative, rationally requisite, if you please the noumenal Germany, "Germanism," was still infinitely remote from actual, empirical Germany, and that every effort must be made to try to approximate the ideal through ethical reformation (or "continuous revolution"), that is, through democratic socialism.[69]

Here, then, we arrive at the final point that is cogent for the problematic of Cohen's "Germanism and Judaism." It is a philosophic, methodological point, and in this context I can only block it out in broad strokes. The decisive term for it is a Marburgian *terminus technicus*: "idealization." In Critical philosophy "idealization" not only does not mean what it generally means in current English ordinary usage—glorification, enveloping grimy reality with a nimbus of ideality, and so on, but, in fact, it means exactly the opposite: "idealization" is the rational, conceptual construction, the postulation of a morally desirable condition (A), for the purpose of measuring against it any actually given condition (B), so as necessarily to reveal that (B) falls short of (A) $[(B) = (A) - x]$, and entailing the categorical challenge that the most strenuous efforts must be made to narrow this gap urgently and increasingly [so that

(B) = (A) - (x - a)]. "Idealization" is then a critical and meliorist tool. (Max Weber's "ideal model" is closely cognate to this.)

"Germanism," thus, (but also any other analogous conception—for example, Judaism) is such a regulative idealization. In this perspective the German state ("Germany"), analogous to any other real state, plays a considerably more complex role in Marburg neo-Kantianism than is commonly credited. The state is, to use the language of the Hegelian translation of Kantian categories, the logical, ethical, and historical "mediation," which particularity performs between individuality and universality. That is, the state is the social organism through which the solitary individual and its needs approach in historical actuality the ideal and infinite goal of universal morality. It performs this mediation by generalizing and moralizing the biological individual and its immediate kin in the relative community—or really "society"—which it establishes and constantly improves.[70] It does all this, however, only on a number of conditions.

Idealization is the word that designates both the goal and the incremental efforts leading to the goal. Under the latter heading, the state must, in the first place, always be in historical motion in the right direction, that is, toward ideality, toward universal morality, for, like all "ideas" in the Kantian sense, idealization has to be not only nonempirical but also "universalized." Thus, for example, when Cohen published the second part of his Kant exegesis, *Kants Begründung der Ethik* (significantly in 1877),[71] he opened it by stipulating that the ultimate and normative unity of mankind is both the criterion and goal of ethics,[72] and he ended it[73] by defining the task of ethics as the "re-creation of man in accordance with the idea of mankind." On the other hand a state that was historically developing in a regressive direction—toward barbarism, immorality, or inhumanity—would obviously be performing what we have come to know in theory and practice as a "negative dialectic."[74]

The most striking example, perhaps, of this directional condition that Cohen demands occurs at the climax of the "critical epilogue," which he added to later editions of his controverted wartime Germanic and anti-Zionist broadsheet *Deutschtum und Judentum*.[75]

> A Germanism that might demand of me that I surrender my religion and my religious inheritance, I would not acknowledge as an ideal peoplehood in which the power and dignity of statehood inhere. Such a peoplehood would not instill in us

the confidence with which we all believe that victory in this world war is a divine judgment in world history. Were I born into such a peoplehood and such a state I would, indeed, regard myself as entitled to claim "a publicly and legally insured home." But a Germanism that might demand such a surrender of religious selfhood, or that could even approve of and project it, simply contradicts the world-historical impulsion of Germanism. And the mission that has even now devolved upon Germanism, of saving the bulk of Russian Jewry, confirms the confidence of the German Jew in the humanist vocation of the German people.

En passant this paragraph happens to underline the peculiarly Jewish motivation that impelled Cohen to endorse German arms during World War I so fervently—a powerful consideration that also impelled many other Jews at that time throughout the world and in Russia itself: the fate of the greatest reservoir of the Jewish people under the whip of the czars.[76]

In our immediate context, however, what that paragraph powerfully bespeaks is that Germanism was understood by Cohen to mean the humanistic values of Kant and Schiller, or what he often called "the nation of Kant."[77] Throughout his life he proclaimed this identification over and over again. "Nationality—if it be humanistic, not Teutonic—is part of humanity."[78] "I am at one in my feelings with the cosmopolitans of all nations."[79] At the beginning of the great war he writes to Natorp:[80] "We have a cosmopolitan nationality. This it is that we must unveil and explicate." And in the contemporary early war-time essay "About the Peculiarity of the German Spirit"[81] he writes: "Germanism is and always remains in the continuity of the 18th century and its cosmopolitan (weltbürgerlich) humanism." (Cohen emphasizes that "About the Peculiarity of the German Spirit" and *Germanism and Judaism*, written respectively at the beginning and in the middle of the war, are, as it were, "twin" productions, one more concerned with Germany as such and the other with the German-Jewish symbiosis).[82]

Germanism does not designate the narrow and, as Cohen knew only too well from his own lifelong experiences, historically disastrous reality of Germany but the intermediate embodiment, as he wished to see it, of the progressive development of humanistic values from Plato through Maimonides to Kant, the French Revolution, and the socialist movement, which had, by that time, achieved greater political successes in Germany than anywhere else.[83] Were Germanism something contrary to what he conceives it to be, or when it has in fact proved to be something contrary, Cohen adopts verbatim the first and fundamental sentence of the Basle-Program of the First Zionist Congress of 1897 to lay claim to "a publicly and legally insured home" somewhere other than in Germany.[84]

Another way of putting this is to say that the Germanism that Cohen is talking about is not the real Germany but a future Germany, which will have been raised to a moral, humanistic, cosmopolitan level on which all viable socio-historical entities will not so much merge into one as live peaceably and creatively with one another. This is the conception of a worldwide federation of social republics as Kant had projected it in *Toward a Perpetual Peace*, that Cohen advocated, and which a year or so after Cohen's death was visualized in the League of Nations.[85] On this level not only Germany and Judaism but also England and France, Spain, America, Russia in which the revolution had already begun and was hailed, the Moslem world, and so on, will interrelate productively out of the ethical "sources," which they each have searched out within themselves and "idealized" as their peculiar historico-cultural contribution to the universal polity.

Cohen himself tried hard in his various works to ferret out such ethical sources in diverse historical cultures: he worked almost like a professional at Christian theology;[86] in his *Ästhetik des reinen Gefühls*, as an example, the Spanish Don Quixote (recommended to him by his student Ortega y Gasset), the English Shakespeare,[87] the French impressionist painters as spokesmen of the working class,[88] and so on, are interpreted as building-stones for the edifice of the temple of mankind; Newton and scientists of other nations throughout history, not to speak of the Greeks, are treated in his *Logik der reinen Erkenntnis* and elsewhere as the pioneers of universal and ultimately moral; "practical" reason.[89] In all of these historic cultures their past and present chauvinistic and immoral features are, as it were, locked away from future historical effectiveness, be this the pantheistic danger in Judaism and in German Romanticism[90] no less than the empiricistic one in England, feudalism in Russia, and so on. It would not be very hard to show how Cohen, had he been, say, a Frenchman and immersed in French historical culture as he in fact was in German sources, would doubtless have written about "Frankism and Judaism," in which he would have said in principle precisely what he said in *Deutschtum and Judentum*:

let us use the best resources put at our disposal by the historical cultures and political structures into which history has placed us in order therewith to create a decent cosmopolitan human society. He stated this program paradigmatically at the very end of his *Ästhetik*[91] and therewith at the highest peak of his philosophical "system": "The unity of the consciousness of culture is . . . the task of not only specifying respectively but also of tracing and making translucent in their reciprocal relations all kinds of consciousnesses of culture as they come down to the individual person and to individual peoples, as they mutually permeate and affect one another."

Cohen's social philosophy also provides a number of conceptual mechanisms by means of which the positive state is always to reform itself *in actu* in the direction of the humanistic ideal. Cohen follows Kant in preferring the concept of "society" (*Gesellschaft*) to that of "community" (*Gemeinschaft*)[92] (*pace* Guenther: "Community, central motto of fascism . . .").[93] "Society" designates the totality of all human relations and social relationships, and the state is called upon increasingly to serve societal needs rather than being a self-serving, self-justifying supreme value (as it turns out to be in Hegel and Hegelianism, including historical Marxisms).

Socialism plays a major part in this socialization of the state.[94] Even Karl Marx, as "the fiery prophet of justice," performs a significant function in this process,[95] though, to be sure, his philosophic materialism and historical determinism must be reduced to their ethical motivations. And "reform and revolution" (!)[96] are the channels of this socialization.

The increasing preponderance of societal values over communal and especially statist values in any given state will also increasingly transform the actual *Machtstaat* ("power state") into the ethically imperative *Rechtsstaat* ("legal/constitutional state").[97] One passage in Cohen's *Ethik* states this doctrine so eloquently that it deserves quotation at length:[98]

> This is what matters—that justice become the virtue of the law, as the virtue of the state, so that the state become the state of justice. Our ethics (*Ethik*?) may perhaps be regarded as being infected with the oppressing odium of orienting the consciousness of the self by the state,[99] while in fact the empirical state corresponds so little to this ideal and so frequently and emphatically makes a mockery of it in fact. Nonetheless,

even this state must, in the logic of its own impulsion and however unwillingly, tend toward and serve that ideal—even at the risk of sounding hypocritical. *It is true that the empirical state is the state of the estates and of the ruling class—not the legal state.* The power state can become the legal state only by developing the law in accord with the idea of the state rather than in the interest of the estates and classes. The latter are relative communities. And the mediaeval ideals with which they adorn themselves reveal their armed selfishness.

The state of justice has only one goal: the moral self-consciousness. [...] *The self-consciousness of the state is the self-consciousness of all its members.* [...] Restriction on property is added as its second condition. [...] (T)he law of justice becomes the right of man (le droit de l'homme) in the state. [...] *Without the state no right of man* ("human rights"). *Also, however, without the right of man no law of the state as the state of justice.* Without the right of man in the state only the right of power, class right rules in the state. Thus the state is a shadow of the state. And its fate is sooner or later to perish—by conquest or by dissolution. . . .

Or again, at the very end of his life and in the middle of his own, war-euphoria Cohen writes in his *Neue Jüdische Monatshefte*:[100] "For me the ideal of every legal state is humanity. . . . The positive state must let itself be guided also in its political affairs by this ideal conception of the world-state."

The neo-Kantian method of idealization entails a further number of *modi operandi* that are noteworthy. In the first place, since the postulation has been constructed on the basis of *a priori* criteria, that is, *sub specie* "the primacy of practical reason," it constitutes a literally "ideal," that is, infinite goal. Therefore, not only empirical condition (B) but every other empirical state of affairs (C–Z) will also necessarily fall short of the ideal (A), though perhaps less so. The ideal can and must be approached asymptotically, as Cohen and Kant liked to put it. (Cohen identified this perspective as Jewish messianism.) In other words, the historically given condition of Germany, of Judaism, any state, any stage of science, and everything else in the phenomenal universe always stands under the judgment of being at least inadequate and in crying need of improvement; satisfaction with any status quo is mortal sin.

In the second place, idealization is also a precise historiographical methodology. (Kant had in fact worked it out with a high degree of sophistication in his historiographical and political essays.)[101] Having stipulated ideal condition (A) as the goal, this is then used as an historiographical principle of selection from the welter of past and present actual conditions (B-Z) of those elements (α-β), which tend most strongly in the direction of (A) and which, when serialized chronologically and conceptually, constitute the direction of past history that is to be normatively extrapolated into the future. Historiography has thus become idealistically prescriptive.[102]

Not only the quasi-political writings of Cohen and his associates but also their numerous and important studies in the history of philosophy and of ideas have, since the time of their original publications to this day, constantly been subjected to the heaviest criticism. The usual refrain is that "the Marburgers" always misinterpret past texts and events as precursors to or deviations from their own eventual philosophic position. Thus, for example, Natorp's presentation of Plato (at least in the first edition) is decried as "Platorp." Cassirer's interpretation of Descartes and Leibniz, among others, is condemned as a Kantianization of these rationalists. Isaac Husik excoriated Benzion Kellermann's translation and interpretation of Gersonides as "unhistorical."[103] (Husik had an axe of his own to grind to the effect that the mediaeval Jewish philosophers held views which are untenable under all conditions of modernity and that, in fact, there can no longer be any such thing as "Jewish philosophy.")[104] Hermann Cohen himself continues to our own time to be rejected on philological grounds for his (and, in his footsteps, Zvi Diesendruck's) exegesis of, among others, Maimonides[105]—not to speak of the Bible and Judaism as a whole.

There are also still further complexities in the Cohennian model of the development of "humanity" out of the state. Prior to the state the "people"(Volk) is the biological socialization of the individual,[106] and this Volk is then ethicized through the state. In 1917, perhaps under the influence of the then current Wilsonian discussions of "the nationalities policy," Cohen even speaks of a "Jewish nationality," which, like others, enters—in this particular case—into the German state.[107] By the same token there are other intermediate steps between the state and "mankind," such as the federation of states.¹⁰⁸

An approximate schema of this entire, rather complex normative model of the good society might be sketched like this:

> individual, i.e. "natural man"—> "nationality"—> Volk (territory)—> state (from "power state" to "legal state" = from "community" to "society," i.e. socialism)—> federation of states—> humanity.

How Cohen could have matured further in his unpacking of the idea of the healthy German state had contemporary political conditions shown him other options or had he lived into the 1920s does not have to remain a matter of counterfactual speculation; as it happens, we can legitimately infer this from what Paul Natorp was to say on these questions.

Natorp came very close to a Marxist-anarchist thesis of the desirable, ultimate transformation of the state into a nonviolent system of "councils" (i.e., "soviets"). J. Klein describes his overall view as follows:

> The idea will live, though the world perish. This also applies to the Volk, for the Volk is no manner of thing, which could easily die, but it is an idea. Natorp's demand for non-violence is nought but post-war pacifism integrated into his system¹⁰⁹ and the idea of liberalism with its doctrinaire faith in the conquering power of freedom in eternally growing development, which, too, is connected with the system. He advocates this with revolutionary pathos. But all he is doing is extrapolating to the end Cohen's concept of the state, when he perceives in the state the instrument "of the effectuality of the idea in time."¹¹⁰

It is true that by the time Natorp thought like this he was no longer a Cohennian, and what I implied earlier about Klein¹¹¹ remains true; but on the score of the political ideology that may be regarded as the logical result of Cohen's political philosophy this sounds entirely convincing: the state as the federation of local democratic groups, pacifism, the "people" as a moral idea, liberalism in the sense of growing political and social freedom, and so on.

At this point we can return to our narrower theme of Cohen's "Germanism and Judaism." Historical Germany and historical Judaism, too, are, of course, subject to the methods of idealization. They, too, are not simply accepted in the crude forms of their historically conditioned givenness at any one time or even at all times. They, too, are subjected to a philosophical, rational, ethical process of "purification." One could write a history of the Jewish concept of an *emunah tzeruphah* ("refined, purified faith") from before the times of the Biblical prophets[112] through, of all people, R. Yehudah HaLevy and Nachman Krochmal in the nineteenth century. In any case, at the hands of Hermann Cohen it comes to mean, in the strict Kantian sense of the term *rein*, the processing of the empirical and historical facts by *a priori* reason, so as to select, cleanse, and order them into a ratio-morally desirable "system."

In Critical idealism history and idealization relate to one another generally as empirica and reason relate to one in Kantianism as a whole: history without idealization is blind, and idealization without history is empty.[113] The accusation of tendentious subjectivism that is so widely leveled at Marburgian historiography—quite apart from leaving itself wide open to the *tu quoque* reply—would be valid only if, counterfactually, the Marburgers had not done their historical homework very carefully. But, in fact, whether with respect to the Bible, philosophical texts, or history in general, Cohen used to insist with his students that "you have to square away your philology before you can go on to your philosophy."[114] Nineteenth-century German historical methodology, by which he was surrounded all his life, and perhaps also his early training at the Breslau rabbinical seminary and his association with Wellhausen at the University of Marburg, would have made it impossible for him to tackle problems in any other way. And this was then applied to all, what are nowadays called "hermeneutic," tasks—"Germanism" no less than Judaism, in the instance with which we are here primarily concerned.

When, therefore, Jewish Zionists, German anti-Semites, and others quickly jumped to the attack on Cohen's "Germanism and Judaism" on the ground that "Germany," for example, is not, or at least is not only, Luther's individualistic autonomy, Kant's moral reason, Schiller's passion for freedom, and Mozart's and Beethoven's paeans to the beauty of universal humanity—then they entirely miss the point. In the instance of Judaism, the very title of his magisterial ethico-philosophical theology *Religion of Reason—Out of the Sources of Judaism* should be translated with a dictionary of the idealistic method of historical idealization at one's side, and this title will then turn out to mean something like this: "Universal Morality, concretized in history as religion, constructed with the literary and historical material originated, i.e., produced *a priori*, in Judaism." When critics then argue that there are important elements in Jewish texts and experience that conflict with Cohen's version of Judaism—such as ultimate particularistic loyalties, irrationalities, and even immoralities—Cohen would reply that he is, of course, entirely, indeed, painfully aware of these historical anomalies but that the point of philosophy is to change the world and, therefore, also to moralize, to "idealize" historical Judaism.

I said at the outset of this study[115] that in the last decade or so of Cohen's life opposition to his ideal of the German-Jewish symbiosis also began to come forth from intensely Jewish quarters. The clash between his ideology of rationalist, universalist liberalism, on the one hand, and the new ideology of Zionism or other forms of Jewish ethnicism, on the other, found classic expression in the polemic between Cohen and Martin Buber in the years that brought to a close both World War I and Cohen's life.[116]

Cohen's controversialists—Zionists like Buber and Klatzkin, but also some others, including non-Zionists like Rosenzweig—reacted to the correctly perceived discrepancy between his normatively moralized sublation of the German-Jewish synthesis on the one hand and the empirical reality of the antithetical German-Jewish relationship on the other in a manner, which was itself, on the one hand, antithetical to Cohen's view and, on the other, perfectly analogous to, if not identical with, the attitude of German ethnicists and even racists. That is to say, all three—Cohen and his type of ethical, cosmopolitan rationalism, the Zionists and other Jewish folk-ideologists, and the anti-Semites—could not but acknowledge the grave tensions and even hostilities between Jewry and Germany. However, whereas Cohen concluded from this state of affairs that all efforts ought to be made to eliminate this divisiveness between them, his opponents were at one in concluding—sometimes in concert and sometimes at loggerheads with one another—that, for the benefit of both, the division between Germany and Jewry—and, for that matter, "the nations of the world" in general and the Jewish people— is and by rights ought to be maintained and even radicalized, culturally, politically, and even geographically.

Thus Zionists developed an ideology of peoplehood ("Volkstum"), which was derived from much the same sources (Hegel, Nietzsche, etc.) as and paralleled the theories of German ethnicism.[117] Not infrequently they even expressed their Jewish approval of at least some of the planks in the anti-Jewish platform—in the spirit, say, of Herder's early-nineteenth-century liberal nationalism and of Nachman Krochmal's mid-nineteenth-century philosophy of the Jewish *Volksgeist* (*ru'akh ha'am*); the hope would then be that all ethnic cultures would develop their own respective indigenous "spirits" separately and fully and that they would then, out of that posture, cooperate with one another to universal advantage. The motto then was *Micah* 5:5: "For all the nations will each go in the name of its god, and we shall go in the name of the Lord, our God, forever and ever" (Cp. Is. 2).[118] Not infrequently, too, German "civilized anti-Semites" reciprocated such good will by, as it were, bidding the Jews "hail and farewell!"[119]

Returning to the technicalities of the method of idealization, even some purely stylistic consequences flow from it in Cohen's work. It is often pointed out that one of Cohen's literary peculiarities is his use of the auxiliary verb "to be" as a copula. It is frequently not at all clear whether he is using it as an existential qualifier, as identity, the introduction to a syllogistic or inductive proof, or as what. If one runs across a sentence of the form "Germany is the spirit of Kant and Beethoven," what is one to make of this? Readers will complain that no evidence has been adduced for this claim. It also seems to claim identity—which obviously neglects much and even contradictory evidence, and so on. In fact, this sentence is—consistent with and, as a matter of fact, resultant from the epistemology and philosophy of science of Critical idealism—the most radical application of Kant's "primacy of practical reason."

All concepts, like "Germany" or "Germanism," for example, but, for that matter, also "tree" and even "this tree," are the rational, conceptual utilizations of some set or other of "givens" (or *sensa*), sensible and historical, in the form of prescriptive notions, whose purpose is "practical" in one way or another; that is, a challenge to scientific investigation or to moral action. In the former of these two cases we use "regulative" concepts and in the latter "normative" ones. (It goes without saying that there can be and are, therefore, also false and bad concepts—namely such concepts as, if acted upon, lead to scientific nonsense or to humanly injurious results.)[120]

Such "'is'-sentences" also possess another "practical," even tactical property. They are really "'ought'-sentences." For example, "Germany is the spirit of Kant and Beethoven" really means: people ought to act with respect to Germany on the basis of the belief that Kant and Beethoven correctly articulated the historical and moral goals of German culture and society. But many, perhaps most, people will not act in this manner unless, given that they regard themselves as good Germans, they believe that such behavior is in fact in keeping with and consistently required by the past record of their German sancta. We are face-to-face with a peculiar literary form of the Kantian "as if"[121] and even of Leo Strauss's esotericism: "Germany is the spirit of Kant and Beethoven" is now seen also to imply that in fact Germany is at least also a lot of other things—most of them probably highly undesirable from a moral point of view—but we must make people believe, rightly or in part wrongly, that Germany "is" ("being" having been understood as, in the Platonic/radically Kantian tradition, an ultimately ethical term)[122] only the spirit of Kant and Beethoven and their likes, because then they are likely to act accordingly and thus in fact make it into what it is already (normatively and "ideally") claimed to be.[123] (Such conscious esotericism is illustrated in practice in the difference in tenor between Cohen's public and his private expressions in the middle of the war regarding his hopes for Germany, of which we gave an earlier example.)[124] Fully explicated, our model sentence thus means: Germany ought to be as the ideals of Kant and Beethoven would have it be, and, therefore, people ought to believe that this is "the true Germany" ("Germanism"), so that they will act in this spirit and thus increasingly really make it so.

In this light we can finally translate into our language what Cohen's thesis of "the German-Jewish symbiosis" was meant to signify. It was not essentially a descriptive proposition but a regulative one. It said in effect: there are a number of social and intellectual forces at work in both the German and the Jewish historical cultures, which can and should be used so as to advance as much and as quickly as possible whatever dynamic force they possess toward the goal of a cosmopolitan, humanistic, ethical world society—*Weltbürgertum* in Kant's eighteenth-century term, a federation of social republics, in the spirit of Kant's vision in *Toward a Perpetual Peace*, which Hermann Cohen extrapolated.

It is, of course, the case that in the twentieth century nothing of the sort happened. To the contrary, both Germany and Jewry, and, for that matter, literally every other social body of which our world is constituted, have strongly developed in the direction of ethnic, particularistic nationalism, and *sacro egoismo*.

This is commonly taken to be a refutation of Cohen's interpretation of the essential nature of these two cultures and of his projection of the future. But normative propositions are not in fact refuted by descriptive propositions. To reply to the statement "A ought to be x" by saying that "A is not x" is not to refute it but, if anything, to lend greater urgency to the original statement. Normative propositions can really only be argued against with contradictory normative propositions and the reasons that undergird these.

In our case, Cohen's thesis of 1871–1918 that Germany and Judaism should pool their resources so as to have the rest of mankind join them in creating a morally just and peaceful world order can only be argued against by claiming, and justifying the claim, that it were better, or in fact was better, to have proclaimed in those years or to proclaim at the present time a program under which Germany instead becomes an expansionist, biologically self-defined, and eventually unlimitedly revanchist power and Jewry withdraws to a bastion in the Near East where, at an incredibly high past, present, and future price to its people and historic cultural values, it is to preserve its existence—without guarantee or security—apart from the cultures of the West and of the Arab world that surround it. It would have to be shown that the actual history of Germany, of Jewry, and of the rest of the world in the twentieth century was humanly more desirable than what Cohen and the program of eighteenth-century rationalist, ethical cosmopolitanism set out—and failed—to achieve. This strikes me as an exceedingly unlikely undertaking.[125]

In short, the tragedy of Cohen's love affair with the two values of Judaism and Germanism—to him really the one confluent value of universal, rational, social, ethics, derived from Biblical-Jewish culture, Greek Platonism, liberalized Christianity, and cosmopolitan German rationalism—was that he personally experienced and felt most sensibly the general tragedy of Germany, Judaism, and of the world that failed to act anywhere near his guidelines. That Germany and the Jewish people in turn came to feel at least as painfully the effects of their actual courses of action would seem to add to, not to detract from, the persuasiveness of his program.

The very least that one must say is that the thesis of the German-Jewish symbiosis is nothing to be retrospectively snickered at. It was a serious and reasonable program in its time.[126] The history of the twentieth century has left it in bloody shambles, at the sight of which "there is nothing left but boundless tears."[127] The century cannot be done over. Whatever may prove to be the future fate of Germany and of Judaism, their symbiosis is water over the dam, or ashes in the crematoria.

It might be argued that Cohen made a mistake not so much in regarding just Germany as rather in regarding any state whatsoever as the proper "mediation" between biological and moral humanity. Our experiences in this century with other states, including most emphatically our own, whichever this may be, would certainly seem to lend strong credibility to such a thesis. Cohen was compelled to look to the state not primarily because of his political situation and beliefs but because he reasoned philosophically that ethics have to be extrapolated from the positive law, and the positive law is to be found only in the state. If one were then to leave the state aside, where would one look for positive law? And where else could one hope to find general historical mediation? One might think of the socialist movement. But, of course, one would find positive law there only in an extremely attenuated sense, and, in any case, the role played by organized socialism in the twentieth century is scarcely more attractive than that of the states. Religion and its "canon law" (*halakhah*) offer themselves as a third alternative. But also the part that religion has played in our time is surely very dubious on many counts. Still, this should, perhaps, be taken much more seriously as a possibility by serious social thinkers.

Certainly one has to admit that Cohen's tactics did not work. For one thing, the esoteric use of "is" to mean "ought" can backfire, and it did backfire. That is, a proposition such as "Germany is the nation of spirit," instead of being taken to mean that German culture ought to foster ethical values in social life, is more likely to be and has been taken to mean that whatever Gemany in fact is and does is spiritually justified—even as the claim that the Jewish people is the chosen people, instead of being taken to mean that special moral obligations devolve upon Jews (in the spirit of Amos 3:2), is in fact commonly taken to mean that what would have to be regarded as obnoxious when done by others is, when done by Jews, justified by some special theological validation. In philosophical language, Hegel's conflation of "is" and "ought" comes close to being here recapitulated by Hermann Cohen, not for Hegel's metaphysical but for regulative reasons. The philosopher, on Cohen's own view, ought to remain more the "critic" than the affirmer, as Cohen let himself be seduced into being too much. As Luebbe put it correctly, though speaking of Natorp:[128] "the pathos of criticism is transformed into the pathos of identification."

No doubt, also, Cohen tended to fall prey to the seductions of patriotism. As World War I dragged on some people awakened to the real role that Germany was playing in modern history earlier and more than he.[129] Instead of choosing between Germany and Czarist Russia one could, alternatively, face the option between imperial Germany and the Western democracies—and how much of a factor the numerically small groups of Jews in the West as compared with the large Jewish communities in the East should be in one's evaluation could be disputed.[130] Even here, though, in fairness one ought to recall that the vice of patriotism was and is not limited to Cohen and his time and that his rationalization of his posture could reasonably be argued for on moral and Jewish grounds at his time.

In any case, I want to hold that also in our time there are at least two elements in Cohen's thesis of "Germanism and Judaism" that ought to be heeded. For one thing, Jewish-Western symbioses are still being attempted—for example, at least de facto in America. The ethical and methodological principles that Cohen worked out for this kind of enterprise still demand careful attention. In the second place, even in the absence of symbioses (if this be possible and desirable), that is, if Israel and Jewry, Germany, the U.S., and all sorts of other socio-historical entities go their own respective separate ways, "idealization" in Cohen's sense, that is, self-moralization, is surely incumbent upon them, if not in order that they be able to grow into one then at least so that they may achieve decent lives for themselves and viable coexistence together.

Chapter 11 | 1981

Ethics of the Pure Will—
Introduction

I. The Primacy of the *Ethics of the Pure Will*

The *Ethics of the Pure Will*[1] constitutes the peak, the dominating height, of Hermann Cohen's philosophic system, a system that largely follows Immanuel Kant's system both in structure and in substance.

Cohen devoted the first major stage of his life's work to writing exegeses of Kant's three Critiques. The point of this exegetical reconstruction was to refurbish the entire rational, scientifico-philosophic enterprise by, as it were, cleaning up and strengthening its foundations as laid by Kant in the Critical philosophy and thereupon to rebuild the upper stories more firmly. The essence of Cohen's new form of Kantianism that was thus in the making resides in the conception that all three "directions" of reason that Kant had educed and explored, namely thinking, willing, and judging, and the worlds that they determine, namely science, ethics, and art, are exhaustively conditioned by rational constructions that are themselves not derived from but "transcendentally" prerequisite for and creative of their respective realities. Implied in the *a priori* character of these rational, transcendental constructions is, of course, also that they are no more derived from the empirical nature of the human mind (for they would otherwise be psychological dispositions) than from any other empirical state of affairs. What they are has, therefore, to be transcendentally educed from how in fact they must rationally be shown to operate in their respective fields.

The second major stage of Cohen's work consists of a rewriting, as it were, of Kant's three Critiques, again in sequence, in the light of the conception that we have briefly adumbrated. Thus we have "Logic of Pure Reason" (1902, 1914), *"Ethics of the Pure Will"* (1904, 1907), and his *"Aesthetics of Pure Feeling"* (1912).

First published in *Hermann Cohen, Werke*, vol. 7, Olms, Hildesheim, 1981, VII–XXXV.

Cohen's Logic and his Ethics are correlated in a special way. All thinking finds its rules in the effective work of, primarily mathematical, science (and it is, of course, produced by reason precisely for such work); therefore, also thinking about morality must be based on scientific logic. On the other hand, ethics (the Ethics) also retro-effect logic (the Logic). One relatively obvious way of exemplifying this is to direct attention to the interpretation of the noumenon not as, in the so-called orthodox interpretations, a quasi-ontological notion (which causes all sorts of exegetical, philosophic, and historic problems) but as an ideal, rational construct, useful and, indeed, indispensable to the progress of science but, on the other hand, clearly in itself an ethical concept, an "ought." The noumenon is a methodological, heuristic "idea" (318), which, as an infinite task, constitutes the ought of the scientific ideal of the perfect, mathematical, "pure" constitution of its object. Thus, by virtue of an ought in the very methodology of science, theory requires ethics. The noumenon can thus, as pars pro toto, stand for both the ethics of science as well as for the scientificity of ethics. Kant's "infinite progress of science" has now been built into the *a priori* epistemology of science, instead of being either an hypothetical, empirical condition or a postulate added to, even though produced by, that epistemology. Ethics—not only meta-ethics or "formalistic" ethics but substantive, though, to be sure, theoretically well-grounded substantive ethics—then not only constitute the loftiest results of the philosophic system (and its methodology) but also determine the system from the beginning and constitute its ultimate, creative criterion.

Cohen's ethics are, to be sure, in some ways a rigorous "methodism," and this methodism is thus admittedly, nay professedly, derived from the mathematical and natural sciences, but that the "Ethics" is far from remaining "abstract" and "formalistic" can be conveniently exemplified in two areas. First, religious doctrines in general, and Jewish ones in particular, interlace the ethics frequently and systematically, though with respect to the Jewish ones often in very generalized language (cf. 453). To give some examples of Cohen's veiled manner of using Jewish nomenclature: the whole notion of "the other/the thou/the neighbor" and so on revolves around the fact that in German "the neighbor" is "der Nächste," that is, "the nearest one" (in the superlative), whereas its Biblical/Hebrew source is an absolute nominative, "re'a" (cf. 218); Cohen's entire identification of "God" with "truth" is one extended philosophical commentary on the famous talmudic dictum that "the seal of God is truth"[2] and, indeed, on the kabbalistic game with the letters of the Hebrew word for truth (e-m-t) as the first, middle, and last letters of the Hebrew alphabet.

To turn to a second illustration of the concreteness and "relevance" of Cohen's ethics that may engage the religiously less and politically more interested philosophers of our time better, the present work formulates in considerable detail and systematically derives from its basic philosophic operations an ethically idealist program of socialism, non-Marxist or at least heavily neo-Marxist, which, though making a significant impact at the time and noted in the secondary literature, has been neglected to our loss, and, in any case, it has been historically tragically ineffectual. " 'Act in such a way that at all times you use your own as well as every other person as a purpose, never merely as a means.' In these words [Kant's third formulation of the categorical imperative] the deepest and most profound meaning of the categorical imperative is expressed. They contain the moral program of the new aeon and of the future of all world-history" (320, cf. xiii). Kant "is the true and real originator of German socialism."[3] This socialism was then also launched into programmatic practice by Cohen himself and by his disciples in their nonacademic endeavors.[4] Eduard Bernstein, Karl Vorländer, and the martyred Kurt Eisner[5] were among the most notable fighters in this movement.

II Ethics and Jurisprudence

The broad outlines of Cohen's ethics are not difficult to sketch. Ethics, like scientific theory, begins with an *a priori*, necessary and universal, hypothesis or regulative idea. Since the subject matter of ethics is man, the regulative idea for ethics, as the infinite task, which ethics as a philosophical discipline is to conceptualize and morality as practice is increasingly to approximate, is "humanity." As in scientific theory individual objects of cognition are conceptually derived from the class, as terms of the function, formulated by its respective idea and then empirically constituted as integrals of the purely conceptual, rational infinitesimals (the zero that is oriented toward them, their "origin," "Ursprung"), so the members of the universal class "humanity," that is, individual men, the empirical agents of ethics, are the derivative instantiations of their ratio-ethical class. The rule—analogous to the mathematical rule with which physico-mathematical science determines its own operations—in compliance with which the concept of the individual human being is derived from its class-concept is, in turn—and here perhaps the chief innovation and creative turn is made in Cohen's Kantian ethics—derived from the history of the positive law.

To put it broadly again, the positive law, too, deals with individual man, as one equal member of the subclass of all its legitimate subjects, in his capacity as a persona, not as a homo, that is, as a ratio-legal, not as a physical, entity (74). More broadly, the law deals with legal persons—corporations, for example—although in fact Cohen prefers to use trade unions and cooperatives ("Genossenschaften") as his ideal model of legal persons (thus laying the foundation for his orientation of social ethics toward socialism).[6] Most broadly, the law defines the widest existent subclass of humanity as the state, again not a sensuous entity, of course, but an humanly, purely constructed one (78). (Cohen also projects the future of the historic progress of ethics toward the realized ideal of humanity, from the state to—in the footsteps of Kant's "Toward a Perpetual Peace"—the universal federation of republican, social states.)

All of these are regulative, not descriptive, moves. They are "fictions," in the technical Marburg-sense of fiction, that is, a rational, heuristic prescription for, not an empirical description of, reality (78, 243 f.). Under the law the accused has responsibility "imputed" to him (despite the fact that, by virtue of causal explanations, he could presumably be exempted from responsibility); so in ethics we look upon man from a point of view different from the cognitive, scientific, causal one, in order thus increasingly to order human and social life in accordance with ethical demands (392). By this token freedom of the will is not a "given," somehow to be sought physiologically or even conceptually in a putative human nature, but it, too, is an ideal notion: freedom is increasingly to be achieved as autonomous, rational self-determination by means of the transformation of phenomenal (= causal) reality (315 ff.). As Cohen put it with his usual aphoristic felicity, this is the (regulative) noumenon of freedom, not the (quasi-descriptive) freedom of the noumenon. Freedom is a project ("Vorsatz"), not a posit ("Satz," "Gesetztes") (143). Causality is thus the explanatory route toward freedom, as the phenomenon is the growing unpacking of the noumenon. And Cohen may, therefore, speak of "the freedom of causal thinking" (361).

Within the wide structure of this argument, one of Cohen's most important achievements is what might be called "the concretization of Kant's categorical imperative." Kant himself emphasized the formalistic character of the categorical imperative, hence its very name. Much of what he does with and says about it (though far from everything, and the rest is at least as important) remains intentionally abstract, theoretical, meta-ethical (in the broader sense of this term). As a result post-Kantian literature has been and still is full of the criticism that the categorical imperative is, if not totally nonsensical, at best a negative criterion by which concrete moral maxims have to be measured.

If this were true, the moral maxims themselves would have to be derived from elsewhere, not *a priori* from the categories, and thus ethics would, for actual purposes and substantively, be thrown back on some sort of ethical empiricism. This conclusion would, of course, contradict Kant's own claims and the essential point of his entire argument.

It is true that Kant himself often pointed out that, unlike the concepts purely constructed that may be taken to be valid as regulative, methodic tools in science, since they can be shown to be empirically applicable and productive there, the ethical analog of cognitive concepts, that is, the moral law, can, by definition, never be observed in practice (since all actions can be causally explained). This leaves a gaping hole in his argument, since, by his own transcendental criteria, any rational construct that cannot be shown to be applicable to the phenomenal universe is a rationally unjustifiable indulgence in metaphysics. Partly, no doubt, in order to try to fill this hole und partly also, perhaps, because he has not yet discarded all of the language of the philosophic ethics that preceded him, Kant then often still speaks of "the fact of practical reason," "the consciousness of duty" (and similar locutions). Within his total systematic context such expressions should not really be susceptible to the misinterpretations and misuses to which they have been put; in fact, however, they have given rise to all sorts of explications of Kant's ethics in terms of the human psychology and even of traditional religion to which they seem to point.

To this philosophic, systematic Kantian and ethical problem Cohen addresses himself now in a highly creative fashion. He handles the problem in what may be regarded as two phases. The first phase provides a Kantian "derivation" of the categorical imperative from "the primacy of practical reason" (which, as it were, replaces Kant's own "metaphysical deduction" that Cohen eliminates). As we have previously noted, a proper (Cohennian) understanding of Kant's noumena is that these are rational constructions that can be shown to serve as guides for the scientific, causal, lawful explanations of phenomena. Therein lies their validity. As purely rational constructs, they are, however, invented, as it were, by and for human purposes, not derived from some sort of objective nature. Thus, science itself is rightfully seen to be a "practical," and—if rational—as an ethical, enterprise. The moral law is thus in principle presupposed for the acknowledged validity of the natural sciences and hence "deduced" (or validated). Its application to human relations turns out to be really only another "direction" from its application in science. Both scientific concepts and moral freedom are, as again we have seen, not descriptives but regulatives, whose validity is established by their functional applicability. The "pure will" is a task, a rational goal to be striven for (27), even as the noumenon is the goal of a phenomenon, totally constituted by rational and ultimately mathematical means.

Here the second phase of Cohen's revision—better perhaps: his reconstruction and improvement—of Kant's ethics comes into force. The analogy of scientific method, indeed, its universal logical imperativeness, is again applied to ethics. As the purely rational, theoretical law must be crystallized as underlying the actual, positive scientific work in order to be transcendentally valid—that is, in application, and must then be used in order to try to bring positive science incrementally more and more into conformity with its ideal rationality (thus motoring "the eternal progress of science"), so also the moral law, if it is to be validated, cannot be satisfied with having been "derived" by means of a purely analytic treatment of "the experience of duty"[7] but must also be susceptible to exemplification in, transcendental deduction from, and practical, that is, reforming, application to an actual rational, scientific enterprise in human history. Since ethics deals with human actions, we are, however, looking not for a natural science but for a social science—specifically a science that deals with human, social prescriptives. These prescriptives are in fact to be found, as we have previously intimated, in the law. The science of law is jurisprudence. Therefore, whereas the natural-mathematical sciences are the matrix out of which transcendental philosophy extracts the methodic concept of the "object," jurisprudence will be the matrix out of which it extracts the "subject."

Kant had still argued at the beginning of the *Second Critique* that there can be no critique of pure practical reason, on the ground that reason can no longer be seen to be pure as soon as it is put to phenomenal practice. Cohen has now enabled himself to claim an "*ethics of the pure will*" precisely as a "critique of pure practical reason"—indeed, not only as a "critique" (which is to say, a rational delimitation of previously made claims) but even as a philosophic "origination" (that is to say, a rational production) of pure practical reason, since he finds it in the actual history of the law.

In short, in Cohen's Kantianism this equation can be formulated: noumena : phenomena = ethics : law, for ideas are now known to be extended noumena and tasks, and from these tasks emerge laws according to which the tasks are to be carried out. And the transcendental sequence which Cohen has followed can be put in the following diagram:

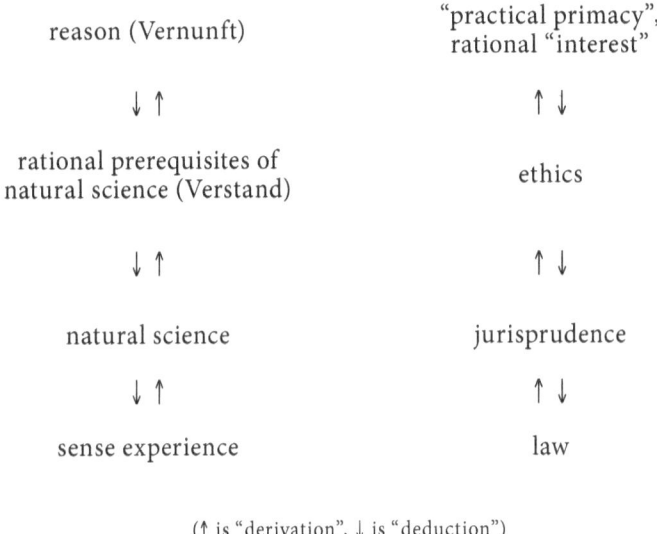

($\uparrow$ is "derivation", $\downarrow$ is "deduction")

Thus, jurisprudence is "the mathematics of the 'Geisteswissenschaften'" (vii). But, complains Cohen, jurisprudence is as yet in its baby shoes; it possesses little of the rigor and of the widespread consensus that the natural sciences have attained. At this time, therefore, philosophers still have to try to do jurisprudence, at least initially, the way philosophers were "natural philosophers" until science had formalized and systematized itself sufficiently. One day jurisprudence, too, will become an independent discipline, and when this has happened it will accrue to the greater precision, progress, and productivity both of the science of jurisprudence itself and of its philosophic, transcendental comprehension.

We have thus noted the central place of law and jurisprudence in Cohen's philosophic ethics. In the present book and elsewhere, also, incidentally, with respect to the centrality of the law, "halakhah," in Jewish philosophical theology—jurisprudence pervades virtually every significant philosophical move that is made in his ethics.[8] We have also heard his call for systematic work in jurisprudence (on the basis of critical idealism). One of his, and especially Paul Natorp's, associates, Rudolf Stammler, took up Cohen's challenge and published a series of jurisprudential works, based on the neo-Kantian epistemology and ethics of the Marburg School.[9] Also, Albert Görland, a close disciple of Cohen's, launched in part on this endeavor.[10] The trouble was that Stammler had taken Cohen's philosophy of law in a direction of which Cohen disapproved,[11] and as a result a serious split opened up within the school, which even subsequent history has not healed.

As we have seen, on Cohen's view the philosophical desideratum was that the positive law be conceptually analyzed so as to reduce it, or rather so as to elevate it, to its systematic, rational principles. These would constitute the science of law, or jurisprudence. The philosopher's task would then be to investigate the transcendental conditions of this jurisprudence, that is, the pure, *a priori*, rational and ethical presuppositions, which alone would validate that jurisprudence. Also and importantly, by laying bare the ideal forms of the ultimate goals of the law the many and sore discrepancies that inevitably creep in between the ideal law and the actual law would be revealed, and this would constitute the incentive for the continuous reformation and ethical improvement of the positive law. Thus would be constructed what Cohen would then be justified in calling, "a pure doctrine of law" ("reine Rechtslehre"). It is "pure" in the precise Kantian sense that it can be shown to be ultimately produced by *a priori*, that is, necessary and universal, canons of ethical, normative reason.

Stammler now began by criticizing Kant for not having gone far enough in distinguishing and separating law from ethics and the legal content of the positive law from its rational form. He defined "pure jurisprudence" as meaning, in the first place, that the jurisprudence would deal exclusively, purely, with the law itself, not with any other materials, which might seem to conjoin with it, such as philosophy, ethics, economics, sociology. In the second place, he extrapolated Kant's distinction between law and "virtue" to the point that "pure law" was to be analyzed totally in terms of its own methodological procedures—basic norm, statutes, and rules—rather than by reference to ethical or historical purposes beyond itself.

Thus the separation of jurisprudence from philosophy, like that of natural science from "natural philosophy," seemed to come about much more quickly than Cohen himself had envisaged, and immediately with the same theoretical strains that have also always weighed on the other paternal relationship. In any case, Stammler had gone far beyond what Cohen had asked for. Cohen wanted what might be called a tactical separation between ethics and jurisprudence, so that strategically the two could mutually improve and strengthen one another the more in advancing toward their common goal.[12] Stammler instead seemed to divorce jurisprudence as purely a science of law forever from philosophy and ethics. More specifically, Stammler went even further than Kant in relegating morality, "virtue," to the private, extra-legal realm and thus in effect identified it with religion (225f.).

In this dispute there are some elements that were not completely articulated. Paul Natorp (and to a lesser degree also Stammler) played a role in "the Marburg School" that can be compared, *pari passu*, to that of Jung in Freud's school in Vienna. On some very deep level Cohen was always on guard against Christian religious, or at least non-Jewish ideological, if not actually anti-Semitic, purposes not only among his philosophic and professional opponents but even among the proportionately very few non-Jewish members of his own school of thought. In the "Ethics" (268) he explicitly draws an historic line between Paulinian antinomianism, Kant's relegation of the law to an inferior status compared to inward morality, and (by implication) to Stammler's bifurcation of ethics and jurisprudence. Thus Kant's criterion for distinguishing law and virtue is compulsion; this is to say, legally acting "in accordance with the law" is heteronomously caused, whereas morally acting "because of (out of) the law" is autonomously produced. This distinction Cohen rejects, too. Also the autonomous act is, after all, compelled, not, to be sure, by external powers but by the power of reason; compulsion cannot, therefore, in any case, bring about a fundamental cleavage between law and ethics (269f.). Indeed, even "theonomy" is not only not incompatible with but is positively conducive to Kantian autonomy properly understood—if, that is, the God who is regarded as issuing imperatives is understood as the "God of truth," that is, the God of philosophical reason (335ff.). (The Jew Cohen has thus salvaged his fundamental commitment to *halakhah*, the law, for his ethics of rational autonomy.) And Vorländer, himself not a Jew, pointed out[13] not only that Stammler's book positively crawled with Christian textual and historical references (the usually implicit Jewish allusions in Cohen's own writings probably escaped most people's notice but would, today, deserve uncapping) but also that his dichotomy of inner and outer man, moral and legal values, follows an entrenched Christian tradition. One might add that, without forgetting all the important differences between the two cases, Cohen's philosophical wariness of Natorp proved in the longer run to be no more bereft of justification than Freud's of Jung.

The controversy bore consequences that went far beyond the confines of the brief period before World War I during which it took place and beyond the narrower confines of the Marburg School. Natorp, while arguing in favor of his teacher's and colleague's view in this matter, also tried to reconcile the divergent sects that seemed to be forming.[14] Vorländer, the outstanding theoretician and activist of socialism to come out of the Marburg School, stuck by his teacher. Görland and others followed Stammler's lead, on the other hand. And before long one of the most important jurisprudentialists of the twentieth century emerged from this latter line in the person of Hans Kelsen.

Max Weber subjected Stammler's, "Wirtschaft und Recht nach der materialistischen Geschichtsauffassung. Eine sozialphilosophische Untersuchung" (1st ed., 1895) to a withering review.[15] The gravamen of his critique was that Stammler retained, and—in Weber's view—even strengthened, the ultimate rootage of the law in ethics and cognate social concerns and that he thus violated the dichotomy between "value-free" science and "dogmative, normative" commitments. (According to Weber, the latter are beyond the reach of reason.) Stammler thus found himself plunk in the middle—Cohen, on the one hand, condemning him for divorcing the law too much from ethics and Weber, on the other hand, condemning him for not divorcing them enough.[16] Hans Kelsen then accepted Weber's dichotomy between theory and values, but he went on to argue (in Weber's own journal, incidentally) that norms, which exhaustively constitute the law, "possess their own rationality."[17] (Thus, where Weber had introduced sociology as the empirical science of jurisprudence, Kelsen could eliminate it again.) On the other hand, Kelsen continued to reject the Marburgian deduction of law and ethics from a common, transcendental (i.e., "practical") reason. He has often, and not without justification, been accused since then of thus having succored a state-positivism that resulted in much of the tyranny that our century has experienced: "Every order is legitimate,"[18] for the state is the real God.[19] One could schematically say that the Stammler-Kelsen line is the unilateral continuation of the phenomenon = law side of the Cohennian equation: noumenon : phenomenon = ethics : law. (The Nazis were quick to condemn the entirety of the intellectual development from Cohen through Kelsen as one long Jewish, lifeless, degenerate destruction of "reality.")

Since some years after the end of World War II the heritage of the Marburg School has begun to be refurbished to some extent and even, quite rightly, to be put to productive use in the revitalization not only of the philosophy of science but also of philosophical ethics. Even in Anglo-American philosophy a whole renaissance of renewed rigorous, ethical thinking is taking place, instantiated by people like Rawls, Donagan, Charles Fried, for which Kantianism and jurisprudence constitute the proclaimed foundations. How long can it be before also Hermann Cohen will not only be given his historical due but also used, as he would want to be used, to correct and further to stimulate productive philosophico-ethical work?

III. Ethical De-Ontologization

Cohen's radical, albeit critical, that is, science-oriented, idealism results, as we have seen, in the stipulation of "ideas," ideals, noumena, and so on, as rational constructs, of which, though they are never adequately instantiated in the empirical world, true "being," in some sense, eternal being, the being of ought-to-be, must be predicated—toward which, as their ideal model and goal, all actually existing realities must be oriented in their serialization—and toward the infinite, asymptotic approximation of which the latter must incrementally be improved, in science, ethics, and in history. In a very real sense, therefore, ideas and oughts can be said to possess being more than the objects of experience, for the latter are clearly effervescent, transient realities, while the former are, if true, if, that is, correct hypotheses, eternal, or at least they are likely to endure longer—until, that is, having turned out to be false, they are discarded. The objects of experience are, according to Cohen, constituted by and thus dependent on ideal notions literally from beginning to end—from the ideas which define, as it were, their ideal telos, end, and thus their ideal definition, to their infinitesimally incremental emergence out of the "nothing" of their conceptual projection (itself a rational, ideal construct, according to Cohen's "philosophy of origin"). This is readily recognized as a highly modernized version of Platonic idealism. In it the objects of experience exist really only as terms of functions—from their respective 0 to their particular integer, and "being" then appertains to the functions rather than to their terms.

In a philosophic situation in which this analysis is accepted in principle, one misinterpretation, out of many, lies particularly near at hand. It seems that the virtually ineluctable ontologizing proclivity of at least those minds that have been formed by our particular culture induces us to infer that, if the objects of experience with which we are familiar in our presystematic, naive worldview must be conceded not to possess ultimate reality, or "being," then certainly the alternative kind of entities with which we are dealing, in this case the ideas and their various functions, must be regarded as possessing that being. Thus the Platonic ideas, which Kant had regulativized, if one may so put it, in the *First Critique*, are re-hypostatized. This interpretation—as we are about to see, really thoroughgoing misinterpretation—soon caught up also with Cohen's doctrine, and it has continued to be held as correct in relatively wide circles to this day. In short, whereas the universe had been meant to be transformed from one consisting of substances into one consisting of functions, substances were brought back—almost literally through the backdoor—by eventually substantializing the functions.

In the ground-laying first chapter of Cohen's "Ethics," entitled "The Basic Law of Truth," the connection between the scientific epistemology of the first volume of his "system," the "Logic," and his ethics is formulated. Simply put, his thesis is that scientific theory claims "validity" ("Geltung"), not "truth." This is to say, a theory is accepted in science if and only if it can be shown to fit with the other relevant knowledge that we believe we possess, with the evidence that scientific experience provides for the specific theory under consideration, and with the canons of logic that apply to the connections between these two bodies of knowledge. In the "Ethics," now, another body of knowledge is about to be formulated; here it is not knowledge of what is (the objects of cognition) but knowledge of what rationally ought to be and ought to be brought about (the subject of ethics). This second kind of knowledge also must conform, of course, to the canons of reason and of logic and is thus conditioned by the first, though, as we have noted, by virtue of the primacy of practical reason, there will be some retro-effects on scientific cognition and its operations at the hand of ethical reasoning.

This retro-effect must be handled, Cohen repeatedly emphasizes, however, with the greatest of care. We are dealing with a retro-effect on logic by ethics, not with a supersession of logic by ethics (23, 38). Ethics is thus logic appropriately reoriented and reformulated in order to enable it to handle satisfactorily the rational requirements of human relations. It is, one might say, a particular variant on logic, an "Eigenart." Ethics is, then, in the first place, different from, in the second place, however, always unseverably conditioned by, and, in the third place, eventually taken into due account by, scientific logic.[20]

In any case, also ethical reasoning, taken by itself, can only argue for validities, that is, the "fit" of its concepts with the subject matter to which it addresses itself, the procedures used in basing each step on its predecessor, and the consistency of the total argument. The great theoretical and practical question that then inevitably arises is whether and how ethical knowledge and scientific knowledge interact with one another. Theoretically put, the question becomes: Can that which ought to be be shown in principle to be subsumable under the canons which determine that which is? And the practical version of it is: Can that which ought to be be operationalized in the world that is? Only a theory—really a meta-theory—which provides a satisfactorily positive answer to this double-barreled question, the question of the compatibility, or more rigorously: the question of the ultimate identity, of the two sets of validities of which we have spoken will provide "truth." Truth, in short, is the possibility in principle and the actualization of the principle of the unification of ethical and scientific claims. Truth is the verification of theory and will by one another. This also conforms, at least in part, with the notion of truth as used in much of the ordinary discourse in the history of our culture: we say, for example, that a man may have behaved in a certain lamentable manner but that, were it not for corrupting and distorting influences from his environment, his "true" nature would have made him act otherwise.

We do not here need to rehearse the specifics of Cohen's arguments to this effect in the first chapter and elsewhere in his "Ethics" and in other writings of his. He can be let speak for himself. The conclusion is, in any case, that the answer to this question is and must be in the affirmative. It is also plausible that he should so conclude, for we have seen in another context that his rational ideals, both cognitive noumena and ethical oughts, have been, after all, transcendentally arrived at from their actual, empirical, historical (though partial) instantiations, and it then stands to reason that also their more adequate realizations in the future are at least in principle susceptible to actualization in the empirical world. Using the historic vocabulary of Judaism in the very pores of the flesh of his philosophic ethic, Cohen calls the ultimate, universal, ideal condition of the total identity of the realm of the "is" with the realm of the "ought" "the messianic kingdom" = "the ideal" (chapter 8), and he calls the rational ground for the belief in the principled possibility, indeed the scientific and ethical necessity, of its attainment "the idea of God" (= "God") (chapter 9). (In this, too, Kant had, of course, paved the way for him.)

In the "Ethics" Cohen raises this question by way of pointing out, among other things, that the ideal states of affairs (an ideal model, somewhat in the Weberian sense, of the universe) is, of course, as again we have seen, an "infinite goal." Within finitude, within time, it can, therefore, in principle not be attained. The empirical universe, for which the ideal is stipulated, is, however, finite: physis is finite not only in the traditional philosophic sense that it is by definition defined but also because it is subject to scientific anti-tropisms. Thus it would seem that the infinite tasks of science and of ethics are in principle unachievable for finite humanity. To this difficulty Cohen responds by reminding us that, as he puts it in the "Ethics" (426ff.), the idea of God is precisely the affirmation of the feasibility—not necessarily the achievability, the "completability"—of the infinite tasks.[21]

This entire armamentarium of terms, concepts, and theses—God, the messiah, or at least the messianic kingdom, and so on—has proved to be an open invitation to re-ontologize, to re-hypostatize, Cohen's functional concepts. Thus, for example, Cohen develops in the "Ethics" a definition of the true individual as a person that "realizes itself" fully as a member of mankind and is, in this capacity, of infinite significance. Not only "the late Cohen" of his posthumous theological work but the emphatically neo-Kantian Cohen of the philosophic system as manifest in the "Ethics" relies on the book of the Biblical prophet Ezekiel and its doctrine of individual guilt "before God" to expound this doctrine. Franz Rosenzweig then made the claim[22] that the God in relationship to whom (in correlation with whose idea) the human being is thus absolutely individualized, rather than being functionally serialized by the idea of humanity, cannot be and for "the late Cohen" was not an idea; rather he had to be a "real God," for, Rosenzweig asserted, ideas cannot and do not "act," whereas "absolutization" is here attributed to God. (He failed to pay sufficient attention to the fact that according to Cohen it is the man that acts, albeit "before God," that brings it about.)

In Rosenzweig's footsteps Martin Buber extracted Cohen's entire ethico-epistemological vocabulary of "I and thou" from the "Ethics" (cf. 248f.) and (without ever making proper acknowledgment, incidentally) turned it into a sort of mystical description of phenomenological, antiscientific ontology, while it had in fact been intended and argued as a methodological, heuristic, functional analysis of interpersonal relations. Julius Guttmann, the historian of Jewish philosophy, asked[23] whether an idea can be said to give guarantees about the future and whether it can in fact preserve nature, implying what seemed to him to be the obvious answer that, again, the late Cohen was forced by the logic of his own arguments to stipulate a "real God," that is, a metaphysical hypostasis, rather than what Arroyo[24] felicitously called "un dios functional."

It was not only Jews, however, who, for their theological purposes, re-ontologized Cohen; also Christians, for their religious purposes, and non-Jewish philosophers for their respective reasons, took this path. Wilhelm Herrmann, in his early critique of Cohen's "Ethics," said on behalf of his evangelical faith and of its religious individual, what Rosenzweig argued in Jewish terms. Even Natorp, after Cohen's death, re-ontologized the Marburgian concept of nothing (0) and of (true) being and thus came to expound a neo-Platonic mysticism. Also Heidegger's ontology can be seen, as he himself at the time at the least implied, as an extrapolation (and total reversal) of neo-Kantian functionalism and of a purely regulative ontology.

All of this could not be further from Cohen's intentions and, above all, from the logic and purpose of his analyses. This can conveniently be demonstrated in the case of "the basic law of truth."

"The basic law of truth" does not stipulate any possible future unity of the good and the actual, nor, therefore, the eternal existence of nature. This would be a dogmatic prediction of what the temporal, even infinite, future holds, to which neither the philosopher nor the religionist is rationally entitled. The future of nature is simply a scientific question, to which no scientific answer may be possible with finality, or the answer to which is, at best, subject to all the vicissitudes of scientific scholarship. In fact, we are here, too, face-to-face with a normative, regulative, ideal proposition: the scientist, the jurisprudentialist, and the moral man are to act "as if" the unity of ethics and nature, of an infinitely imperative ethic in an infinitely perduring universe, were possible. Infinity turns out to have little, if anything, to do with the future; in fact, it structures every present. Unification as a task and function, not unity as an accomplishment, is the significance of the law of truth. The truth of "the basic law of truth," which Cohen puts forward is the truth of Lessing's God of the left hand, which holds out the eternal search of truth, rather than the truth of the other hand—its possession (91). The operational meaning of the law of truth is not any prediction of a perfect future but, to the contrary, the always present-time applicability, in incremental fashion, of the "ought" to the "is." This is to say, the fact that historical actuality manifested the applicability of the ethical imperative to a lesser degree yesterday implies its applicability, or at least the imperative of its applicability, to a greater degree tomorrow, not their perfect identity at any (dogmatic) day-after-tomorrow.

"Eternity" is thus de-ontologized itself, as it were. It, too, is defined as eternal work—ethical and scientific work (adumbrated, if we want to keep the Kantian/neo-Kantian system in mind, by the works of art—aesthetics as the anticipatory embodiment of the ideal and as the physical incentive to the active pursuit of that ideal) (408). In no uncertain words did Cohen attempt to prevent the ontologizing misinterpretation to which his often metaphoric, religious, and vestigially substantival language lent itself, and was immediately put to use. "The eternity of the ethical self-consciousness [the perfect flowering of humanity] does not imply a theoretical question regarding the duration of the human race" (415). In other words, whether mankind will in fact perdure is not susceptible to treatment by his or anyone else's analysis; this is a cognitive, scientific question, and (one might add) Hegel's and Marxist stipulations of a present, an imminent, or of a delayed actualization of the putative ideal state are both dogmatic and invidious. "Heaven and earth may pass away, but morality will remain," Cohen exclaims twice in short order (411, 425) (thus revising both the Biblical prophecy and the classic dictum which also Kant used to like to quote: *fiat justitia, et pereat mundus*); that is, the moral ought is infinite, not necessarily the universe in which it has to be enacted. This Cohen explicitly calls "the religion of the Biblical prophets" (438f.), relying on the Biblical term "acharit ha'yamim," which literally means "that which follows the days," rather than the conventional rendering "the end of days." And this is for Cohen the real significance of religious messianism in ethics, history, and politics (406f.).

Thus, Cohen translates Kant's doctrine of a postulated, regulative "kingdom of ends" into his typically programmatic, activist, political language: it is a question not of optimism about the assured eventual triumph of the good in the world but of socialism in history looking toward such a triumph, that is, the insistent, although incremental, social, moral, and intellectual improvement of the lives of men in the real world.[25]

Eduard Bernstein then spoke famously of "socialism—not the goal but the way." At the time and during Cohen's own lifetime this argument was clearly intended and generally perceived as a Jewish explication of a messiah always yet to come, in distinction from a Christian messiah who has, or ever can have, come. That the superstructure of Jewish theorizing later in the twentieth century was increasingly interested in trying to get "to the things themselves," "zu den Sachen," is another—and ironic—commentary on our history.

IV. The "Ethics" in its Time

The biographical and historical setting in which the "Ethics" was produced is worth keeping in mind. Cohen was inextricably involved not only with the intellectual, cultural, and religious but also with the political developments that occurred around him throughout his lifetime—and he wanted it this way. For one thing, he wanted and thought that he ought to play a part in them. For another, they affected him, of course, very directly. The wave of democratic liberalism that had carried him into the university during Bismarck's "liberal honeymoon" receded not only in the German economic and political crisis from 1873 onward (which made his life and that of his associates a struggle ever afterward) but received another grim setback in the 1890s and thereafter. Nationalism, militarism, growing ethnicism, even racist antisemitism, and generally increasing conservatism determined the life and culture of the Second German empire throughout his lifetime. The effect that this sociopolitical environment had on Cohen personally and on the Marburg School as a whole can be gauged by their professional problems, the strains that they experienced within their university and even in their own department, and in their personal relations and correspondences.

As for the specific circumstances under which the "Ethics" was composed, all one need do is to compare Cohen's introductory words to its first edition in 1904 with the changes that he inserted in the second edition of 1907. The first edition ends on these words (vi f.):

> All ethics that strove for classicity of foundations have conceived and handled [their] methodical labor as a searching. And this searching neither is nor remains exclusively theoretical, a question of research, but it is at the same time a desire for the unveiling and mining of that treasure—and like a courting of it—which the spirit acknowledges as the highest, as the only value of human existence: humanity in all peoples and

in every man. However thoroughly the reality of morality may be disguised, defamed, and restricted in the empirical world of men, the moral spirit will not despair of its inalienable possession. Ethics has no other task than to guard humanity against the doubts and the befuddlement of moral culture about itself, about its truth and veracity, and about the incomparable value of its highest good.

If there is an unmistakable note of pessimism about contemporary conditions in that paragraph, compare it with the following words that are taken from the introduction to the second edition:

> While I must take a principled posture of opposition to this modern style of Germanism, I feel fortified by the knowledge that I am harking back to the original power of the essence of the German spirit, contrary to its ephemeral distortions. . . . This book swims in all directions of our time against the current. . . . In politics, in religion and art, and above all in philosophy this book cannot agree with the voices that today dominate the scene. . . . The youthful generation and people abroad should not really think that today's prevailing tone of voice is the genuine, basic spirit of Germany. . . . (p. x)

Indeed, Natorp, in a letter dated September 24, 1904, describes Cohen's usual deep depression about the actual state of affairs and adds that his associates—especially graduate students that were helping him to compile the index to the "Ethics"—are, on the other hand, amazed at his gay state of mind whenever he dealt with his new book, or with philosophical matters in general. A real example of mind lifting a man beyond the afflictions of the flesh! (Cohen had increasingly been turning blind.) Also, the heavily underplayed Jewish component of the book provides Cohen with some satisfaction. On February 4, 1905, he reports to one of his most favored and devoted disciples, Benzion Kellermann (who became a leading radically Reform rabbi), that the new book had been offered to rabbis at a specially reduced price and that, as a result, one-hundred orders had come in within one week.

When one looks at the reception that was extended to the "Ethics" upon its appearance, one can summarize it exhaustively as following the pattern that one would expect, conforming in each and every instance to the independently known ideological position of the respective reviewer.

Natorp himself, in his private correspondence, finds much to criticize in the book, both substantively and stylistically. On the other hand, his personal and philosophical loyalty to Cohen puts limits on these criticisms, restricting them to relatively minor issues within the school. Also, he wants to keep this sort of thing "within the family." The fact was—and they both knew it deep-down—that, despite the powerful personal and philosophical attachment that bound Cohen and Natorp together, Cohen's profound, though very liberal, Jewishness, on the one hand, and Natorp's equally profound and liberal Christianity, on the other, with all their respective wide-ranging philosophical consequences, kept open a gap between them which would occasionally come to the surface on the theoretical and political levels, though both strained very hard (and while both were living succeeded) at pushing such considerations aside.

In the second edition of his "Religion within the Limits of Humanity" (1908), the personal intimacy and intellectual kinship between Natorp and Cohen, together with their no doubt religio-culturally conditioned psychological differences, are sensitively expressed during the course of Natorp's discussion of Cohen's "Ethics"[26] and of his *Religion and Morality*" (1907). Natorp, the Christian, is not, after all, ultimately satisfied with Cohen's typically Jewish "eternal seeking" and waiting. He wishes to find some feeling of "rest in the eternal." On the other hand, loyal Marburgian that he is, he, too, rejects a "religion of the transcendent," of course, and stays "within the limits of humanity," that is, the three directions of human reason. He reconciles these two opposite goals by wishing to stress more than Cohen the present-time function of eternal futurity—as he quotes Schleiermacher: "To be eternal at every moment."

This differential impact on their common ethics of their respective Judaism and Christianity found public expression quite fully also in the review published by Wilhelm Herrmann, a colleague and friend of theirs and a liberal professor of Protestant theology at the University of Marburg.[27] This is a lengthy, serious, immensely respectful and laudatory discussion of the "Ethics." At the same time it puts into words what is rightly recognized as the Jewish program that underlies the book and what Herrmann, as a pious Protestant, would want to alter about its philosophical theses, so as to bring them into accord with his own Christian program.[28]

Religiously and theologically less committed non-Jewish disciples of Cohen's exposited and reviewed the book wherever they could in unboundedly enthusiastic terms, always stressing the progressive social effect which it could be expected to produce. This is true first and foremost of Walter Kinkel.[29] It is also true of briefer reviews by more marginal members of the school.[30]

Jewish reactions to the "Ethics" in turn followed the lines that one would expect. At the time Cohen was, of course, the chief object of cultural pride and the greatest philosophical influence among German (and Russian as well as other) Jews, across the religious spectrum from the radical Reform Jew Kellermann, through (the younger) Franz Rosenzweig somewhere in the center, to the Orthodox rabbi of the Frankfurt Jewish community, Nehemiah Nobel. They naturally emphasized the Jewish ethos in Cohen's philosophy. A good illustration of this reaction, in a moderately popular tone, is B. Wolf's "Die Lebensanschauung des Idealismus."[31]

The subsequent history of Cohen-reception among Jews would itself constitute an illuminating history of the twentieth century. In broad strokes one can say that immediately before Cohen's death a combination of vitalistic reinterpretation and critique set in, combined with the beginnings of what was to become known as existentialist thinking. Simultaneously, and not unconnected with that, a Zionist opposition arose. The former is probably best exemplified by Rosenzweig and Buber, reaching down to Emil Fackenheim today. In turn, the names of Buber and Fackenheim,[32] and in between that of Jacob Klatzkin,[33] can also exemplify the overlap of the philosophical and political opposition to Cohen's trend of thought among Jews.

In view of the content of Cohen's "Ethics" it stands to reason that two additional groups would be particularly interested in it. The first of these were jurisprudentialists and, to a limited extent, historians. These, too, ranged across the spectrum, from very favorable,[34] to mixed,[35] (we have earlier considered the reaction of Max Weber to Stammler's jurisprudence and of Kelsen to Cohen's "Ethics"), all the way to a wildly antagonistic (empiricist and professionally supercilious) one.[36]

Finally, and perhaps of most interest in terms of the current climate of opinion, socialists were, of course, bound to pay attention to the only politically committed and Left-leaning academic school of philosophy precisely at the time that "the revisionist debate" in socialism was raging at its fullest. The socialist "Dokumente," April 1905, discussed Cohen's "Ethics," for example. It is characteristic that Cohen, who certainly opposed Marxist theoretical orthodoxy, nonetheless wrote to Natorp in a letter dated September 9, 1905, that he preferred orthodox socialists to his contemporary revisionist sympathizers. The most important and thoughtful critique of the "Ethics" to originate in such quarters must be Ferdinand Tönnies', as part of a monographic discussion of the cognate literature under the title "Ethics and Socialism."[37] Again one finds there what one would reasonably expect: a sympathetic overview of Marburg neo-Kantian socialism, beginning with Cohen's academic patron Friedrich Albert Lange through Natorp, a summary of the relevant discussions in the "Ethics," a defense of Tönnies' preference of "Gemeinschaft" as over against Cohen's preference for "Gesellschaft," and some mild ideological arguments in favor of greater socio-political analyses as against Cohen's "theology" and Kantian ethics.

Chapter 12 | 1986

The Title of Hermann Cohen's *Religion of Reason out of the Sources of Judaism*

Hermann Cohen devoted the long introduction of his *Religion of Reason out of the Sources of Judaism* (R.o.R.) to what he called "An Explication of the Title and of the Structure of the Task: A. Reason—B. Religion—C. The Sources of Judaism." Even now it is still worth the trouble to give an explication of the title of the work.

In the first place, the work is correctly entitled *"Religion of Reason,"* not "The *Religion of Reason."* The latter was the title when the book was first published, while in all later editions, though unfortunately not in all later references to it, this fundamental mistake was rectified.[1] It had truly been a fundamental distortion, for Cohen held that there can be only one rational religion, which would have to be as universal and necessary as pure reason itself, and that consequently all human beings, at least regulatively speaking, would subscribe to it. This one *religion of reason* could and should be crystallized from Judaism, to be sure, but also from Christianity and from other religious, historical, and cultural configurations. Whether and to what extent, on Cohen's conception, Judaism might be the most favorable climate in which to nurture the universal religion we shall have occasion to see shortly.

First published in *The Life of Covenant—The Challenge of Contemporary Judaism: Essays in Honor of Herman E. Schaalman*, ed. Joseph A. Edelheit, Spertus College of Judaica Press, Chicago (1986) 207–220.

* I dedicate this essay gladly to my friend Rabbi Hermann Schaalman on his professional retirement. Not only have he and his family and my family been good friends all our lives, but his parents and mine were lifelong friends before us. All of us, as thorough-going "Yekkes," devoted German Jews, share some fundamental values. This short paper is, therefore, appropriate to the purpose. It even, as it happens, has occasion to deal with the concept of the Jewish covenant, the theme of this volume. I wish Hermann and Lotte a long life of continued satisfaction and productivity.

The phrase "out of the sources" in the second part of the book's title refers, in the first and obvious place, to the fact that, in matters of religion as in every other area of philosophic truth, reason has to extract *a priori* truth from historical realities by means of the transcendental method, and this entails, of course, that the historical realities need to be studied and analyzed. Cohen would always say: "One has to square away one's philology before doing one's philosophy."[2] More concretely, this conception of the relationship between religion, history, and philosophy was formulated by Cohen in his *Ethics of the Pure Will*[3]; but also in his *Religion and Morality* (1907), and finally in the present work, as the thesis that religion produces notions in history, and philosophy's task is in the course of time to refine and to validate them. (With all the important differences between them, there are thus significant parallels between Hegel's and the neo-Kantian approach to history.) Thus, for example, biblical religion produced the very notions of history[4] and of a universal humanity (which Greek philosophy was never able to do),[5] though it was Enlightenment rationalism that finally brought them to their fullest conceptual and social exfoliation. Specifically in the present work, "the (historical) sources of Judaism"—that is, first the Bible, along with the Bible authoritative rabbinic/talmudic and medieval Jewish philosophical sources, and the texts of the Jewish liturgy, must be shown to justify the claims being made in the name of theologico-philosophical religion. (Those sources are abundantly adduced in Cohen's text itself and then supplemented in the appendix, in the original, compiled by Leo Rosenzweig.)[6]

The phrase "out of the sources" should, however, also be interpreted on a second level of philosophic discourse. "Source" and "origin" are very close synonyms in any language, and Cohen used them as such (*Quelle* and *Ursprung*). "Origin" (*Ursprung*) was so decisive a technical, philosophic concept in his fully matured thought that he called his entire system a "philosophy of origin."[7] Here origin does not primarily mean historical beginning; rather, it means the transcendentally logical ground, the rational presuppositions, which are the only conceptual basis from which the subsequent historical events could transpire.[8] This rational origin is perhaps best symbolized by "O"—the letter O for origin and zero for its mathematical significance: it is empirically nothing, because purely, *a priori*, rational, and it is also the infinitesimal, which, though de facto zero, is a differentiated zero, with the potentials of all the various "functions" that are derived from it and that produce the natural and other numbers, which are then treated as names of actual phenomena, as, indeed, is the case in the mathematico-physical sciences.[9]

The Jewish theological background to this conception is only intimated by Cohen: what in Western scholasticism is known as the doctrine of *creatio ex nihilo* is known in Jewish scholasticism as *yesh me'ayin*—that is, "what-there-is (the given) from nothing"—and in both traditions, by both rationalists and mystics, God himself is then often regarded as the *nihil*, the *'ayin*, the Nothing by which all is produced. This "originating" (productive, "constructionalist") power then also actually manifests itself in the concrete life of religion. For example, in the climactic, concluding chapter of *Religion of Reason*, entitled "Peace"—written, *nota bene*, at the height of World War I—Cohen writes: "Peace, which is the *goal* of the moral world, must also be valid as its *own originating power*. God is peace. (Cf. Meg. 18a, Lev. R., 9:9: "Rabbi Yudan b. Rabbi José said: 'Great is peace, for God's name is peace, as it is said in Judges 6:24: "And he called him God-peace.'") God stands for *harmony* between the moral powers of the universe and their material conditions" (Cohen's typical italics).[10] Or, for another example, the people of Israel are the "pure [i.e., atemporal] origin" of monotheism, which, naturalistically considered, would be a "miracle."[11] We may thus substitute the word origin for the word "source" in the title of this work. In this way the implicit claim is put forward that biblical Judaism and the later talmudic Judaism that evolved consistently from it are in fact the historically closest instantiation of the pure, *a priori*, rational conception—indeed of the "construction"—of God and all that this conception entails—primarily an ethic.[12] To be sure, other historical religions and cultures also partake of that universal, rational "ethical monotheism" (as nineteenth-century Jewish philosophers favored speaking of Judaism), but, they attained to it with neither the same philosophical purity nor the historical immediacy that distinguishes Judaism. (Historical immediacy is here of logical significance, since, to use Cohen's notation, $0 + (dx/dy) = 0$ still.) In order to crystallize the universal "*religion of reason*" out of their respective sources, these other religions consequently are compelled to work harder at shedding the mythological, immoral, pagan, irrational, and other barnacles that they accumulated on their voyage through history, by means of the process called "idealization" in Marburg neo-Kantianism,[13] and they were well advised to use Judaism as their (relatively) ideal model in performing this task.[14] "Judaism is an indispensable historical force 'toward' moral progress" together with "practical [!] Christianity, which is literally and historically practical Judaism."[15] And it is part of Israel's mission to mankind in turn that Jews must continue to help Christianity "idealize itself" and thus "come nearer to Judaism."[16]

Cohen, passionate and outspoken Jewish believer that he always was, did not then shrink, in an age and place far from receptive to candid discussions between what nowadays are called "faith communities," from arguing publicly, fully, and often very polemically, about Christian theology and history.[17] On the positive side, he believed that Protestant Bible scholarship, Bible "criticism" (as preeminently conducted by his colleague at the University of Marburg Julius Wellhausen, and which discerned the height of religious development in "prophetic religion") together with contemporary Protestant theology (as practiced most persuasively by his other local colleague and intimate fellow worker Wilhelm Herrmann, and which resulted in a liberal, social Christianity) constituted very valuable contributions toward *religion of reason* out of the sources of Christianity.[18] But his vision encompassed much more than Judaism and Christianity. He quarried building blocks for the edifice of a universal culture of reason in all of his works primarily also from German culture, as he conceptualized it (the culture of Luther, Leibniz, Mozart, Kant, Beethoven, and social democracy), and as well from Greek, scholastic, French, Spanish, and other societies.[19] Thus, for example, in *Religion of Reason* (282), the Bible, Christianity, the Renaissance, the French Revolution, scientific humanism, and Kant's categorical imperative are cited as precursors of modern ethical humanism. On the other hand, Cohen did not hesitate to level biting criticisms at those traditions (those other than the Jewish and the Platonic-Kantian) that, on his philosophico-ethical analysis, went in wrong directions and therefore required fundamental "purification."[20] Even a century later so-called interreligious dialogue still has a lot to learn from the debates that took place in and beyond his circles.

It is further useful in this connection to realize that the place that *Religion of Reason* occupies in Cohen's philosophic system is precisely analogous to the place that *Religion Within the Bounds of Reason Alone* occupies in Kant's. It can be argued that Kant's system was not formulated only in the three Critiques but actually in four: though overtly the title of his philosophical theology has a different form, when "reason alone" or "mere reason" (*blosse Vernunft*)[21] is seen to be synonymous with "*a priori* reason," and when "within the bounds of" is seen to be a paraphrase of "critique," then the title of the fourth work turns out to be conceptually translatable as "Critique of Practico-Religious Reason."[22] As Kant's *Critique of Pure Reason* then becomes a *Cognition of Pure Reason* at the hands of Marburg-neo-Kantianism—its constructive function emphasized more than its critical function by also reducing sensibility to functions of originating, pure reason—and as similar treatment is bestowed on the other two *Critiques*, so his "Critique of Practico-Religious

Reason" is transformed into a *Religion of Reason*.[23] Neither the one nor the other breaks with its respective system. Each extrapolates and crowns the system, contrary to the bulk of interpretations and uses to which they have been put subsequently.

The theory that the *Religion of Reason* is the work of "the last Cohen," that is, that it is post-neo-Kantian and pre-existentialist, was dreamt up by Franz Rosenzweig and canonically expounded in his introduction to Cohen's collected *Jewish Writings*.[24] Jews and non-Jews have taken up and spread this misrepresentation, until it has become accepted wisdom.[25] One genus of this species holds that Cohen did not actually take the step out of the neo-Kantian system but that logically and philosophically he should have taken it. Either way, this has served as a basis on which to make larger ontological claims on behalf either of some Hegelian/Marxist form of "realism"[26] or of quasi-Husserlian ontology,[27] even of Christian incarnationist doctrines,[28] or of a sort of Jewish metaphysical naturalism.[29]

The fact is that no ontological claims about God or man or the world are made in this work. For one thing, the title itself stresses with indubitable clarity the intention to provide a *religion of reason*—as, indeed, do all the other titles of Cohen's writings even in the last decade of his life. More specifically, Alexander Altmann has shown canonically that "the concept of the correlation signifies a methodological concept for Cohen, in the pregnant sense that methodology possesses in idealistic thinking. It is and remains a concept of origin and of production and cannot, therefore, in any way be interpreted in the sense of dialogical thinking. God as a member of the correlation is then no personal Thou but an idea. . . ."[30] In other words, religion produces out of its *a priori* rational "origins" the concepts, the ideas, of God, creation, revelation, redemption, the human self, and so on, all of which entail rational and religious obligations for human beings.

We have earlier noted the religious backdrop to the neo-Kantian notion of origin. Here the notion of "correlation" should be seen as a variant on the biblical notion of *b'rit/Bund*.[31] In this correlation/covenant, empirical man obtains ethical imperatives from his ideal partner through reason, which is what the two share. The latter is, of course, an entrenched doctrine in philosophical theology it is systematically explicated by Cohen under the term "the spirit of holiness" ("the holy spirit").[32]

The ideality of God in the correlation is even further abstracted by Cohen: if man and God are held to stand in relation, in "correlation," with one another, and though it even be kept in mind that it is ethical man that stands in relationship with the idea of God, not two empirical terms, it might nonetheless be inferred that God and man are members of one and the same class of concepts (for otherwise would their asserted relationship not be a "category mistake"?), and such an implication would bring God altogether too close to some form of immanentization. Cohen, therefore, goes on to argue that (the idea of) God is not in the relation but is its (rational) ground.[33] In other words, what was done typically in the history of neo-Platonism by way of ontological claims—namely, to build new, additional rungs into the ladder of emanations in order to keep spirit and matter as far apart as possible and yet to relate them—is here done in conceptual terms: God is now (Kant and Kantians would say "even"; traditional religionists and realists would say "only")[34] the regulative idea of universal ethical reason, which in Cohen's fully articulated philosophy of religion is then functionalized through the ideas of creation (from which the scientificity of nature is "correlatively" derived), of revelation (from which the imperatures of ethics are derived), and of redemption (from which the program of the good society, socialism, is derived). A diagram should here be helpful:

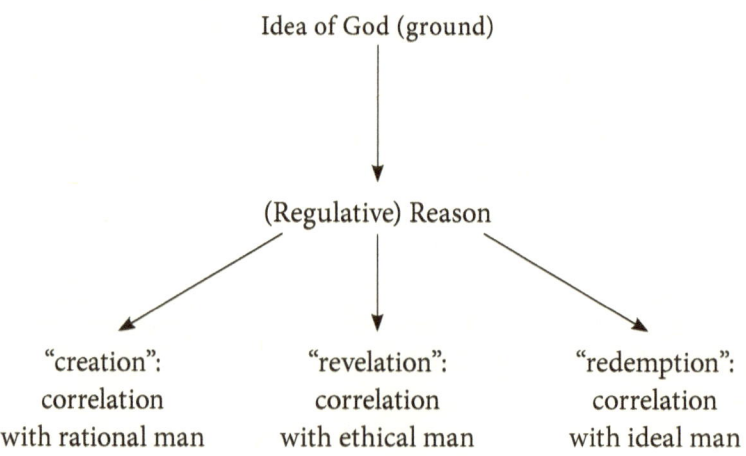

All in all, thus, Cohen's theological concepts are justified/validated by him not as possessing any kind of cognitive status but, in line with Kant's own "primacy of practical reason," as transcendentally necessary presuppositions for man's total ethical life—ethics themselves having, in turn, been rationally, philosophically, validated. As he says in *Religion of Reason* "God is not real, and He is also not alive in the sense of human beings being alive. Maimonides put a clear stop to this. Only the truth is the valid value that corresponds to the being of God."³⁵ And the ethical ultimacy of that being is stated in the somewhat earlier *Religion and Morality*: "Thus the Jewish idea of God is exhaustively defined by the ethical meaning of the idea of God."³⁶ We are thus still dealing with "ethical monotheism," as was the case all along in Cohen's earlier Kantian and neo-Kantian works. Cohen's religion is strictly ethical religion or, better, religion of ethics.³⁷ Indeed, he wanted to incorporate this truth into the very title, or subtitle, of his final work: the Society for the Advancement of the Science of Judaism, which was the patron of the book, wanted it subtitled "Jewish Philosophy of Religion," but Cohen was ready to concede only "Jewish Philosophy of Religion and Ethics."³⁸

That *Religion of Reason* is a consistent extrapolation of, not a deviation from, Cohen's formal philosophic system can also be shown in other ways. For one thing, religious doctrines in general and Jewish ones in particular interlaced his *Ethics of the Pure Will* and other earlier works so frequently and so systematically that one cannot but be reminded of how a professed theology also underlay Kant's *Critiques* and other writings (though in Kant's case this theology was an explicitly, however rationalized, Protestant one).³⁹ For another, the last third of Cohen's *Ethics* consists of chapters in which he goes through what might appear as the very old-fashioned ethical, indeed, the moralistic exercise of reciting the table of virtues (though what he does with them is philosophically, culturally, and even politically very sophisticated); and he does precisely the same thing, though this time in unabashedly Jewish, rabbinic, traditional terms, in the last third of his *Religion of Reason*.⁴⁰ Indeed, the parallelism between *Religion of Reason* and "the system" is all-pervasive: for example, Cohen's treatment of the religious doctrine of "creation" not only recapitulates his analysis of "nothing," infinity, the infinitesimal, "infinite privative judgments" of his *Logic of Pure Cognition*, but also explicitly cross-refers to it (as he cross-refers to "the system" and its appendages throughout).⁴¹

The analogy between the places of their respective *Religions* in the total systematic oeuvres of Kant and Cohen then also extends to the fact that religion is for both of them a rationally necessary consequence of, emphatically not the basis for, ethics. Cohen calls religion a philosophical

Eigenart (a subspecies)[42]: it stays within the philosophical realm of rational ethics, although it adds to and retro-affects the latter.

In sum then, "*Religion of Reason* (1) out of the Sources of (2) Judaism" (3) is intended to convey briefly that (3) historical Judaism will be treated as the empirical matrix out of which (2) the rational, *a priori* (necessary and universal) concepts are transcendentally educed, which (1) are in turn the "synthetic" producers of the universal human religion of ethics.

It is finally then only proper that we cast a glance at two other items that precede the text of this work: the motto and the dedication.

The book is dedicated by the author to his deceased father.[43] Gerson Cohen was the long-time cantor and Jewish teacher, the de facto rabbi, in the philosopher's small native town of Coswig/Anhalt. From the local schools and his father's Jewish training Cohen went to Breslau, in order to study primarily not at the local university but at the rabbinical seminary. As long as his father lived, and indeed in a sense afterward, their warm relationship centered on their common Jewish devotion.[44] It was then fitting that what turned out to be the philosopher's posthumous work, a Jewish philosophical theology and, by general consent, the most important and seminal such work in the century (with two or three possible competitors), be dedicated to his father.[45] This dedication was not, as is sometimes claimed, an act of contrition for having for many years allegedly strayed from the path of Judaism but, as we have by now sufficiently seen, a summation of his entire life and work.

The epigraph is a famous passage from the Talmud: Mishnah tractate "Day of Atonement," 8:9: "Rabbi Akiba said: 'Well off are you, oh Israel! Who purifies you, and before whom do you purify yourselves? It is your Father in Heaven.'"[46] (This is in fact the coda and climax of the mishnaic tractate, which, for the rest, like almost all of the Mishnah, is a technical legal code.)

The passage displays a number of important religious and literary aspects. Here we have to be concerned with the chief point that Cohen wanted to make—a point which, from another angle, we have discussed previously. The passage raises two questions, to both of which one and the same answer is given. Actually, Cohen has reversed the sequence in which the two questions are posed in the original text, but he explains in the body of the work, where he uses what is here the epigraph, what he takes to be its logical sequence: God purifies you, but, on a higher level of truth, you purify yourself, albeit exclusively "before" God. "God purifies no more than he forgives"; you yourself do this, ethically.[47]

(Cohen continues in the text by emphatically distinguishing this from Christianity and other forms of pantheism: "No man purifies you, and also no man who is supposed to be also a god. No son of God is to purify you: An unbridgeable gap must loom before [man]. . . . Truly, the Day of Atonement is the day of monotheism."[48] Man is the agent of his self-purification, though he executes this act only within the correlation. A dialectical relationship is humanly enacted between morally acting human beings—in fact, human beings striving for the ideal of "purity"— and the idea of the morally acting God, and the moral actions of this god, are uniquely predicated of him in the sense that human beings could not logically perform their acts if there were no second person in ideal, not empirical, relationship to whom ("before whom") those acts are performed.[49] (The sentence before the one that Cohen quotes from the Mishnah—that only "before God shall you be pure" on the Day of Atonement—declares in the name of Rabbi El'azar ben Azaryah: "Sins between a man and his fellow [as distinguished from sins between man and God] the Day of Atonement does not forgive until [!] he has reconciled him"—and from here Rabbi Akiba's exclamation takes off. In other words, temporal or other empirical relations between human beings come first ethically, and then only does the logical relation of standing "before God" begin to operate as the superstructure of ethics.)[50] In short, atonement does not precede but is in fact constituted by the moral action of repentance.[51] (At the end of the full study in which this paper is the first section the massive impact of Cohen's philosophical theology of repentance on contemporary Jewish Orthodoxy, namely, Rabbi J.B. Soloveitchik and the late Rabbi Hutner and others, is illustrated at some length—not to speak of Rabbi Nehemiah Nobel, the Orthodox community rabbi of Frankfurt o/M, who took a year off from his rabbinical duties to study with Cohen in Marburg.) "Pure" in the classic Jewish sense has been joined by "pure" in the Kantian sense.[52]

Chapter 13

History of the *Religion of Reason*

Part II of the Introduction

A. Philosophical History

The *Religion of Reason* is, like everything else, the result of historical and intellectual processes that led up to it.

Cohen had had to grapple all along with a philosophical problem that besets especially idealistic thinkers—the problem of individuation. That is, if one starts idealistically with ideas, concepts, and so on, how does one ever reach empirical individuals, which, on the one hand, seem to constitute the actual world in which we live and which a philosophical theory must satisfactorily explain, but which, on the other hand, seem to be generically so different from mental, rational entities that they can hardly be derived from these. In order to answer this question the concept of individuality itself does not suffice, for it is not a question of the concept of the individual but a question of the empirical, "actual," sensuous individual. Scholastic Aristotelianism and Neo-Platonism, therefore, resorted to a philosophical dualism, in which the principle of materiality was invoked as the principle of individuation, and modern dualism in the Cartesian and even the Kantian forms continued this tradition. In Kant the empirical aspect of the individual was supplied by sense-experience, while ideas, and so on, were provided by reason. For the radical, though neo-Kantian, idealist, and rationalist Hermann Cohen this manner of coping with the problem of individuation would not work anymore, however, because, if only in order to overcome the built-in irrationality and thus the ultimate unsusceptibility to scientific explanation of empirical individuals produced by a power independent of *logos*, he discarded the independence of the senses, which Kant still upheld as one of two "sources of knowledge," and insisted instead that also sense-experience is "originated" by reason alone. Thus the problem of individuation arose for him with renewed force. "The principle of the infinitesimal method"[1] was intended to resolve the problem: that is, "reality" was now seen to be itself a rational category—a philosophical "problematic," and real individuals came to be seen then as the rational applications of this category. But this is, of course, still a very general manner of handling the problem. One had to go on to deal with specific types of individuals—first and foremost, humans.

In his "system of philosophy" (i.e., the three components of his neo-Kantian system: the *Logic of Pure Cognition*, *Ethics of Pure Will*, and *Aesthetics of Pure Feeling*) Cohen began by going further in the direction indicated by Kant in order to satisfy this demand. Kant had argued in the *Critique of Judgment* that, though the empirical aspects of individuals in theoretical cognition were, per the *Critique of Pure Reason*, supplied by sense-experience, individuals as they occur in scientific and other human enterprises were actually provided by teleological categorialization (in the life sciences and especially in art). In short, "judgments," even what we these days call value judgments, construct individuals. Art objects, for example, are certainly empirical individuals: we hang them on walls and listen to them in concert halls; but their artistic values do not inhere their material component; rather are these introduced into the material by the artists' conceptions and imputed to them by the art-consumers' values. In Cohen's radicalized Kantianism, once the sense aspect of the individuals of cognition had itself been subordinated to the all-embracing power of reason, individuals then turned out to be quite literally human artifacts: they were (1) rational constructions, (2) constructed for human usage, (3), like works of art, physical exemplifications of values, and (4) qua values, ultimately ethical projects. In short, individuals are regarded as aesthetic units. Even human individuals are works of art, and insofar as religion concerns itself with human individuals it is really a form of aesthetics. At this stage of his thinking Cohen then actually discusses religion in general and Jewish religion in particular in aesthetic terms: "About the Aesthetic Value of our Religious Education," "The Lyricism of the Psalms," "The Style of the Prophets," and so on. (Much from these essays was transferred into the *Religion of Reason*.) Even what is commonsensically regarded as the characteristic predicate of empirical human individuality, and traditionally as the highest value of religion, namely feeling in all its particular human forms of personal love, despair, and so on—even this is "produced" by pure reason through the a*esthetics of pure feeling*.

There was still something unsatisfactory about this aesthetic theory of individuation to Cohen. Aesthetic objects are enjoyed; they are not challenged to moral purposes, nor are they even appropriately used for such purposes. Cohen's primacy of practical reason had to make the actionable challenges of ethics central to his perspective on man and the world rather than the quietism of sublimation and enjoyment, which is taken to characterize the realm of art.

We are at the turn of the century. Now, too, the spirit of the age seemed to be changing: a new realism (in the philosophical forms of naturalism, positivism, "life-philosophy," etc.)[2] demanded a philosophy descend from its ethereal idealism and come to grips with the earthy realities of contemporary life. This spirit manifested itself not only in religious and political circles at large but also in Cohen's most immediate intellectual and philosophical proximity. In 1892 Cohen had said about this that it was "the bad spirit of the cult of persons, which has of late taken the place of the celebration of ideas,"[3] and in "The Ethical and Historical Motifs of Religion"[4] he still warned against the revolt against ideas in philosophy, culture, politics, and religion and contrasted the then prominent "search for the historical Jesus" in Protestant thought[5] with the Deuteronomic condemnation of a visible God. Nonetheless, he was forced to address the problematic further.

Paul Natorp had been Cohen's student and disciple; he became his closest colleague, associate, and friend. Withal, there were real strains in their relationship, largely due to their very different cultural backgrounds—the one a Jew, the other a Protestant. Although Natorp always advocated strict "Marburg neo-Kantianism" while Cohen was alive, these differences nonetheless asserted themselves increasingly as the years went by even in matters of philosophy and politics. After the war was over and Cohen dead, Natorp deviated so significantly from his teacher's basic views that the philosophical tendencies of Nikolai Hartmann, Heinz Heimsoeth, and even of Husserl and Heidegger either issued from or at least converged with his.

In 1894 Natorp published *Religion within the Bounds of Humanity—A Chapter toward the Foundation of Social Politics*. As the very title makes clear, it was in overwhelming measure a philosophical theology in the spirit of Marburg neo-Kantianism. Despite this, it granted a certain autonomy from ethics and philosophy to religion, which Cohen's later *Ethics of Pure Will* (1904, 1907) would still reject. This led to a whole series of exchanges between the two, cordial and even in agreement on philosophical fundamentals they tried to settle their differences in those exchanges: Cohen's *Religion and Morality* (1907), Natorp's original book with a new epilogue that basically addressed itself to Cohen (1908),[6] Cohen's *Concept of Religion within the System of Philosophy* (1915), all sorts of notes and correspondences between them on this subject that have been found in Natorp's literary estate, and finally the *Religion of Reason*, with which we are here primarily concerned.

The original issue between Cohen and Natorp in this respect may be summarized as follows. To be sure, argues Natorp, also religion must, of course, remain under the ultimate rule of reason, and reason cannot go beyond the boundaries of the three human activities that are verifiable in the phenomenal universe: cognition, ethics, and culture. However, Cohen's own doctrine of pure feeling should not be limited to art. As the (different) Kantianism of Schleiermacher and their contemporary Rudolf Otto shows, feeling has a wider domain in religion, in which the human individual and even God are individuated—become, like art—objects, objects of experience—and rather than being infinite values, regulatives, toward which we can and ought to strive but which we cannot experientially attain. In religion, therefore, God and man are, as it were, concrete universals, or, as Natorp puts it in the aforementioned appendix, entitled "Feeling as the Root of Religion":[7] "Ultimately it all depends only on the fact of the demand for eternal rest, a rest in the eternal."[8] That is, the pursuit of the ideal, though into infinity, must be felt to have been completed—thus to end in an (Hegelian) completed infinity. The triumph of the good must be guaranteed, not only assigned as a task. As Natorp cites their common friend Wilhelm Herrmann, the Protestant theologian, if the self, for example, is a task, then there has to be a self, so that it can have a task.[9] Though he generally agrees with Cohen, Natorp wants to stress more than the latter the present-time function of infinity, whereas Cohen always wants to stress the radical uncompletion of present time in the perspective of eternity.[10]

Wilhelm Herrmann, the third in their band at the University of Marburg, did indeed argue very much to the same effect. For him, too, religion was (in a very Protestant, individualistic yet socially engaged, way) the personal experience, thoroughly and even historically Christian, of the infinite God, of the human self, as well as of the moral obligations, which he held issued forth from the encounter between God and man.[11] In this spirit he reviewed Cohen's *Ethics of Pure Will*.[12]

Fortunately we have Cohen's own notes to these arguments.[13] He rejects all rest and reliance on alleged experience ("Erlebnis") of "life," self, and God. He insists to the contrary: "'Rest in the Eternal?' No, eternal work,"[14] and by "work" he means, of course, moral effort. "Micah says it all, in fact" (i.e., Micah 6:8: *It has been told you, oh man, what is good and what the Lord requires of you—to love mercy, to do justice, and to walk humbly before your God.*)[15] In other words, he perseveres in proposing that "God" means the endless tasks of human morality, and he does not even hide (at least from himself, in his private notes) that, when his Christian friends and colleagues insist on the "reality" of God and the religious experience, rather than on their normativity, they really are giving expression "ultimately to Christian pantheism [i.e., the doctrine that God/the ideal has been 'incarnated' in a man/the actual] that here, too, substitutes feeling as the *Ur*-force of life for ethics";[16] that is, it is "pantheistic identity."[17]

Up to this point Cohen's reply is essentially negative. It also contains a strong positive implication, however, namely the ultimacy of ethics, as understood by these neo-Kantians, also for religion. This positive dimension must now be explicated. That is, where and how does religion function so as to individuate ethically, rather than aesthetically?

Cohen's answer to this question runs basically along the following lines. In his *Aesthetics of Pure Feeling* he had shown how art rationally produces/constructs individuals as members of humankind, but these individuals are purely aesthetic objects.[18] In his *Ethics of Pure Will* he had shown how human persons as ethical individuals, that is, as distinguished from all other objects that we experience in the world, are conceptually constructed in relationship with second persons—that is to say, as responsible, interacting entities. These individuals are thus produced in the process of applying universal, ethical categories to them. In this way they are individuals, to be sure, but only in the sense of being members of their class, rather than as possessing absolute value in each by himself or herself. In *The Concept of Religion in the System of Philosophy* the idea of God is added to this conceptual process so as to constitute the second person, now of absolute value (as entailed by the very notion of God), in correlation with whom the first person, and all "I's," acquire absolute value in and by themselves. Specifically, in *Religion and Morality* the correlation is actually a particular and actional event: man's (social) crimes are now treated as (religious) sins—they can, therefore, not be rectified by mere social rearrangements—sin, repentance, forgiveness, and self-improvement are then the activities that can be carried out only "before God" by completely individuated persons.[19]

Paul Celan, after the Nazi cataclysm, was to write this conception into his poem "The Syllable Pain": "Ein Du, todlos/an dem alles Ich zu sich kam."[20] Human relations thus occur between human beings not as sensuously given "fellow-men" (*Nebenmenschen*) or even as ethically stipulated fellow-class-members but as "co-men (correlational men) (*Mitmenschen*), and together they make for moral progress. All of the central section of *Religion of Reason*, chapters 8–10, are devoted to the detailed explication of this doctrine,[21] but there is nothing new in those chapters. In 1908, in his study *Characteristic of Maimonides' Ethics*[22] Cohen had so interpreted Maimonides in a passage worth quoting in full if only because it formulates what Martin Buber claimed fifteen years later to have revolutionarily discovered "For this Self there is no 'I' without thou. *Re'a* (neighbor) is what the other is called, he is like thee, *he is the Thou to the I* (Cohen's italics). The self is the result of the eternal relationship between I and Thou, the infinite ideal of this eternal relationship. [And here Buber will diverge into his metaphysical direction.] The ideal remains ideal, it is true, the task always remains task, but the *ideal* is an ideal precisely also only by demanding, and insofar as it demands, emulation,—and thus it makes it possible to approximate it. . . ."[23] As part of this exposition Cohen rehabilitates even the prophet Ezekiel, who had been downgraded by the Biblical Critics as post-exilic, nationalistic and cultic, but whom Cohen came to cherish not primarily because his own Hebrew name was Ezekiel,[24] but because of the centrality that this prophet assigned to the centrality of the individual atonement in religion.[25]

This fundamental move of Cohen's draws wide circles. The God before whom alone such absolute individuation of persons can be realized is, as we have by now abundantly seen, strictly a rational idea. As an idea he is a regulative concept, and as a regulative idea its exhaustive function is ethical: that is, God is defined by his ethical attributes (Maimonides' only legitimate, other than negative, "attributes of action"), which are to be humanly emulated (*imitatio Dei*, again, the correlation).[26] God is, in the strict sense of Kant's *Third Critique*, a teleological concept, that is, a concept that tells us not how the world is, but how it ratio-ethically ought to be and how we ought to remake it.[27] Since the "meaning" of things, as distinguished from their "existence," is what we believe, or rationally ought to believe, they ought to be, God is thus in fact the "meaning" of our lives. All human beings are, of course, defined as persons in the process, and thus Judaism originates the universal concept of transtribal, transnational, man in the form of the "Noachite."[28] "Noachite" is the Jewish term for the universal term "human being," ethical, rational person. The

Noachitic covenant is the originating/original ("ursprünglich") Torah, that is, the a priori conception that produced and continues to produce the regulative conception of mankind.[29] And the relationship between *Mensch* and *Mitmensch* concretizes itself in the relationship between *Leid* and *Mitleid*: suffering and compassion;[30] that is, my own suffering can only be understood as a derivative of my participation in the suffering of others. Thus religion and ethical socialism come to be indistinguishable.[31]

This, in broad outline, is the specific function of religion within the boundaries of critical epistemology, ethics, and aesthetics. It is a "subspecies" (*Eigenart*) within rational philosophy—distinct, yet a part of the whole.[32]

B. Social History

Naturally, also the history of Cohen's lifetime fed into the writing of the *Religion of Reason*. Throughout the forty years of his incumbency at the University of Marburg he had continued his specifically Jewish commitment, both intellectually and practically, alongside and as part of his philosophical, German, and social commitments.[33] The long chain of "Jewish essays"[34] are the record of that Jewish concern. In practice, he attracted a large number of Jewish students from Germany and abroad, especially from Russia. His early monograph on "The Neighbor"[35] resulted from his involvement in a trial at Marburg that revolved around the new, and since then notorious, classic of antisemitism, Rohling's *Talmudjude*, and involved one of the chief founding fathers of German anti-Semitism, Paul de Lagarde. Cohen always entertained close relations with the local, and other rabbis, and he actively participated in their communal projects and in national and scholarly Jewish affairs.

In the earliest years of the present century the philosophico-religious discussions took place that we have followed in the outline. As though directed by an invisible hand, Cohen was both ready and intellectually compelled to concentrate on religious questions when, analogously to Kant in his lifetime, his philosophic system as a whole had been constructed and its religious implications could, and historically now had to be, explicated. In 1912 Cohen retired at the university, before he had to, because he felt politically rebuffed by galloping German chauvinism, philosophically alienated by the new "realism," and religiously antagonized by the newly respectable anti-Semitism. (Over his resistance the empiricistic psychologist Erich F. Jaensch was in fact appointed as his successor in the chair of philosophy. Jaensch was to influence students like Ortega y Gasset and Julius Ebbinghaus and ended as a Nazi professor.) From a personal point of view he finally wanted to live in the big city, and, ideologically, moving to Berlin (his wife's hometown—daughter of the famous chief-cantor of the Berlin Jewish Community, Louis Lewandowski) meant that he would have a large Jewish and also otherwise liberal audience. He taught at the religiously liberal rabbinical seminary there, the Lehranstalt für die Wissenschaft des Judentums. He was soon coopted into the Rabbinical Selection Committee of the Jewish Community, as he had been when he first came to Marburg. From here on until his death he gave courses in Jewish philosophy at the seminary.

New political developments pushed Cohen even more powerfully toward concentrating on Jewish questions. As part of the general European and particularly German tendency toward a new realism, also among Jews the idealism and universalism of the earlier part of the previous century came under increasing attack. Not only German ethnicism but also the developments that climaxed in the Dreyfus-Affair and the waves of Russian pogroms produced political Zionism and its ideology. Biologicistic mysticism, like Martin Buber's, was adopted by the intellectual and cultural avant-garde. In the first volume of Buber's since then famous monthly *Der Jude* (1916) Raphael Seligmann, for example, argued[36] that Cohen, having outdone Kant himself in idealism by denying the givenness of the given, also eliminated from Judaism all history and "myth" and thus made an ideology out of the assimilationist dissolution of the Jewish people. Buber himself, in an article significantly entitled "Concepts and Reality,"[37] declared: "The idea cannot be realized unless first peoplehood (Volkstum) is realized," and the words "blood" and "ethnos" occur often and favorably in Buber's response to Cohen's reply.[38] On philosophic as well as political grounds Cohen obviously would feel constrained to resist and to counterattack such tendencies.

In May 1914, immediately before the outbreak of the great war, the interests of German propaganda and profound concern for the Jewish masses in Eastern Europe united in Cohen's triumphal tour through Russia.[39] Cohen returned from this trip, 72 years old, deeply moved, for the rest of his life. (This was the model for many younger German Jews who were to meet the reality of Eastern-Jewish authenticity for the first time as soldiers in the German army and were permanently changed by the experience. Usually this is cited as an argument against

Cohen's ideology!) Once the war got going, large numbers of Polish, Lithuanian, Russian, and other Jews came under German rule, and many of them pressed westward. German chauvinistic resistance to their immigration greatly increased. Cohen and other German-Jewish religionists agreed with Jewish nationalists in advocating the rights of such immigrants and of their fellows in the occupied areas. At the same time that Buber and his associates founded *Der Jude*, Cohen and his associates founded the non-Zionist and since then totally and unjustly ignored *Neue Jüdische Monatshefte* (I/1, October 10, 1916).[40] Though the two journals propounded generally opposite intellectual and Jewish-political programs, they agreed not only on the centrality of Jewish values but also on "the Jewish—Polish question"—so much so that Buber and Cohen, who otherwise argued vehemently against one another, exchanged their own articles on this subject in the two journals.[41] The notorious census of Jews in the German army during the war directed attention again to "the Jewish question," and Cohen and Natorp almost came to a basic break over this, which they avoided only by strong reciprocal efforts.[42]

The lectures that Cohen continued to give at the rabbinical seminary during the war began to be published in the *Neue Jüdische Monatshefte*;[43] and were eventually incorporated into the *Religion of Reason* in only slightly altered form. *Neue Jüdische Monatshefte* II, May 10, 1918, immediately but posthumously still carried an excerpt of what was to become chapter 3 of the *Religion of Reason* about the concept of creation. Also toward the end of the war, one of Cohen's prewar students, now a soldier and young friend of his, Franz Rosenzweig, published first in the *Neue Jüdische Monatshefte*, and then as a separate pamphlet[44] a proposal, in form of an open letter to Cohen, *Zeit ist's* (*It's Time*), to organize general Jewish education around a new Academy for the Science of Judaism, to which Cohen responded affirmatively in *Neue Jüdische Monatshefte* II, March 10, 1918, in an article "Toward the Founding" (of such an academy). Ernst Cassirer, surely the most important disciple of Cohen's in the subsequent history of philosophy, then reported that, "beginning the end of 1917, Cohen gathered round him a small group of supporters of the idea of the Academy. The first draft of its statutes was produced in this circle after Cohen's death,"[45] and Cassirer himself became a founding member of the executive committee of the academy. One event, or rather nonevent that occurred during the World War needs to be treated here, both historically and philosophically. Because a number of university teachers were serving in the army, universities would call on retired professors to take over courses. Cohen, too, was called on for such purposes.[46] All we seem to know of is one Kant course that he gave, in which he apparently "recited" the text in Marburg.

What is interesting philosophically about this nonevent is that most of the courses announced on his behalf bore titles referring to (philosophical) psychology. He had stated in earlier works that his systematic philosophy of culture would be completed in a psychology. Thus, for example, the very last words of his *Ethics*[47] project a psychology as "the psychology of the unity of the consciousness of culture,"[48] and in his *Aesthetics*,[49] volume 2, he says: "Thus, in conformity with the systematic concept, the task of psychology widens into that of an *heuristic encyclopedia* of the system of philosophy."[50] He had also taught courses under psychology titles down through the years.[51] Thus Cohen, who is not without justification regarded as the great philosophical antipsychologicist, was, in fact, deeply concerned with psychology throughout his life. His idea of what psychology is had changed drastically, however, from his earliest years, when he was under the influence of his teacher Steinthal, to his final view of it as a transcendental philosophy of culture. In the end, no such psychology was ever written, nor have any records been found of his lectures on the subject. An e-silentio-argument has been made out of this circumstance, to the effect that the "Psychology" was abandoned, and therewith also the neo-Kantian system, to be replaced by the proto-existentialist *Religion of Reason*.[52]

The faults of this reasoning are obvious. We can, on the other hand, form a pretty clear idea of what his psychology would have looked like. Analogously to the titles of the three other systematic works it might have been entitled "Psychology of Pure Culture:" that is, from the culture(s) created by the human, rational activities of cognition, will, and feeling—from what the Hegelian tradition called "objective spirit"[53]— its/their normative transcendental, a priori, pure presuppositions in the human psyche would be educed, and these would then constitute the ideal model of the human psyche, which all empirical psychology ought to endeavor incrementally to realize.[54] Natorp's works on philosophical psychology,[55] written while still intimately identified with Cohen, provide us with one version of what might be called "Marburg psychology." Ernst Cassirer's *Philosophy of Symbolic Forms*[56] presents another somewhat deviant yet extremely suggestive form that a philosophy of culture, traced back to its psychological foundations, could take in Marburg neo-Kantianism—in this case, however, taken beyond the boundaries of rational (i.e., scientific and ethical) culture and extended backward even into the realm of mythology.[57]

In any case, what is clear from such a reconstruction of Cohen's projected psychology and from a proper understanding of his *Religion of Reason* is that neither could or was intended to take the place of the other and that both would have constituted or do constitute the final and valuable components, indeed, the completions, of his consistent, though growing, life's work. This is also documented in the congratulatory article on Cohen's seventieth birthday and retirement that Natorp published in a Berlin daily newspaper, *Berliner Tageblatt*, July 1, 1912, in which he announces that Cohen's philosophic system is "shortly to be completed with a philosophy of religion and a psychology."

We can follow Cohen's progress in writing the *Religion of Reason* literally till the day of his death. We have earlier followed the theoretical debates about religion in the early years of the century, internal to the Marburg school. Even the mechanics of those debates are documented in some measure. In Natorp's literary estate at the University of Marburg,[58] among much other material and a considerable amount of Cohen-Natorp correspondence, there is, for example, an envelope[59] containing hundreds of chits of paper, written by Cohen himself, much of them in Hebrew (although letters were usually written for him by his wife) with Biblical, Talmudic, Jewish-philosophical quotations, references, phrases, and so on. The envelope is dated 1907, addressed to Cohen, with the rubber stamp of A. Lewandowski (Cohen's brother in law), and the penciled subject-title "Atonement." How and why this envelope got into the Natorp estate is a puzzle. But what emerges from it, in any case, is that Cohen was collecting, quite early in the century, material that eventually found its way into *Religion of Reason* in general and in the chapter "Atonement,"—and that, but for convenience, Cohen did not really need the help of Leo Rosenzweig, with his thorough Lithuanian training in Rabbinic literature. When, therefore, Cohen wrote to Natorp in 1914[60] that he now wanted to write his monograph *Religion and Morality*, "worin ich mich mit Ihnen ins Einvernehmen auseinandersetzen will," this is only another stage in an intimate and drawn-out discussion, fed on Cohen's side by Jewish sources no less than by contemporary philosophy.

Now we have collected the Cohen–Natorp exchanges and the prepublications of his lectures at the rabbinical seminar that went into the making of the *Religion of Reason*.[61] In 1917 he reported that the book was almost finished and on January 23, 1918, that half of it was in print.⁶² (One always has to remember that by this time he was almost totally blind and all reading and writing were being done for him by his wife.)⁶³ In checking galleys he used the marginalia of both Franz Rosenzweig and Rabbi Nehemiah Nobel to improve the text, as Bruno Strauss reports.⁶⁴ But death stopped him from reading the galleys of the later sections of the book.⁶⁵ In a letter to Rabbi Kellermann of April 6, 1920, Martha Cohen reported that he had been working on them the last Sunday of his life. Cassirer and Natorp eulogized Cohen at his graveside in the absence of other academic honors.⁶⁶

C. Reception History

Religion of Reason Out of the Sources of Judaism was published as soon after Cohen's death and the end of World War I as conditions allowed.⁶⁷ This was pious, but it also turned out to be a catastrophe for the book itself, because, as we have seen, its text thus appeared in horribly distorted and misleading form: its very title came out wrong, and the many pages of textual corrections, added to the second edition by Bruno Strauss,⁶⁸ illustrate this further⁶⁹—without even then by far exhausting the necessary corrigenda.

A few of Cohen's Jewish disciples remained true to his standard philosophical views. One was Benzion Kellermann, a radical Reform-rabbi.⁷⁰ Others were Sinai Ucko, a Zionist,⁷¹ Zvi Diesendruck, Samuel Atlas, et al.⁷²

The most significant consequence of Cohen's death over the galleys of his *Religion of Reason* was, however, that, since Rabbi Nobel himself died only a few short and turbulent years later, Cohen's brilliant young disciple of earlier years, to whom he had remained very close through the war years,⁷³ Franz Rosenzweig, assumed the role of quasi-canonical interpreter of "the late Cohen," at least in German-Jewish circles, through various occasional lectures and articles and then in his "Introduction" to Cohen's collected *Jewish Writings*. Rosenzweig was thus in a position to revise the public estimate of the intellectual thrust of Cohen's later works in a "post-Kantian," proto-phenomenologist, preexistentialist sense. The tendentiousness of that interpretation⁷⁴ became, if only because it expressed the spirit of the new "realism" of the period, with few and infrequent exceptions, the standard view among Jews.⁷⁵ That view took on two different forms: either it was claimed that "the late Cohen" actually changed his mind and left Criticism behind in favor of a germinal ontologism, or it was claimed that, though subjectively he did not actually think that his philosophical position had changed, the logic of his arguments and analyses was incompatible with Criticism and, because it was valid, led to views that would now be expounded by his critics. Rosenzweig himself basically endorsed the first of these forms.[76] An example of the second form is encountered in Joseph ben-Shlomoh's epilogue to the Hebrew translation of the *Religion of Reason*:[77] he admits that Cohen did not change his mind[78] but argues that a) Cohen's personal piety was incompatible with his intellectualism and b) his rationalism was incapable of doing justice to the profundity of religion[79] or the validity of "concrete" messianism, Jewish peoplehood, and the State of Israel.[80] (By the 1970s organized Jewry had possessed itself of a "concrete universality" such as Natorp's Christianity and Hegelian Germany had proclaimed much earlier in the century!)

We have earlier made short shrift of the philosophical side of this argument. As for Cohen's personal piety, there can be no question about its reality.[81] But what these interpreters fail to understand is that for Cohen proper emotion was itself one important product of reason ("pure feeling"). (Most of the Jewish readers neglected or totally passed by his systematic works.)

The possibility of a radically rational man leading an intensely emotional life precisely by virtue of and as a consequence of rationality was splendidly exemplified in Hermann Cohen[82] (though it is clearly a difficult human model for most people to believe in).

One welcome by-product of this cooptation of Cohen for the cultural and political aims of postrationalism and of Zionism later in the century, whether read into his texts or argued against it, is the translation into other languages of his Jewish writings. His technical, philosophical, systematic writings, on the other hand, linger untranslated in the original German, for Jews and non-Jews in the world alike.

Hostility to Cohen's radical rationalism continued unabated through the twenties. When the second edition of the *Religion of Reason* appeared in 1929 the *Frankfurter Israelitisches Gemeindeblatt—Amtliches Organ der Israelitischen Gemeinde* (VIII/9, May 1930) devoted the first five pages to new critical discussions of the book—the first by Leo Löwenthal[83] (thus a "Frankfurt-School" exercise in more than one literal sense), who, while informative, fair, and even admiring, ultimately reduces Cohen into a superstructuralistic ideologist of the Jewish bourgeoisie, the second by A. Gurwitsch,[84] who naturally uses more phenomenologistic language in order, in a quite unrestrained vocabulary, to attack the "groundlessness" in history and epistemology of such ideology—that is, without a piece of concrete earth under its philosophical feet, unlike peasants.

The power of Cohen's thoughts, far beyond the intellectual and Jewish religious circles usually associated with him and well into our own time, can be illustrated, on the other hand, by the fate of his treatment of Mishnah, "Day of Atonement," 8:9, that we have considered earlier. Thoroughly German and religiously "liberal" that he proudly was, he always had attracted a large number of devoted students especially from Russia[85] (where Jews were virtually barred from the universities, and these were, of course, usually orthodox or at least from orthodox backgrounds. Leo Rosenzweig (at the time referred to as "Rosenzweig-East," in order to distinguish him from Franz Rosenzweig, "Rosenzweig-West"), mentioned earlier, is one example. From the many others that could be mentioned, Boris Pasternak could be picked out as well-known to the general public. Even a generation later, when the scions of great rabbinical dynasties in the East came to study at German universities, Cohen's thought continued to exert tremendous power. Thus Rabbi Joseph Beer Soloveitchik, probably the outstanding legal and intellectual authority in present-day orthodox Judaism, wrote his dissertation at the University of Berlin in 1932 under the title *Das reine Denken und die Seinsbestimmung bei Hermann Cohen*[86] and recently still he published a study of repentance in Judaism, which is clearly, though only implicitly, based on Cohen's theology of repentance, as derived from the Mishnaic passage under title "Well off are you, oh Israel: Before whom Do you Purify Yourselves."[87] Another great authority in Jewish orthodoxy, Rabbi Isaac Hutner, also a student at the University of Berlin around 1930, developed a much more intricate and daring such theology of repentance, again based unmistakably, though only implicitly, on Cohen's treatment of the Mishnaic passage.

From here, the rest of this unpublished manuscript was later in-cooperated in Schwarzschild's published essay The Theologico-Political Basis of Liberal Christian-Jewish Relations in Modernity, *in the next chapter.*

Chapter 14 | 1986

The Theologico-Political Basis of Liberal Christian-Jewish Relations in Modernity

I can here only hope to offer a broadly brushed description and a partial analysis of liberal Christian and Jewish theologies (and religions), with emphasis on the turn of the nineteenth and twentieth centuries, in their historical and philosophical contexts and with particular emphasis on Germany (the latter specification being justified by the facts of the case).

It is notorious how fuzzy, multivalent, and changeable the very notion of liberalism is. As Th. P. Neil wrote: "Liberal . . . A Term of Many Meanings Whose Sense Must be Defined When Used."[1] This is as true of religious as of political liberalism. (I will leave completely aside the additionally complicating factor that in the second third of the present century the term "liberalism" acquired in America an enduring signification that is essentially different from and even contradictory to its enduring significance in Europe. The American meaning was determined by the efforts of the Franklin D. Roosevelt administrations in creating a very limitedly welfare state[2] and is best exemplified by the Liberal Party in New York City.) Most broadly, it can perhaps be said that liberalism, especially in the later nineteenth century and thereafter, locates itself somewhere in the middle—in the middle between the Right of conservatism and the Left of socialism. Such political terms are, however, convenient labels rather than conceptually precise definitions—not to mention the logical problems that have pertained to the notion of the medium ever since Aristotle's "golden mean." Consider then how exponentially vague a middle-of-the-road notion of liberalism must be that is defined by such

---

First published in *Das deutsche Judentum und der Liberalismus*, Dokumentation eines internationalen Seminars der Friedrich-Naumann-Stiftung in Zusammenarbeit mit dem Leo Baeck Institute, London Comdok-Verlagsabteilung, Schriften der Friedrich-Naumann-Stiftung, St. Augustin (1986), 70–95

labels! In any case, such political and religious liberalism, located in the middle of the spectrum, however fluid on all its peripheries, is in turn typically upheld by the middle classes, especially the upper middle class (to which in turn all the previous definitional problems adhere). And it is then characteristic of liberal, centrist constellations (as again political philosophers since Aristotle have noted) to slide off to the Right or to the Left, and commonly in both directions, thus splitting themselves in the process, if they do not disappear altogether.[3]

In the economico-political crisis in Germany that began in 1879 Bismarck's "honeymoon" with liberalism came to an end in more than one respect, also as far as German Jews were concerned. Treitschke demanded that Jews not only be responsible citizens in return for their political emancipation but also that they be baptized into Protestantism on the ground that (and this will be one of the chief ongoing themes of German-Jewish debates for the next half-century) the German State and Protestant Christianity were now of one substance, so that one could not participate in one without the other. Hermann Cohen, in his famous reply to Treitschke,[4] in turn laid down what was to remain the essence of the Jewish reply to the German Christians—that enlightened Judaism was, as a matter of fact, a purer expression of social ethics and of political responsibility than Christianity and that, therefore, both Germany and Christianity required Judaism for their social health, and Jews ought to remain Jews, of course, precisely for the sake of their political, German duties. On this score, though, Cohen and his liberal Jewish cohorts then and subsequently lost the public battle. As a result and so early in the history of the Second Empire Jews and the National Liberals began their political divorce. To be sure, in the 1890s official establishment German Jewry entered into what Marjorie Lamberti calls an "alignment with the Progressives,"[5] but, as she immediately goes on to show, this was always an extremely tenuous, short-lived, often useless and even counterproductive, alliance.[6]

In any case, the formal liberal party in Wilhelmine Germany, in the period with which we are here primarily concerned, then split, on the logical pattern, which I have stipulated, between the so-called National Liberals (with its big-business and sometimes anti-Semitic associations) to the conservative Right[7] and the so-called Left Liberals toward the Left, especially revisionist Social Democracy. (Friedrich Naumann, too—very important as he was in all these developments—had started out in the antisemitic Christian Social Movement around the turn of the century)[8] In fact and throughout the history of united Germany Jews generally found their political home among the socialists.[9]

On a much wider historical and philosophical scale, covering the end of the eighteenth century down into the twentieth and, therefore, also embracing the shorter period with which we are here centrally concerned, the following broad structure can be discerned[10]: The conventional histories of modem philosophy describe fairly enough how German "absolute idealism" and especially Hegel and Hegelians used (or misused) especially Kant's "Critique of Judgment," mostly in order to close the gap that, as they saw it and still see it, Kant had opened up between experienced reality and theoretical, to them "metaphysical," truth—including under the latter heading matters that are usually regarded as the meat-and-potatoes of religion. Somewhat simplistically one can say that the nineteenth and twentieth centuries attempted philosophically to close the gap between noumenon and phenomenon, rationality and actuality, God and the world, and so on, in one of two fashions (which sometimes came to the same thing): either reality was made to collapse into ideality (e.g., Hegel), or ideality was made to collapse into actuality (Marxism, historicism, positivisms, etc.). And from the outset of this nineteenth-century German development the distance that intellectuals put between themselves and Kant also measured their hostility to Jews and Judaism. Uri Tal's study "Young German Intellectuals on Romanticism and Judaism—Spiritual Turbulence in the early 19th century"[11] summarizes the trend between 1807 and 1820 so aptly that it can be reduced to the formula: romanticism is antirationalistic, organicistic, self-consciously Germanic/Teutonic, and, therefore, vehemently opposes the French Revolution and liberalism and thus also turns anti-Semitic.

As soon as one sees things in this light it becomes clear that Jewish philosophers and religious thinkers would want to stipulate, as, indeed, they did, some significant reservations about the thesis that the actual is the rational or that there is naught but the actual, for at least two reasons—one historical, the other conceptual: historically, Jews continued to live in a real world that they could scarcely regard, at least from their perspective, as ideal,—and, conceptually, the absolute transcendence of God and everything He is taken to stand for is massively embedded in the very foundations of historic Jewish culture. As a consequence even the Jewish Hegelian or quasi-Hegelian thinkers of the first half of the nineteenth century all held, in one way or another, that Judaism differed from Christianity (and paganism) in that it preserved the discreteness of God from nature and, what amounts to the same thing, of the power of reason and moral freedom in the world.

For German philosophical politics and real politics on the broad canvas from the later eighteenth century down to our time, on the other hand, all one really needs to do is to look, for example, at Georg G. Iggers, *The German Conception of History—The National Tradition of Historical Thought from Herder to the Present*,[12] (within its own limitations) to see how things developed there. One can summarize that development in formulaic fashion: from late eighteenth-century cosmopolitanism (e.g., especially Kant) to Romantic but still cosmopolitan nationalism (e.g., Herder, von Humboldt) to chauvinistic nationalism (e.g., Ranke, Treitschke, etc.) and the National Liberals, of whom Iggers treats in some detail Dilthey, Max Weber, Troeltsch, Meinecke, and Naumann, to the beginning of racist nationalism,[13] dictatorship (e.g., Meinecke's *temporäre Vertrauensdiktatur*)[14] and to politico-historical anti-Semitism even beyond World War II.[15] Meinecke recapitulated in his own person the development that Iggers traces and that Meinecke himself narrated in his famous book "Cosmopolitanism and the National State."[16] (His *Diltheyan empathy* with his historical material is presumably responsible for his uncritical attitude, contrary to Iggers.) Naturally all of those political ideologies were always elaborated in characteristically "German," that is, "profound," even in metaphysical, terms.[17]

In the era with which we are here mostly concerned, the Second Reich, German Christians, increasingly before and particularly after 1870, were in a different situation from that of the Jews both politically and philosophico-religiously. Politically they had now acquired, through the accretions of size and power extending over half a century, something close to what since Napoleon's time they had striven for, namely an unified Germany. On this score, therefore, it was tempting for them to believe that their political ideal had become a political reality, or something quite close to it.[18] Of course, it was primarily a Prussian Germany and, therefore, as independent Austria (the Austro-Hungarian Empire) and Bismarck's *Kulturkampf* exemplify, a dominantly Protestant Germany.[19] On the religious and theological score the central Christian doctrine of the incarnation, which always lies underneath and often even on the surface of Hegel's secularized, philosophized theology, easily seduced them into an even more absolutist position: (1) if, as they believe, God and the world have become identical at one time at least and in one place, namely in the person of Jesus, then it is in principle possible, and the doctrines of the *corpus Christi mysticum* and of the second coming in fact announce, that God, on the one hand, and more time and space, on the other, can become or have become identical again; (2) if, furthermore, as again they believe, now in their capacity as German Protestants, Protestant Germany is the highest and best, perhaps the ultimate or near-ultimate, expression of Christian truth, then the realization, either in process or in a state of near-completion, of a culturally and politically unified Germany constitutes the *corpus Christi* at this stage and at least a close approach to the second coming; therefore, (3) and in short, the Prusso-German Second Empire incarnates the universal Christian truth, if not in all concrete details then certainly in its essential spirit?[20] (The possible gap between the "actuality" of the essential spirit of "the end of history," that is, the millennium, the third and last thousand-year-long Reich, and the vestiges of pre-eschatological but "mere" "reality" was also the point in Hegel on which subsequent interpreters parted as to whether or not he still had room for an open, ongoing history beyond his own period.) With the equation "the spirit of Germanism" = "the holy ghost," by dint of the symmetry of the equation, one could infer from the nature of Germany to the truth of Christianity as well as from the truth of Christianity to the destiny of Germany. (John B. Freed's important "Reflections on the German Medieval Nobility"[21] shows how the proto-Nazi and Nazi historiography of medieval Germany *Führertum* continues to be effective even among non-German historians. He concludes[22] with some comments on German historiography at large, using primarily J. Sheehan. What Freed/Sheehan then say about the ideology of the intellectuals of the Second Reich is a somewhat more secularly formulated version of the formula "the spirit of Germany = the holy ghost." "The unquestioned assumption that the unification of Germany in the form of the Second Reich was the inevitable destiny of the German folk. . . ."[23]

Historians in our time have noticed how, as the mid-nineteenth century neared, the emancipationist thrust of classical, eighteenth-century German, enlightened philosophy grew ever weaker. Now, in the second half of the century and under the drastically altered politico-historical circumstances, the mainstreams of philosophy and theology repoliticized themselves, but it was a repoliticization that, in one way or another but always to a very high degree, justified the establishment and the status quo.

Patriotic German Jews were tempted to join the national and intellectual *Einsegnung* /"ritual confirmation," the chorus of jingoistic "Amens" and "Hallelujahs." Indeed, there were some who did. On the other hand, it was characteristically usually Jews who, in philosophy as in politics, in the second half of the century sounded, in Otto Liebmann's famous phrase, the call to "return to Kant." And by general consent it is then the greatest of the Jewish philosophers of the closing nineteenth and the opening of the twentieth centuries, Hermann Cohen, who carried out the program of philosophically and Jewishly reopening the "infinite" gap between ideality and reality and of explicating in technical detail what the actionable consequences of that gap are for science, ethics, aesthetics, religion, and for social policy. His disciples were typically Jews—Germans, like Ernst Cassirer, and Eastern-Europeans, down to Samuel Atlas and, in a more complicated way, the contemporary R. Joseph Baer Soloveitchik—so that other schools of neo-Kantianism, which typically sought some sort of compromise between Kantianism and Hegelianism, spoke of "the Marburg School" as a Jewish distortion. For Cohen Judaism was "religion of reason" par excellence, and the task of the Jewish people was not only to "purify," to "idealize," the actual Germany but also[24] to carry Jewish "ethical monotheism" through history and to the ends of the earth.

Generally it is true that Kantianism in this period split between Germans and German Jews. The canonical Academy-edition of Kant's collected works demonstratively left out the Marburg School from among its editors, so that the "Cassirer-edition" had to be initiated during World War I. The census of Jews serving in the German army[25] directed attention again at that time to "the Jewish question," and Cohen and Natorp almost came to a basic break over this, which they avoided only by strong, reciprocal efforts.[26] Even more importantly, a wave of ethnicist and actually racist Kantianism washed over cultured Germany. That wave had been prepared by a century of German cultural endeavors to "aryanize" Christianity—that is, to show that Christianity was born in Greece, not in Judaea (as Hegel's youthful essay put it in its very title: "Athens and Judea—Should Judea be the Teuton's Fatherland?" 1795, and as later he was to identify Jesus with Socrates; cf. also Goethe,[27] Eugen Dühring,[28] etc.). The ideologist Houston Stewart Chamberlain, Richard Wagner's son-in-law, had systematized this well before the World War,[29] but now, at the height of the war, even so good a philosopher as Bruno Bauch, one of the two chief editors of *Kant-Studien*, published an article, "About the Concept of a Nation,"[30] in which he pitted a "Jewish (misinterpretation of) Kant" against a Teutonic Kant—therefore, of course, hereticizes Cohen, Cohen's (Jewish) followers, and "Marburg"—and wants to separate the Jewish and the German peoples neatly, sending each off in its respective Teutonic and Zionist direction. During this nasty episode Cohen and Cassirer resigned from the *Kant Gesellschaft*. It is an eerie anticipation of the catastrophic historic separation of the German and the Jewish peoples and of the bifurcation of the historic image of Hermann Cohen into the philosopher and the Jew.

Germany was afflicted by another pronounced economic crisis around 1900. Not accidentally this crisis was accompanied by strong antisocialist policies in society and by strong antirationalist forces in German culture. Therefore, also all of the developments that we have broadly sketched up to this point came to a head in the twenty years that surround the beginning of the present century, what Dubnow, in the subtitle of Volume X of his great historical work calls "The Age of the Second Reaction (1880–1914)." The best-known episode in this climax is Adolf von Harnack's "Essence of Christianity," with its extrapolations (Ernst Troeltsch, etc.) and the numerous reactions it evoked especially among liberal Jews, peaking in Leo Baeck's "Essence of Judaism." There is a good deal of secondary literature about this episode, and I will treat of it, therefore, rather summarily.[31] For philosophical and historical reasons of my own I am more interested in a parallel debate, which took place within the Marburg School of neo-Kantianism itself in the first 15 years of the century between the very Jewish Cohen and his very Protestant disciple/colleague Paul Natorp, and I can offer an overview of that debate that is either unknown or very little known to most.

Before turning to such specifics, however, we have to understand a little bit more fully the cultural situation of the Jewish community and of its intelligentsia at this juncture. The Russian pogroms of 1881 had flabbergasted Jewry, and, as is well-known, the reactions to these events among Eastern-European Jewry, with some overlap to Western Jewry, had polarized to the Left in the form of Jewish political radicalisms (communism, the Band, territorialists, etc.), to the Right in the form of Zionist nationalism, and to forms mixed of the two in the middle. At the same time a new wave of German conservatism and of political and/or racist antisemitism arose in Germany and France, whose symbolic climax was reached in the "Dreyfus-Affair." Western culture generally was going through a phase of "fin de siècle" pessimism—as Sheehan puts it in his political study: not only Meinecke perceived decline and twilight; "the newly popular writings of Nietzsche and Schopenhauer, novels such as Thomas Mann's 'Buddenbrooks,' and social analyses like

Tönnies' 'Gemeinschaft und Gesellschaft' all point to this diffuse sense of uneasiness within German culture. Even Max Weber, who was much too tough-minded to embrace the fantasies sometimes provoked by this fashionable pessimism, based his view of social change on the belief that 'rationalization,' once thought to be the source of liberation and enlightenment, was in fact producing even more restrictive limits on individual freedom."[32] A rising wave of Jewish realistic self-assertion, therefore, also set in to accompany the other ethnic, linguistic, cultural, and political self-assertions that were spreading through Europe.[33]

It is in this situation at the turn of the century that Adolf von Harnack affirmed, in an essentially Hegelian fashion, that German Protestantism = the true spirit of Christianity = the quintessence of the Prusso-German state. One inference from this equation was that all other political and religious forms were mere historical atavisms = Zombies, the traditional "Wandering Jew." Another inference was that whatever strengthened Germany strengthened Christianity and was, therefore, a divine duty. Most importantly, the equation, simply put: "real Germany = metaphysical Christianity," had the obvious advantage that it could claim to be both a descriptive as well as a prescriptive, an empirical as well as a normative, truth. As Hegel put it, "the true now is the actuality of true eternity."[34] In Iggers' less philosophical and theological language, "German historicism assumed that the existing institutions and positive laws themselves represented rationality and morality."[35] In Troeltsch's proclamation "Only history reveals value."[36] *Am deutschen Wesen soll die Welt genesen*. Or to put it aphoristically: these people wanted to have their "ought"-cake and eat the "is"-cake, too.

Parallel to the Harnack-Baeck debate, which we have mentioned and to which we shall briefly return, we may also look at the less well-known Troeltsch-Marburg neo-Kantianism polemic.[37] They are of a piece. Troeltsch reviewed Hermann Cohen's "The Concept of Religion within the System of Philosophy" in the *Theologische Literaturzeitung* rather late, in 1918.[38] He comes to the conclusion that he, Troeltsch, and Cohen cannot really understand one another, because as Jew and as Protestant German respectively their histories are too different, and, of course, truth and value are produced if not by then certainly in history—he calls them "historico-psychologically conditioned."[39] This being the case, the obvious question must arise whether other Protestant Germans, like Wilhelm Herrmann and Paul Natorp, must not be in error when they identify themselves more than he does with Cohen's "Jewish thinking."

Troeltsch answers this question in the affirmative, with varying degrees of irony, rejection, and sympathy. Natorp is said (rightly, as it turned out) to be somewhat alien and mystical in comparison to standard Marburgianism. Herrmann is ironically described as "one of the deeper representatives of Protestant theology." In any case, the philosophico-theological difference between the Jew and the German Christian is (again rightly and well) said to be that Cohen has no "real community with God," nor has he a notion of divine "substantiality," and he totally rejects any idea of religion as autonomous in relationship to philosophy and ethics beyond "the rational idea of God" and beyond internationalist, messianic socialism. In all these respects and others Cohen goes counter, said Troeltsch, to the German-Christian historical and cultural substantiality, that is, German actuality.

The Marburg School replied directly to Troeltsch. Cohen himself published a polemic on Troeltsch's sociological and, therefore, to Cohen's way of thinking empiristic theology in what was in effect his own journal, *Neue jüdische Monatshefte*.[40] In this short piece Cohen calls Troeltsch's thought "materialist" sociology. He declares both German racism and Jewish nationalism the enemy, and he continues to insist that the religion of the Biblical prophets is identical with Kant's ethics. (We must keep in mind that these polemics were going on inside Germany at the height of World War I, 1916–1917, just while a new, strong wave of anti-Semitism was rising—namely, the census of Jews serving in the army, the Bruno Bauch-episode in the *Kant-Studien* previously mentioned, etc.) Indeed, just now Cohen had been moved to exclaim in print: "What has happened to German liberalism?!"[41]

More systematically Cohen's favorite Jewish-religious disciple, Benzion Kellermann, wrote a monograph, "Der ethische Monotheismus der Propheten und seine soziologische Würdigung," which he submitted for publication to *Logos* but, when rejected there, he published as a separatum.[42] The argument boils down to this: the canonical Bible-criticism of the time, for example, Cohen's admired colleague Julius Wellhausen, held that the Biblical literary prophets had arrived at an ethical universalism which was to remain for all time the absolute ideal of true religion[43] (though, according to this scholarship, postexilic and Rabbinic Judaism were then regarded as a "Pharisaic" degeneration of prophetic religion, and pristine Christianity had to come along to purify religion again—a process repeated by the Reformation in relation to the Roman Church and by German Protestant Liberalism with respect to the established, institutionalized churches). Troeltsch rejects this view of the Hebrew prophets and, instead, puts them back in their particularistic, historical, ethnic, and sociological contexts (Max Weber, Werner Sombart, and the "pariah-people" are adduced)[44]— as, indeed, Troeltsch reads all religious history, including even Jesus himself, as superstructural expressions of historical sociology, and thus its latest (and highest) expression, German liberal Protestantism, is and ought to result from current German real politics.[45] Cohen/Kellermann, to the contrary, insist,[46] on the historical score, that Wellhausen's thesis of prophetic universalism was correct, and they insist, on the philosophical score, that history is a question not of Dilthey's *Verstehen*, which has to be subjective and empiricistic, but of Kantian rational, ethical ideals, that are in turn identical with the values of the prophets[47] and in the light of which present history, like all history, ought to be criticized and reformed. (My own view is, anyway, that these liberal Jews made the mistake, in varying degrees, of conceding to Bible-criticism that *Spätjudentum*, that is, Judaism after the literary prophets and through "Pharisaism" and Talmudism, was a decline from "prophetic Judaism," whereas, in fact, when rightly known and understood, Rabbinic Judaism is the full exfoliation of Biblical Judaism at its highest. This is the *emunuh tzeruphah* "refined faith" from the prophets through and beyond Nachman Krochmal.)

Generally, Jews obviously would not accept the exhaustive equation "Protestant Christianity = the German state = the consummation of all human history." There were too many factors in this equation that violated their most fundamental values. They had to choose from among basically five possible alternative options with which that equation confronted them: (A) they might accept the proposition that Germany was in fact (a close approximation of) the ideal state but would add that its spirit, its "essence," was either Judaism or, at most, the Jewish component in Christianity (i.e., "purified Christianity" is Judaism, certainly purified Judaism);[48] (B) they might look on Germany as merely another historical state in the endless succession of social organizations in human history, without tying it positively either to Christianity or to Judaism; (C) they might use the same structure that Harnack used, that is, ultimate truth is incorporated in a particular historical people (comp. the notion of *Volksgeist*) but instantiate it in the Jewish people and in (Jewish) truth. Jewish option (C) would, however, have to differ from Harnack's analog in that, of course, even the notion of Jewish peoplehood, in the contemporary sense, was difficult to instantiate, and certainly there was not even the beginning of a Jewish state as its historical realization. Option (D) would simply stand pat—that is, hold on to the original, eighteenth-century "enlightened," rationalist-ethical cosmopolitanism and demand as well as work for a better, fuller realization of its political program. In other words, this approach, while sharing the disappointment and even disillusionment with how the initial program had been realized or defeated during the course of the nineteenth century, inferred not that the program was wrong-headed but that its execution had been at best faulty and perhaps even prevaricatory. There is finally option (E), which would accept the ideology of German Protestantism and submit to Treitschke's demand of 1880 that truly emancipated German Jews also would be baptized as Protestants.

The bulk of the Jewish liberal response to the dilemma that, typically, Treitschke and von Harnack had put before them at that time chose option A. In this manner they were able to combine German patriotism with Jewish faithfulness. But one has to note that in the best expression of that view, for example, Leo Baeck's "Essence of Judaism," the formulaic definition of the Jewish part of the option, namely "mystery and commandment," while holding to Mendelssohn's and Cohen's universalistic ethicism under the heading of "command," adds the metaphysical factor of "mystery," that is, the election of Israel as a "religious people." That metaphysical actor was meant to respond to the then-spreading criticism among self-affirming Jews of what they perceived as "abstract," ultra-universalistic rationalism. (Christianity, on the other hand, is criticized by Baeck as what he later, 1922, called "Romantic religion"[49]—that is, the drastic reduction of ethicism in favor of the expansion of "mystery.") If one reformulated Baeck's talk of the election of Israel in more rationalistic terms, as Cohen himself was doing on his own, the fundamental postures of Baeck and Cohen were in fact very similar in theology (whatever their other differences).[50]

Option C, in several different versions, was elected by a number of intellectuals and has come to fruition really only later in the twentieth century. The different versions have in common that, whatever their sociological infrastructure and their metaphysical superstructure, they all put their worldly hope and their spiritual faith in the Jewish people, where Protestant Germans were putting theirs in the German, Orthodox Christians in the Russian people, ceteris paribus. (The foundations for such ideologies had been laid earlier in the century by liberal nationalist thinkers like Herder and von Humboldt, and Abraham Geiger[51] among the Jewish theologians.) The Jews, for reasons mentioned earlier, tended to retain the cosmopolitan framework for such Romantic nationalism longer than the bulk of the Germans. Such liberal Jewish nationalism, mainly, though not exclusively, Zionist, itself came in different versions: Achad Ha'am's secularized Jewish religiosity, Martin Buber's respiritualized version of Achad Ha'am, even the emphatically pagan, Nietzschean nationalism of the poets of the first generation of the Hebrew renaissance, Saul Tchernikowsky, M. Berdyczewski (bin-Gorion), down to the German, Oskar Goldberg, and the Russian, Ze'ev Jabotinsky.[52] (How also Jewish "liberalism" will slide off either to the Right or to the Left is then fully symbolized by the later political platforms of Jabotinsky and Buber in the history of Zionism and for the State of Israel.) The very young Franz Rosenzweig, while he was still holding somewhere in the middle between Hermann Cohen, his teacher, and Buber, later his associate, sighted the target of what I am calling option C dead-center when he criticized Buber's "folkishness" under the title "Atheist Theology." (The mature Rosenzweig joined that cultural move toward a new "realism," away from Cohen's rationalism, and used Jewish peoplehood as one of the very pillars of his philosophical theology, without, however, drawing Buber's Zionist inferences therefrom.)

Hermann Cohen himself stuck to his guns—what I have designated as option D. That is, he adhered to Kantian/neo-Kantian cosmopolitanism, now including (ethical) socialism, and in fact identified this with rational religion, to be transcendentally derived in its purity "from the sources of Judaism" and in less pure forms also from Protestant Christianity and, indeed, from all other historico-cultural configurations, primarily German culture as defined by him (Nicolas of Cusa, Luther, Mozart, Kant, Beethoven, Schiller, social democracy, etc.) that were in line with Platonic-Maimonidean-Kantian ethicism. The widespread impression that Cohen was, or became in August 1914, a jingoistic worshipper of the German state is largely false. He always insisted that the Kantian-Jewish ideal of the good society was, and had to be, infinitely superior to and, therefore, always radically critical of every given reality, including the reality of Protestant Prussian Germany. (This was, therefore, also the decisive role that Cohen assigned to the law and its philosophy,[53] and this underlies his ongoing polemics with Rudolf Stammler, Max Weber, and even Hans Kelsen.)[54]

Some of the members and associates of the Marburg School not only remained loyal to Cohen's position but radicalized it in his spirit. The political dimension of this syndrome is represented by the socialist activists, like Eduard Bernstein, Kurt Eisner, Karl Vorländer, Dimitri Gawronski, Austro-socialism, and so on—most, though not all, of them Jews.[55] (Görland at an early stage also belonged to this group.) The philosophical and Jewish-religious dimension is represented in very different ways by people like Ernst Cassirer,[56] Benzion Kellermann, Leo Rosenzweig, Sinai Ucko, Samuel Atlas. The problem of former students of his who chose what I call option C, that is, who wanted to find some sort of "reality," usually an ethnic-cultural or political entity, in which to locate the unicity of value and worldliness—of whom I have so far only mentioned the Jewish example of Franz Rosenzweig—is, in fact, most instructively exemplified in the long-lasting and deep-ploughing controversy between the two chief heads of the Marburg School themselves, Cohen and Natorp. (One could say that Natorp and Rosenzweig were the Christian and the Jewish paradigms respectively of the electors of option C in the most sophisticated forms.)

We are, let us remember, at the turn of the century. The spirit of the age seems, as we have seen, to be changing: a new realism (in the philosophical forms of naturalism, positivisms, "life-philosophy," etc., what Holzhey calls "the anthropological turn")[57] demanded that philosophy descend from its ethereal idealism and come to grips with the earthly realities of contemporary life. In 1892 Cohen had said about this changing *Zeitgeist* that it was "the bad spirit of the cult of persons, which has of late taken the place of the celebration of ideas"[58] and in "The Ethical and Historical Motifs of Religion"[59] he still warned against the revolt against ideas in philosophy, culture, politics, and religion and contrasted the then prominent "search for the historical Jesus" in Protestant thought with the Deuteronomic condemnation of a visible God. Nonetheless, he was forced to address this problematique further.

Paul Natorp had been Cohen's student and disciple; he became his closest colleague, associate and friend. Withal, there were real strains in their relationship, largely due to their very different cultural backgrounds—the one a very self-conscious Jew, the other equally a Protestant. Although Natorp always advocated strict Marburg neo-Kantianism while Cohen was alive, these differences nonetheless asserted themselves increasingly as the years went by even in matters of philosophy and politics. After World War I Natorp took a philosophical direction that diverged drastically and publicly from Cohen's.

In 1894 Natorp published "Religion within the Bounds of Humanity—A Chapter toward the Foundation of Social Politics." As the very title makes clear, it was in overwhelming measure a philosophical theology in the spirit of Marburg neo-Kantianism. Despite this, it granted a certain degree of autonomy from ethics and philosophy to religion, which Cohen's later "Ethics of the Pure Will" (1904, 1907) would still reject. This led to a whole series of exchanges between the two. Cordial and even in essential agreement on philosophical fundamentals as they remained, they tried to settle their differences in this exchange: Cohen's "Religion and Morality" (1907), Natorp's original book with a new epilogue that basically addressed itself to Cohen (1908),[60] Cohen's "The Concept of Religion within the System of Philosophy" (1915), all sorts of notes and correspondences between them on this subject, which have fortunately been found in Natorp's estate, and finally Cohen's "Religion of Reason out of the Sources of Judaism" itself. When Cohen wrote to Natorp in 1914[61] that he was writing his current religious works, "worin ich mich mit Ihnen ins Einvernehmen auseinandersetzen will," it was quite true that an intimate and drawn-out discussion was taking place, which was fed for both of them by their religious as well as philosophical sources. The original issue between Cohen and Natorp on this score may be summarized as follows. To be sure, argued Natorp, also religion must, of course, remain under the ultimate rule of reason, and reason is restricted exhaustively within the boundaries of the three human activities that are verifiable in the phenomenal universe—science, ethics, and culture. However, Cohen's own doctrine of pure feeling should not be limited to art. As the (different and notably Christian) Kantianism of Schleiermacher and their contemporary Rudolf Otto show, feeling has a wider domain in religion, in which the individual and even God are individuated—become, like art-objects, objects of experience—rather than being infinite values, regulatives, toward which we can and ought to strive but which we cannot experientially attain. In religion, therefore, God and man are, as it were, concrete universals, or, as Natorp put it in the aforementioned appendix, entitled "Feeling as the Root of Religion"[62]: "Ultimately it all depends only on the fact of (the) demand for eternal rest, a rest in the eternal."[63] That is, the pursuit of the ideal, though into infinity, must be felt to have been completed—thus to end in an (Hegelian) "actual infinity."[64] The triumph of the good must be guaranteed in fact, not only imposed as a task. As Natorp cites their common friend and colleague, Wilhelm Hermann, the Protestant, liberal theologian, if the self be a task, for example, then there has to be a self, so that it may have a task.[65] Though he generally agrees with Cohen, Natorp wants to stress more than the latter the present-time function of infinity, whereas Cohen always wants to stress the radical incompletion of present-time in the perspective of eternity.[66]

Wilhelm Herrmann, the third in their band at the University of Marburg, did, indeed, argue very much to the same effect. For him, too, religion was (in a very Protestant, individualistic yet socially engaged way) the personal experience, thoroughly and even historically Christian, of the infinite God, of the human self, as well as of the moral obligations that he held issued forth from the encounter between God and man. In this spirit he reviewed Cohen's "Ethics of the Pure Will."[67]

Fortunately, we have Cohen's own notes to these arguments.[68] He rejects all rest and reliance on alleged experience (*Erlebnis*), of "life," self, and God. He insists to the contrary: "Rest in the Eternal? No, eternal work,"[69] and by "work" he means moral effort. "Micah says it all, in fact" (i.e., Micah 6:8: "It has been told you, oh man, what is good and what the Lord requires of you—to love mercy, to do justice, and to walk humbly before your God").[70] In other words, Cohen perseveres in proposing that "God" means the endless tasks of human morality, and he does not even hide (at least from himself, in his private notes) that, when his Christian friends and colleagues insist on the "reality" of God and of the religious experience, rather than on their normativity, they really are giving expression "ultimately to Christian pantheism (i.e., the doctrine that God/the ideal has been 'incarnated' in a man/ the actual) that here, too, substitutes feeling as the Ur-force of life for ethics"[71]; that is, it is "pantheistic identity."[72] (Cohen's negative reply to Natorp is accompanied by a positive, philosophical doctrine of the relationship between the human individual and [the idea of] God, but this is a complicated and technical subject, which I shall here leave aside.)

In Christian and in general, nonreligious circles a few sparse attempts were made to appreciate Cohen's work on its own terms—for example, Hinrich Knittermeyer's review of *Religion of Reason* in *Christliche Welt*, 1922. Cohen's identification of religious messianism with ethical, non-Marxist or at most neo-Marxist socialism clearly made an impact on Paul Tillich and contributed to the rise of religious, Christian socialism during the period of the Weimar Republic. (Martin Buber also transmitted this influence, in his way.) But the bulk of non-Jewish reactions, philosophical as well as religious, went (like the Jewish ones) in the direction of either reading him as a precursor of a new ontologistic realism or of criticizing him for not having been such a precursor. As Buber had used the whole structure of fellow-man/co-man/correlational-man in order to develop his own "dialogicism" of *I and Thou* (without acknowledging his indebtedness),[73] so Karl Löwith pushed this line of thought further toward a religious personalism.[74] Many years later he, too, claimed that the "Religion of Reason . . ." went "beyond the System"[75] and argued[76] that the purely conceptual God was, in the first place, insufficient for religious and historical purposes and could, in the second place, be found concretely and universally in nature. Albert Görland, in turn, went off in such a re-ontologizing, quasi-pantheistic direction. For instance, he wrote a book as late as 1947, *Die Grundweisen des Menschseins*,[77] in which he makes the punning distinction between *unendlich* (infinite, literally "unending") and *ohnendlich* (infinite, literally "without end"), the former what Kant called "indefinite," the latter what Hegel then called "actual infinite" and identified by Görland as "the all-life" of ultimate truth and reality, that is, God, that, contrary to Kant, can in fact be reached by spirit as its "origin"[78] and in which man is safely at home/geborgen.[79]

"Community" is then the bearer of ethics. Natorp himself came to deviate so much from Cohen's philosophy after the war and Cohen's death, in a mystical, re-ontologizing, semi-pantheistic direction, that his own later philosophizing, as exemplified in the second and totally revised edition of his "Plato" (Platorp), with its "Metacritical Appendix: Logos–Psyche–Eros" (the hyphens might just as well be equal-signs) and talk about "the ontically being of being,"[80] became the bridge from "Marburg" to Hartmann,[81] Heimsoeth,[82] and even to Husserl and Heidegger. Ortega y Gasset had earlier left Marburg in order to study with Husserl, although he always preserved some piety for Cohen.[83] Roger A. Johnson's "The Origins of Demythologization—Philosophy and Historiography in the Theology of Rudolf Bultmann,"[84] chapter 2, "The Philosophical Origins of Demythologizing: Marburg neo-Kantianism,"[85] traces the Christian theological side of this post-Cohennian development with special reference to Bultmann, without forgetting Karl Barth,[86] Wilhelm Herrmann, Natorp, and Gogarten, and so on.[87] What happened to Marburgian critical epistemology at the hands of these existentialist thinkers might be described as a reversal of prefixes: they acknowledge the basic distinction between law-ruled explanations, what is called "objectification," and, on the other hand, subjective, psychological "experience" (Natorp's emphasis on *Erlebnis* vs. *Erfahrung*[88] and Gadamer's extrapolations therefrom),[89] but, as Johnson puts it,[90] whereas in Marburg "the concept of objectifying appears as a creative, dynamic term laden with the substance of being. . . .

In Bultmann this ontological pattern is reversed. Objectification, in all its spheres, is stripped of any positive ontological significance and is left standing as an empty shell, bereft of Being"; now, to the contrary, Being is found, however brokenly, in private, nonlaw-ruled experiences, outside the scientific, causal universe, in "subjectivity." What it is that subjectivity finds may be religiously transcendent reality in Bultmann—Being in Heidegger[91] and Gadamer[92]—or God/ Christ in Barth.[93]

A belated and deeply ambivalent manifestation of this reaction to Hermann Cohen is still to be found in Joseph Klein, "Die Grundlagen der Ethik in der Philosophie Hermann Cohens und Paul Natorps—eine Kritik des Neukantianismus," 1976.[94] This thorough and intelligent treatment, written by an N. Hartmann admirer, sometime Roman-Catholic, was written originally early in the Nazi years, published at that time with prudential selectivity,[95] and argues a very complex and highly dubious thesis: (1) strict Marburg neo-Kantianism never reaches "reality"[96]; (2) being essentially Jewish, it is an ideology of the "Judaism of emancipation and assimilation"[97]; (3) often basing himself on F. Rosenzweig, Klein subscribes to the thesis of an "old Hermann Cohen,"[98] who found his way back to the reality of his (Jewish) people; (4) the (non-Jewish) Germans in the Marburg School, on the other hand (e.g., Görland,[99] Kinkel,[100] and especially Natorp),[101] unlike Cohen, did not find their ways back to their (German) people (although "the old Natorp" did go in a new but equally unsatisfactory direction)[102]; and (5) what is really needed, therefore, is a *philosophia teutonica* for the Volk,[103] which, as Klein ends his book,[104] "is no more identical with the Enlightenment-impoverished and ethico-juridically impoverished Jewish philosophy of religion of the old Cohen than with the pantheistic philosophy of coincidence (identity) of the late Natorp."[105]

We may at this point make some meta-historical observations about the history of liberalism in Germany. We have taken a bird's-eye view of German (and, indeed, wider) history—intellectual and in some measure political—from the eighteenth to the twentieth century. The last book we have had occasion to refer to, Joseph Klein's, brought us, as it happens, down to the Nazi era and beyond. James Sheehan's book, often cited in our study, covers in its way the same ground that we have covered. He, too, ends his analysis by summarizing the aftereffects of Wilhelmine liberalism in the Weimar Republic and the Nazi end—from National Liberals and even Left Liberals to the *Volkspartei* and from the latter's Right-wing to the Nazi party in 1930 and thereafter.[106] He ends his study with these words: "The liberal constituency proved to be especially susceptible to Nazism after 1930. This is, I think, the clearest indication of German liberalism's bankruptcy and the most consequential effect of liberalism's failure to provide the ideas and institutions with which Germany could understand and master the problems posed by their nation's long journey to modernity."[107]

Three quasi-metahistorical observations seem justified when one tries to evaluate the reception-history of Hermann Cohen's philosophy at the hands of non-Jewish Germans and, together with Cohen, also of radically ethicist Jewish liberalism in the course of the twentieth century: (1) just as immediately after Kant's death, and even during the last years of his life, the climactic work of his Critical philosophy, the Third "Critique," was interpreted or attacked so as to develop the "concretism" of Absolute Idealism—also called "the German philosophy"—so also Cohen's final work was immediately interpreted or attacked so as to develop a new "realism." (2) Non-Jewish Germans and Jews took this new realism in different and ultimately in opposite directions—at least politically and geographically. (3) The image of Hermann Cohen in subsequent history has really remained totally bifurcated to this day[108]: general philosophy knows Cohen (when it knows him at all) only as the father and grandest exponent of Marburg neo-Kantianism—a movement that fell apart during the early Weimar Republic, was suppressed with increasing vehemence in the later years and, of course, destroyed under the Nazi regime as both Jewish and "Left-liberal" (J.M. Bochenski rightly says: "The rule of National Socialism dealt (the Marburg School) a fatal blow, because its representatives, largely of Jewish extraction (?), were fiercely persecuted"[109]), and has been rehabilitated as a foundation for contemporary philosophizing by only very small circles (in Germany especially "transcendental philosophy"), while, on the other hand, Jews know him only as a Jewish thinker, for good and usually for ill. That Cohen's Jewish essays were collected and separately published under the editorship of Franz Rosenzweig, while his philosophical and political essays were separately collected by Ernst Cassirer and Albert Görland,[110] despite the fact that all of them were written in chronological and thematic interconnection, heavily contributes to the bizarre result of two Hermann Cohens in reception-history: on one side the German philosopher, and on the other side the Jew. Nothing could have been more obnoxious to him!

One would like to be able to make a fourth meta-historical observation, when one writes as a Jew, as this writer does—namely that the Jewish stream that flowed out of Hermann Cohen's fountain preserved his insistence on the radical primacy of ethics and his liberalism, while the German stream unfortunately took a metaphysical and wildly historicist direction. There would be some evidence to substantiate such an interpretation. Knittermeyer, for example, came to trace himself back via Heimsoeth and Natorp—thus conspicuously omitting all the Jews, and, even as Rosenzweig kidnapped Cohen's "Religion of Reason..." for his own metaphysics, so Knittermeyer and Natorp even wanted to claim that Cohen's "Ethics of the Pure Will" was already "on the way to metaphysics and ontology."[111] Friedrich Niewöhner, in a study entitled "Primacy of Ethics, or, Epistemological Grounding of Ethics? Theses regarding the Kant-Reception in Jewish Philosophy,"[112] even makes the claim proudly that one would here like to advance.[113] Hans Ludwig Ollig, "Religion und Freiheitsglaube—Zur Problematik von Hermann Cohens später Religionsphilosophie" (!) as late as 1979 and once again pits the "German ontological Kant-interpretation" against Cohen[114] and makes no bones about the Christian, theological stake in this.[115] Similar treatments are continuing to be published in Germany.[116] But our survey of the Jewish Cohen-reception shows that such a claim is actually contrary to fact. Jews, too, as the twentieth century grew older, increasingly insisted that "life," survival, self-assertion, and so on, were not only more important but also more ultimate than reason, ethics and universal fraternity. Since World War II in particular two extraordinary developments describe the thrust of contemporary Jewish history—the establishment of the State of Israel and the ensconcement of the bulk of surviving Jewry in the middle-classes. Both these conditions provide more comfort in the real world than one could have dreamt of in or before 1945. One of the most striking current formulations of Judaism under these circumstances is Michael Wyschogrod's "The Body of Faith—Judaism as Corporeal Election,"[117] whose very title exhibits its thrust toward incarnationalism. Wyschogrod affirms the divine physicality of the people and the land of Israel (and he does not mind conceding the Christian doctrine of the incarnation as an option either). The reception of Hermann Cohen in Hebrew, in Israel, and in Zionism goes in the same direction: the peoplehood and the Land of Israel are so decisive that a philosophy of Judaism in which they play little or no part is thereby *eo ipso* disqualified.[118] Whether, under such conditions, Jews can renew and continue their historic affirmation of the wide gap between how things ought to be and how they actually are may then be the central question for Judaism and Jewish life in the foreseeable future.[119]

Whether in Germany, on the other hand, especially since Willy Brandt's chancellorship, a fundamental "Scandinavian turn" has really taken place not only in politics but also in culture and even in religion, and whether rationalistic liberalism, in the Left-wing and American sense of this term, has finally become an integral force in German thinking, feeling, and willing,[120] or whether their histories will continue to overwhelm Germany and Europe—these may well be the decisive questions for the future of Central Europe. As Theodor Heuss said in 1959,[121] "the decisive question is for Germany to emerge from the romanticism of the 19th century," and, one might add, to re-appropriate the rational, cosmopolitan values of the eighteenth-century Enlightenment, which reached its pinnacle in Immanuel Kant. To conclude with a moving statement by Freed/Sheehan,[122] whom we have had occasion to use repeatedly throughout the present study, it could also be put this way: "Above all, the time has come for medievalists as well as for scholars of modern Germany . . . to abandon the primacy of politics and to accept the diversity of the German-speaking world's rich heritage in all of its aspects (Jews as one of them). The legacy of Bismarck's defunct state does not have to shape forever our understanding of a thousand years of German history."

Chapter 15 | 1987

The Religious Stake in Modern Philosophy of Infinity

Hegel's philosophy is from beginning to end a secularized religious philosophy—indeed, a secularized Christian philosophy. As such it is also a sustained argument against Kant(ianism), and the latter is in fundamental ways identified with Judaism by Hegel himself and in subsequent Hegelianisms.

In the philosophy of the mature Hegel a central tenet emerges from the battle he wages against Kant—the dichotomy between what he calls respectively "good infinity" and "bad infinity," with a great many systematic ramifications, metaphysical, logical, epistemological, mathematical, and ethical. Underneath all its various formulations it is in fact a question of the nature of God.

"Bad infinity" is, on Hegel's definition, an infinity constituted by an interminable series. (It is thus what Kant calls "indefiniteness," rather than infinity.) In it every x is followed by an $x + 1$. It is a mere "mechanical," additive function and can, by definition, not come to a conclusion.[1] "Good infinity," on the other hand, is an entity—infinite but, as it were, self- enclosed.[2] One example of Hegel's bad infinity are endless human "needs."[3] Good infinity, on the other hand, in turn and even yet not a very intuitive idea, can perhaps be illustrated by several similes: the circumference of that ancient symbol of infinity, the circle, is, in Hegel's sense, infinite, but it encloses a determinate area[4] (the line is "bent round"),[5] unlike an infinite ("bad") line, which gets nowhere and circumscribes no area; a black hole approaches an infinity of mass-pressure, but this mass-pressure, instead of exploding and dispersing its matter into infinite space (bad), "implodes" into itself and thus creates a (good) physicalist entity; an object standing in front of a mirror and then infinitely remirrored in a series of mirrors placed at an angle to the first

---

First published in *Daat* 22–23 (1987), 63–83. Dedicated respectfully to the memory of Professor Moshe Schwarcz.

will decrease in size as the mirroring process continues *an infinitum* without reflecting any greater details in it (bad), whereas such an object, if placed in the center of a circle of minors, will also be reflected and re-reflected an infinite number of times, but, in the first place, the object (given a proper set of eyes) will be able to see, and thus "reappropriate" for itself, all its images, and, in the second place, a literally innumerable number of aspects of itself will thus be directed back at it from all directions (good).

We see thus that a good infinity reabsorbs into itself all of its external relations; indeed, it "sublates" its relations and brings them, and itself in the process, "home."[6] "It never leaves its own ground."[7] It completes the dialectical process: having started out "in itself," it extruded its relations "for (to) others," and now it has achieved its fullest "real(!)ization" "in-and-for-itself."[8] It contains all its relations within itself and is, therefore, also called "intensive," as distinguished from "extensive," infinity.[9] As the simile of the black hole may illustrate most concretely, the infinite has thus taken up residence in the finite ("in-finite").[10] Transcendence, that which is beyond the individual, has collapsed into the individual (e.g., the ego)[11]; the infinite has become incarnate.

Bad infinity thus turns out to be the rationalistic, quantitatively infinite, unsublatedly transcendent, alien God of Judaism,[12] the God of "dead nature" (dead, because God is outside of it),[13] and of Kant.[14] It is a God thought, not sensed (because he is perfectly immaterial and unencompassably infinite).[15] He cannot be "tasted" (*geschmeckt*—comp. the eucharist), even as the negative infinite judgment is *widersinnig und abgeschmackt* ("self-contradictory/antisensuous and of bad taste").[16]

To Kant all these characterizations of the uncompletable "potential" infinity are not derogatory but positively laudatory. His distinction between the infinite and the indefinite, from which Hegel has taken off, is, as it were, procedural: if the infinite were given as a whole then one could, of course, regress from it to its finite parts, since the finite is by definition determinable; from the finite part, on the other hand, one could never reach the infinite (again by definition), and this latter progress is, therefore, *ad indefinitum*, not *ad infinitum*.[17] But the infinite is, in fact, never given. It is, therefore, always a regulative idea, that is, a limit that one can and should try to approximate ever further, asymptotically, though one can never reach it. It is an heuristic notion, an "as-if."[18] And this is precisely its functional value in science, ethics, and so on, that it is an incentive to never-ending progress. It is truly *erhaben*, sublime in the transcendent sense,[19] as conceptually beyond all possible reality and, therefore, always a rational, purely constructed notion, by means of which men ought to improve reality incrementally. Thus Kant says about the mathematical idea of infinity exactly what he says about the idea of the ethical God: "The infinite is never given, only the condition of the possibility of the *progressus in infinitum* or *indefinitum* is."[20]

Hegel's Christian God is, on the other hand, incarnated.[21] This is to say, in him transcendence and infinity have self-contracted into immanence and finitude.[22] Finitude in form and infinity in essence,[23] they have collapsed into their metaphysical "substrate."[24] God is no longer *ein Jenseits* (a transcendent),[25] and the previously external relations between God and the world have been reabsorbed into his own essence, where he is both God (beyond the world) and human (in the world)—that is, they are now relations within himself. He is now a sensuous God, who can be seen and tasted.[26] Indeed, he is the "substrate," which, through all changes, always remains the same.[27]

One might say that on the question of infinity Hegel and Kant recapitulate the classic struggle between Athens and Jerusalem. For Hegel as for the ancient Greeks the idea of an uncompletable, inexhaustible reality was obnoxious; it violates their sense of form and order. For Kant, as for classical Judaism, to the contrary, a true infinity inexhaustible and even unconceivable in content, is the most majestic conception possible. Its very "irreality" is held to be the origin of all reality.

The debate between Hegel and Kant on the nature of infinity continued throughout the nineteenth century and has not abated to this day. It always has two faces—a metaphysical one and a mathematical one,[28] the latter in the form of the debate in the philosophy of mathematics about "potential" or "actual" transfinite numbers, as advocated respectively by intuitionists and at least some constructionalists, on the one hand, and by logicists, at their head Georg Cantor himself, on the other.

Cantor held that there are three kinds of infinity: (1) the extramundane God, or "absolute infinity," *Infinitum aeternum in creatum Absolutum*, which is "the actual set of all, even and especially of, contradictory, sets,"[29] (2) ontologically actual infinite numbers, *Infinitum creatum sive Transfinitum, in concreto seu in natura naturata*; and (3) concepts of transfinite numbers, these being identified with Kantian syncategorematic, heuristic ideas.[30] All three are, according to Cantor, "actual," and he makes no bones whatever about the religious stake that, for him, turns on this: God could otherwise not be believed to exist, and the human intellect could otherwise not cognize him.[31] In a letter to Cardinal Franzelin he even makes the mind-boggling assertion that an infinity of actual persons can "probably even (be found) ... in one region of the world, in my firm conviction," only to go into some Biblical exegesis on the book of *Proverbs*.[32]

Though: Cantor stipulated some reservations about Hegel's conception of infinity (which amount to an affirmation of theism against Hegel's pantheism),[33] he enlists on the side of Hegel and against Kant by consistently attacking the latter[34] and by speaking of Kantian infinity explicitly in Hegel's vocabulary, that is, by calling it "bad infinity."[35] More usually he speaks of *eigentliche* and *uneigentliche* infinities,[36]—what in English has come to be rendered in Bertrand Russell's terminology as "proper" and "improper" infinities[37] but what is really the language of the later existentialists that Theodor W. Adorno excoriated as *The Jargon of Authenticity* and of inauthenticity.[38] Cantor protests his place in the historical line of Plato and scholastic realism.[39]

Marburg neo-Kantianism was at its height simultaneously with Cantor.[40] Hermann Cohen quotes Cantor's phrase "free mathematics" approvingly in his decisive *The Principle of the Infinitesimal Method and its History—A Chapter in the Foundation of the Critique of Cognition*, 1883,[41] and the two even agree that mathematical constructs derive their value / validity from their scientific applicability. On the other hand, Cantor reviewed this work of Cohen's negatively,[42] as Bertrand Russell was to do a little later.[43] The theory of infinitesimals, which is at issue between them, though systematically and philosophically of a piece with the theory of infinity, is, on the other hand, too complex and too discrete to be taken up here.[44] On the question of the concept of infinity itself one can turn to Cohen's closest disciple and colleague, Paul Natorp, who, in his *Die logischen Grundlagen der exakten Wissenschaften*,[45] chapter 4, addresses himself directly and systematically to Cantor's doctrine of actual infinities. He shows here that on this score, as well as on the problem of infinitesimal-theory, the Kantian-Cohennian regulative interpretation serves Cantor's very purposes much better than Cantor's own.[46] Cantor's disciple Abraham Fraenkel later in effect conceded this point,[47] and so does the editor of Cantor's collected writings.[48]

Paragraph 25 in Natorp's "Logic" (*Foundations and Logical Construction of Mathematics and of Mathematical Natural Science*), in *Leading Propositions for Academic Lectures*[49] summarizes his analysis as follows:

Paragraph 25. The Mathematically Infinite.

The purely methodological meaning of number is best expressed in its characteristic of infinity. This signifies first only that the procedure of number, with all that it includes, is valid precisely as procedure once and for all, therefore always in itself without limit, and that it demands application, or that the relations of number exist unlimitedly. From this results in the place-relationship the endless continuity of the numerical series in the positive as well as negative direction and in the metrical relationship the infinity of number in respect to multiplication and division. What is thereby excluded, however, is the exhaustibility of the infinite in quantitative respect and excluded also is the presupposition of an infinite that exists like a thing and that merely cannot be reached by means of the procedure of counting, which always has to remain finite. For nothing exists in mathematics that cannot be defined by a mathematical procedure. This strongly "methodological" conception of the mathematically infinite in no way coincides with the widely adopted opinion of Aristotle that an infinite is admissible in "potentiality" (the potential infinite) but inadmissible in "actualization" (as an actual infinite). There "is" the infinite in that methodological sense, and not because of an allegedly uncompletable succession. For it can rightly be asserted that the relations of number "are," they do not "become" (comp. paragraph 23, first section), into infinity. The methodologically infinite is thus to be regarded as actual in the full sense of the word, not as merely potentially infinite, if the modal distinction between possibility and actuality has any place in mathematics altogether. In the new doctrine of the infinite (of Georg Cantor's) not that it dares assert an actual infinite ("transfinite") is to be challenged as rather that it permits by its side a potential infinite to which no actual infinite corresponds (especially for an explanation of the infinitesimal) (an inconsistency which, by the way, has already been overcome by Guiseppe Veronese).[50] The assertion of the transfinite rests securely on the basis of the always unchangeable existence of the relations of numbers. Resistance to this assertion is essentially due to the attempt to understand the infinity of numbers by mere means of quantity, which was recognized as invalid even by the founders of the mathematics of infinity (Galileo, Newton, and Leibniz, Kant agreeing with them). The rigorously scientific meaning of the mathematically infinite is to be caught only by means of the method of qualitative universality (cf. paragr. 16), i.e. through the function of the law that logically superordinates itself as the set (*Gattung*) of every differentiation of the quantitatively distinguishable values of any magnitude and that produces the latter in the first place as their originating unity (paragr. 17)...

The above passage brings out clearly the philosophically strongly, though limitedly, positive position taken by "Marburg" toward Cantor. Infinites are "actual" in the sense in which all mathematical entities are actual—that is, as ideal models, or as Kantian/neo-Kantian regulatives.[51] Infinites are not and cannot be "potential" in the sense of "potential" that implies a potential, practicable or inpracticable, empirical instantiation, any more than any mathematical entity can ever be anything but an "idea." The value and validity of all such ideal constructions are their possible scientific "application."[52] Joseph Bloch, in his monograph, arrives at precisely the self-same position.[53] He concludes: "Cantor's theories, which ... have discovered clearly independent qualities in the infinite, seem to be a sign of the independence of pure cognition."[54] That is to say, transfinite numbers, like all mathematical entities, including infinitesimals (of different orders, like infinites),[55] are, precisely because they are "pure," aprioristically rational, "actual" and as such "produce," construct, "reality." They are not *Dinge*/"things" but *Bedingungen*/conceptually "conditioning" tools, as he quotes Ernst Cassirer.[56] In short, Cohen and Cantor have, in effect together, worked out the philosophy and the mathematics of infinity (though Cantor went further in several technical mathematical respects, while Cohen is correcting him in one mathematical and in several important philosophical respects). This entire way of analyzing the problem can then, perhaps, be summarized in the following formula: transfinite numbers are mathematically, not empirically or ontologically, actual, and they possess validity inasmuch as they are useful first in mathematics, then in science, and ultimately also in ethics, and so on.

At the very time that we have now reached in our brief historical survey the underlying religious, indeed, the theological, issue in the dispute about "good"/"actual" infinity came to the fore again—and within the Marburg School itself! Hermann Cohen had published his *Religion and Morality* in 1907,[57] in which God functions as the unattainable, only approximatingly, infinite end (*telos*) of ethics. God is a "pure idea" and as such, but only as such, "actual."[58] Cohen's intimate Protestant associate Natorp, who, until Cohen's death in 1918, always stuck loyally to his senior's philosophical guns, added an epilogue in the second edition of his own *Religion within the Bounds of Humanity—A Chapter toward the Foundation of Social Politics*,[59] in which he reacted to Cohen's thesis about philosophical religion. This reaction of his still stays, strictly speaking, within Cohen's criticistic boundaries—religion wants to have a completed infinity (i.e., God),[60] but it can in practice only strive toward it;[61] still, Christian that he is and future Platonic mystic,[62] Natorp wishes to stress more than Cohen does the actual, as he says, "present-time," function of the infinitely future limit-concept of God.[63] He adduces their common friend and colleague Wilhelm Herrmann, professor of Protestant theology at the University of Marburg,[64] to imply even more "actuality" for the God-concept than this.[65]

A number of factors enter into this originally incremental but eventually fundamental divergency between Cohen and Natorp: (1) Cohen was a very self-conscious Jew, while Natorp was equally self-consciously a Christian[66]; (2) it was precisely at the turn of the century that a full-fledged philosophical and ideological rebellion erupted, which has not ended even now, against what was and is derogated as Kantian/Marburgian abstractionism, theoreticism, critical rationalism, constructionalism, and so on[67] and in favor of one form or another of vitalism, positivism, empiricism, realism, existentialism, and so on, and even within the Marburg School lots of defections took place toward metaphysics and "to the things themselves"; and (3) the domination of Hegelianism in the first half of the nineteenth century in and beyond Germany had not, of course, been totally turned hack with the rise of the various neo-Kantianisms in the second half, and for all sorts of reasons, philosophical, historical, political, and sociological, it was now coming to the fore again in different forms and with renewed vigor, Natorp's Protestant Christian desire for "reality," including a practicable infinity, was soon and thereafter increasingly to be accompanied by an analogous Jewish backlash, for analogous,

Jewish, and general reasons. We cannot here review the development of Jewish vitalistic, Nietzschean self-assertions, like Martin Buber's, or Jewish existentialist, quasi-Kierkegaardian "absolute empiricism" like Franz Rosenzweig's.[68] We want to try to limit ourselves to the narrower and technical question formulated in our title, Buber's essay about and against Cohen's philosophical "idea of God" versus (the real) God,[69] via the entrenched divine attribute of infinity, brings us back closer to our subject. We can get back to the precise subject through Buber's partial but significant follower, Emanuel Levinas.[70]

Levinas is, on the one hand, what I have called a "post-phenomenologist,"[71] that is, a thinker based on but going well beyond and even against Husserl, and, on the other hand, an emphatically and pervasively Jewish philosopher. As the very title of his book *Totality and Infinity*[72] implies, Levinas commits himself to the Hegelian doctrine of real infinity: "The Kantian notion of infinity figures as an ideal of reason, . . . without the incomplete being confronted with a privileged *experience* (Levinas' italics) of infinity. . . . The infinity referring to the finite marks the most anti-Cartesian point of Kantian philosophy as, later, of Heideggerian philosophy. Hegel returns to Descartes in maintaining the positivity of the infinite. . . ."[73] "In returning to the Cartesian notion of infinity, the 'idea of infinity' put in the separate being by the infinite, we retain its positivity. . . ."[74] (With all this, however, it is to be decisively noted that, while falling back on the ontological tradition of Anselm, Descartes, Spinoza, and Hegel, Levinas asserts, on the other hand, that he is putting forward an anti-Occidentalist [i.e., anti-Greek and anti-Christian], Jewish, "prophetic," philosophy; he thinks he does this by identifying the real infinite, God, with ethics, and that God "persecutes" men, rather than "reconciling" them with himself in an ever premature peace).[75]

Jacques Derrida makes a very strong case against his friend Levinas on this score (though I would hold that, on the whole, Levinas' case against both Husserl and Heidegger is stronger than Derrida's rehabilitation of these two): "Violence et métaphysique—essai sur la pensée d'E. Levinas."[76] Derrida argues that, contrary to Levinas' (and F. Rosenzweig's) rejection of history as "totality" (that is, as "dead matter," contrasted with "subjecthood"),[77] history is in fact the infinite "horizon" within which subjectivity must and does occur. It is the "history of exits from totality,"[78] and philosophy is then such as "to know itself increasingly as *historical* (in a sense which tolerates neither a completed totality nor a positive infinity).[79] Thus Husserl is more right, because if "the other" could ever be turned into an "actual infinite" he would, therefore, being "actual," have become part of "the same" and therewith of totality.[80] Derrida then explicitly puts himself on record as, in the first place, vindicating the "Kantian" potential infinite, which is the "opening into infinity, the work of objectification"[81]: "(A) confrontation (between Levinas and Kant) is called for not only because of the ethical subjects but already by the difference between totality and infinity, about which Kant, among others and perhaps more than others, also had some thoughts"[82]; and, in the second place, Derrida defends and, indeed, identifies himself with, "Hebraism" *versus* "Hellenism": "But precisely the God of the classics, whose actual infinity was intolerant of the question, had no vital need of writing."[83]

Now we have dealt once more for a while with matters of religion, theology, history, philosophy. One thing, though, seems to be agreed on by the writers whom we have adduced on these high-flown questions—they all turn decisively on the notion of infinity, potential or actual, bad or good. We and they know that this is a much more delimited and technical subject. We must, therefore, return one final time to our central subject—the nature of infinity. Depending on what the best, competent, and for this stage most sophisticated explication of infinity turns out to be, also the high-flown philosophical and religious doctrines derived from it will have to be judged.

We left matters around the time of the early Bertrand Russell. In *Principles of Mathematics*[84] he reasoned that there are no useful "infinite unities" or "infinite wholes"—only "infinite aggregates." In *Our Knowledge of the External World as a Field for Scientific Method in Philosophy*,[85] chapter 6 is devoted to "The Problem of Infinity Considered Historically": "But just as an infinite class can be given all at once by its defining concept, though it cannot be reached by successive enumeration,"[86] " . . . in the case of infinite collection: they may be known by their characteristics although their terms cannot be enumerated. In this sense, an unending series may nevertheless form a whole. . . ."[87] In chapter 7, "The Positive Theory of Infinity," he then, nonetheless, accepts Cantor as the last word on the question.

In arriving at this at first blush self-contradictory conclusion Russell refers to Frege and adds: "In the above remarks I am making use of the unpublished work by my friend Ludwig Wittgenstein."[88] D.S. Schwayder has shown[89] that the invocation of Wittgenstein for this purpose is invalid and that, to the contrary, Wittgenstein rejected the notion of actual infinities from the time of the *Tractatus* on to the end. In fact, Wittgenstein,'s conversations with L. E. Brouwer showed "tendencies toward 'intuitionism'" in general and that he disliked set-theory and the "theology of *Mengenlehre*."[90] On his view, infinity is but a feature of our conceptualization—"a highly Kantian theme." "An infinite possibility is not the possibility of an actual infinity." "It is a confusion of 'the elements of cognition' with physical questions."[91] In general, about Wittgenstein's mathematical views the same must be said that is said about his linguistic views, namely that the meaning of a mathematical concept is its use—not its Platonizing metaphysical ontology, as in the case of actual infinities.

Schwayder refers to, among others, Michael Dummet's study "Wittgenstein's Philosophy of Mathematics" and, while clearly agreeing with it, calls it rightly a "well-known but widely disbelieved interpretation."[92] Dummet's fullest argument against set-theoretical infinities is naturally to be found in his *Elements of Intuitionism*.[93] Here he repeats the application to mathematics of the linguistic principle that meaning is use.[94] Also he rejects Russell's limitation of actual infinities to the other side of "medical impossibility": that Russellian limitation implies that actual infinities are a logico-mathematically perfectly valid conception and that the only trouble with them is that, by definition, they cannot be physically instantiated, while Dummet's and Brouwer's argument against them is methodological, that is, logico-mathematical.[95] The intuitionistic argument itself against actual infinities, explicitly in the Kantian tradition,[96] is, of course, simply an application of the basic intuitionistic methodological requirement that every proposition must be constructable[97]; therefore, "an infinite structure is always to be thought of as something in process of generation, not as something the construction of which can be completed."[98] In short, "in intuitionistic logic, all infinity is potential infinity: there is no completed infinity."[99]

The situation is significantly different in Quinean constructionalism.[100] Provoked in no small measure by Russell's paradoxes of set-theory, W.V. Quine and Nelson Goodman started out with a radically nominalist position: "We do not believe in abstract entities. . . . (N)o construction will depend upon the existence of classes." "Renunciation of Infinity. We decline to assume that there are infinitely many objects. . . ."[101] Quine recognizes, at least in a general way, what we have been stressing here—the ancient metaphysical issues underlying our current academic concerns: "Classical mathematics . . . is up to its neck in commitments to an ontology of abstract entities. . . . The great medieval controversy over universals has flared up even in the modem philosophy of mathematics"[102] and in our time produces basically three approaches—logicism/realism (e.g., Cantor), intuitionism, and formalism.[103] While Goodman will continue to maintain this position,[104] Quine, already in the 1948 essay just cited, guardedly expresses himself in favor of formalism (Hilbert) and is ready to accept sets, even transfinite ones, to the extent, though only to the extent, that they are useful to science.[105] As time has gone by Quine has accepted transfinite numbers to a pragmatically, that is, scientifically, minimum point of need—without any one single, necessary logic to underlie them—and with no necessary ontological commitment implied.[106] In any case, though, from Quine's point of view the bottom line can be said to be that "actual infinities," while nominalistically at best dubious, are pragmatically, that is, scientifically acceptable.

Our survey may be held to lead to a consensus on the question of the nature of infinity at this stage, which can even be shared by technicians in the field as widely divergent otherwise as logicists and constructionalists (though, to be sure, excluding set-theoreticians of Cantorial orthodoxy and intuitionists): Plato's ideas—in this case mathematical ideas—are, indeed, real in the sense that they are logically consistent, or non-self-contradictory, and they are functional in the actual world as, but only as "regulatives," ideal, in this case scientific, models.[107] But this is what Kant and "Marburg" said all along about Platonic ideas in general and about the concept of infinity in particular.

Let us just round out this conclusion by a glance at what appears to be the current state of the debate. Steven Körner, in *The Philosophy of Mathematics*[108] speaks of "methodological transfinitism" as "a program," not a dogma (in other words, what we have just called regulatives).[109] Agreeing with Hilbert, Körner holds that such infinities are "without full ontological status" and are Kantian ideas.[110] He then renders an open ended final verdict: "But the logical status of an actual infinity, as opposed to the readiness of some and the hesitation of others to accord it full metaphysical honors, is still left in the dark—or it is left in the twilight into which Kant had moved it from obscurity," for purely mathematical and logical reasons.[111] If one then adds to this final verdict of Körner's and Hilbert's Hermann Cohen's insistence that mathematics is at the service of physics,[112] then we have come back to our conclusion.[113] Paul Lorenzen concludes,[114] as we, too, have done, that our question can and should thus be amicably settled even between theoreticians that seem to be far apart. Lorenzen even recognizes in passing[115] what we have here tried to put in focus—the religious stake in the affirmation of actual infinities. Of Georg Cantor himself one might say that he recapitulated in his life and in his work the quintessential heresy of Christianity: he rightly recognized the infinite God, and he then wrongly wanted to see him incarnate in the world.[116]

Chapter 16

Book Reviews

Samuel Atlas, *From Critical to Speculative Idealism: The Philosophy of Salomon Maimon* (1966)

The Hague: Martinus Nijhoff, 1964, 335 pages

This is the first full-length study in English of the philosophy of Solomon Maimon (1754–1800), by a professor at the Hebrew Union College-Jewish Institute of Religion. Hitherto, only German, Hebrew, and French studies have been available, save for the scholarly articles, which Professor Atlas has published preparatory to this volume. The book is strictly limited to basic and technical philosophical concerns; it does not enter into the well-known romantic biography of Maimon and his place in Jewish history.

As the title indicates, Atlas analyzes Maimon's thought in relationship to Leibniz, Hume, and, most especially of course, Kant before him, and to Hegel, Fichte, and Schelling after him. The name of Hermann Cohen occurs frequently. Indeed, Maimon is in one sense shown to be the bridge between "orthodox Kantianism" and Cohen's "Marburg neo-Kantianism," while in several respects he is interpreted in light of the latter. Unfortunately, no complete, systematic chapter is devoted to the kinship and continuity between the two. This is the more regrettable, because we clearly have here the most productive of Maimon's extrapolations in history.

The most important problem for immediate post-Kantian philosophy was the nature of the noumenon, which threatened to split, and in fact did split, the philosophical world picture and the world of philosophy into "metaphysics" and "experience." Maimon anticipated in reasoned detail much that the Cohenians were to say on this subject: that the noumenon is not a metaphysical entity but a limiting concept of the full rationalization of the data of experience toward which reason strives into infinity.

First published in *Journal of Bible and Religion* 34:1 (1966), 64–68, © Oxford University Press.

The "given" itself is produced by the mathematically, that is, scientifically, patterned infinitesimals of sensation, and it is therefore capable of rationalization. The author's chapter on the infinitesimals is perhaps the best in the book. It is most useful as a general introduction to this difficult but seminal concept.

A number of consequences follow from the earlier view of the nature of reality. For one thing, if the mind produces the stuff of sensation, this guarantees the creativity of reason and therewith the very principle of human and divine creation. In addition, the ethical nature of cognition is understood: cognition is an imperative directed toward an infinite. Although Atlas does not point all this out explicitly, one may say that both the Jewish and the more specifically Cohenian character of this epistemology is underscored. This becomes even clearer when one turns to Maimon's consistently deduced definition of God as in turn a "limiting concept," the totality of all cognitions toward which human reason strives.

Furthermore, cognition is now seen to arise out of a relationship, the relationship between subject and object, which creates reality. Neither subject nor object precedes the other. In one respect this is similar to Buber's dialogical, relational reality, but in another respect the two are totally different in that the latter transpires between empirical, subjective individuals whereas the former transpires in the realm of objective, scientific thought. And hence, finally, scientific laws are recognized as "acts, not facts" (250), as rational functions, not descriptions of "being." The connection with Cassirer and even with pragmatism is thus highlighted.

Even as cognition is an act between science and the given, rather than one performed by empirical individuals, so also the categories of cognition are deduced by Maimon from actual scientific experience rather than, as Kant proposed, from formal Aristotelian logic. So, too, the forms of intuition, time, and space are not eternal structures of the human mind but concepts that the mind has developed, with all other concepts, in order to organize experience. Thus, in the end all three—the noumenon, God, and reason—turn out to be not eternal, metaphysical entities but historical functions.

Two criticisms must be leveled at Atlas' treatment of these questions, however. The first is merely historical. He mentions Bishop Berkeley only once (310)—and then only to say that the identification of neo-Kantian idealism with Berkeleyan idealism is "untenable." Atlas proposes that the incongruence resides in the fact that for Berkeley "mind" is a metaphysical reality, which is also encountered in man, whereas for Maimon it is the principle of experiential, scientific labor. Clearly, the relationship between the two is considerably more positive than this. For one thing, the concept of Infinite Mind plays a significant part in Maimon's philosophy, a point to which we shall return. Even apart from this, the fact remains that for Maimon as for Berkeley ultimate reality is the "identity of thought and being" (290), the dissolution of experience in thought, and mathematical science is the god of both."[1]

The second criticism refers to a substantial doctrine, which Atlas does not elaborate but obviously presumes and, which, indeed, he learned from Hermann Cohen. That the forms of intuition are no more than concepts is what makes possible the progress of science, for it now becomes possible to conceive at least the possibility that other forms of intuition may be evolved, and thus a better and fuller penetration of the given attained. Even the religious concept of a God beyond time and space becomes more rational, once these forms are understood not as metaphysical necessities but as rational tools.

On the other hand, Maimon and Cohen—and it would seem Atlas as well—consistently pay homage to the nineteenth-century, optimistic doctrine of "the progress of science" (93, 97, 277f., Z81, 328). Cohen, in turn, always claimed that the very concept of God guarantees the apparently unilinear progress of knowledge. Such a notion has acquired an unsavory odor in our time; our experience of the twentieth century has made us wary of identifying the passage of time with progress. More significantly, why should this assumption even be necessary in terms of neo-Kantian epistemology itself? What these thinkers really mean is that the progress of science consists of the ever increasing unification of experience and knowledge. But why must we assume that this experience and knowledge will always move in a forward direction in order to be unified? Experience and science also can, and in fact do, regress. Presumably, reason will then come along and at one point or another unify the progressions as well as the regressions within one growing structure. In other words, the curve may well dip any number of times and to any depth before it finds its asymptotic axis.

Other factors as well militate against this simplicistic assumption of unilinear progress. The Cohenians always assume that unless a man is guaranteed the attainment of his epistemological as well as his ethical strivings he will not try to further either of them. (See Cohen's postulation of the very concept of God as the guarantee of the attainability of ethical goals.) But is not this a kind of rarified eudemonism, which they otherwise emphatically and rightly reject? Why can I not strive for the truth and for goodness without any guarantee that I will reach them? Quite apart from Sartrean heroism, is this not actually a condition of the ethical character of both truth and goodness?

Furthermore, Atlas argues in Maimon's name that unless the forms of intuition are metaphysically valid they are incapable of the ideal reduction from synthetic into analytic propositions. But this does not necessarily follow. It is perfectly conceivable that time and space may at the present moment be the best tools at our disposal for the unification of data that lend themselves, in measure, to such ministration. But this is not to gainsay the possibility that the same data may at some future time be found to be better cognizable through other forms of intuition. Indeed, we have been shown earlier that it is precisely through the formulation of new forms, understood as concepts, that the progress of science may well come about. The dogmatic and reactionary danger of "natural philosophy" always raises its head, before which Maimon also did obeisance at one point, in alleging that "the human spirit is, in its essence, always the same" (252).

One other major point needs clarification, insofar as it concerns both Maimon himself and Atlas' interpretation of him. Maimon constitutes the bridge from Kant to the German idealists, rather than to criticism, to the extent of his doctrine of the Infinite Mind. Even as he postulates the metaphysical validity of the forms of intuition in order to guarantee the reduction of synthetic to analytic propositions, so he postulates the Infinite Mind in order to guarantee the ideal of the rationalization of the stuff of experience: unless it is metaphysically rational before God it cannot be scientifically rationalized by men. And the human mind is then a part of the Infinite Mind.

This doctrine, congenial as it was to the German absolutists, is a sore embarrassment to the antimetaphysical neo-Kantians. Atlas therefore makes every possible effort to reinterpret Maimon's statements in a methodological sense: Infinite Mind is not to be regarded as an ontological reality but as a scientific, limiting concept; it is a "symbolic" expression of the hope and intent of reason to rationalize experience fully (cf., e.g., 326, 330). But this reinterpretation runs headlong into Maimon's own positive statements, which make it clear that he thought of Infinite Mind as a necessary metaphysical postulate—and Atlas is uncomfortably conscious of this (cf. 87, 95f., 98, 101). Certainly Maimon also thought of the infinitesimals in the Leibnizian sense, as metaphysical realities, not as methodological tools (cf. 117, 119).

Therefore, one may, in the first place, have to draw a clearer distinction between Maimon's own intent and the interpreter's use of his statements than Atlas does. But this is a mere matter of historicity. In the second place, and more important, one will have to work out a philosophy of reinterpretation: When, how, and why is it legitimate and useful to reinterpret a philosopher in a sense other than the one which he originally had in mind? (This would also be very helpful for a proper appreciation of Hermann Cohen's own textual studies, in the Bible, Plato, and in the general and Jewish classical philosophers.) In any case, what is sauce for the goose is sauce for the gander: once we reinterpret Maimon in the spirit of Cohen, we cannot very well object as strenuously as does Atlas to Klement's reinterpretation of Reinhold's philosophy (298) an objection made, I suspect, in order to raise Maimon above his contemporary Reinhold.

From the point of view of Jewish philosophy, Hermann Cohen's supreme achievement was that he proved all philosophy to be dependent on Judaism: philosophy can only progress on the basis of Jewish doctrine. In this, he was unlike almost all other Jewish philosophers who measured Judaism against the supreme and independent yardstick of philosophy. Professor Atlas' book can lead us back into this universe of discourse, something that is badly needed for the sake of the health of philosophy as well as that of Judaism.

William Kluback, *Hermann Cohen—The Challenge of a Religion of Reason* (1987)

Chico, CA: Scholars Press (Brown Judaic Studies 53), 1984. 96 pp.

The ongoing importance of the philosophic work of Hermann Cohen (1842–1918), founder of "Marburg neo-Kantianism," is far too little (if at all) known or appreciated. This is also true of the extension of his systematic work to philosophy of religion, and among Jews his philosophy of Judaism is largely misunderstood.

William Kluback's small book helps remedy this state of affairs, although limitedly so.

The chief job done by the present treatise is very well chosen and carried out. The author exposits and compares Kant's treatment of the virtues in "The Doctrine of Virtues" in the *Metaphysics of Morals* and Cohen's treatment of the same subject matter in his *Ethics of the Pure Will* (1904/1907) and in his *The Concept of Religion within the System of Philosophy* (1915) and *Religion of Reason out of the Sources of Judaism* (posthumously 1919/1929). The systematic ramifications of these two treatments are also adumbrated, although, due in part perhaps to the brevity of the book, not sufficiently so, and at that usually without the analytic explications that these very technical texts require. In the process a good example of careful and specific philosophical ethics is offered to a contemporary literature, which stands in need of it. At least once (27ff.) an instructive contrast is drawn between such Kantian/neo-Kantian ethics and opposite postures in their and in our time.

That chief job performed by the book is framed by the author's thesis that "the later Cohen" was more "religious," less strictly "Critical," than he had been in his neo-Kantian works. This thesis was canonically put forward in a much more drastic form by Franz Rosenzweig in his "Introduction" to Cohen's collected *Jewish Writings* (3 vols., 1924): the *Religion of Reason* was in fact no longer neo-Kantian at all in its essence but proto-existentialist, and Rosenzweig's interpretation has generally been accepted by Jewish intellectuals. Kluback is much too knowledgeable

---

First published: *Idealistic Studies*, vol. 17, issue 1, January 1987, 83–84, doi: 10.5840/idstudies198717110.

and responsible to advocate it *simpliciter*, but even in his qualified version it is, in this reviewer's considered view, false. Cohen's posthumous and epochal philosophy of Judaism is in fact an exfoliation, specification, and broad historical instantiation, in terms of Judaism, of his mature, radical, Critical Idealism. The very continuity between Kant's and Cohen's treatment of the virtues through the various stages of the latter's development that is demonstrated here contradicts rather than supports Kluback's thesis. Also his own plentiful citations, when more systematically understood, often show this. In his bibliography, Kluback cites an article by Alexander Altmann, "Hermann Cohen's Concept of Correlation" (German), but he unfortunately does not use it; this, and lots of other evidence, would belie his thesis further. The author repeatedly puts down Kant's religion in favor of Cohen's. This is quite wrong since both "idealized" the religions to which they were respective historical heirs, with their *signa rememorativa, demonstrativa, prognostica*. (To speak of Cohen's "conviction that Israel was the embodiment [!] of an eternal truth" (78) is dangerously careless language and, in any case, removes the critical sting from Cohen's always normative conceptuality.) Sure, God is being, but that being is "ought-being." Sure, Cohen feels the passion of faith, but it is "pure, i.e., a priori, rational feeling" that he feels (cf. his *Aesthetics of Pure Feeling*, 2 vols., 1912, not cited by Kluback). Sure, he believes in Judaism, because Judaism, properly, regulatively understood, is identical to (ethical) reason.

The author ends with a brief comparison of Hermann Cohen with Troeltsch and Otto. This is a peculiar thing to do because, as Kluback goes on to show, the latter two diverge decisively, though differently, from the former. In view of his Jewish religionist interpretation of the alleged "late Cohen," why not Jewish thinkers in Cohen's succession, and why not subsequent "transcendental philosophy"?

Hermann Cohen also has serious technical problems. It is as good as not edited. The massive, and probably supererogatory, German quotations teem with errors, and not they alone. Maimonides is once quoted in a French translation (67). The bibliography is selective and unnecessarily in foreign languages. Some diversionary sources are adduced. The nadir is reached when (60) *Concept of Religion* becomes *Contempt of Religion*. Kluback obviously does not share Cohen's thorough familiarity with the classic Jewish sources.

I have dwelled longer on the faults of this book than on its very real value. This is due only to the fact that one would like to see a worthwhile job done better.

Mechthild Dreyer, *Die Idee Gottes im Werk Hermann Cohens* (1989)

(Monographien zur Philosophischen Forschung, vol. 230), Königstein/Ts., Hain, 1985, 244 pp.

This is a study of "The Idea of God in Hermann Cohen's Work," an important subject not previously treated in full, here competently carried out and well-written. Three general considerations must be kept in mind from the outset: (1) Cohen's and his followers' "Marburg neo-Kantianism," a radically Criticistic, science-oriented idealism, was a minority school of thought at the time, then and thereafter generally perceived and attacked as a "Judaization" of Kant—which pretty much died out in the early 1920s and was exterminated, of course, in the rise and rule of Nazism (though some significant aftereffects, for example, Ernst Cassirer and postwar, German "transcendental philosophy" give it an afterlife). In Jewish circles Cohen's philosophy of Judaism, not his general philosophy, has continued to be very influential, however controversially so. (2) The relationship between Cohen's philosophical work and his Jewish, religious work has always been difficult to determine with any precision, and this is one of the chief purposes of Dreyer's enterprise. (3) In Christian as well as Jewish circles the view has widely been accepted that in his last works, especially the posthumous *Religion of Reason out of the Sources of Judaism*, Cohen in effect broke out of his neo-Kantian "system" into a form of religious, metaphysical quasi-existentialism. This question, too, is tackled in the present book.

The author provides solid summaries of Cohen's thought as it bears on her subject in the three stages of his work as conventionally stipulated: (a) his Kant exegeses, (b) his neo-Kantian system, and (c) his late, religious writing. She argues essentially two theses: (I) Cohen's thought was continuous throughout his life, although his concern with Judaism increased significantly as time went on (II) by the last stage, (c), two Jewish, religious doctrines had become so important to Cohen that he made them central to his thinking, despite the fact that they could

---

First published in *International Studies in Philosophy* 21:1, 1989, 76–78.

not be accommodated in his radical transcendentalism—namely messianism and a metaphysical God.

She is certainly right on (I). On (II) she is wrong.

Before we can get down to the brass tacks of (II) some other criticisms of the book should be taken care of.

Though it is not surprising that in post–World War II Germany authors have to get their knowledge of Judaism from secondhand sources, and in an extremely superficial manner, it is objectionable that any should dare to expound on subjects on which they are not qualified. They then must be even warier than this author is in criticizing the Jewish authenticity of a man like Cohen, and to quote the criticism of a man like Joseph Klein, with his record of moral dubiousness during the crucial years; Dreyer furthermore claims to have surveyed "completely" the relevant literature as far as they are "generally accessible." This is certainly untrue. Also, the book lacks a broader historical and philosophical context, and some parts of Cohen's work are not fully taken into account, but this could not be expected in a dissertation. There are other minor matters that one might argue with.

The occasion allows a generalization beyond the present book on the question of contemporary German treatments of Jewish subject matter. There is no reason at all to assume that Dreyer bears the subject ill will. Rather is it a matter of ignorance and of an alien, parochial perspective—and this is in fact fairly typical of the kindred literature.

One additional factor plays a role here. We all draw on the historic culture that has produced us when we extrapolate that culture to the present and for the future. In Germany this is then largely German culture; and German culture is notorious not only for ignorance and ethnocentrism but also for hostility when it comes to Jewish matters. Thus there is, for example, a book by Hans Ludwig Ollig, *Religion und Freiheitsglaube: Zur Problematik von Hermann Cohens später Religionsphilosophie* (1979, no. 179 in the same series of dissertations as Dreyer's book). It, too, is not at all a bad book. Apart from smaller matters to which one might object in it, however, what mainly sticks in one's craw is that it treats and judges the passionate Jew, Cohen, in terms of its own declared Christian, religious concerns (e.g., 4, 172, 361).

Relevant to the present point, Ollig quotes Ebbinghaus, of all people, as saying of Cohen that he came from a Jewish, Orthodox background, "devoted to the service of the synagogue," where people "did not live, like the rest of their coreligionists, from lowly trade and particularly from the money-trade" (9). In a handbook on *Der Neukantianismus* (Stuttgart, 1979, 29), Ollig expands that Ebbinghaus quote, comparing Cohen to those assimilated Jews "whose moneybags enabled the fathers of baptized daughters to marry them off to aristocratic officers of the royal guard-regiments." (Ebbinghaus wrote all this after World War II.) Here Ollig also quotes Max Scheler, a biographically dubious source, who wrote in 1922 that Cohen's writings were "characterized as much by Talmudic sharp-wittedness as by a peculiar obscurity, even abstruseness...." And Ollig even feels compelled to quote Kuno Fischer's notorious piece of anti-Semitism that Cohen's work is "more a matter of race than of philosophy." To be sure, he allows that this was a "tasteless" observation.

Klaus Christian Köhnke, in his new and important *Entstehung und Aufstieg des Neukantianismus: Die deutsche Universitätsphilosophie zwischen Idealismus und Positivismus* (Suhrkamp. 1986, 487, n. 55) says about this: "Ollig rehearses once more, apparently without malice, Kuno Fischer's antisemitic swipes..." and finishes by asking "Why?" The answer to this question is, as his own, ultimately also unsatisfactory, work again illustrates, that, however cavalier their attitude toward things Jewish, on German matters such scholars are very particular about their historical sources. They feel obligated to survey their predecessors before going on to make their own new contributions. And thus all the flotsam of the past keeps floating down and polluting the river of history, unless some really courageous and independent minds come along, as a very few do, to break with their infected tradition.

To return to the book under review, the decisive point in Dreyer's book is her thesis II. She claims continuously throughout the second half of her book that Cohen's "idea of God" cannot perform the function that is assigned to it, namely to guarantee the total convergence of nature and ethics "in infinity," that is, in temporal eternity, and that it must, therefore, refer to a metaphysical God. In fact, however, that is not the function assigned to it by Cohen. As I showed in a passage to which the author refers, but which she obviously did not use, also, indeed, in a quotation from *Ethics of the Pure Will* that she adduces herself, and systematically it should be perfectly clear that the idea of God is propounded by Cohen as an heuristic regulative to the following effect: act, or try to act, as if the rational will can be actualized in the natural world—and then see what happens. This is also the point of her mistaken claim that Cohen's talk about providence in the world entails a metaphysical God. She should know from Kant's own talk of this sort ("the cunning of nature," etc.) that this is all heuristic, regulative language. Finally, that Cohen's idea of God is inadequate to the real asseverations of what she repeatedly calls "Jewish-Christian religion"—it is, indeed, to the latter, but Cohen (and Maimonides, etc.) are far from alone in holding that it is more than adequate to (well-understood) Judaism. In general, Dreyer's view seems to be that if a man builds a unified edifice of his religious and his philosophical convictions he must have gerrymandered at least one set of his convictions, either beforehand or afterward. That, of course, is not necessarily the case. Cohen believed ("regulatively") that the philosophical tradition through Kant and the God (and culture) of Judaism—both properly understood—did, as a matter of fact, converge to the point of identity, without any fundamental gerrymandering of either. Lots of people once thought similarly. The reviewer holds that they are essentially right.

EPILOGUE | 1987

Entry on "Cohen, Hermann" in the *Encyclopedia of Religion* (ed. Mircea Eliade)

COHEN, HERMANN (1842–1918), Jewish philosopher of religion, founder and exponent of Marburg neo-Kantian philosophy. Born into a cantor's family in the small-town Jewish community of Coswig/Anhalt, Germany, Cohen received intense religious training from his father, in addition to the general education typical of his time and place. The transition from these beginnings to the modern rabbinical seminary of Breslau was natural. Part of the seminary's curriculum was the requirement of university studies. At the University of Breslau, Cohen decided that philosophy, rather than the rabbinate, was his *métier*.

Transferring to the University of Berlin, Cohen first fell under the influence of the "folk-psychological" epistemologists Heymann Steinthal and Moritz Lazarus, but he quickly progressed to a more Kantian and logicistic outlook. His habilitation thesis on Kant's theory of experience was published in 1871, and in the context of the "back to Kant" movement of the day his ideas had a revolutionary impact. He particularly impressed the radical social reformer and professor of philosophy at Marburg Friedrich Lange (author of the famous idealistic *History of Materialism*). Through Lange, a committed Protestant, the committedly Jewish Cohen received his first appointment at the University of Marburg in 1873. He stayed there until his voluntary, albeit disgruntled, retirement in 1912, thereafter to teach at the Liberal rabbinical seminary in Berlin, the Hochschule für die Wissenschaft des Judentums, where he wrote his last works. Shortly after his arrival in Marburg he married Martha Lewandowski, daughter of the chief cantor of the Berlin Jewish community and liturgical

---

From Mircea Elaide. *Encyclopedia of Religion* 1 16V SET, 1E. © 1987 Gale, a part of Cengage Learning, Inc. Reproduced by permission.

composer, Louis Lewandowski. (She was to die in the concentration camp of Theresienstadt.)

During his long incumbency in Marburg, Cohen not only produced the bulk of his own philosophic oeuvre but also gathered around him a group that came to constitute the Marburg school of neo-Kantianism. Among the many scholars associated with him in this undertaking were his student and subsequent colleague Paul Natorp and, later, Ernst Cassirer. Cohen attracted many devoted students and disciples, particularly Jews from German-speaking countries, from eastern Europe, and even America. However, his personal, philosophical, and social relations at the university became increasingly strained down through the years, not least because of growing political reaction during that period against the overtly ethical, that is, Kantian, anti-Marxist, and antimaterialist socialism of the Marburg school. (In the politics of the time the names of Cohen's students Kurt Eisner and Eduard Bernstein became quite well known.)

Throughout his life Cohen never ceased to be active in Jewish matters. For example, he published his *The Love of Neighbor in the Talmud: Affidavit before the Royal Court of Marburg* in 1888 (in German) in response to the notorious Rohling/Delagarde anti-Semitic episode in which the old "blood libel" and Jewish xenophobism combined with the then nascent German racism. He wrote voluminously on Jewish subjects; in 1924 his writings were collected in three volumes, edited, and introduced by Franz Rosenzweig, author of *The Star of Redemption*. Just before the outbreak of World War I Cohen made a triumphal tour of the largest Jewish communities in Russia, a trip that the German government supported for political reasons. Cohen hoped also by means of this tour to advance in the East the enlightened Jewish social and educational values of the Jews of the West.

Cohen's Writings. Cohen's work can be divided into three parts: his exegetical readings of Immanuel Kant, his "system of philosophy," and his specifically Jewish work.

Exegetical readings of Kant. Several of Cohen's books crystallized and solidified the aprioristic, transcendental, "critical" foundations of the Kantian system: *Kants Theorie der Erfahrung* (1871), *Kants Begründung der Ethik* (1877, 1910), and *Kants Begründung der Ästhetik* (1889). In 1883 he published *Das Prinzip der Infinitesimalmethode und seine Geschichte: Ein Kapitel in der Begründung der Erkenntniskritik* (The Principle of the Infinitesimal Method and Its History: A Chapter in the Foundation of the

Critique of Cognition), in which he argues that "the (sensuous) given," which Kant treated as the separate, empiricist source of knowledge, is also a rational construction, and thus that "reality" is totally an aprioristic, regulative product.

The "system of philosophy." Cohen's radicalized, neo-Kantian understanding of reality and of ethics that developed directly from his critiques of Kant found expression in his *Logik der reinen Erkenntnis* (Logic of Pure Cognition: 1902, 1914), *Ethik des reinen Willens* (Ethics of the Pure Will, 1904–1907), and *Ästhetik des reinen Gefühls* (Aesthetics of Pure Feeling: 1912). Here the universe is determined by the three "interests" of reason (cognition, will, and feeling), which strive for the traditional ideals of truth, goodness, and beauty. All three operate under what Kant had called "the primacy of practical (i.e., ethical) reason." The infinite task of the attainment of practical reason produces the unending history of regulatively progressive science, progress toward the good society (as in ethical socialism), and the synthesis of the two in a world perfectly true and perfectly good, that is, messianically beautiful.

Cohen's specifically Jewish work. His work in this area, intimated in his philosophizing and, increasingly, explicitly identified with it, was systematically elaborated in the final decade of his life and was consummated in the posthumously published *Religion aus den Quellen des Judentums* (Religion of Reason out of the Sources of Judaism: 1919, 1929). Cohen's Jewish philosophical theology (although he did not use this terminology) consists of a translation back into classical Jewish terms of the philosophical position Cohen held he had extracted from Judaism with the help of the progressive line of thought running from Plato through Maimonides to Kant. Thus God is the idea (in the neo-Kantian, regulative sense) of the normative, infinite realization of the good in the world. This realization is known in religion as the establishment by means of "the imitation of God" of the messianic kingdom on earth. The Law (*halakhah*) is the historical Jewish specifications of the categorical imperative and the foundation of the universal human moral brotherhood of the "Noachide covenant," which is also the religious, "Prophetic," goal of socialism. The last third of *Religion of Reason*, leading up to the religious virtues of truthfulness and peacefulness, is, together with the cited and appended texts, a Jewish restatement of the last third of *Ethics of the Pure Will*. The role of the Jewish people in history is then to represent "ethical monotheism" physically and to disseminate it morally throughout the world. Therefore, Cohen rejected the Zionism that was nascent at the time: the conflict between the two views is well expressed in the classic debate between Cohen and Martin Buber in "Answer to the Open Letter of Dr. M. Buber" (1917) and in the writings of Cohen's former student Jakob Klatzkin, who became the leading theoretician of the radical Zionist "negation of the Diaspora."

Influence of Cohen's Work. Cohen's influence in matters of religion was not limited to Jewry, although here it was magisterial. At the University of Marburg he interacted strongly with the Protestant theology faculty, first with Julius Wellhausen, whose Bible criticism he esteemed highly as a good scholarly undergirding to "Prophetic Judaism," and then especially with the liberal, proto-Social Gospel philosophical theologian Wilhelm Herrmann. Paul Natorp himself became increasingly active in liberal Protestantism. A second generation of Christian thinkers resulted from what might be called this Marburg school of Kantian liberal theology, albeit largely by way of dialectical antitheses: Karl Barth and Rudolf Bultmann deliberately place primary emphasis on the subjectivity of faith in place of Cohen's argument for the objectivity of ethical and social values.

Cohen's philosophical and Jewish influence is scattered in diverse and embattled manifestations. Around the turn of the century a rebellion emerged against what was perceived as the extreme scientific, rationalistic theoreticism of Marburg neo-Kantianism. In reaction there appeared positions that asserted the ultimate power of "reality" over reason in "life-philosophy," re-hegelianizing historicism, positivism, and nascent existentialist phenomenology. In German circles the value of historical and even metaphysical "Germanism" (*Deutschtum*) was apostrophized, and in Jewish circles a parallel affirmation of the peoplehood of Israel and the historical or even metaphysical "genius" of the Jewish people was pitted against "bloodless" and "lifeless" assimilationist universalism. The fact that Franz Rosenzweig, a disciple of Friedrich Meinecke and author of important studies on Hegel, became Cohen's last important, brilliant disciple added another complicating element, for Rosenzweig interpreted the "late Cohen" as the precursor of a total break with systematic rationalism in favor of a Schellingian form of metahistoricism.

Politically, religiously, and philosophically very different extrapolations continue to this day to be made from Cohen's fundamental analyses. Leading Jewish Orthodox authorities like Joseph Ber Soloveitchik and Isaac Hutner (d. 1980) never ceased drawing on their Cohenian studies in the 1920s, while rationalistic Reformers like Benzion Kellerman and fully acculturated Westerners like Ernst Cassirer struck out in their own directions from Cohen. These varied approaches demonstrate how decisive the intellectual experience of Cohen has remained for subsequent Jewish thought. Cohen's Jewish writings have been translated into Hebrew, English, and other languages, but the technical philosopher Cohen has remained within the confines of German-language culture. Even there he has suffered many depredations. The Weimar backlash against "cold, brainy" rationalism forced a number of Marburg- influenced figures such as Natorp, Nicolai Hartmann, and Ortega y Gasset, into Husserlian, Heideggerian, and other positions. The Nazi period saw the final destruction of the neo-Kantianism of Marburg. Since World War II, however, a new, qualified appreciation of "transcendental philosophy" has arisen, through the work of men such as Hans Wagner, Helmut Holzhey, Werner Flach, Wolfgang Marx, and others. But the contributions that Cohen's work can still make toward a fully developed and effective constructionalism in the areas of philosophy of science, ethics, and even of religion, have not yet been fully realized.

Notes

Preface

1. Albany: 1990.
2. Norbert M. Samuelson, "The Jewish Philosophy of Steven Schwarzschild," in *Modern Judaism*, vol. 12, no. 2 (May, 1992), 185.
3. Provided by Prof. Maimon Schwarzschild, San Diego.
4. http://digifindingaids.cjh.org/?pID=475354–Subseries 2: Teaching and Research Materials, 1932–1989, box 5, folder 10. (Held physically in the archive of the Center for Jewish History, New York.)
5. State University of New York, 1989, 162–181.
6. Samuelson acknowledged on p. 177, note 9 his dependence on a yet-unpublished manuscript by Schwarzschild.
7. Hermann Cohen, *Werke*, Herausgegeben vom Hermann-Cohen-Archiv am Philosophischen Seminar der Universität Zürich unter der Leitung von Helmut Holzhey, (so far) 17 Bände in 19 volumes, Hildesheim, 1987–2012.

Introduction

1. Torsten Lattki has recently published a letter by Cohen to his disciple Benzion Kellerman from 1905, which seemed to indicate that Cohen did not write on Shabbat. Cohen had read Kellermann's article in a periodical, which caused him *Sabbathlust*, but wrote to him about it only after nightfall. See Torsten Lattki, *Benzion Kellermann–Prophetisches Judentum und Vernunftreligion*, Göttingen, 2016, 217.
2. Isaac Breuer, "Was lässt Hermann Cohen vom Judentum übrig," in *Der Israelit*, March 16, 1911, 2–3. Cf. George Y. Kohler, "Keine Brücke zwischen Begriff und Welt - Orthodoxe Kritik an der Religionsphilosophie Hermann Cohens," in Eveline Goodman-Thau und Hans-Georg Flickinger (ed.),

Zur Aktualität des Unzeitgemäßen - Beiträge zum Jüdischen Denken, Reiner Wiehl zum Andenken, Nordhausen, 2013, S. 111–140.

3. Cf. Emil Fackenheim *Hermann Cohen-After Fifty Years*, New York, 1969, or Eugene Borowitz, *Choices in Modern Jewish Thought*, West Orange, 1995, 51.

4. See for the history of this development the biography of Kellermann by Torsten Lattki, *Kellermann*, 333–338.

5. See here Michael Zank, *Reverberations of Hermann Cohen in Contemporary Jewish Philosophy*, paper on the second annual panel of the Academy for Jewish Philosophy at the American Philosophical Association, Atlanta, December, 1996.

6. See in the current volume the essay on "The Tenability of Herman Cohen's Construction of the Self" from 1975 (p. 69–92 of this volume) where Schwarzschild brings Cohen's thought into dialog with contemporary American philosophers like Sydney Shoemaker and Wilfrid Sellars, the English philosopher P.F. Strawson and the German psychologist Erik Erikson.

7. See Helmut Holzhey: *Cohen und Natorp. Ein Beitrag zur Geschichte des Neukantianismus*, Basel/Stuttgart, 1981.

8. Schwarzschild: "Here the Germanic philosopher, and there the Jew. Nothing could have been more obnoxious to him!" (p. 182 of this volume).

9. Four years later Menachem Kellner edited and published a volume with Schwarzschild's "Jewish Writings," called *The Pursuit of the Ideal*, New York, 1992. This collection of articles, however, excluded all essays Schwarzschild had written on the Jewish thinker he himself deemed the most important of all: Hermann Cohen. Those essays are collected in the present volume.

10. For a good summary of Schwarzschild's "Jewish thought," see the extended review of his "Jewish Writings" by Norbert M. Samuelson, "The Jewish Philosophy of Steven Schwarzschild," in *Modern Judaism*, vol. 12, no. 2 (May, 1992), 185–201.

11. See Zank, *Reverberations*, and others.

12. Cf. Steven S. Schwarzschild, "Moral Radicalism and "Middlingness" in the Ethics of Maimonides," in *The Pursuit of the Ideal* (ed. M. Kellner), New York, 1992, 137–160

13. See especially Schwarzschild's introduction to Cohen's *Ethik des reinen Willens*, pp. 119–139 of this volume.

14. See, for example, Gershon Scholem's famous letter "Wider den Mythos vom deutsch-jüdischen Gespräch" where he writes of Cohen, the German patriot, as of a "unglücklich Liebenden, der den Schritt vom Erhabenen zum Lächerlichen nicht gescheut hat" (an unhappy lover, who

did not shrink from taking the step from the exalted to the ridiculous), in *Bulletin des Leo Baeck Instituts*, no. 27 (1964), 27, and in this volume, p. 257, note 54.

15. See the fifteen-line-long endnote no. 25 he adds in "The Title," p. 272 of this volume. It is interesting to note that they are all German and Israeli, while Americans usually did not follow Rosenzweig (e.g., William Kluback) on this point. But even those critics who did not claim that Cohen changed views at the end did take Cohen to task for his idealistic God idea in accordance with Rosenzweig's interpretation (e.g., Mordecai Kaplan and Emil Fackenheim).

16. Schwarzschild, *Rosenzweig*, p. 37 of this volume.

17. Hermann Cohen, *Kants Begründung der Ästhetik* (Berlin, 1889), 415–427 (reprinted as vol. 2 of Cohen, *Werke*, Hildesheim, 2011). See also Schwarzschild's introduction to Cohen's *Ethik*: not only "the late Cohen" of his posthumous theological work, but the emphatically neo-Kantian Cohen of the philosophic system as manifest in the *Ethik* relies on the book of the Biblical prophet Ezekiel and its doctrine of individual guilt "before God" to expound this doctrine (p. 132 of this volume).

18. Cf. here a third theory on how to read Cohen as a "textual and liturgical reasoner," developed by Steven Kepnes in critical dialogue with Schwarzschild's rational theological understanding of Cohen. (Kepnes, *Jewish Liturgical Reasoning*, Oxford, 2007, 46–48.)

19. The only scholar consistently credited by Schwarzschild with a true understanding of Cohen's idealism is Alexander Altmann, especially because of his "canonic" essay "Hermann Cohens Begriff der Korrelation," in *In Zwei Welten—Bishnay Olamot*, ed. Hans Tramer, Tel-Aviv, 1962, 366–399.

20. Cohen, *Kants Begründung der Ästhetik* Berlin, 1889, 125 (reprinted as vol. 2 of the *Werke* edition). Cf. Cohen, *Kants Begründung der Ethik*, 74f., where he writes that we should say: "only a phenomenon," as opposed to the errant "only an idea." Also cf. *Ethik des reinen Willens*, (Berlin) 1904, 417 (Cohen, *Werke*, vol. 7).

21. For Schwarzschild and Maimonides, see Menachem Kellner, "Steven Schwarzschild, Moses Maimonides, and Jewish Non-Jews," in Görge Hasselhoff (ed.), *Moses Maimonides, His Religious, Scientific and Philosophical Wirkungsgeschichte in Different Cultural Contexts*, Würzburg, 2004, 587–606.

22. As the academic rediscovery began earlier with Manuel Joel, most nineteenth-century German Jewish Reform thinkers, most prominently Geiger and Graetz, rejected the *Guide's* cold intellectualism. Cf. George

Y. Kohler, *Reading Maimonides' Philosophy in 19th-Century Germany*, Dordrecht, 2012.

23. The most extreme version of Cohen "misunderstanding" Maimonides is probably the chapter on Cohen in Eliezer Berkovits's *Major Themes in Modern Philosophies of Judaism*, (New York, 1974, 21–23). But also Shlomo Pines and many other Maimonides scholars held similar views of Cohen. Pines, for example, following in the footsteps of Leo Strauss, fiercely attacked Cohen's attempt to attribute the view of an idealistic God of morality to Maimonides (Moses Maimonides *Guide of the Perplexed*, Chicago, 1963, translator's introduction, cxxii).

24. Schwarzschild: " . . . Cohen would reply that he is, of course, entirely, indeed, painfully aware of these historical anomalies, but that the point of philosophy is to change the world and, therefore, also to moralize, to "idealize" historical Judaism" (p. 113 of this volume).

25. Schwarzschild, "Germanism," p. 104 of this volume. Cf. here Kenneth Seeskin, who supported Schwarzschild by pointing out that not only is idealization not a glorification, but "on the contrary, making the ideal explicit often shows how much the real thing suffers by comparison." Kenneth Seeskin, "The Rational Theology of Steven Schwarzschild," in *Modern Judaism* 12, 1992, 277–286, here 286, note 30.

26. Fackenheim, *Hermann Cohen-After Fifty Years*, 6, my emphasis.

27. Cf. the extensive debate about God being "alive," from Maimonides onward down to Heschel and Herberg in postwar America.

28. For a short discussion of Schwarzschild's account of Cohen's idealizing method, see Daniel H. Weiss, *Paradox and the Prophets: Hermann Cohen and the Indirect Communication of Religion*, Oxford, 2012, 21–22, where it is also applied to Cohen's rejection of Kabbalah, that is, against the well-known critique of Gershon Scholem.

29. Schwarzschild, "Germanism," p. 104–105 of this volume.

30. See, for example, Jaques Derrida, "Interpretations at War: Kant, the Jew, the German," in *New Literary History*, vol. 22:1 (1991), 39–95, where he even goes so far as to compare Cohen's wartime patriotism with Heidegger's supporting the Nazis (81). David Novak, in discussion of Derrida, is still writing of Cohen's "unfortunate naivety in uncritically endorsing German militarism," (Novak, "Hermann Cohen on State and Nation," in *Hermann Cohen's Critical Idealism*, ed. R. Munk, Dordrecht, 2006, 262, note 6).

31. Another important example in Schwarzschild's thought is the application of *regulative idealization* to *halacha*. For explanation and discussion, see Menachem Kellner "Torah and Science in Modern Jewish Thought:

Steven Schwarzschild vs Yeshayahu Leibowitz," in Gad Freudenthal (ed.), *Torah et science–perspectives historiques et théoriques*, Paris 2001, 235–236.

32. Schwarzschild, "Germanism," p. 93 of this volume.

33. For support of Schwarzschild, see here: Andrea Poma, "Hermann Cohen's Response to Anti-Judaism," in Poma, *Yearning for Form and Other Essays on Hermann Cohen's Thought*, Dordrecht 2006, 11.

34. Newer studies show that in the second half of the nineteenth century, Cohen's lifetime, this gap was not only closed, but that Jews clearly took the lead in educational matters in Germany. Jewish families investing extensively in the education of their children caused a situation where more than 10 percent of the children attending institutions of higher education were Jewish, while Jews made up only 1 percent of the German population. All this, and especially many Germans' inferiority complex resulting from this development, fostered the new wave of anti-Semitism, beginning in the 1880s. See Götz Aly, *Warum die Deutschen? Warum die Juden?: Gleichheit, Neid und Rassenhass - 1800 bis 1933*, Frankfurt, 2011.

35. Cohen, *Jüdische Schriften*, Berlin, 1924, vol. II, 79.

36. Cohen, *Schriften zur Philosophie und Zeitgeschichte*, (eds. A. Görland and E. Cassirer) Berlin, 1928, vol. l, 559f. (Schwarzschild's translation). Following Schwarzschild to similar conclusions, cf. Hartwig Wiedebach, *The National Element in Hermann Cohen's Philosophy and Religion*, Leiden, 2012, 120 and 152.

37. Schwarzschild, *Radicalizes*, p. 47 of this volume.

38. Ibid., p. 44 of this volume.

39. p. 47 of this volume.

40. Schwarzschild in his afterword of *The Pursuit of the Ideal* (ed. Kellner), 253.

41. Schwarzschild, *The Pursuit of the Ideal*, Afterword, 253. Rosenzweig, he claims there, "fell prey to himself in this sense" and never recovered. Clear traces of this detour can still be found in the essay "To Recast Rationalism" (1962/1970) (pp. 23–27 of this volume).

42. For an interesting comparison between Cohen and Rosenzweig on Messianism, see Benjamin Pollok, "To Infinity and Beyond–Cohen and Rosenzweig on Comportment and Redemption," in *Rethinking the Messianic Idea in Judaism*, ed. M.L. Morgan, S. Weitzman, Bloomington, 2014, 174–194.

43. Schwarzschild, *The Pursuit of the Ideal*, Afterword, 254. See Schwarzschild's early Rosenzweigian critique of Cohen on this point in "Democratic Socialism" (pp. 1–21 of this volume).

44. Cf. here the discussion of Daniel Weiss, in Schwarzschild's favor (*Paradox and the Prophets*, 200).
45. Schwarzschild, *Afterword*, 254.
46. Schwarzschild, "Germanism," pp. 102–103 of this volume.

Chapter 1. The Democratic Socialism of Hermann Cohen

1. Hermann Cohen, *Ethik des Reinen Willens*, Berlin, 1904, 279, reprinted in Hermann Cohen, *Werke*, vol. 7, Hildesheim, 2012 (using the second editon from 1907 but giving the pagination of the 1904 edition).
2. Friedrich A. Lange, *Geschichte des Materialismus*, 7th ed., Einleitung mit kritischem Nachtrag von Hermann Cohen, Leipzig 1896, 527. (Reprint edition in Hermann Cohen, *Werke*, vol. 5, Hildesheim, 2012.)
3. Cohen, *Jüdische Schriften*, 3 vols., Berlin, 1924, vol. 3, 174.
4. Cohen, *Ethik*, 295 (*Werke*, vol. 7).
5. Quoted in Walter Kinkel, *Hermann Cohen—eine Einführung in sein Werk*, Stuttgart 1924, 168; cf. also Cohen in Lange, IX, 446 (*Werke*, vol. 5).
6. Cohen, *Ethik*, 276 (*Werke*, vol. 7).
7. Ibid., 287, 280 (*Werke*, vol. 7).
8. Ibid., 296 (*Werke*, vol. 7).
9. Cohen, *Religion und Sittlichkeit*, Berlin, 1907, 16. (New edition: Cohen, *Werke*, vol. 15, 21.)
10. Cohen, *Jüdische Schriften*, Berlin, 1924, vol. 2, 398.
11. Cohen, *Ethik*, 36f. (*Werke*, vol. 7).
12. Cf. Cohen in Lange, 523 (*Werke*, vol. 5).
13. Cohen, *Ethik*, 43, 314 (*Werke*, vol. 7).
14. Cohen in Lange, 463 (*Werke*, vol. 7).
15. Ibid., 521f. (*Werke*, vol. 5).
16. Cohen, *Logik der reinen Erkenntnis*, 2nd ed., Berlin 1914, 388. (Reprinted in Cohen, *Werke*, vol. 6.)
17. Cohen, *Ethik*, 43 (*Werke*, vol. 7).
18. Ibid., 41f. (*Werke*, vol. 7).
19. Cf. Simon Kaplan, *Das Geschichtsproblem in der Philosophie Hermann Cohens*, Berlin, 1930, 53.
20. Cohen, *Logik*, 113 (*Werke*, vol. 6).
21. Cohen, *Ästhetik des reinen Gefühls*, Berlin, 1912, vol. 2, 8. (Reprinted in Cohen, *Werke*, vol. 9.)
22. Cohen, *Ästhetik*, vol. 1, 398 (reprinted in Cohen, *Werke*, vol. 8).

23. Ibid., vol. 2, 94ff. (*Werke*, vol. 9).
24. Ibid., vol. 2, 415 (*Werke*, vol. 9).
25. Cohen, *Ethik*, 31 (*Werke*, vol. 7).
26. Ibid., 236ff. (*Werke*, vol. 7).
27. Ibid., 32 (*Werke*, vol. 7). Cohen, *Logik*, 203 (*Werke*, vol. 6).
28. Cohen, *Religion der Vernunft aus den Quellen den Judentums*, 2nd ed., Frankfurt, 1929, 292 (Schwarzschild's own translation) English edition, *Religion of Reason out of the Sources of Judaism*, trans. Simon Kaplan, New York, 1972, 249 [pages of this edition will be given in brackets]. See also: Cohen, *Logik*, 586. (Reprint *Werke*, vol. 6.)
29. Cohen, *Jüdische Schriften*, vol. 3, 198.
30. Ibid.
31. Cohen, *Religion der Vernunft*, 15 [English ed., 13], Cohen, *Ethik*, 1–5 (*Werke*, vol. 7).
32. Cf. Kinkel, 251.
33. Cohen, *Ethik*, 53 (*Werke*, vol. 7), Cohen, *Jüdische Schriften*, vol. 3, 173.
34. Max Brod, *Heidentum, Judentum, Christentum*, Munich, 1921, makes a similar distinction between the Christian emphasis on "ignoble suffering" that could be prevented or remedied, and the Jewish emphasis on "noble suffering," which is unavoidable and in the nature of things. (English ed.: *Paganism, Christianity, Judaism: A Confession of Faith*, trans. from the German by William Wolf, Alabama, 1970.)
35. Cohen, *Jüdische Schriften*, vol. 1, 313f., Cohen, *Religion der Vernunft*, 26 [engl. 23].
36. Cohen, *Ethik*, 528f. (*Werke*, vol. 7).
37. Cohen in Lange, VIIIf. (*Werke*, vol. 5).
38. Julius Guttmann, *Die Philosophie des Judentums*, Munich, 1933, 351, (English ed.: *Philosophies of Judaism: the History of Jewish Philosophy from Biblical Times to Franz Rosenzweig*, Garden City, 1966), Cohen, *Ethik*, 426f. (*Werke*, vol. 7).
39. Cohen in Lange, 527 (*Werke*, vol. 5).
40. Cohen, *Ethik*, 32 (*Werke*, vol. 7).
41. Cohen, *Logik*, 544 (*Werke*, vol. 6).
42. Quoted in Kaplan, *Geschichtsproblem*, 85.
43. Cohen, *Religion der Vernunft*, 16 [engl. 14].
44. Cohen, *Deutschtum und Judentum*, Giessen, 1916, 49. (New edition Cohen, *Werke*, vol. 16, Hildesheim, 2012, 543.)
45. Kaplan, *Geschichtsproblem*, 31.
46. Cohen, *Ethik*, 57 (*Werke*, vol. 7).

47. Cohen in Lange, 530 (*Werke*, vol. 5).

48. Cohen, *Religion der Vernunft*, 277 [engl. 237], Cohen, *Logik*, 203 (*Werke*, vol. 6).

49. Cohen in Lange, 525, 529 (*Werke*, vol. 5).

50. Cohen, *Jüdische Schriften*, vol. 3, 171, 174.

51. Ibid., vol. 1, 330.

52. Ibid., vol. 2, 70.

53. Ibid., 48.

54. Kaplan, 32.

55. Cohen in Lange, 525 (*Werke*, vol. 5).

56. Cohen, *Ethik*, 305 (*Werke*, vol. 7).

57. Ibid., 293f. (*Werke*, vol. 7).

58. Kinkel, 241.

59. Samuel Atlas, "Zur erkenntnistheoretischen Grundlegung der Geschichte," in *Archiv für systematische Philosophie und Soziologie*, vol. XXXI, no. 3, 232.

60. Kinkel, 197.

61. Cohen, *Ethik*, 74 (*Werke*, vol. 7).

62. Cohen, *Deutschtum und Judentum*, 48 (*Werke*, vol. 16, 541–542).

63. Cf. Kinkel, 215.

64. Cohen in Lange, 534 (*Werke*, vol. 5). Chayim Greenberg, *The Inner Eye, Selected Essays*, New York, 1953, 264, tells of an actual encounter on the field of socialist controversy between Cohen and Lenin. He gives no source, but the character of Greenberg and the internal verisimilitude of the story commend it: Lenin wrote that Cohen's demand for the teaching of higher mathematics in the last years of German high schools was a bourgeois attempt to befuddle and direct the minds of young adults just when they are ready to become associated with revolutionary activities.(!)

65. Cohen, *Religion der Vernunft*, 39 [engl. 34].

66. Ibid., 28 [engl. 24].

67. Ibid., 300 [engl. 257], Cohen, *Ethik*, 58 (*Werke*, vol. 7).

68. Ibid., 295 [engl. 253].

69. Cohen, *Jüdische Schriften*, vol. 2, 335.

70. Cf. Kinkel, 264.

71. Cohen, *Religion der Vernunft*, 304, 312 [engl. 260, 267], cf. Kinkel, 255.

72. Guttmann, 351.

73. Cohen, *Religion der Vernunft*, 16 [engl. 14].

74. Cohen, *Deutschtum und Judentum*, 57f. (Cohen, *Werke*, vol. 16, 557).

75. Immanuel Kant, *Streit der Fakultäten*, 2, 3–7.

Chapter 2. To Recast Rationalism (1962/1970)

1. Hugo Bergman, *Faith and Reason*, Washington, 1961, 22.
2. "The Basis of Franz Rosenzweig's Philosophy," *Al Franz Rosenzweig-Bimlot 25 Shanah Liftirato*, Jerusalem, 5716, 83ff.
3. Moshe Maisels, *Thought and Truth: A Critique of Philosophy, its Source and Meaning* (trans. from the Hebrew), New York, 1956.
4. Cohen, *Religion der Vernunft*, Frankfurt am Main, 1929, 17, cf. also 22ff. [engl. 14, 19].
5. Julius Guttmann, *Philosophie des Judentums*, Berlin 1933, 360ff. (English ed.: *Philosophies of Judaism*, 1966).
6. Franz Rosenzweig, *Stern der Erlösung*, Frankfurt 1921, I, 27–31. (English: *The Star of Redemption*, trans. Barbara E. Galli, Madison, 2005).
7. "The Personal Messiah—Toward the Restoration of a Discarded Doctrine," *Judaism*, vol. 5, no, 2, 127, and "The Democratic Socialism of Hermann Cohen," *HUCA*, vol. XXVII, 436ff., in this volume p. 1–21.
8. Guttmann, 351.
9. Cf. Ernst Simon's most helpful and illuminating study, "James, Fechner and Jung on Religious Experience and Divine Education," *Judaism*, vol. 3, no. 3, where he says: "In my view, he [Thieberger, in his introduction to the Hebrew translation of *The Varieties of Religious Experience*] could have gone much further by showing the lines that run from James to Buber and to Rosenzweig," and then goes on to cite a Jamesian passage about the *I and Thou*, which also brings us right back to Hermann Cohen. The intimate connection is not limited to the field of psychology; it also exists in the field of logic and ethics, even in epistemology. For Cohen the idea is the hypothesis: the hypothesis is to be derived from science and jurisprudence; and the validity of the idea, or hypothesis, is always measured by its effectiveness in helping toward the realization of the (ethical) purpose which it enshrines. For the idealist Cohen, therefore, the value of the idea is not very different, basically, from what it is to the pragmatist Dewey.
10. F.A. Lange, *Geschichte des Materialismus*, 7th ed., *Einleitung mit kritischem Nachtrag von Hermann Cohen*, Leipzig, 1896, 463. (Reprint ed.: Hermann Cohen, *Werke*, vol. 5, Hildesheim, 2012).

Chapter 3. Truth

1. See, for example, Alexander Altmann, "Hermann Cohen's Begriff der Korrelation," in *Zwei Welten*, Tel Aviv, 1962.

2. "From Critical to Speculative Idealism" [review], *Journal of Bible and Religion*, January 1966, and "The Democratic Socialism of Hermann Cohen," *HUCA*, 1956, 436 (pp. 197–201 and pp. 1–21 in this volume).

Chapter 5. Franz Rosenzweig's Anecdotes about Hermann Cohen

1. Parts of this essay were read at the American Academy of Religion, October 1968, Dallas, Texas.

2. Rosenzweig was perfectly aware of the fact that he was conjuring up a mythical Cohen: in *Stern der Erlösung*, (Frankfurt a.M.) 1921, 29f., he states explicitly that he is taking Cohen somewhere he does not want to go; Franz Rosenzweig, *Briefe* (Berlin) 1935, 399, admits that Cohen would not have liked his reinterpretation of him and wonders whether his historiographical procedure is legitimate, and p. 617 calls his Cohen "a legend" about which Mrs. Cohen, by then widowed, was very angry. Bruno Strauss, in his introduction to Hermann Cohen, *Briefe* (Berlin) 1939, 4, calls Rosenzweig's a "daring" biographical sketch, "based (too) much on anecdotes."

3. Cf. Franz Rosenzweig, *Kleinere Schriften* (Berlin) 1937, 530: "Cohen said (unfortunately he only said it and did not write it): . . ." cf. ibid. 352; Hermann Cohen, *Jüdische Schriften* (Berlin) 1924, vol. 1, "Preface," L: "my fortunate ears heard him. . . ."

4. Rosenzweig tells the story at least twice: *Jüdische Schriften*, vol. 1, xxxv, Rosenzweig, *Jehuda Halevi, Zweiundneunzig Hymnen und Gedichte*, Berlin, 1926, 239.

5. . Cf. for example, Emil Fackenheim, *Hermann Cohen - After Fifty Years* (Leo Baeck Memorial Lecture 12), New York, 1969, 7ff.

6. Rosenzweig, *Briefe*, 594.

7. Cf. Also, Rosenzweig, "Ein Gedenkblatt," *Kleinere Schriften*, 291; *Jüdische Schriften*, xiii, xix, lii. Cf. Samuel H. Bergman, "Franz Rosenzweig on Hermann Cohen's Death" (Hebrew), *Hadoar*, Tishri I: 5729, 739.

8. This argument, too, continues to be carried forward: cf. Martin Buber "The Love of God and the Idea of Deity," *Israel and the World*, New York, 1948, and his disciple E. Fackenheim, *Quest for Past and Future* (Boston), 1968, 33ff., and *God's Presence in History*, New York 1970, 35–41.

9. Ernst Simon, *Brücken*, Heidelberg 1965, 214: "Thus it was with Hermann Cohen. His messiah was false; his messianism was genuine." In

Briefe, dated April 7, 1918, Rosenzweig tells another anecdote about the messianism of the two men, in which their positions are curiously reversed.

10. Rosenzweig, *Jehuda Halevi*, 191; Samuel H. Bergman, *Faith and Reason: An Introduction to Modern Jewish Thought*, Washington, DC, 1961, 41.

11. As ought to be better known, Pascal's distinction was long and precisely anticipated by R. Yehudah Halevy in *Kuzari*, iv/16, where, instead of "God of the philosophers," he speaks of the "God of Aristotle." In the context of Halevy's philosophical theology, however, contrary to what most mid-brow historians do with him, his God, that is to be "tasted and seen," is just the same the God of the negative and ethical attributes, not, heaven forfend, Pascal's Eucharistic God. (Unfortunately we cannot unpack this here.)

12. Strauss, *Philosophie und Gesetz - Beiträge zum Verständnis Maimunis und seiner Vorläufer*, (Berlin) 1935, 39, n. 1.

13. Cf. "A Giving of Accounts: Jacob Klein and Leo Strauss," in *The College*, St. John's College (Annapolis, MD, Santa Fe, NM), April 1970, 2. On p. 3 Strauss also tells of how he reported on his way home to Rosenzweig about Heidegger. The same motivation, which Rosenzweig had for believing the anecdote at issue also works for Strauss: in this article the latter makes clear his preference for Heidegger's existentialist ontology over Cohen's rationalism, as did Rosenzweig in "Vertauschte Fronten," (*Kleinere Schriften*), opting for Heidegger rather than Ernst Cassirer. (Cf. also Carl Hamburg, "A Cassirer-Heidegger Seminar," *Philosophy and Phenomenological Research*, xxv–2, December 1964, and K. Loewith, *Gesammelte Abhandlungen*, Stuttgart, 1960, "Martin Heidegger und Franz Rosenzweig—Ein Nachtrag zu 'Sein und Zeit,'" 68–92.) Indeed, between Strauss' present article and his *Spinoza's Critique of Religion*, including the dedication to Rosenzweig in 1930 and the quasi-autobiographical "Preface" to its English edition, New York, 1965, the Rosenzweigian motivation for Strauss' work in general becomes quite clear and should be explicated by someone soon.

14. There are two *loci classici* in Kant that deal with this point, one is the *Critique of Pure Reason*, Cassirer ed., (Berlin) 1922, 265, and the second is so stunning and also Jewishly so important that it deserves to be quoted here *in extenso*, *Critique of Judgment*, loc. cit., 347 (my translation):

> There is perhaps no more sublime passage in the law-book of the Jews than the command: You shall not make for yourself

an image, nor anything resembling that which is in heaven or on earth or underneath the earth, etc. This command alone can explain the enthusiasm which the Jewish people during its civilized epoch felt for its religion when it compared itself with other peoples and the pride with which Mohammedanism embues men. The same applies to the notion of the moral law and the disposition to morality within us. It is an entirely erroneous anxiety to worry that if men were deprived of all that the senses can commend they would retain nothing but cold, lifeless approval and no moving power or emotion. To the contrary: only where the senses can no longer see anything, but the unmistakable and imperishable idea of morality still remains, there it might be necessary to moderate the élan of an unbounded imagination, so that it will not grow into enthusiasm, rather than to look for help in images and other childish apparatus out of fear of the powerlessness of these ideas. It is for this reason that governments have gladly and richly supplied religion with all possible implements and thus sought to deprive their subjects of the need as well as of the capacity to expand their spiritual powers beyond the limits which have been arbitrarily imposed upon them and by means of which they could more easily be treated as passive objects. This pure, soul-elevating, merely negative representation of ethics, on the other hand, creates no danger of enthusiasm, which is the illusion of wishing to see beyond all limits of sensibility, i.e. to dream according to principles (to rave rationally), precisely because it is a merely negative representation. For the unfathomability of the idea of freedom cuts off all possibility of representing it positively...."

(The passage deserves a most careful explication.) That such an "idea of God," really "the ideal," is implicitly and necessarily quasi-personal is seen in the *Critique of Pure Reason*, loc. cit., 396, 402, *Critique of Practical Reason*, ibid., 95, 136, 151—and the *Critique of Judgment*, ibid., 523–556.

15. Berlin 1889, 125. reprint edition in Cohen, *Werke*, vol. 3, Hildesheim 2009. Cf. also Cohen, *Ethik des reinen Willens* (Berlin), 1904, 417, *Werke*, vol. 7.

16. *Religion der Vernunft - aus den Quellen des Judentums*, Frankfurt a.M., 1929, 480 [engl. 414].

17. Cf. *Jüdische Schriften*, xlv ff.; in "Ein Gedenkblatt," 293 he speaks of "Cohen's last theological epoch," and in "Hermann Cohens Nachlasswerk - Ein Brief," *Kleinere Schriften*, 295, of "the last Hermann Cohen"; cf. also Rosenzweig, *Briefe*, 299, 499. Opposed to his thesis cf. Julius Guttmann, *Philosophie des Judentums*, München, 1933, 346, 351, 361; Leo Strauss, *Philosophie und Gesetz*, 35–41; S. Schwarzschild, "To Re-Cast Rationalism," *Judaism*, xi/3 (Summer 1962), 207, and ib., xv/4 (Fall 1966), 466; especially Alexander Altmann, "Hermann Cohens Begriff der Korrelation," in *In Zwei Welten*, Tel-Aviv, 1962. More, however, remains to be said about this point, which is decisive not only for a correct understanding of Cohen but also for what is again very much alive in the current discussions of the ontological function of "episteme."

18. For the time being let it suffice to point out that *Kants Begründung der Ästhetik*, 415–427 (reprint: Cohen, *Werke*, vol. 3) argues virtually the entire thesis of the *Religion of Reason*—that religion is rightly concerned with "the individual *quand même.*"

19. *Jüdische Schriften*, xxi; Rosenzweig, *Briefe*, 499; cf. also *Davke*; (Yiddish), xxiii–xxiv/9, (Buenos Aires) 1958, "Hermann Cohen's 40th Yahrtzeit," especially the articles by Aron Steinberg and Jacob Mase, the chief rabbi of Moscow at the time of Cohen's visit, and Schwarzschild, "Davke," *Judaism*, ix/1, Spring 1960, 169–173.

20. Cf. Michael Meyer, "Great Debate on Antisemitism–Jewish Reaction to New Hostility in Germany 1879–1881," *Year Book* XI, Leo Baeck Institute, 1966; Hans Liebeschütz, *Das Judentum im deutschen Geschichtsbild*, Tübingen, 1967, 203–227.

21. Cohen, *Briefe*, 24.

22. Ibid., 27.

23. *Jüdische Schriften*, xxii.

24. Cohen, *Briefe*, 47.

25. Ibid., 56.

26. Ibid., 62.

27. Ibid., 51f.

28. Cf. S. Schwarzschild, "The Democratic Socialism of Hermann Cohen," pp. 1–21 of this volume.

29. Cf. S. Schwarzschild, "A Note on the Nature of Ideal Society - A Rabbinic Study," in *Jubilee Volume to C. C. Silberman*, eds. H. Strauss and H. Reissner (New York), 1968, 86, note.

30. Cf. also *Jüdische Schriften*, xxxiii, ff.

31. Cf., for example, the incident with Rickert told in *The Autobiography of Nahum Goldmann* (New York), 1969, 69, that Hermann Cohen is "more race than philosophy."

32. *Jüdische Schriften*, 333, Cohen, *Briefe*, 71.

Chapter 7. Historical Excursus

1. Hermann Cohen, *Das Princip der Inifinitesimal-Methode und seine Geschichte*, Berlin 1883, new edition in Cohen, *Werke*, vol. 5, Hildesheim, 2012. For a recent discussion of this work see: Marco Giovanelli, *Reality and Negation - Kant's Principle of Anticipations of Perception*, Dordrecht, 2010, 178-197.

2. Cf. the use of Genesis in the "Introduction" to Cohen, *Logik der reinen Erkenntnis*, Berlin 1902, p. 28ff. (*Werke*, vol. 6).

3. I found the book to which Cohen refers in his surviving library (cg. n. 4): *Versuch einer logischen Auseinandersetzung des mathematischen Unendlichen*, 2nd ed., Berlin: Christian Gottfried Schoene, 1796. Cohen's marginal notes show how thoroughly he worked this volume through. There are several original editions of Bendavid's publications in Cohen's collection.

4. I found also in Cohen's library a copy of Marcus Herz's *Grundlage zu meinen Vorlesungen über die Experimentalphysik*, Berlin: Christian Friedrich Voss & Sohn, 1787 (COH 530.9 [P] H 58), interpaginated with extensive manuscript notes that clearly represented the basis of the author's medical lectures.

5. Also found in Cohen's library is Heinrich Witte, *Salomon Maimon: die merkwürdigen Schicksale und die wissenschaftliche Bedeutung eines jüdischen Denkers aus der kantischen Schule*, Berlin: Mecklenburg, 1876. The latter item is particularly interesting as there has been some debate as to whether Cohen was at all aware and, if he was, to what extent he consciously took up some of Maimon's views. (Cf. S.H. Bergmann, *The Philosophy of Solomon Maimon*, Jerusalem, 1967.) In a letter of June 10, 1917, Cohen writes to Natorp (Holzhey, *Cohen und Natorp–Ein Beitrag zur Geschichte des Neukantianismus - Texte, Briefe, Interpretation*, Zurich, 1974, ccxvif.) that he likes Friedrich Kunze, the author of a book about Maimon, "although he misrepresents me over against Maimon and even ignored my note in *Kants Theorie der Erfahrung* (p. 424). [3rd ed. 540, n.]."

6. *Infinitesimalmethode*, 136 (*Werke*, vol. 5).

7. Cf. Alexander Altmann, *Moses Mendelssohn - A Biographical Study*, University of Alabama Press, 1973, 153.

8. Other Jews were occupied with this subject at this time: for example, Moses Ensheim = Moses Brisac of Metz, *Recherches sur les calculs différentiels et integrals*, Paris, 1799.

9. Cf. Altmann, *Mendelssohn*, 112–130.

10. Ibid., 155.

11. Ibid., 144, 153, 179.

12. Ibid., 179.

13. Ibid., 669.

14. Ibid., 689.

15. Ibid., 267.

16. Cohen, *Infinitesimalmethode*, 128f., reprint Cohen, *Werke*, vol. 5.

17. Cf. L. de Villefosse and J. Bouissounouse, *The Sourge of the Eagle— Napoleon and the Liberal Opposition*, London: Sidgewick & Jackson, 1972, 108, 171, 226f. Both doctrinally as well as anecdotally it is then wryly amusing to find the American Secretary of State, Henry Kissinger, in his doctoral study *A World Restored—The Politics of Conservatism in a Revolutionary Era*, London: Victor Gollancz 1973, 23, admiringly cite his *beau ideal* Prince Metternich, the epitome of conservatism, about "an alliance *infiniment limité*"—referring to understandings with Napoleon that intentionally meant "nothing" at all.

18. Cf., for example, Platon, *Timaeus* 370–380.

19. *Meister Eckharts Mystische Schriften*, trans. Gustav Landauer, ed. Martin Buber, Berlin: Karl Schnabel Verlag, 1920, 127.

20. Cf. how Glendower's Welsh mysticism was eliminated from "Henry IV" in the rationalist eighteenth and nineteenth centuries: *The First Part of the History of Henry IV* (*The Works of Shakespeare*) ed. John Doner Wilson, Cambridge: University Press 1946, XXXVII, XLV.

21. Cf. Frances A. Yates, "The Hermetic Tradition in Renaissance Science," in *Art, Science and History in the Renaissance*, ed. C. Singleton, Johns Hopkins University Press, 1968, and idem, *The Rosicrucian Enlightenment*, Routledge, 1972, 228; Ernst Cassirer, "Giovanni Pico Della Mirandola: A Study in the History of Renaissance Ideas," in *Journal of the History of Ideas*, vol. 3, no. 3 (June, 1942), 319–346.

22. Cf., for example, Blaisio Ugolini's *Thesaurus of Rabbinic and Kabbalistic literature*. [*Thesaurus Antiquitatum Sacrarum*, 34 vols., Venice, 1744–69.]

23. A volume of Boehme is still preserved in Cohen's library.

24. Cf. Eugene Gadol, "The Idealistic Foundations of Cultural Anthropology," in *Journal of the History of Philosophy* XII/2, April 1974, 210f; Johann Georg Wachter, *Der Spinozismus im Jüdenthumb, oder die von dem heutigen Jüdenthumb und dessen geheimen Kabbala Vergötterte Welt*, Amsterdam, 1699, and idem, *Elucidarius cabalisticus sive reconditae Hebraeorum philosophiae*, Rome, 1706. To the latter work Leibniz wrote *"Animadversiones"*; cf. Altmann, 866, n. 12.

25. Frank E. Manuel, *The Religion of Isaac Newton and Portrait of Isaac Newton*, Harvard University Press, 1968; Herbert McLachlan (ed.), *Sir Isaac Newton's Theological Manuscripts*, Liverpool 1950; J.M. Keynes, who calls Newton "the last of the magi": "Newton the Man" in his *Collected Writings* X, Essays in Biography, 1972, 363; Christopher Hill, "Sir Isaac Newton and his Society" in *Change and Continuity in 17th Century England*, London: Weidenfeld and Nicolson, 1974, 272, that in the millenarian period of the "troubled years 1656–6, Newton, away from it all, was discovering the calculus..."—and 273f. on Newton's apparently somewhat contradictory attitudes toward color as a "secondary quality," and so on.

26. In Cohen's library a lot of literature by and about Bruno and most especially by and about Newton is to be found. Newton's works are there in several multivolumed editions, in Latin, English, and German.

27. Ed. J. Ph. Wolfers, Berlin, 1872.

28. Newton, 506.

29. Ibid., 509f. It is amusing to note that in Newton's footnote to this passage, where references are made to the Church fathers, the Bible, and Philo, Cohen picks the last, the Jew, to underline.

30. Cf. Hill, "Sir Isaac Newton and his Society," 277.

31. Cf. Benzion Kellermann, "Ideal, Schema und Hypothese," in *Das Ideal im System der Kantischen Philosophie*, Berlin, 1920, 308ff.; and Albert Görland, *Die Hypothese - Ihre Aufgabe und ihre Stelle in der Arbeit der Naturwissenschaft*, Göttingen, 1911, in Cohen's library (H 67) autographed "Seinem Meister Hermann Cohen in selbstverständlicher Treue"—a telling dedication in view of the history of the relationship between the two men and of Cohen's political situation at his university in this final period.

32. *Sir Isaac Newtons Mathematische Prinzipien in der Naturlehre* (ed. Wolfers), 511.

33. Cf. Shmuel Sambursky, "Kepler in Hegel's Eyes," in *Proceedings, The Israel Academy of Sciences and Humanities*, V/3, Jerusalem, 1971,

100. Sambursky's conclusion is to be noted, that Hegel consistently denigrated Newton in favor of Kepler, as part of his "essentially Romantic," antimathematical posture. (Ibid, 191ff.) (Cf. Friedrich Engels' unsuccessful attempt to defend Hegel's philosophy of mathematics against Lange's attacks: Lange, op. cit., 74, 82.) In general, a curious ambivalence must be observed about Marburg neo-Kantianism's attitude toward Hegel: the two share many basic notions, on the one hand; on the other, Hegel is strongly disliked, (cf. Steven Schwarzschild, "Hermann Cohen's Construction of the Self," pp. 69–92 of this volume) and the fundamental difference between Hegel's ontologizing and Cohen's heuristics must be kept in mind.

34. Harry A. Wolfson, *The Philosophy of Spinoza*, New York, 1969, vol. 1, p. 17, vol. 2, p. 304ff.

35. See, for example, Gershom Scholem "The Career of a Frankist: Moshe Dubroshka and his Metamorphoses," (Hebrew) in *Zion* 35, 1970, 127–181.

36. Trans. H.G. Broun, Stuttgart, 1870, with additions by Darwin that were not as yet to be found in the then extant English editions, inscribed "Seinem Freunde Hermann Cohen—Hermann Lewandowsky (a lifelong friend and medical scientist) zum 25. Juli 1870," that is, immediately upon publication, and fulsomely annotated by Cohen.

37. *I. Physikalischer Teil*, plus Marcel Grossman's *II. Mathematischer Teil*, Leipzig and Berlin: B.G. Teubner. This is especially interesting in view of the cliché often, and wrongly, thrown at Kant and Kantians that their philosophy, particularly of science, is conditioned exclusively on Newtonian physics. Also to be found in Cohen's library is Ewald Sellin, *Die erkenntnistheoretische Bedeutung der Relativitätstheorie*, Kantstudien, Ergänzungsheft 48, 1919, but by this time Cohen was, of course, dead. He may still have ordered it shortly before his death, and in that case he must have made a special point of doing so, since he ceased receiving the *Kantstudien* automatically when he resigned from the Kantgesellschaft during the Bauch-fight. It is also possible that, as in the case of a few other later accretions to his library, this item was later added by his widow. As for the substantive issue raised by this cliché, cf. Ernst Cassirer, *Zur Einsteinschen Relativitatstheorie—Erkenntnistheoretische Betrachtungen*, Berlin: B. Cassirer Verlag, 1921. (Cohen references are on pp. 12, 28, and back cover. Einstein had reviewed this book in manuscript. [p. 5] In a postscript Cassirer stipulates wide-ranging agreement between himself and Hans Reichenbach, although he reserves his disagreement on the subject of Kant [p. 134]. This fact is more illuminating than Vaihinger's

somewhat facile dichotomy between neo-Kantianism and empirico-positivism [cp. footnote 6].) In a letter dated July 21, 1913, Cohen writes to Benzion Kellermann (the letter is in possession of the latter's son, Prof. E. Walter Kellermann, Leeds University [England], Physics Department): "Now I am finally clear about the relativity principle and can talk about it on my own." On November 28, 1914, Cohen writes to Natorp (Holzhey p. clxxv); "it is very interesting that Buek (cp. Otto Buek, "Michael Faradays System der Natur und seine begrifflichen Grundlagen," *Philosophische Abhandlungen zu Hermann Cohens 70. Geburtstag*, Berlin, 1912) attends Einstein's lectures and that he gets together with him frequently and has thorough discussions with him. He does think that Einstein is philosophically unclear [an opinion that can also be justified from his later quasiphilosophical writings], and he still has not been able to form a proper judgment of the whole thing; only the difficult mathematics of it is *extra jures*." (Cassirer adds his personal greetings to this letter.)

38. Cohen, *Infinitesimalmethode*, 121 (reprint Cohen, *Werke*, vol. 5).

39. Third revised ed., Braunschweig: Friedrich Vieweg & Sohn, 1870. Cohen studied theoretical physics and acoustics with Helmholtz at the University of Berlin in 1872 (cf. Lange, op. cit., 366, 369). One may assume that this book was his text at the time.

40. See infra.

41. First published in *Kultur der Gegenwart*, III, part 3, vol. 1, Leipzig Teubner, 1914—the volume that also contains the first edition of Einstein's "Die Relativitätstheorie."

42. Cohen, *Infinitesimalmethode*, 149 (reprint: Cohen, *Werke*, vol. 5).

43. Ibid., 162–169.

44. As compiled at the Hermann-Cohen Archive in the Philosophical Seminar of the University of Zurich.

45. Cf. Holzhey, "Philosophie und Wissenschaft," loc. cit., 50, col. 2. Müller died in 1888 and thus could not continue this line of investigation.

46. Altmann, *Mendelssohn*, 668–671.

47. Cohen, *Infinitesimalmethode*, 169 (reprint Cohen, *Werke*, vol. 5).

48. *Georg Christoph Lichtenbergs Vermischte Schriften*, eds. L.C. Lichtenberg and F. Kries, Wien, 1817, vol. 1, 110.

49. *International Herald Tribune*, September 10, 1975.

50. Cf. Jacob Fleischman, "Two Eternities - Franz Rosenzweig on Judaism and Christianity" (Hebrew), in *Iyyun* V/1, 78–86.

51. Cf. *The Guardian* (London), August 28, 1975, 6, for a summary.

Chapter 8. Applications of the Infinitesimalistic Theory in "the System"

1. Hermann Cohen, *Logik der reinen Erkenntnis*, Berlin, 1902, new edition in Cohen, *Werke*, vol. 6, Hildesheim, 2005.

2. Concerning the modern dispute between a logic of judgments and a logic of syntactical calculi cf. Werner Flach, "Urteil," in Handbuch philosophischer Grundbegriffe, eds. H. Krings, H.M. Baumgartner, and C. Wild, Koesel, vol. 6, 1556–1571, which ends with the sentence: "The logical calculus is, within the limits indicated, a logic of judgments after all."

3. Cohen, Logik, *Erste Klasse, Die Urteile der Denkgesetze* ("Judgments of the Laws of Thought"), p. 68ff., *Werke*, vol. 6. Holzhey wants to claim that there is a significant philosophic difference between Cohen's infinitesimalistic theory as expounded in the *Infinitesimalmethode* and as expounded in the *Logic*, but I cannot see this.

4. See Schwarzschild, "The Tenability of Hermann Cohen's Construction of the Self," pp. 62–63 of this volume.

5. Cohen, *Logik*, 67, *Werke*, vol. 6.

6. The principle of anticipation: this is a model of objective, mathematical qualitative perception. The principle is an "anticipation" in the same sense in which the spatial and temporal forms of intuition (i.e., space and time as pre-requisite to sensuous experience) are not derived from the object itself but exist logically prior to, independent of, a priori to it and are prerequisite to its experience; and mathematics is in turn the most consistent and the broadest such logical, rational construction. See Cohen, *Infinitesimalmethode*, 27f.: "The principle of anticipation contains, rolled in one, the entire problem of the critique of knowledge" (reprint Cohen, *Werke*, vol. 5).

7. Cohen, *Logik*, 65–75, *Werke*, vol. 6.

8. Cf. Schwarzschild, *Tenability*. There, however, its place in the infinitesimalistic system was not considered. The philosophical absence of an "unconscious self" would be the locus of the self-infinitesimal.

9. Friedrich Eckstein, *Das Phänomen der Verdichtung - eine naturphilosophische Studie*, Mainz 1885, 27–47.

10. Ibid., 37.

11. For Mendelssohn and Helmholtz, see above, p. 66.

12. For a discussion of Cohen's "pure affect," cf. also Cemach Feldstein, *Cohens Begruendung der Ethik. Erster Teil: Methode und Prinzipien*, dissert., University of Bern, 1907, Breslau: H. Fleischmann, 1914, 55–59ff.

13. See Schwarzschild, "The Legal Foundations of Jewish Aesthetics" *The Journal of Aesthetic Education* 9,1 (January 1975): 29–42.

14. Naum Gabo's famous "Kinetic Construction/Virtual Kinetic" (1920) consists of a steelstrip set in motion by a bell-magnet and thus creates a space. Her sound produces (or could produce) motion that infinitesimally creates a space; it is thus an extraordinarily good "realization" of a Cohennian object d'art. It has also been called an instance of "upper threshold movement," because the motion of the strip is so fast that it becomes almost invisible. This is an approximation of infinite speed. There are also kinetic art-objects built on "lower threshold movement," that is, movement so slow that it is virtually invisible. This would be an approximation of infinitesimal speed.

15. Cohen, *Religion of Reason - Out of the Sources of Judaism*, trans. Simon Kaplan, New York, 1972, 141, 404. Notice the cross-reference to the *Ethics* here. There is much to be improved about the Kaplan translation: here, for example, the use of "pity" for "compassion."

16. Alexander Altmann, "Hermann Cohens Begriff der Korrelation," in *In Zwei Welten—Bishnay Olamot*, ed. H. Tamer, Tel-Aviv, 1962, 377–399.

17. Cf. Schwarzschild, "The Function and Limits of Reason in Contemporary Jewish Theology," *Central Conference of American Rabbis Yearbook* 73 (1963), 199–214.

18. Cohen, *Religion of Reason*, 88.

Chapter 9. The Tenability of Herman Cohen's Construction of the Self

1. For example, this triple classification coincides essentially with T. Penelhum's use of "memory criterion" and "bodily criterion" and a combination of these two in "Personal Identity," *Encyclopedia of Philosophy*, vol. 6, and that of Charles Landesman in "The New Dualism in the Philosophy of Mind," *Review of Metaphysics*, XIX (December 1965), 329–331.

2. A.J. Ayer says, talking about Hume (Ayer and R. Winch [eds.], *British Empirical Philosophers* [London: Routledge, 1952], 28): "The idea of self as substance is to be discarded not because it is uncommonly difficult to verify in practice but because it is in principle unverifiable. . . . Of all the problems of philosophy, this is one of the most difficult. But I think it is soluble, although I do not think that it has yet been solved." Cf. also Dennis Wrong, "Identity: Problem and Catch-words," *Dissent*, September–October 1968, and the literature there adduced.

3. *Ethik des reinen Willens* (Berlin: Cassirer, 1904); subsequent citations to this text in this section are in parentheses. This work is "the second part" of Cohen's "System of Philosophy." The first part is his *Logik der reinen Erkenntnis* (Berlin: Cassirer, 1902; 2nd ed. 1914). The third is *Ästhetik des reinen Gefühls* (2 vols.; Berlin: Cassirer, 1912). New edition as volumes 6–8 of Hermann Cohen, *Werke*, Hildesheim, 2005. For how his own philosophical construction of the self-emerged seamlessly out of his still entirely convincing Kant-exegesis, see particularly "The Reformulation of the Second Edition: The I," *Kants Theorie der Erfahrung* (Berlin: Ferdinand Dümmler, 1871), 137–146. This was the fundamental work that put Cohen on the map at the time. On Cohen in general see Walter Kinkel, *Hermann Cohen: Eine Einführung in sein Werk* (Stuttgart: Strecker and Schroeder, 1924). For our subject in particular cf. Jacob Gordon, *Der Ichbegriff bei Hegel, bei Cohen, und in der Südwestdeutschen Schule* (Berlin:Akademie-Verlag, 1927), and J. Agus, *Modern Philosophies of Judaism* (New York: Behrman, 1941), especially 76–82, 96–103, 108–117.

4. References to the works more extensively treated in the text below are provided *in locu*. In the summaries of Cohen's argument some lengthy historical excursi and philosophical polemics are omitted, although they are actually of considerable historical, methodological, systematic, and especially Jewish interest.

5. Cf. Jakob Gordin, *Untersuchungen zur Theorie des unendlichen Urteils* (Berlin: Akademie-Verlag, 1929).

6. Cf. Thomas Nagel, *The Possibility of Altruism* (Oxford: Clarendon, 1970), 106.

7. The entire armamentarium of Buber's *I and Thou* is provided by Cohen in this section and elsewhere in his "system of philosophy."

8. *Ursprung* is a central concept and methodological tool for Cohen: *Logik*, Introduction, chap. 7, and Part I, chap. 1; cf. Walter Kinkel, "Das Urteil des Ursprungs," *Kantstudien*, XVII, no. 3 (1912).

9. Cf. Karl Popper's practitioner of "epistemology without a knowing subject" (*Philosophy Today No. 2*, ed. J. Gill [New York: Macmillan, 1969], 273): "Everything depends upon the give and take between ourselves and our work . . ." (unfortunately Sir Karl misreads Kant, as usual, and seems to be unaware of Cohen); and especially, J.R. Jones' excellently argued "cognition without a subject," in which the self is a "logical construction": "The Self in Sensory Cognition," *Mind*, LVIII (1949), 40–61 (despite A.G.N. Flew's petulant animadversions; ibid., 355–358, and Jones' reply, ibid., LIX [1950], 233–236).

10. Gilbert Ryle's well-known put-down phrase about "the ghost in the machine" was verbatim preempted by Kant and Cohen: see *The Concept of Mind* (New York: Barnes and Noble, 1949), especially 162–169, Cf. 376. 378–379 infra.

11. London, 1968; review in *The New Statesman*, Jan. 3, 1969, p. 20.

12. Cf. Kurt Lisser, "Der Begriff des Rechts bei Kant: Mit einem Anhang über Cohen and Görland," *Kantstudien*, no. 58 (1922); S. Wielikowsky, *Die Neukantianer in der Rechtsphilosophie* (Munich, 1914). For the juristic sources of the term "person," and for a very interesting history of the term in general, cf. A. Trendelenburg, "Zur Geschichte des Wortes Person," *Kantstudien*, XIII (1908), especially 6, 8.

13. Cf. my "The Democratic Socialism of Hermann Cohen," *Hebrew Union College Annual, XXVII* (1956), pp. 417–438; pp. 1–21 of this volume, and Henning Günther, *Philosophie des Fortschritts: Hermann Cohens Rechtfertigung der bürgerlichen Gesellschaft* (Munich: Goldmann Verlag, 1972), 17, 19, 30.

14. See Cohen's *Begriff der Religion im System der Philosophie* (Giessen: Töpelmann, 1915), 53; (reprint in Cohen, *Werke*, vol. 10, Hildesheim, 2002), also cf. Ernst Cassirer, *Rousseau, Kant, Goethe* (Princeton: Princeton University Press, 1945), and John Rawls' explication of the social contract as an heuristic device, in *A Theory of Justice* (Cambridge, MA: Harvard University Press, 1971), for example, 12, 138f., 350, passim.

15. Cf. H.L.A. Hart, "The Ascription of Responsibility and Rights," in *Logic and Language*, ed. A.G.N. Flew (First Series; Oxford: Blackwell, 1960), 145: guilt is not descriptive but a judgment of "ascription," that is, "imputation." Hart has since withdrawn this thesis (see *Punishment and Responsibility: Essays in the Philosophy of Law* [Oxford: Oxford University Press, 1968],"Preface") because of the criticism of P.T. Geach and G. Pitcher in *Philosophical Review*, LXIX (April 1960). (Alan Gewirth, in "The 'Is-Ought' Problem Resolved," *Proceedings and Addresses of the American Philosophical Association* [1973–1974], 50, therefore concludes that it "has, by general agreement, been definitively[!] refuted.") I continue to hold with Hart-the-ascriptivist as against Hart-the-nonascriptivist. Neither he nor Pitcher seems to be willing to face up to the problem of what we mean by "cause"; and Geach, though realizing that this is the issue, declares that he cannot handle it (*Philosophical Review*, LXIX, 224f.). It is here being argued, as did Kant, that causes are in fact always categorial "judgments," and that for the sake of science itself not only juridical judgments but all concepts must, contrary to Pitcher (ibid., 234), be "defeasible."

16. See above. Cf. Locke's use of "self" as a "forensic term" (*Essay* [Oxford, 1894], II, chap. 27, 467), and Kelsen's definition of the juridical object as "a localization of a point of imputability" (Erich Kaufmann, *Kritik der neukantischen Rechtsphilosophie* [Tübingen, 1921; Aalen, 1964], 81).

17. William James, *Principles of Psychology* (London, 1891), vol. I, chap. 10, especially 360–365, "The Transcendentalist Theory [of the Self]," gives, on the whole, a correct exposition of the Kantian view, quoting Cohen's *Kants Theorie der Erfahrung*, 365. James' own view, however, seems to oscillate back and forth. On the one hand, he speaks of the self "as a logical postulate" (304, 327f.), which is all that is needed for ethical purposes (350). On the other hand, he wants to say that it is "no mere *ens rationis*" but something "with which we have direct sensible acquaintance" (298f.). He identified this something with the primary stream of thought (302, 338, 342). Yet, "nothing can be known about it" (341f.), and it may only be taken as "some vague problematic ground" (350). (I am indebted to my colleague Prof. Herbert Spiegelberg for originally giving me this reference.) James' friend and neighbor Josiah Royce, while doing some of the same things, comes a good deal closer to Cohen at least in his "third self," the self as an ethical task (cf. Peter Fuss, *The Moral Philosophy of Josiah Royce* [Cambridge, MA: Harvard University Press, 1965], chaps. 4, 7, especially pp. 83f., 110, 165).

18. One feels in Schiller's formulation, unlike with Kant or Cohen, a presentiment of the state as the ultimate value, as it was to become in Hegel: "The state is the actuality of the ethical Idea. [. . .] The state exists immediately in custom, mediately in individual self-consciousness . . . while self-consciousness in virtue of its sentiment toward the state finds in the state, as its essence and the end and product of its activity, its substantive freedom" (*Philosophy of Right*, trans. T.M. Knox [New York: Oxford, 1967] §257, p. 155). And Marx writes in early July of 1842; "The state educates its members . . . by the individual finding his satisfaction in the life of the whole and the whole in the attitude of the individual" (Easton and Guddat [eds.], *The Writings of the Young Marx* [New York: Doubleday, 1967], 120). A little later, however, Marx criticizes this view of Hegel's harshly (*Critique of Hegel's "Philosophy of Right,"* ed. J. O'Malley [Cambridge: Cambridge University Press, 1970], 103). For the notion of the "species-individual," cf. Kant's *Ideas for an Universal History with Cosmopolitan Purpose*, §2.

19. *Kants Begründung der Ethik* (Berlin, 1877), 237; cf. Cohen, *Werke*, vol. 2, Hildesheim, 2001.

20. *Vorsatz* means literally "presetting." In the context of Cohen's thought it is, therefore, part of the rational activity of hypothesizing, that is, conceptual setting-up. If the word had not come to be used for somewhat different purposes later by phenomenologists and existentialists, "pro-ject" might have been a good rendering of *Vorsatz*. Cf. note 21 infra. For a radical, extremely complex, but also prototypical exposition of the concept and methodology of hypothesis in the Marburg school with scientific, historical and philosophical applications, cf. Benzion Kellermann, *Das Ideal im System der Kantischen Philosophie* (Berlin: Schwetschke, 1920), chap. 7, "Ideal, Schema und Hypothesis," 308–340.

21. My translation of this passage (the best that I could come up with) loses, however, much of the original (320): "Der Vorsatz ist die Vorwahl, die Vorwegnahme, die Vornahme des bestimmten Inhalts der Handlung. Der Vorsatz ist nicht Überlegung, sondern Entscheidung; Entscheidung in der Wirklichkeit, in der einzelnen Tatsache. Daher ohne Vorsatz kein Wille, keine Handlung. In dem Vorsatze aber scheinen sich Aufgabe and Wirklichkeit zu berühren. Dies darf nicht auffallen; das ist richtig und notwendig. So fordert es der Begriff der Aufgabe, dass sie in Lösung übergehe; und ebenso wiederum in Aufgabe zurückgehe."

22. Cf. Kant's *Metaphysics of Morals*, ed. Cassirer (Berlin: Cassirer, 1922), VII, 24: "A person is that subject whose actions are capable of being imputed. The moral personality is thus nought but the freedom of a rational being under moral laws (whereas the psychological person is merely the capacity of being conscious of one's own identity in the various states of one's existence).... An object is something that is incapable of imputation." (Subsequent references to Kant's works, except the *Opus Posthumum*, are to the Cassirer edition.)

23. Cf. *Ethik*, chap. 6; also *Kants Begründung der Ethik*, 233. For a summary of the complex juridical status of *mens rea*, cf. Orlan Lee and T.A. Robertson, *"Moral Order" and the Criminal Law* (Hague: Nijhoff, 1973), 83–91.

24. Cf. Morris Stockhammer, *Kants Zurechnungsidee und Freiheitsantinomie* (Cologne: Universität-Verlag, 1961).

25. On this cf. particularly the emphasis on voluntary acceptance of punishment in Maimonides, *Code*, "Laws of Theft and Loss," 1:13, and generally N. Rakover, *The Status of the Violator who has Accepted his Punishment* (Hebrew, mimeographed; "Series of Studies and Analyses in Jewish Law," no. 5; Jerusalem: Ministry of Justice, April 1970), especially 7, 20f.

26. Cohen's use of the term *Selbsterhaltung* could be misunderstood as "self-preservation." In fact he means the preservation of the self. Cf. *Logik*, 93, and his *Religion der Vernunft* (Frankfurt: Kaufmann, 1929), 264 [engl. 226].

27. *Religion der Vernunft*, 194 [engl. 167]. Citations in parentheses in this section are to this text. *The Religion of Reason* was preceded in Cohen's *oeuvre* by his war-time study, *The Concept of Religion within the System of Philosophy*; cf. note 14 *supra* and Cohen, *Werke*, vol. 10. In the latter work he deals with the present problem on 52–84, 118f, passim. The physical centrality of Cohen's massive treatment of what it means to be human in all of his major works may, then, be taken as symbolic of his profound humanism.

28. Cf. "Charakteristik der Ethik Maimunis," in *Moses ben Maimon*, ed. W. Bacher et al. (Leipzig, 1908), vol. I, 117, 120, new edition in Cohen, *Werke*, vol. 15, Hildesheim, 2009, 161–269, here 243, 248. Cohen's entire lifework can be seen as an arc from his early court affidavit on the Talmudic treatment of "the love of neighbor" (*Die Nächstenliebe im Talmud* [Marburg: Elwert, 1888]) to the posthumous *Religion of Reason*, in which this doctrine is the cornerstone.

29. At this point Cohen's use of the term *Nebenmensch* undergoes a small change from what it was in the *Ethik* (cf. 362, *Werke*, vol. 7), in the light of the higher notion now introduced of the *Mitmensch*, but this would appear to be only a displacement of terms. Karl Löwith's *Das Individuum in der Rolle des Mitmenschen* (Munich, 1928; Darmstadt: Wissenschaftliche Buchgesellschaft, 1962), his inaugural dissertation, works this notion out in considerable detail. He bases himself, however, only inadequately on Cohen (2, n. 1, 55, n. 1, 124) and not entirely along, though close to, the latter's lines. The unsatisfactory character of his Cohen-treatment must be due to the fact that this dissertation was written under Heidegger in Marburg in 1928. (Cf. C. Hamburg, "A Cassirer-Heidegger Seminar," *Philosophy and Phenomenological Research*, XXV [Dec. 1964], 208–222). Toward the end of his life he made some kind of amends in "Religion der Vernunft und Religion der Offenbarung: Hermann Cohen, dem deutschen Judentum zum Gedächtnis," *Neue Rundschau*, 4, (1968), 644–660.

30. In earlier approximations of his philosophic system Cohen had emphasized the role of art at this point, that is, that art "produces" "the ideal self" as a real individual, a unity of the duality of body and soul (*Ästhetik des reinen Gefühls*, II, 45f., reprint *Werke*, vol. 9), out of the ideal "lyrical" relationship between the duality of an isolated "I and

thou" (ibid., 23f; cf. Günther, *Philosophie des Fortschritts*, 72–74). This is another link in the argument that many have made (of note 39 *infra*) that "the old Cohen" made a turn away from radical neo-Kantian idealism to religious metaphysics. But in fact this is not the case. At most one can speak of a shift of evaluative emphasis. Even in the *Ästhetik* he saw the individual of art as only the typical individual, the individual as a member of the species (cf. *Ästhetik*, I, 168). In *Begriff der Religion* (85–107, especially 87, reprint *Werke*, vol. 10), he then stresses that this aesthetic individual, the species-individual, has thus been prepared for the truly and ultimately individualizing love of religion—the point that he is developing at this point of our exposition.

31. It has occasionally been pointed out that there is a good deal of crypto-Hegelianism in Cohen, despite the fact that Cohen regarded Hegel as the archenemy in philosophy. (Cf. *Hebrew Union College Annual*, XXVII, 421ff.; Donald P. Verene, "Kant, Hegel and Cassirer," *Journal of the History of Ideas*, XXX, [January–March 1969], 33–46). Thus here, Cohen's three-tiered person—*Nebenmensch, Mitmensch,* absolute self—is undoubtedly related to Hegel's "three selves" on their various levels: the self of the person, the *gebildete* self, and the divine self (*Pänomenologie des Geistes* [3rd ed., Jubiläumsausgabe; Stuttgart: Frommann, 1951], "Conscience, Beautiful Soul, etc.," 484–501; also 354–375, 515113). Hegel also holds that individuality arises from guilt: cf. *Philosophy of Right*, §§220f. For the theologico-religious sources of the persistent triadic theme in the history of philosophic discussions of the self cf. Trendelenburg, loc. cit., 12, and Sigmund Schlossmann, *Persona und Prosopon im Recht und im Christlichen Dogma* (Kiel and Leipzig, 1906; Darmstadt: Wissenschaftliche Buchgesellschaft, 1968).

32. Cf. Günther, *Philosophie des Fortschritts*, 82f., 87, 91. Cf. also Paul Natorp, "Bruno Bauchs 'Immanuel Kant' und die Fortbildung des Systems des kritischen Idealismus," *Kantstudien*, XXII (1918), 455: "Even the moral self is not yet the self as such. The latter is the theoretical and esthetic as well as the practical 'subject.' It knows itself as the ultimate—one need not avoid the word: absolute individuality, as religious, i.e. in mutual relation with the last, absolute universality. It exists in its ultimacy and knows itself to be doing so only in this mutual relation; in the language of all peoples that have raised themselves, if only intuitively, to this highest point: in the confrontation with 'God.' For this reason 'God' is for the self that knows itself not a mere matter of 'faith' in some sense or other, thus leaving open the possibility of reasonable doubt, but it knows 'God'

as surely and in quite the same ways as it knows itself, since it can know itself in its ultimate selfhood only through and by virtue of this confrontation." Henry W. Johnstone Jr.'s development of the notion of "self" in *The Problem of the Self* (University Park, PA: Pennsylvania State University Press, 1970), parallels in its entirety Cohen's explication. That the former's argument is entirely independent of and significantly different from Cohen's, yet quite persuasive in itself, and that it arrives at essentially the same conclusions, may be regarded as a supportive consideration for both. For Johnstone, too, the self is a "problem" (xi) in the sense of an "hypothesis" (16), "presupposition" (110), or "regulative idea" (131), which serves as the conceptual unity (9) of humanly necessary contradictions for "pragmatic," actionable purposes (12, 39, 71). It arises on occasions of "regretting" (pp. 8f.), blame (9), "sinning," "repenting" (23), changes of mind (146), and responsibility (65). Only when regarded not as reflexive but as "absolute" (e.g., "before God"), is it spoken of as "soul" (36). Apart from details, the only argument that Cohen would have with Johnstone is that he does not see the full rationality of his own concept of the self. He insists on regarding it as a "primitive" (*pace* Strawson, cf. infra.), while he ought to say that it is precisely for the unifying and other ethical purposes previously adduced that we construct this notion of the self. In this way he would also relieve himself of the necessity of repeatedly having to stipulate the "subjectivity" of selfhood (cf. 78, 89).

33. *On Trial: Fidel Castro, Régis Debray*, ed. M. Alexander (London: Lorrimer Publishing Co., 1969), 90.

34. Cf. Emma Goldman, *Living My Life* (New York: Dover, 1970), I, 190: "When he was face to face with the Prime Minister, he shot him dead. Mme. Canovas ran in at that moment and hit Angiolillo full in the face. 'I did not mean to kill your husband,' Angiolillo apologized to her, 'I aimed only at the official responsible for the Montjuich tortures.'"

35. Cf. *supra*; also *Begriff der Religion*, 63, *Werke*, vol. 10.

36. Cf. the classic distinction in Toennies, Buber, and so on, between "Gesellschaft" and "Gemeinschaft," but cf. Günther, *Philosophie des Fortschritts*, 19. (Ferdinand Toennies, as is little known, made his extended obeisance to Cohen in "Ethik und Sozialismus," *Archiv für Sozialwissenschaft und Sozialpolitik*, XXIX [1913], 895–930.) Kinkel, *Hermann Cohen*, 247 passim, objects that everything that Cohen adds to the concept of the self in his "theology" could also be done under the rubric of a philosophical ethic. (As a non-Jew himself, he apparently

felt a little left out at this point in Cohen.) I think this becomes a mere matter of nomenclature.

37. Citations in parentheses in this section are to Cohen's *Ethik der reinen Vernunft* (1904), Cohen, *Werke*, vol. 7.

38. Cf. note 12 *supra*.

39. Gordon, *Ichbegriff*, 48–68, like others, stipulates a development between Cohen's *Kants Theorie der Erfahrung* and his *Logik*. If he were right, then a difference could also be stipulated between Cohen's *Kants Begründung der Ethik* and his *Ethik*. However, even as we show here that there is no substantial difference between the latter two, so also his differentiation between the former two is not tenable.

40. *First Critique*, ed. Cassirer, 30f., note; also 130.

41. Ibid., 125, 276. To see how even in Kant's own time Solomon Maimon felt he had to safeguard the "phenomenal self," especially against Reinhold, see Samuel Atlas, *From Critical to Speculative Idealism* (Hague: Nijhoff, 1964), chap. 4 and 284–301. H.J. Paton makes the same mistake about Kant as Cohen; cf. *The Categorical Imperative* (New York: Harper, 1967), 254, 269.

42. *Werke* (Akademie-edition; Berlin: De Gruyter, XXII; hereafter cited as *Werke*, for all references to the *Opus Posthumum*. Cf. Gerhard Lehmann "Ganzheitsbegriff und Weltidee in Kants Opus Posthumum," in *Beiträge zur Geschichte und Interpretation der Philosophie Kants* (Berlin: De Gruyter, 1969), and Ted B. Humphrey, "Internal Structure in Kant's Thought," *Journal of the History of Ideas*, XXXIII (January–March 1972), 43–60, especially 52.

43. *Werke*, XXII, 33, 73. Cf. *Prolegomena*, §46: "The I" is the experienced subject as an "unknown . . . regulative principle."

44. *Werke*, XXII, 22, 96, 105, 323, 326, 404, 438f.

45. At one point, speaking of phenomenal objects, Kant actually says they are "= a oder *non a* des Setzens oder Aufhebens" (ibid., 31).

46. *Werke*, 11f., 16f., 19, 31, passim; Lehmann, "Ganzheitsbegriff," *Beiträge*, 248, 263.

47. Lehmann, "Ganzheitsbegriff," *Beiträge*, 253, 266f.

48. P. 286; *Religion within the Limits of Reason Alone*, ed. Cassirer, 166, 216f.

49. *Werke*, XXII, 415f. passim.

50. *Werke*, 289–292; *Second Critique*, ed. Cassirer, 133, 140. Cf. Cohen's *Religion of Reason*, 220.

51. This explication of Kant on the self also ought to take care of R.P. Wolff's thesis of "The Four Selves in Kant's Philosophy," in *The Autonomy of Reason: A Commentary on Kant's "Groundwork of the Metaphysics of Morals* (New York: Harper, 1973) 9–15 (repeated from R.P. Wolff [ed.], *Kant* [Garden City, NY: Doubleday, 1967], xi–xix [also in this volume is S.J. Todes, "Knowledge and the Ego," 156–171], and *in nuce* in his *Kant's Theory of Mental Activity: A Commentary on the Transcendental Analytic of the Critique of Pure Reason* [Cambridge, MA: Harvard University Press, 1963]. One would want to recommend Cohen's reading of the *First Critique, Kants Theorie der Erfahrung*, to Wolff. [I pass by a number of other important refutations of Wolff's interpretations and arguments, much as one appreciates his basic thrust.])

52. Cf. note 12 *supra*.

53. Cf. Ucko in the Hebrew translation of *Religion der Vernunft* (Jerusalem: Mossad Bialik, 1972), 9f.; also Ryle, *Concept of Mind*, 159; in a lovely paragraph, Ryle traces the dogmatic notion of consciousness from the Protestant notion of conscience.

54. Erik Erikson, *Identity, Youth, and Crisis* (New York: Norton, 1968). Citations in parenthesis in this section are to this text.

55. Cf. Helen Merrell Lynd, *On Shame and the Search for Identity* (New York: Harcourt Brace, 1958), 203, 206n, 207, 210, 219.

56. Cf., for example, Dimitry Gawronsky, "Ernst Cassirer: His Life and His Work," in *The Philosophy of E. Cassirer*, ed. P.A. Schillp (La Salle, IL: Open Court, 1949) 1–38.

57. Cassirer, *Leibniz System in seinen wissenschaftlichen Grundlagen* (Marburg: Elwert, 1902).

58. Cassirer, ix, 400, passim.

59. Cassirer, chap. 7 and chap. 10, sec. 1.

60. Trans. Ralph Mannheim (New Haven: Yale University Press, 1953, 1955, 1957). Citations in parentheses in this section are to this text.

61. *Leibniz System*, p. xi. Vol. II is dedicated to Natorp.

62. Eugene T. Gadol, "The Idealistic Foundations of Cultural Anthropology," *Journal of the History of Philosophy*, XII (April 1974), 222.

63. Cf. *An Essay on Man* (New Haven: Yale University Press, 1944), especially chaps. 2, 3, p. 32, and *Philosophy of Symbolic Forms*, especially III, 63f.

64. *Languages of Art* (New York: Bobbs-Merrill, 1968), 76f. His Cassirer references seem, on checking, to be somewhat awry.

65. Cf. notes 2, 9, 10, 87.

66. Bradley, *Ethical Studies* (Oxford: Clarendon, 1927), 64, 73, 193, 199ff., 319 passim; 323ff. (Citations in parenthesis in this section are to this text.) Cf. Hegel's *Philosophy of Right*, Preface.

67. Cf. Richard Wollheim, *F. H. Bradley* (Baltimore, 1969), Index under "self"; but Wollheim does not really properly come to grips with the problem. G.L. Vander Veer, *Bradley's Metaphysics and the Self* (New Haven: Yale University Press, 1971), Part II, is a dogmatic, incoherent argument with all sorts of other philosophers and leaves out all the interesting parts of Bradley.

68. This famous phrase, too, is from Hegel: *Philosophy of Right*, trans. Knox, §150, 107.

69. As Bradley differs from Cohen for his Hegelian reasons, so Ortega y Gasset, though at one early stage a student with and deeply influenced by Hermann Cohen, came to differ with Cohen to essentially the same effect for his own essentially "völkisch" reasons. (Cf. *The Dehumanization of Art* [Princeton: Princeton University Press, 1968], 147 n.) What in Bradley are "my station and its duties" are in Ortega "I and my circumstances," and both are then absorbed in one's "fate" (ibid; 151, 169). This fate then turns, at the hands of an historian like Américo Castro, into the metaphysical destiny of the Spanish people. Cf. also Gerhard Krüger, *Die Herkunft des philosophischen Selbstbewusstseins* (Darmstadt: Wissenschaftliche Buchgesellschaft, n.d. [1958]), 57f.: a reassertion of the substantiveness of the "I" for the sake of some sort of neo-Christian ideology. One could well place Bradley, Natorp, Ortega et al., in one group, trying for an ideological return to Christianity.

70. Cf. *Theologico-Political Tractate*, ed. Elwes (New York: Dover, 1951), 200, 204f., passim, and my unpublished study of Spinoza and political Spinozism.

71. *Thus Spake Zarathustra*, trans. R. Hollingdale (Baltimore: Penguin, 1961), 55.

72. This also is a profound passion with Hegel: cf., for example, *Philosophy of Right*, § 187; "Philosophy of History," in Friedrich (ed.), *The Philosophy of Hegel* (New York: Modern Library, 1953), 114ff., 144, also 463, 487, passim. Cf. M. Buber, *Das Problem des Menschen* (Heidelberg: Lambert Schneider, 1948), 46, 56f.

73. *Individuals* (Garden City, NY: Anchor, 1959), 100, 104f.; see especially chap. 3. Citations in parentheses in the first three paragraphs of this section are to this text. Cf. B. Williams, *Problems of the Self* (Cambridge: Cambridge University Press, 1973), 66, 122, 124f.

74. Cf. Williams, *Problems*, 70.

75. For a substantive argument on why Strawson should by rights abandon the notion of the primitivity of "person," see Norman Burstein, "Strawson on the Concept of a Person," *Mind*, LXXX (July 1971), 449–452. Cf. Donald Sievert's devastating critique in "Strawson on Persons," *The Modern Schoolman* XLVIII (March 1971), 237–262, and his "How Well Can One Get to Know a Strawsonian Person?" with its potent Kantian criticism (*Philosophy and Phenomenological Research*, vol. 34, no. 4, June 1974), 515–527). Arthur Danto's attempts to defend Strawson on this score ("Persons," *Encyclopaedia of Philosophy*, vol. 6, 112f.) turn out to be quite weak.

76. Cf. note 9 *supra* and various thinkers—Kant, Cassirer, Sartre, et al.—treated in the present study.

77. In *Wittgenstein and the Problem of Other Minds*, ed. H. Morick (New York: McGraw-Hill, 1967).

78. Cf. note 10 *supra*.

79. Roderick M. Chisholm, repeatedly relying on Strawson, also renews a claim for "the observability of the self," in *Language and Human Nature*, ed. P. Kurtz (St. Louis: W.H. Green, 1971). His arguments against Hume are entirely unconvincing, as, among others, D. Sievert shows in his appended comments. Chisholm's argument is a peculiar mixture of linguistic analysis, phenomenology, and traditional metaphysics. Under the last rubric his consistent reliance on Leibniz ought to be noted; indeed, it is true that the self becomes a true monad under his ministration. Naturally, then, he has to criticize Kant and Sartre. Characteristically, it is two Frenchmen, Henri Lefebvre and Gilbert Varet, who point up in the subsequent discussion the privatistic, bourgeois worldview, which is manifest in Chisholm's thesis.

80. *The Bounds of Sense: An Essay on Kant's "Critique of Pure Reason"* (London: Methuen, 1966). Citations in parenthesis in the remainder of this section are to this text. Cf. W. Cerf's review in *Mind*, LXXXI (October 1972), 601–617.

81. *Opus Posthumum*: "Amphiboly, mistaking a logical reason and the causal law" (*Werke*, XXII, 313).

82. Cf. note 49 *supra*. If this were a study of Kant's, rather than of Cohen's "construction of the self," one would, at this point, have to enter into an explication of the *Third Critique*. In brief, what would result from such an explication is that a person is of course an individual *qua* "organism," and that a human organism, like any other, is of course a regulative concept applied to a set of sensa carved out of the world for the purpose

of thereafter subjecting this set to increasingly causal analysis (Cf., e.g., *Third Critique*, ed. Cassirer, 452f.).

83. Cf. *supra*.
84. *Werke*, XXII, 26f., 74, 94, 414, 420, passim.
85. Cf. Williams, *Problems*, 123.
86. *Self-Knowledge and Self-identity* (Ithaca, NY: Cornell University Press, 1963). Citations in parentheses in this section are to this text.
87. Cf. J.O. Nelson, "Criteria and Personal Identity," *Ratio*, XV (June 1973), 102–106; A.J. Ayer, *The Concept of a Person* (New York: St. Martin's Press, 1963), 115: to call a concept "indefinable" is to hide its failure.
88. Cf. "Self-Reference and Self-Awareness," *Philosophy Today* no. 3, ed. J. Gill (New York: Macmillan, 1970), 32–90.
89. Wilfred Sellars, "Metaphysics and the Concept of a Person," in *The Logical Way of Doing Things*, ed. K. Lambert (New Haven: Yale University Press, 1969), 252; and " . . . this I or he or it (the thing) which thinks . . . : I. Kant's *Critique of Pure Reason* [A346; B404]," in *Proceedings of the American Philosophical Association*, XLIV (1970–1971), 11ff.
90. Sellars, "Metaphysics and the Concept," *Logical Way*, 252. Sellars calls this a "neo-Peircean" position, whereas we have shown it to be at least "neo"-Kantian.
91. Sellars., 251.
92. Ibid., 252.
93. Sellars, *Proceedings of the American Philosophical Association*, XLIV, 25f.
94. "Metaphysics and the Concept," *Logical Way*, 226–238, 246; *Proceedings of the American Philosophical Association*, XLIV, 12.
95. Sellars, *Proceedings of the American Philosophical Association*, XLIV, 11.
96. Ibid., 12, 19n, 23n.
97. Sellars, "Metaphysics and the Concept," *Logical Way*, 252; in this spot he also refers to the view that the "I" is a serialization of experiences as a "Cartesian" view, a view that he believes to be false, though compatible with Kant's basic position; but I cannot see either how Descartes "thinking substance" can be reconciled with the notion of the "I" as a series, or, for that matter, why serialization may not be regarded as synonymous with a definition in terms of function.
98. Sellars, *Proceedings*, XLIV, 30.
99. Cf. *supra*.
100. Cf. note 61 *supra*.
101. Quoted from Herbert Spiegelberg, *The Phenomenological Movement* (Hague: Nijhoff, 1965), I, 140.

102. *Ideas* (London: Allen and Unwin, 1969), §57, 157n, and *Ideen* II at the very end. Cf. Herbert Spiegelberg, "Husserl's Phenomenology and Existentialism," *Journal of Philosophy*, LVII (January 21, 1960), 71–74.
103. *Husserl: An Analysis of His Phenomenology* (Evanston, IL: Northwestern University Press, 1967), 180.
104. Cf. Gerd Brand, *Welt, Ich und Zeit: Nach unveröffentlichten Manuskripten E. Husserls* (Hague: Nijhoff, 1955), especially chaps. 9–14, 20, 24–26; better, Eduard Marbach, *Das Problem des Ich in der Phänomenologie Husserls* (Hague: Nijhoff, 1974), especially §26, Excursus, 29, 33–40, 43e. (Marbach has Kant wrong, however; his views of the matter are contradicted in the present study.) For the relations between Husserl and Kantianism, cf. in addition to Marbach especially Iso Kern, *Husserl und Kant* (Hague: Nijhoff, 1964). Marbach (§43e) would appear to bring Husserl around the time of World War I quite close to Cohen, but for how the absolute ego continues to play its fundamental part even in the latest Husserl of *The Crisis of the European Sciences*, see Werner Marx, *Vernunft und Welt* (Hague: Nijhoff, 1970), 45–62. This philosophical line from Natorp to Husserl continues through Heidegger: see, for example, *Kant und das Problem der Metaphysik* (3rd ed.; Frankfurt: Klostermann, 1965), 138, 177; *Die Frage nach dem Ding* (Tübingen: Niemeyer, 1962), 130. My colleague Herbert Spiegelberg argues along such egological lines even now: see "On Some Human Uses of Phenomenology," in *Phenomenology in Perspective*, ed. F.J. Smith (Hague: Nijhoff, 1970); "A Phenomenological Approach to the Ego," *The Monist*, XLIX (January 1965), 1–17. Cf. however Gurwitch in note 111 and Löwith, *Das Individuum*, 108 n. Emanuel Levinas, in *Totalité et infini* (Hague: Nijhoff, 1961), and in *Autrement qu'être; ou, Au-dela l'essence* (Hague: Nijhoff, 1974), especially chap. 4, see 3 passim, presents an essentially Jewish, ethical argument against Heidegger, and also a rectification of Husserl.
105. Michael Sukale, "The Ego and Consciousness in Rival Perspectives," *Iyyun*, XXII (October 1971),193–214, 274–276 (English summary), tries to vindicate Husserl by criticizing Sartre.
106. Cf. note 8 *supra*.
107. Trans. F. Williams and R. Kirkpatrick (New York: Noonday, 1957); French edition, 1936–1937. Citations in parentheses in this section are to the English text.
108. Sartre, like so many others, tends to reverse Kant's technical use of "transcendent" and "transcendental."
109. Sartre's extraordinary philosophical consistency over the years, despite all apparent and all real (though minor) changes, can be shown

to stretch all the way from *The Transcendence of the Ego* through *Being and Nothingness* (New York: Washington Square Press, 1966) to the *Critique of Dialectical Reason*. Thus, the above summary of his theory of the self also correctly summarizes *Being and Nothingness*: the self is "mediated" through "others," and these others are themselves a "regulative concept" (Part II, 272, 278, 374, 352). The self is an "asymptotic," infinite task (Part II, see. iii, especially 106–116, 351; cf. *The Problem of Method* [London: Methuen, 1963], 5). And man is "praxis," "being in quest" (90–96; *Problem of Method*, 167f., 174).

110. Cf. note 61 *supra*.

111. The French literature on Cohen is available: Leo Rosenzweig, *La Restauration de l'a priori par Hermann Cohen* (Paris: Presses Universitaires, 1927); Jules Vuillemin, *L'Héritage Kantien et la Révolution Copernicienne: Fichte, Cohen, Heidegger* (Paris: Presses Universitaires, 1954); H. Dussort, *L'Ecole de Marbourg* (Paris: Presses Universitaires, 1963). For further summaries of Sartre's polemic against Husserl on this score, see Herbert Spiegelberg, *The Phenomenological Movement*, I, 140f.; II, 479–486; Wilfrid Desan, *The Tragic Finale: An Essay on the Philosophy of J.-P. Sartre* (New York: Harper, 1960), 16–20, 144–149, 157f.; A. Gurwitch, "A Non-Egological Conception of Consciousness," *Studies in Phenomenology and Psychology* (Evanston, IL: Northwestern University Press, 1966), 287–300, rehearses and endorses Sartre's view. Cf. also note 79 *supra*.

112. In Ulrich Sonnemann, *Negative Anthropologie: Vorstudien zur Sabotage des Schicksals* (Reinbeck bei Hamburg: Rowohlt, 1969), a book that is itself excessively opaque and yet significant; see especially 168–177.

113. Sonnemann is close to "the Frankfurt School" (cf. even the title of Adorno's *Negative Dialectics*), and this Marxist argument against a monadic self is derived from Adorno's and Max Horkheimer's *Dialektik der Aufklärung* (Amsterdam: Querido, 1947), especially 230ff. Cf. Hegel on the *Entzweiung* (*Phänomenologie des Geistes*, 361, 374 ["alienation"]) and on the *Verrücktheit* (ibid., 336, 513 ["dis-placement" = "insanity"]) of the self. See also notes 13 and 18 *supra* for their Marxist references.

Chapter 10. "Germanism and Judaism"

1. The phrase is here used referentially, not as the title of Cohen's famous 1916 brochure.

2. N.L.c., that is: "b" that a reversal of noun and adjective never seems to occur.

3. Cohen's talk about "German Judaism" is often used as evidence for the allegation that there was hostility between German "assimilationist" Jews and Eastern-European "authentic" Jews. This is rubbish. The relations between Cohen and the whole "Marburg School" on the one hand and Eastern-European Jewry on the other deserves full treatment as one instance of the positive mutual relations between these two communities. I can cite here only several of the most obvious highlights of this phenomenon. Jewish students from Poland and Russia flocked to Cohen's lecture-hall—among them Boris Pasternak (see *Safe Conduct* [London, 1959], 186–222), Dimitri Gawronsky, Boris Pines, Leo Rosenzweig (the author of the appendix of Hebrew sources to Cohen's *Religion of Reason*, etc.) and Sergey Rubinstein (see T.R. Payne, *S.L. Rubinstein and the Philosophical Foundations of Soviet Psychology* [Dordrecht-Holland: D. Reidel, 1968], especially 68ff., and W.H. Sahakian, *History and System of Psychology* [New York, etc.: Schenkman Publishing Co., 1957], 405–408 [I am indebted for these references to Prof. H. L. Ansbacher, Department of Psychology, University of Vermont]; Rubinstein's dissertation is announced for publication in the series *Philosophische Arbeiten*, under Cohen's direction, on the back cover of Cohen's own *Begriff der Religion im System der Philosophie* [Giessen: Toepelmann, 1915], and thus with Cohen's approval). See also R.C. Williams, "Russians in Germany: 1900–1914," *Journal of Contemporary History* I/4, October 1960, 126, and Fedor Stepun, *Vergangenes und Unvergängliches—Aus meinem Leben*, 1884–1914 (Munich: Koesel, 1947), 110. To the present time there are disciples of Cohen, or of Cohen's disciples, often combining Lithuanian *yeshivah*-training with Cohennian neo-Kantianism, who have become seminal scholars and intellectuals in centers of Jewish learning all over the world (e.g., Samuel Atlas, Rabbi J.B. Soloveitchik). Cohen's trip to Russia shortly before World War I broke out, whose purpose it was to succor its oppressed Jewry, turned into a triumphal journey through their major communities. (See "Hermann Cohen's 40th Yahrtzeit," *Davke* [Yiddish] XXXIII/IV, no. 9 [Buenos Aires, 1958], especially the articles by Aron Steinberg and Rabbi Jakob Maze.) And Cohen's last major enterprise, the publication of *Neue Jüdische Monatshefte*, was largely devoted to ideological apostrophes and sociopolitical aid to Eastern Jewry; see especially vol. l (1916–1917), 141–156, "Der polnische Jude." (My own copy of this volume, bound, has the penciled marginalia of Leo Rosenzweig.)

Indeed, on this score of proclaiming the basic unity of German and Eastern-European Jewries Martin Buber's Zionist *Der Jude* and Cohen's simultaneous non-Zionist journal, otherwise at one another's throats, collaborated intimately: see *Der Jude*, l (1916–1917), 149–156.

4. Steven Schwarzschild, "S.R. Hirsch—The Man and His Thought," *Conservative Judaism*, Winter 1959, 26–45.

5. Thus Hans Liebeschütz, "Hermann Cohen and His Historical Background," *Leo Baeck Institute Year Book* XIII (1968), 32: "Nobody can doubt that history has made Cohen's case a *causa victa*. . . ."

6. Cohen's mother died in 1873 at the age of 71. (Hermann Cohen, Briefe [Berlin: Schocken, 1939], 57.) The point made here remains the same.

7. See Schwarzschild, "Franz Rosenzweig's Anecdotes about Hermann Cohen," in *Gegenwart im Rückblick*, eds. H.A. Strauss and K.R. Grossmann (Heidelberg: L. Stiehm Verlag, 1970), 213f. (p. 40 of this volume). For a characterization of Louis Lewandowski see Eric Werner, *A Voice Still Heard - The Sacred Song of the Ashkenazic Jews* (University Park/London: Pennsylvania State University Press, 1976), 25–29 and notes.

8. I had some letters restored on the tombstone after the War. The inscription is a poem in Hebrew and in German by the legendary Orthodox rabbi Nehemiah Nobel of Frankfurt a/M, who himself had studied with Cohen.

9. Letter of August 23, 1972, from Jüdisches Komitee (sic) für Theresienstadt in the Hermann Cohen Archive of the Philosophy Seminar of the University of Zurich, Switzerland.

10. *Kant und die Epigonen* (Stuttgart, 1865). A second edition (it is ironical that this was prepared by Bruno Bauch; Stuttgart, 1912), has survived in Cohen's personal library at the Hebrew University, Jerusalem, Israel: COH 1932/Z8C71. (I am indebted to the Deutsche Forschungsgemeinschaft, the Gustav Wurzweiler Foundation, and the Jewish Memorial Foundation for grants which made possible the work that has, in part, gone into the present study.)

11. L.W. Beck, "Neo-Kantianism," *Encyclopaedia of Philosophy* (NY: MacMillan, 1967), vol. 5, 468ff., and I.M. Brochenski, *Contemporary European Philosophy* (Berkeley/LA: University of California Press, 1957), 88.

12. *Politische Philosophie in Deutschland*, Deutscher Taschenbuchverlag 1974, 88; see also his "Die politische Theorie des Neukantianismus & der Marxismus," *Archiv für Rechts- und Sozialphilosophie*, vol. 44 (1958), 333–350.

13. Brochenski, 89: "The rule of National Socialism dealt it (neo-Kantianism) a fatal blow because its representatives, largely of Jewish extraction, were fiercely persecuted."

14. Luebbe, 86f., 113f., 120ff.

15. See my unpublished study "Judaism as the Bone of Contention in the Philosophical Battle between Kant and Hegel."

16. Friedrich Albert Lange, *Geschichte der Materialismus*, 7th ed., introduction and critical epilogue by Hermann Cohen (Leipzig, 1896), 527; see also Hermann Cohen, *Schriften zur Philosophie und Zeitgeschichte*, eds., A. Görland and E. Cassirer (Berlin: Akademie-Verlag, 1928), vol. 1, 546.

17. See the good, albeit insufficiently, sophisticated article by Lawrence S. Stepelevich, "Hegel and Judaism," *Judaism* XXIV/2, Spring 1975, 215–224.

18. See Hans Liebeschütz, *Das Judentum im deutschen Geschichtsbild von Hegel bis Max Weber* (Tübingen: Mohr [Siebeck], 1967), 184, 204, and *Von Georg Simmel zu Franz Rosenzweig* (Tübingen: Mohr [Siebeck], 1970), 35, where the epochal split between Dilthey's *Akademie-Ausgabe* and the "Cassirer edition" of Kant's collected works is adumbrated.

19. Chamberlain was well-acquainted with Cohen's work: see Liebeschütz, "Hermann Cohen and His Historical Background," 19, n. 45, and *Von Georg Simmel*, 33, n. 54. Chamberlain also is represented in Cohen's private library, and the Natorp files in the archives of the University of Marburg contain correspondence between Natorp and Chamberlain in 1906 and 1914.

20. For the Bauch episode see Bruno Bauch, "Vom Begriff der Nation," *Kant-Studien* XXI (1917), 139–162 and his publications along the same line in Leonore Ripke-Kuehn's *Der Panther* (n.b. that this racist anti-Semite approves of Zionism, while disapproving of Polish-Jewish immigration to Germany), 159f. (Cp. below 97). The very first footnote in Friedrich Meinecke's famous *Cosmopolitanism and the National State*, trans. R. Kimber (Princeton University Press, 1970), 10, n. 1, draws favorably on Bauch's 1916 article. (This book and its influential author instantiate the diversion of Germany in the nineteenth century from Enlightenment values of the eighteenth century to the ethnic nationalism of the twentieth, which I am here blocking out. Cp. Shulamit Volkow, "Cultural Elitism and Democracy: Notes on Friedrich Meinecke's Political Thought," *Jahrbuch des Instituts für deutsche Geschichte*, vol. 5, ed. W. Grab [University of Tel Aviv, 1976], 383–418. See also E. Keller, *Die Philosophie Bruno Bauchs als Ausdruck germanischer Geisteshaltung* (!) (Berlin, 1935 [!]). Ernst Cassirer penned a reply, "Zum Begriff der Nation. Eine Erwiderung

auf den Aufsatz von B. Bauch," which, however, seems never to have been published. The Cassirer Collection of the Yale University Library has the manuscript and two slightly different typescripts of it (no. 113), the latter with Cassirer's longhand corrections. The MS notes convey the impression that Cassirer sent the article to Dr. Arthur Liebert, then editor of the *Kant-Studien*, and that Cohen and Cassirer resigned from the Kant-Gesellschaft when the editor declined to publish the reply. (In Cohen's private library two other books by Bauch [cp. earlier n. 10] are extant: COH 171/B33, COH-171. 4/B33.) See the good historical study by Werner T. Angress, "The German Military's Judenzählung of 1916: Genesis-Consequences-Significance," *Leo Baeck Institute Year Book* 23, 1978, 117–135.

21. Cp. Hans Kohn, *The Idea of Nationalism* (New York: Mac-Millan, 1944), 590, n. 41, 596f., nn. 26, 30, 598, n. 32, et passim.

22. "The Weimar Republic is . . . a belated break-through of the Enlightenment into the middle . . . of Europe"—quoted from a Nazi book by Peter J. Pulzer, *The Rise of Political Anti-Semitism in Germany and Austria* (New York: John Wiley, 1964), 311; see also Adam Roeder, *Reaktion und Antisemitismus. Zugleich ein Mahnwort a. d. akademische Jugend* (Berlin: Schwetschke & Sohn, 1921), on "die Judenrepublik."

23. See Schwarzschild, "The Jewish Enlightenment Symbiosis," *The Jewish Spectator* (New York), XL/3, Fall 1975, 26–29.

24. Erich Kahler, *The Jews Among the Nations* (New York: F. Ungar, 1967), 116. See also Werner Jochmann, "The Jews and German Society in the Imperial Era," *Leo Baeck Institute Year Book* XX (1975), 5, and the good economic analysis of the rise and decline of the emancipation ideal in Germany in Reiner Ruerup, "Emancipation and Crisis—The 'Jewish Question' in Germany 1850–1890," ibid., 13ff.

25. Second ed. Berlin: Ferdinand Duemmler, 1885.

26. Chief rabbi Maze of Moscow had exclaimed at the end of his welcoming address (see earlier n. 2); "As is your name ("Cohen" = priest), so are you."

27. A Cohen-Lange bibliography would be a worthy task all its own. As late as 1915 Cohen once more apostrophized his patron: *Der Begriff* p. V, and in *Monatshefte*, 323. Some of Lange's books ended up in Cohen's personal library.

28. Julius Ebbinghaus, "Die Berufung Cohens auf den Marburger Lehrstuhl," *Archiv für Philosophie* IX, 186–222; Liebeschütz, *Von Georg Simmel*, 25 and *Judentum im deutschen Geschichtsbild*, 203; H. Holzhey,

Cohen und Natorp—Ein Beitrag zur Geschichte de: Neukantianismus, lxxiv, cxxvi, cxxxv. Ebbinghaus's "Deutschtum und Judentum bei Hermann Cohen," *Kant-Studien,* LX/1 (1969), 84–96, well-intentioned as it is, is full of factual and philosophical mistakes. It is, in any case, hard to take seriously the 1969 political analyses of a German "Alt-Kantianer" monarchist. See also Karl Loewith, "Philosophie der Vernunft und Religion d. Offenbarung," *Sitzungsberichte d. Heidelberger Akademie d. Wissenschaften, Philosophisch-Historische Klasse,* 1968, 7. Abhandlung, 28, n. 55.

29. Liebeschütz, *Judentum im deutschen Geschichtsbild,* op. cit, chap. 5–6; Ismar Schorsch, *Jewish Reactions to German Anti-Semitism 1870–1914* (Columbia University Press, 1972), chap. 1; W. Boehlich, ed., *Der Berliner Antisemitismusstreit* (Frankfurt, 1965); H.-J. von Borries, *Deutschtum und Judentum—Studien zum Selbstverständnis d. deutschen Judentums 1879/1880,* dissertation at the University of Zurich (Hamburg, 1971). (I have in my private library a bound "convolute" of about twenty pamphlets published in the course of this episode.) See also H. Holzhey, "2 Briefe Hermann Cohens an H. v. Treitschke," *Bulletin d. L. Baeck Instituts* XII/46–47 (1969), 183–204. For Treitschke's general anti-Semitism see Sophony Herz, "Treitschkes kritische Haltung gegenüber Bethold Auerbach, Rahel Varnhagen und Fanny Lewald," *Jahrbuch d. Instituts für deutsche Geschichte,* vol. I (1972), 119–144 (though itself a rather naive study). For a fascinatingly different Jewish reaction to 1879 in Germany see G. Scholem, "Zur Literatur der letzten Kabbalisten in Deutschland," in *Bishnay Olamot—on S. Moser's 75th Birthday* (Tel Aviv, 1962), 366–376. I may cite another interesting and undoubtedly highly ephemeral by-product of this episode in history—*Sem und Japhet—Die hebräischen Worte der Jüdisch-Deutschen Umgangssprache* . . . (Leipzig: G.A. Gloeckner, 1882), paper, 56 pp. The anonymous author ("J.H.M.") argues against Graetz's thesis of a German-Jewish dichotomy (9), and he adduces "Judeo-German" (15ff.) as one important illustration of the profound kinship between the two peoples. This kinship is said to be due to their common spirituality and pantheism and their moral chasteness, so contrary to the ethos of Roman Catholic cultures (15).

30. *Antisemitismus—religiöse Motive im sozialen Vorurteil* (Munich: Chr. Kaiser, 1975).

31. *The Autobiography of Nachum Goldmann* (New York, 1969), 69.

32. Jakob Klatzkin, "Hermann Cohen," *Der Jude,* III (1918–1919), 35, and de Schmidt, *Psychologie u. Transzendentalphilosophie* (see below, n. 35),

76, n. 209. (Klatzkin is himself a revealing study in the psychopathology of the riven Europeanized Jewish mind. He published, among other things, a whole short series of studies on Hermann Cohen.) It might be pointed out that the patriarchs of Zionism, like Goldmann, Klatzkin, and Buber, themselves wrote fervently patriotic pro-German articles during World War I: see Goldmann, 51, and the moving illustration in Gustav Landauer's letter to Buber, May 12, 1916 (*Martin Buber - Briefwechsel aus sieben Jahrzehnten*, I: 1897–1918, ed. Grete Schaeder [Heidelberg: Lambert Schneider, 1972], 433–438 [I am indebted for this reference to Prof. Norbert Altenhofer, University of Frankfurt, Germany]), which demonstrate their support of the war and their ideologization of the German cause (in no small part motivated by their concern, too, for Russian Jewry [see 189]); for these reasons Landauer refuses to participate in *Der Jude*.

33. Knowing what one does, it is more likely that Klatzkin is right in attributing the statement to Kuno Fischer. For Fischer's anti-Semitism see his *Immanuel Kant und seine Lehre* (Heidelberg, 1899), vol. II, 377 (quoted by J. Katz, "Kant and Judaism - the Historical Connection" [Hebrew], *Tarbiz* XLI/2, 222, n. 10). See also Cohen's "Zur Kontroverse zwischen Trendelenburg und Kuno Fischer," *Schriften z. Philosophie*, vol. 1, 229–275.

34. See earlier n. 20. For a contemporary statement of indebtedness to Bauch, see Carnap's "Autobiography," in *The Philosophy of Carnap* (Library of Living Philosophers), ed. P. Schilpp (1963), 4, 11.

35. Henning Günther, *Philosophie des Fortschritts—Hermann Cohen: Rechtfertigung der bürgerlichen Gesellschaft* (Munich: W. Goldmann Verlag [Das Wissenschaftliche Taschenbuch, Abteilung Geisteswissenschaften], 1972), 119f., n. 77; the second part of W. de Schmidt, *Psychologie und Transzendentalphilosophie—Zur Psychologie-Rezeption bei Hermann Cohen und Paul Natorp* (Bonn: Bouvier Verlag Herbert Grundmann, 1976); H.-G. Gadamer, *Philosophische Lehrjahre* (Frankfurt a/M: Klostermann, 1977), 60–63, 233f.

36. There is a stunning example of this way of handling philosophical topics in Joseph Klein, *Die Grundlegung der Ethik in der Philosophie Hermann Cohens und Paul Natorps—eine Kritik des Neukantianismus*, Abhandlungen der Akademie d. Wissenschaften in Göttingen, Philologisch-historische Klasse Nr. 100 (Göttingen: Vandenhoeck and Ruprecht, 1976). For the style and content of this kind of thinking, in a serious analytical work, one sentence may here suffice (13): "Die Ausschaltung der Anschauung zugunsten der Hegemonie dieses mit seinem logisierten Differentialkalkül operierenden Verstandes hängt zweifelsohne mit der Struktur und dem Wesen der

spezifischen Geistigkeit des Emanzipations–und Assimilationsjudentums zusammen, wie der Urheber der Schule (Cohen) es vertrat." See also 99, 159ff., 187, 287, and the penultimate sentence of the book on 294f. (The telling history of Klein's book is intimated on p. 8. De Schmidt, puts it on the record that Klein's dissertation was abbreviated into *Die Grundlegung der Ethik in der Philosophie Paul Natorps. Eine Begründung des Sittlichen im methodischen Idealismus* [Bonn, 1942] (I), and that Klein had published "Der Mensch im System des Marburger Idealismus" in *Das Bild vom Menschen*, F. Tillmann [Düsseldorf, 1934], 119ff.) De Schmidt, 177 (epilogue) has a funny, if not tragic, list of the established dictionary of insults directed at the Marburg School: "subjectivism, purism of the subject, logicism, theoreticism, mathematicism, scientism, positivism, problematicism, pan-methodism, rationalism, relationalism, etc."

37. Holzhey, *Cohen und Natorp*, cxv and cix.

38. See Akiba Mendel, "The Debate between Prussian Junkerdom and the Forces of Urban Industry 1897–1902," *Jahrbuch d. Instituts für d. Geschichte*, vol. 4 (1975), 301–338 (for an American equivalent see *The Education of Henry Adams—An Autobiography* [Boston/New York: Houghton Mifflin, 1918], 238 et passim—Jews as the obnoxious avantgarde of industrial society, at the sight of whom the land-oriented aristocracy retches); W.Z. Bacharach, "Die Ideologie d. deutschen Rassenantisemitismus und seine praktischen Folgerungen," ibid., 369–386; S. Angel-Volkow, "Popular Anti-Modernism. Ideology among Master-Artisans during the 1890's," ibid., vol. 3 (1974), 203–225; and Pulzer, 24.

39. "Dem 50 jährigen Doctor medicinae Hrn. Sanitätsrath Dr. Salomon Neumann ein Festgruß," *Allgemeine Zeitung d. Judentums*, September 16, 1892, 447–448. (Cp. Cohen's eulogy on Neumann in *Jüdische Schriften*, vol. II, 425–438.) (It is interesting to note that immediately preceding Cohen's birthday-greeting this newspaper carries an article by the well-known German-Jewish *litérateur* Gustav Karpeles, "Die Waffen Nieder! Brief an Frau Baronin Bertha v. Suttner," in which the baroness's husband is praised as president of the Austrian Society for the Defense against Anti-Semitism, she is praised for her memorable campaign for activist pacifism, and Karpeles says that, while Jewish hearts are with her, Jewish voices have to be muted on the subject of pacifism for fear of being accused of cowardice and lack of patriotism.)

40. Cohen, "Das Problem der jüdischen Sittenlehre," in *Jüdische Schriften*, introduction by Franz Rosenzweig (Berlin: Schwetschke & Sohn, 1924), vol. III, 27.

41. Walter Kinkel, *Hermann Cohen—Eine Einführung in sein Werk* (Stuttgart: Strekker & Schroeder, 1924), 54: "All his life Cohen suffered grievously of the inhumanity of anti-Semitism, from which also the academic sector did not keep itself entirely free" (sic).

42. He always wrote how much he enjoyed places like Paris and Vienna—if only because Jewish academicians there seemed to be so much less embattled—and particularly Swiss resorts, because of the spirit of freedom in that country and because they were so remote from the political battlefields: Hermann Cohen, "Briefe über Gottfried Keller," in *Gabe Herrn Rabbiner Dr. Nobel zum 50. Geburtstag*, ed., M. Buber et al. (Frankfurt a/M: J. Kauffmann Verlag, 1921), 9ff.; H. Holzhey, "Hermann Cohen und G. Keller," *Neue Zürcher Zeitung*, July 20, 1969, Beilage "Literatur und Kunst."

43. *Mein Leben* (Munich: Brackmann, 1968), 39.

44. Paul Natorp, "Hermann Cohen," *Berliner Tageblatt*, July 1, 1912.

45. Julius Galliner's eulogy on Kellermann, *Jüdisch-liberale Zeitschrift*, September 26, 1924. On March 28, 1913, Cohen had written to Kellermann "Da denkt man an seine Pflicht und hofft sogar auf die Menschen."

46. Fritz K. Ringer, *The Decline of the German Mandarins* (Cambridge, MA, 1969), 305–312, and Helmut Holzhey, "Hermann Cohens Weggang aus Marburg," *Neue Zürcher Zeitung*, March 21, 1971, 49f.—a deeply moving description.

47. The history of Cohen's chair at the University of Marburg is itself an eloquent symbol for the whole historical era, which we are here analyzing. Cohen's immediate successor in fact turned out to be Erich Jaensch, who proved to be a Nazi (Ringer, 441) a philosophical psychologist and thus hostile to Cohen's entire methodology, and, in 1938 at Leipzig, published *Der Gegentypus*. After Jaensch the chair was to be occupied by Martin Heidegger, who, in his "Zur Geschichte des philosophischen Lehrstuhles seit 1866," *Die Philipps-Universität zu Marburg, 1527–1927: 5 Kapitel aus ihrer Geschichte* [1527–1866], H. Hermelink, S.A. Kaehler et al. (Marburg: Elwert, 1927), 681–687, devotes himself to derogating Cohen. Only a little later occurred the notorious meeting in Davos, Switzerland, in which Ernst Cassirer had to face up to the proto-Nazi behavior and ideas of Heidegger. (Toni Cassirer, *Mein Leben mit Ernst Cassirer*, 166). And a little after this Heidegger welcomes Hitler as the incursion of Being into history. He died recently without ever a single word of contrition. His posthumous self-exculpation is both disingenuous and obnoxious; *Der Spiegel*, no. 23, 1976, 193–214.

48. F.A. Lange, *Über Politik und Philosophie—Briefe und Leitartikel 1862–1875*, ed. Georg Eckert (Duisburg: W. Braun Verlag, 1968), 377.
49. "Habilitationsschrift" (University of Zurich, 1974), not yet published.
50. Ibid., viii.
51. Luebbe, 122.
52. Holzhey, *Cohen und Natorp*, ccii.
53. Ibid., cciii.
54. (Kant, too, of course, is usually imagined to have been "an eighteenth-century optimist"—with equal lack of justification.) G. Scholem, "Wider den Mythos vom deutsch-jüdischen Gespräch," *Bulletin des Leo Baeck Instituts*, no. 27 (1964), 27 and *Judaica* II (Frankfurt: Bibliothek Suhrkamp, 1970), Cohen as "typical for the unhappy love of the Christian environment, which did not shrink from taking the step from the exalted to the ridiculous." Against Scholem see Yehiel Ilsar, "Zum Problem der Symbiose. Prolegomena zur deutsch-jüdischen Symbiose," *Bulletin des Leo Baeck lnstituts* XIV/S (1975), especially 124, Buber, writing in March 1939 "Wer hier leichthin verurteilt, hat die tragische Tiefe des Galuth-Schicksals, der Entstehung und Vernichtung echter Synthesen nicht verstanden." For how early in history a genuine German-Jewish symbiosis was stipulated even as a matter of theory, see H.H. Ben-Sasson, "The in Contemporary Jewish Eyes," *Israel Academy of Sciences and Humanities Proceedings*, IV/12, 1970.
55. Holzhey, *Cohen and Natorp*, op. cit., ccxxxix.
56. "Weggang aus Marburg," loc. cit., 50.
57. See Schwarzschild, "From Critical to Speculative Idealism" (review), *Journal of Bible and Religion*, January 1966, 65f., pp. 197–201 of this volume.
58. Holzhey, "Weggang aus Marburg," 50.
59. *Prison Notebooks* (London: L. Wishart, 1971), 418. (I am indebted for this precise reference to Prof. Paul Piccone, Washington University.)
60. Mrs. Cohen writes to B. Kellermann on April 6, 1920, of her late husband's "... double greatness, his lofty, almost tragic dualism...." (I express my thanks here to the sons of Benzion Kellermann, the physicist Walter in Great Britain and the retired diplomat Henry in Washington, D.C., for letting me have copies of their father's papers.) Cp. Hans Bach, *Jakob Bernays* (Tübingen: Mohr, 1974), 214: "Der Riß des Jahrhunderts (i.e., the European Jewish antipathy) ging mitten durch sein Herz;" also Eva Reichmann, "Der Bewußtseinswandel d. deutschen Juden" in *Deutsches Judentum in Krieg und Revolution 1916–1923* (Tübingen: Mohr, 1971), 601.
61. Pulzer, 5.

62. Lucien Goldmann, *Immanuel Kant* (London: New Left Books, 1971). There was, of course, another route that Jews could and did take to try to bridge the gap between their own and their society's condition. Lucien Goldmann is himself a belated exemplar of this—the Marxist insistence that the present world is, in the Hegelian sense of the world, "verrückt," that is, displaced, lunatic, inauthentic. Starting at that point many Jews would go in the Marxist-socialist direction, and others would go in the nationalist direction. Moses Hess embodied both directions in their common starting-out point.

63. Cohen, *Ethik des reinen Willens*, 1904, 333f., new edition: Cohen, *Werke*, vol. 7, Hildesheim, 2005.

64. "Karl Jasper: Citizen of the World," in *The Philosophy of Karl Jasper* (Library of Living Philosophers), ed. P. Schilpp (New York: Tudor, 1957), 548.

65. Cohen, *Jüdische Schriften*, vol. 2, 76.

66. Cohen, *Ethik*, 581ff.; Cohen, *Werke*, vol. 7, S. Schwarzschild, "The Democratic Socialism of Hermann Cohen." Hebrew Union College Annual, XXVII (1956), 417–438, p. 1–21 of this volume.

67. Dimitry Gawronsky, "Ernst Cassirer: His Life and Work," in *The Philosophy of E. Cassirer* (Library of Living Philosophers), ed. P. Schilpp (Evanston, IL, 1949), 15. I have what must be a very rare copy of Gawronsky's *Die Bilanz des russischen Bolschewismus, auf Grund authentischer Quellen* (Berlin; Paul Cassirer, 1919). (The author describes himself on the title page as "Delegierter der Russischen Sozialrevolutionären Partei zur Internationalen Sozialistischen Konferenz" and signs the preface "Jan. 1919.")

68. Peter Gay, *The Dilemma of Democratic Socialism* ... (Columbia University Press, 1970), chap. "From Hegel to Kant"; Bernstein, "Vom Mittlerberuf der Juden,"*Neue Jüdische Monatshefte*, April 25, 1917, 397ff.; "Wie ich als Jude in der Diaspora aufwuchs," *Der Jude* II (1917–1918), 186ff., and so on.

69. Luebbe, like so many others, claims that the neo-Kantian program for socialism necessarily leads to reformism for the purpose of aborting revolution (113) and that it thus undergirds the S.P.D. in a "pseudo-revolutionary" posture (ibid., 120). This really makes no sense at all. Why does a program of literally "infinite" demands necessarily result in compromising, and how does waiting for "developed revolutionary situations" of Communist party orthodoxies engender revolutionary activism?

70. Cohen, *Ethik*, 398. Cohen, *Werke*, vol. 7. In this context a clear distinction must be kept in mind, however, between our use of the notion of

"mediation" and that of Hegelians and Marxists. Here mediation can only mean the use and effect of historical processes toward ideal goals, while the value differential between route and destination is firmly retained. In Hegelianism, on the other hand, the mediation is itself an embodiment of the ideal; see Hegel's *System of Philosophy*, 1, Logic, para. 161: "The concept remains at home with itself in its process . . ." Günther's *Philosophie des Fortschritts*, while certainly a responsible recent philosophical confrontation with Hermann Cohen, thus criticizes Cohen for his lack of "mediation." In the peculiar contemporary philosophical mood in Germany and other European countries, in which "dialectics" and metaphysics creep in almost everywhere, this complaint of Günther's turns out to mean that Cohen is, rightly, alleged to lack "dialectical reconciliation" with reality and to insist on deontological, rather than "hermeneutic," ethics. Günther then reveals the typical Christian religious stake in Hegelian dialectics during the course of his argument, and a number of serious misinterpretations and misunderstandings of Cohen result. Hegel, the ex-student of the Protestant theological seminary, and Cohen, the ex-student of the rabbinical seminary, still face one another in their historical extrapolations.

71. Hermann Cohen, *Kants Begründung der Ethik*, Berlin, 1877. Reprinted in Cohen, *Werke*, vol. 2, Hildesheim, 2011.

72. Ibid., 9.

73. Ibid., 246; cp. Cohen, *Ethik*, 19, 403 (*Werke*, vol. 7), *Religion der Vernunft—aus den Quellen den Judentums*, 2nd ed. (Frankfurt a/M; J. Kauffmann Verlag, 1929), 16 [engl. 14] (prophetic humanism); and *Neue Jüdische Monatshefte* 2 (1916), 50.

74. Pace Theodor Adorno.

75. Giessen: Toepelmann, 1916, 9th and 10th thousands, "with a critical epilogue," 59. (The essay was first written for inclusion in Fr. Thimme, *Vom Inneren Frieden des deutschen Volkes, Von deutscher Zukunft*, Steck 1, 1915, new edition in: Cohen, *Werke*, vol. 16, Hildesheim 2012, 465–560.) The later editions toned down its chauvinistic fervor somewhat. Thus on p. 37 the sentence "We are proud to be Germans" is omitted. It had occurred in the first place, it should be noted, in a passage, which, while stridently Germanic, meant to emphasize the importance of international morality even in the midst of war. The added epilogue, written in a very passionate style, points out that the essay had been attacked by anti-Semites and Zionists—that "Germany" means "ethical idealism," "scientific reason" from Plato through Kant—and it fights against German irrationalism and particularism (52ff.).

76. See, for example, Binjamin Segel, Lemberg, *Der Weltkrieg und das Schicksal des jüdischen Volkes—Stimme eines galizischen Juden an seine Glaubensgenossen in den neutralen Ländern insbesondere in Amerika* (Berlin: G. Stilke, 1915). And, of course, a number of highly placed people in the U.S., Jewish academicians included, paid heavy prices at that time for their sympathy with the German cause, motivated by their opposition to Czarist Russia.

77. *Jüdische Schriften*, vol. II, 79.

78. Cohen, *Ästhetik des reinen Gefühls* (Berlin: Bruno Cassirer, 1912), vol. II, 226, reprint edition: Cohen, *Werke*, vol. 9, Hildesheim 2005.

79. Borries, 147.

80. Holzhey, *Cohen and Natorp*; clxxxvii. (This sentence was italicized in the original.)

81. *Schriften zur Philosophie*, vol. I, 567; *Jüdische Schriften*, vol. II, 285.

82. Franz Rosenzweig also spoke of "the blond" essay that he wrote during the war to go with his essays about Jewish education: *Briefe*, eds. Ernst Simon & Edith Rosenzweig (Berlin: Schocken, 1935), 480.

83. *Schriften zur Philosophie*, vol. I, 559f.

84. Alex Bein, *Theodor Herzl—A Biography* (Philadelphia: Jewish Publications Society, 1948), 239.

85. Cohen, *Ethik*, 411, *Werke*, vol. 7.

86. *Monatshefte*, 106ff., 167, 387ff., 511ff., et passim.

87. Cohen, *Kants Begründung der Ethik*, 433; again in Cohen, *Werke*, vol. 2. Günther, op. cit., 337, 433.

88. Schwarzschild, "Cohen's Democratic Socialism," 424, 429, in this volume pp. 1–21.

89. Cohen, *Kants Begründung der Ethik*, 357. *Werke*, vol. 2.

90. Günther, 348, 368. 168.

91. Cohen, *Ästhetik*, vol. II, 226, 431. *Werke*, vol. 9.

92. Cohen, *Ethik*, 72, 240f., 276, 297f., 430. *Werke*, vol. 7.

93. Günther, 19. Cp. Gustav Landauer's contrast between "Gemeinschaft" and "Gemeinheit" ("community" vs. "commonness," impertinency) in his letter to Buber, 436. Günther's thesis that also in its Jewish version the ideal of "community" can lead to proto-fascism (19) is correct, although one must add that moral subscribers to it, like Buber and Landauer, overcame its dangers at least in their own lives. A history of the philosophical concept of "community," which waits to be written, would have to start with Kant's First *Critique*, A2Bf/B260f. *Metaphysische Anfangsgründe der Rechtslehre*, ed. Cassirer, vol. 7, §62, 159.

94. See above n. 66.

95. Cohen, *Ethik*, 296. (Cohen, *Werke*, vol. 7).
96. Ibid., 311, thus explicitly contradicting Luebbe, for one (see above n. 69); also *Kants Begründung d. Ethik*, 272: ethical man "exploding in revolutions and continual reforms."
97. The notion of the "Rechtsstaat" was developed by pre-1848 liberals like Karl Theodor Welcker: see Frank Eyck, *The Frankfurt Parliament 1848–1849* (London: MacMillan, 1968), 181f., 222. Cp. Otto Kirschheimer, "The *Rechtsstaat* as Magic Wall," in *The Critical Spirit—Essay: in Honor of H. Marcuse*, eds. K. Wolff and B. Moore Jr. (Beacon Press, 1967), 287ff.
98. Cohen, *Ethik*, 429, 581ff. (emphases in the original). (*Werke*, vol. 7).
99. See Schwarzschild, "The Tenability of Hermann Cohen's Construction of the Self," *Journal of the History of Philosophy* XIII/3, July 1975, 364, pp. 69–92 of this volume. The present passage makes it very clear that Cohen was entirely aware of his temptation to trust the state unduly.
100. *Neue Jüdische Monatshefte* 1916, 50.
101. Klaus Weyand, "Kants Geschichtsphilosophie," *Kant—Studien*, Ergänzungsheft 85, 1964. I heroically abstain from giving a longer bibliography of Kant on history.
102. Cp. the last chapter of Kant's First *Critique*, "The History of Pure Reason."
103. Isaac Husik, *Philosophical Essays—Ancient, Mediaeval and Modern* (Oxford: Blackwell, 1952). Preface by M.C. Nahum and Leo Strauss, xxviff. For Cohen's philosophy of history see Simon Kaplan, *Das Geschichtsproblem in der Philosophie Hermann Cohens* (Berlin, 1930) and my unpublished doctoral dissertation, "Two Jewish Philosophies of History: Nachman Krochmal and Hermann Cohen," Hebrew Union College-Jewish Institute of Religion, Cincinnati, 1955.
104. *A History of Mediaeval Jewish Philosophy* (New York: MacMillan, 1930), 432.
105. See, for example, Shlomo Pines in Maimonides' *Guide for the Perplexed* (University of Chicago Press, 1960), cxxii, and S. Rawidowicz, *Studies in Jewish Thought* (Philadelphia: J.P.S., 1974), 286.
106. Cohen, *Ethik*, 32; *Werke*, vol. 7. Schwarzschild, "Cohen's Democratic Socialism," 425, in this volume pp. 8–9, *Monatshefte*, 257.
107. *Monatshefte*, January 25, 1917, 223ff. Cp. Vorländer, *Kant und der Gedanke des Völkerbundes* (Leipzig, 1919).
108. Cohen, *Ethik*, 411, 514. *Werke*, vol. 7.
109. Werner Hänsel, *Kants Lehre vom Widerstandsrecht—ein Beitrag zur Systematik der kantischen Rechtsphilosophie*, Kant-Studien no. 60 (Berlin, 1926).

110. Joseph Klein, 289f.

111. See earlier n. 36.

112. For example, "(t)he idealization of their people . . . by the prophets": *Religion der Vernunft*, 313 [engl. 268].

113. Cp. Kant's famous statement that "concepts without intuitions are empty, intuitions without concepts are blind," First *Critique* A52/B76 Cohen, *Schriften zur Philosophie*, vol. II, 180f.: "Wir fordern für das Studium der Philosophie die Verbindung von Systematik und Geschichte. . . ."

114. Nietzsche: "Ich habe mich längst daran gewöhnt, Philosophieprofessoren danach zu beurteilen, ob sie gute Philologen sind oder nicht."

115. See earlier.

116. Martin Buber, *Völker/Staaten und Zion, Ein Brief an Hermann Cohen* (Berlin/Vienna: R. Loewith Verlag, 1917); Emil Fackenheim, "Hermann Cohen—After Fifty Years," *Leo Baeck Memorial Lecture 12* (New York, 1969). For an evaluation of the Cohen-Buber controversy see Hans Liebeschütz, "Martin Buber und das neue jüdische Geschichtsbild," *Bulletin des Leo Baeck Instituts*, no. 1 (1957), 24–27.

117. George L. Mosse, "The Influence of the *Voelkisch* Idea on German Jewry," in *Studies of the Leo Baeck Institute*, ed. M. Kreutzberger (N.Y.F. Ungar, 1967), and Günther, 90f. To get a proper idea of this kind of German-Jewish ethnicism a whole roster of contemporary books really ought to be analyzed—for example, Oskar Goldberg (*pace* Thomas Mann's *Doktor Faustus*), *Die Wirklichkeit der Hebräer* (Berlin: Verlag David, 1924); Fritz Kahn, *Die Juden als Rasse und Kulturvolk* (Berlin: Welt-Verlag, 1922); David Koigen, *Der moralische Gott—eine Abhandlung über die Beziehungen zwischen Kultur und Religion* (Berlin; Jüdischer Verlag, 1922); S.M. Melamed (he, too, a curious and interesting thinker), *Psychologie des jüdischen Geistes - Zur Völker- und Kulturpsychologie* (Berlin: Schwetschke & Sohn, 1921), and so on.

118. Therefore, Buber's essay about Krochmal is properly entitled "The Gods of the Nations and God," Israel and the World—Essays in a Time of Crisis (New York: Schocken, 1948), 197ff.

119. Thus, for example, Bruno Bauch's vicious attack on Cohen and "the Jewish spirit" contained expressions of approval for Zionism (159) and of strong disapproval for Eastern-European Jewish immigration into Germany (ibid., 160). The highly ambivalent and not infrequently highly dubious political bed-fellowship of political Zionists and political anti-Semites in various parts of the world in the twentieth century—arising

from the convergence of their beliefs that the Jews were a foreign body within the non-Jewish societies—is, of course, a very complex, difficult, and painful subject; it should, nonetheless, be studied more frankly. It is, for example, not insignificant that the non-Zionist Franz Rosenzweig was and always remained a devoted disciple of Friedrich Meinecke (see earlier n. 20).

120. See W. Stegmueller, "A Rational Reconstruction of Kant's Metaphysics," *Ratio* X/1, June 1968, 14f.: "Physical things are themselves something that cannot be perceived or observed; the concept of a physical thing is rather a 'theoretical construction' and in this sense really 'an a priori concept' which relates not to perceptible objects but to objects of a higher order;" see also the references there to N. Goodman and Quine.

121. *Metaphysische Anfangsgründe der Rechtslehre*, ed. Cassirer, vol. 7, 161: " . . . we must act as if something were, though it perhaps is not, . . . in order to bring it about. . . ."

122. Cohen, *Ethik*, 454: "the being of willing" (= God); ibid., 26. *Werke*, vol. 7.

123. The history of the notion of *pia fraus*, the talmudic legal fiction (*ha 'aramah*), Maimonides' "divine deceit" (*'ormah elohit*), Kant's "List der Geschichte" and Hegel's "List der Vernunft," and Strauss's esotericism would really have to be thematized here.

124. See earlier p. 102 of this volume.

125. This might also have to be one's reply to Liebeschütz et al., n. 5.

126. Erich Kahler, *The Jews Among the Nations*, 109, 119. (The original was *Israel unter den Völkern* [Zürich: Humanitas Verlag, 1936]—whatever one may have to say about the generalizing and metaphysicizing that are perpetrated, both methodologically and substantively, in this well-intentioned book.)

127. Cohen, *Ästhetik*, vol. I, 205: "Da bleibt kein Rat als grenzenlose Tränen" (reprint: Cohen, *Werke*, vol. 8).

128. Luebbe, 189.

129. Especially the Marburger Karl Vorländer must be mentioned as such a person. The dissertation of Timothy R. Keck, "Kant and Socialism—The Marburg School in Wilhelmian Germany" (University of Wisconsin, 1975), came to my attention after this study was completed. It is a very valuable contribution to our subject.

130. Prof. Gerald Izenberg, of the History Department of Washington University, has discussed this issue with me very helpfully. Luebbe's chapter "The Philosophical Ideas of 1914," especially 232, n. 227, makes

it very clear, however, how comparatively sane a voice Hermann Cohen's was in the atmosphere of Germany during the war.

Chapter 11. *Ethics of the Pure Will*—Introduction

1. This introduction to this German text has been kept in the English-language form in which it was written, though the author could have reverted to the language of his childhood. Hermann Cohen's philosophy and Marburg neo-Kantianism in general have, after all, suffered the tragically paradoxical fate that German-language culture, out of whose spirit and toward which they were largely oriented, rejected them virtually from their inception and, through the decades, with cataclysmically exponentialized vehemence for not being "authentically German," and in non-German-language cultures, on the other hand, they never had a fair chance in the first place for, among other things, being "too Germanic." The contrast between the two languages in this volume, therefore, mirrors, in the first place, an historical reality. In the second place, it might be hoped that when Cohen is brought to German readers in part in a foreign language he might be given a more conscientious hearing and that in the English-speaking world he will be given, also by Jews, what will amount to the first serious, systematically philosophical attention. For these reasons, too, Cohen's works will here be cited by their titles translated into English. (Translations of his philosophical works, as distinguished from his Jewish writings, are still, and lamentably, completely missing in all languages.) The "Ethics of the Pure Will" is here quoted from the second edition (1907).

2. B. Sabb. 55a, Y. Sanhed. 1, beginn., 18a cf. Hermann Cohen, Religion of Reason..., transl. S. Kaplan, New York 1972, p. 412..

3. Friedrich Albert Lange: *Geschichte des Materialismus und Kritik seiner Bedeutung in der Gegenwart*, 7th ed. Einleitung mit kritischem Nachtrag von Hermann Cohen, Leipzig 1902, 524. Reprint edition: Cohen, *Werke*, vol. 5, Hildesheim, 2012.

4. Cf. S.S. Schwarzschild: "The Democratic Socialism of Hermann Cohen," in *Hebrew Union College Annual 27* (1956), pp. 1–21 of this volume; T. Keck: *Kant and Socialism. The Marburg School in Wilhelmian Germany*. Dissert., University of Wisconsin, Madison, 1975; Thomas E. Willey: *Back to Kant - The Revival of Kantianism in German Social and Historical Thought 1860–1914*, Detroit 1978, 103ff., and so on.

5. Kurt Eisner: Hermann Cohen. Zum 70. Geburtstag des Philosophen, in: *Münchner Post*, July 5 and 6, 1912 (annual 26, nos. 153f.).

6. Cohen, *Ethik des reinen Willens*, (ed. 1981), 73, 229, 252, 239ff., 433, 434ff., = Cohen, *Werke*, vol. 7. Otto F. Gierke's "Das deutsche Genossenschaftsrecht" was a significant basis for Cohen's thinking here. Cohen alludes to his disagreement with Tönnies in preferring "Genossenschaft" to both "Gesellschaft" and "Gemeinschaft," 76f., 218f.

7. Cohen, *Kants Begründung der Ethik*, 2nd ed., Berlin 1910, 17. New: Cohen, *Werke*, vol. 2, Hildesheim, 2011.

8. Cf. S.S. Schwarzschild: "The Tenability of Hermann Cohen's Construction of the Self," in *Journal of the History of Philosophy* 15 (1975), 361–384 (pp. 69–92 of this volume); H. Lilienfeld: Rechtswissenschaft und Ethik in Hermann Cohen's "Ethik des reinen Willens," in *Zeitschrift für die gesamte Strafrechtswissenschaft* 26 (1906), 41–49.

9. Especially *Stammler, Die Lehre von dem richtigen Rechte*, Berlin, 1901, *Theorie der Rechtswissenschaft*, Halle, 1911; *The Theory of Justice*, trans. Isaac Husik, appendices by F. Geny and J.C.H.W. MacMillan, 1925.

10. Albert Görland: *Ethik als Kritik der Weltgeschichte*, Leipzig/Berlin, 1914.

11. Though he accepted Stammler's earlier book: *Wirtschaft und Recht nach der materialistischen Geschichtsauffassung*, Halle, 1896. Cf. Stammler's letter to Natorp of 31.3.1903, printed in Helmut Holzhey: Cohen und Natorp. *Ein Beitrag zur Geschichte des Neukantianismus*, Basel/Stuttgart, 1986, letter no. 79.

12. Cf. Natorp's letter to Görland of 26.5.1903, in Holzhey, letter no. 82.

13. Karl Vorländer, "Rudolf Stammlers Lehre vom richtigen Recht," in *Kant-Studien* 8 (1903), 329–335.

14. Cf. Paul Natorp, "Recht und Sittlichkeit. Ein Beitrag zur kategorialen Begründung der praktischen Philosophie. Mit besonderem Bezug auf Hermann Cohens Ethik . . ." and R. Stammlers "Theorie der Rechtswissenschaft," in *Kant-Studien* 18 (1913), 1–79.

15. "R. Stammlers 'Überwindung' der materialistischen Geschichtsauffassung," in *Archiv f. Sozialwissenschaft und Sozialpolitik* 24 (1907), 94–120; also, "Nachtrag zu dem Aufsatz über R. Stammlers 'Überwindung' der materialistischen Geschichtsauffassung," in Max Weber: *Gesammelte Aufsätze zur Wissenschaftslehre*, 4th ed., Tübingen 1973, 360–S3. Cp. Willey, 126. In English cf. Max Weber: *Critique of Stammler*, trans. and intr. Guy Oakes. New York/London, 1977; Oakes seems to know nothing about the Stammler-Marburg connection.

16. Stammler tried to keep his philosophical peace with Cohen: cf. *Wirtschaft und Recht* . . . , 3rd ed., Leipzig, 1914, 376, 666f., n. 207, replying to Weber ibid., 670–686, and distantiating himself from Kelsen, ibid., 642, n. 79, 662f., n. 201.

17. "Über Grenzen zwischen juristischer und soziologischer Methode" (1911), in *Die Wiener Rechtstheoretische Schule*, eds. H. Klecatzky, R. Marcic, H. Schambeck, Vienna, 1968, vol. I, 3ff.; "Zur Soziologie des Rechtes," in *Archiv für Sozialwissenschaft und Sozialpolitik* XXXIV (1912), 600–614. Cp. Fritz Loos: Zur Wert- und Rechtslehre M. Webers, Tübingen, 1970, 106, 111f. Cf. also Hans Kelsen: Juristischer Formalismus und reine Rechtslehre, in *Juristische Wochenschrift* 58 (1929), 1723. Kelsen, in turn, however, began early to want to dissociate himself from Stammler, too: cf. his "Hauptprobleme der Staatsrechtslehre," Tübingen, 1911, 56–38, 62f., and so on.

18. Hans Kelsen: *Der soziologische und juristische Staatsbegriff. Kritische Untersuchung des Verhältnisses von Staat und Recht*, 1922, 2nd ed., Aalen, 1962, 168, 248.

19. Ibid., 219ff. That Kelsen is quite conscious of his dependence on "Marburg" is made clear in this work by his extensive discussion of Kant, of Cohen's *Ethics*, 12, 14ff., 75ff., 218; Cassirer, *Stammler*, his anti-Weberianism is here formulated on 156ff.,162f.,169.

20. By using the term "Eigenart" ("particular form") here I want to draw attention to the parallelism between the relationship of logic to ethics and the relationship of ethics to religion, according to Cohen (cf. his "Concept of Religion within the System of Philosophy," 1915). Also, religion does not, of course, supersede ethics; it stays within the realm of ethics, although it adds to and retro-effects the latter.

21. In the background here lurks the well-known Mishnaic/Talmudic dictum of Rabbi Tarfon's: "It is not your task to finish the work, but you are not free to exempt yourself from it" (Mishnah Aboth 2:21). In the "Religion of Reason," 251, he puts this in terms of the poetic metaphor of the Bible that God placed the rainbow in the sky as the bond of his promise that he will never (again) destroy the world.

22. Franz Rosenzweig, Introduction to Cohen's *Jüdische Schriften*, Berlin, 1924, vol. 1, xiii–lxiv.

23. Julius Guttmann, *Philosophie des Judentums*, München, 1933, 350f. 360, 366.

24. Civiaco Moron Arroyo, *El Sistema de Ortega y Gasset*, Madrid, 1968, 97.

25. For this reason Cohen had earlier, in *Kants Begründung der Ethik*, 512ff., excised Kant's doctrine of the *summum bonum* from his own reconstruction of the system. (New: *Werke*, vol. 2, Hildesheim, 2011.)

26. Paul Natorp, *Religion innerhalb der Grenzen der Humanität*, 2nd ed., Tübingen, 1908, 96ff., 117ff. The differences between them are also strikingly articulated in the extensive notes which Cohen wrote out in 1908 on the whole postscript of the second edition. These notes are preserved in the Natorp files of the University of Marburg, and transcribed by H. Holzhey, *Quellen*, part V.

27. Wilhelm Herrmann, "Hermann Cohens Ethik," in *Die Christliche Welt* 21 (1907) cols. 51–59, 222–228.

28. Cohen thanks Herrmann in his "Ethics," 2nd ed., xiii. Some of his and Natorp's criticisms clearly had some effect on Cohen's thinking, since one can recognize some corresponding changes in Cohen's views on such matters between the time of his monograph "Religion and Morality" (1907), which had just then appeared but which Herrmann had not yet read, and the *Religion of Reason*.

29. Walter Kinkel: "Die Ethik des reinen Willens," in *Beilage zur Allgemeinen Zeitung*, München, December 19, 1904, 529–532; "Über Hermann Cohens System der Philosophie - 2. Ethik des reinen Willens" in *Philosophische Wochenschrift und Literaturzeitung* II/8, May 26, 1906, 225–230; "Un nouveau fondement de l'Ethique" in *Revue de Métaphysique et de Morale* 14 (1906), 92–108; *Hermann Cohen. Eine Einführung in sein Werk*, Stuttgart, 1924.

30. R.A. Fritzsche, "Eine idealistische Ethik," in *Berliner Tageblatt*, February 10, 1906; A.Ki. in *Literarisches Zentralblatt für Deutschland*, April 29, 1905, 566f.; the humanly very moving review by Adolf Deissmann, in *Die Hilfe. Wochenschrift für Politik, Literatur und Kunst* XII/37, September 9, 1906, 16. Cf. also Fr. Jodl in *Neue Freie Presse*, September 10, 1905 (gratefully acknowledged by Cohen in "Ethics," xii); Johannes Weise: *Die Begründung der Ethik bei Herman Cohen*, Erlangen, 1911.

31. In *Ost und West. Illustrierte Monatsschrift für modernes Judentum*, ed. L. Winz, 5 (1905) cols. 14560, 223–232. Cf. also Julius Guttmann, "Hermann Cohens Ethik," in *Monatsschrift für Geschichte und Wissenschaft des Judentums* 49 (1905), 384–404.

32. Emil Fackenheim: *Hermann Cohen - After 50 Years*. Leo Baeck Memorial Lecture 12, New York, 1969.

33. Jakob Klatzkin, *Hermann Cohen*, 2nd ed., Berlin, 1921, and other versions thereof.

34. For example, H. Lilienfeld, (n. 8).

35. For example, Th. Sternberg in: *Juristische Wochenschrift* 35 (1906), 671f.

36. H. Kantorowicz in *Archiv für Sozialwissenschaft und Sozialpolitik* 31 [n.s. 13] (1910), 602–606 (the journal of Weber and Sombart).

37. In *Archiv für Sozialwissenschaft und Sozialpolitik* 25 (1907), 573–612 (part I), 29 (1909), 895–930 (part II). The last thirty pages of the Second part are devoted to Cohen.

Chapter 12. The Title of Hermann Cohen's *Religion of Reason out of the Sources of Judaism*

1. The first edition was published in Leipzig in 1919. Later editions have been published as follows: 2d ed., Frankfurt, 1929 (reprint, Cologne, 1959); 3rd ed., Wiesbaden: Fourier, 1966; 4th ed., Bonn: Bouvier. The English translation by Simon Kaplan, introduction by Leo Strauss, was published in New York by Ungar, 1972. A Hebrew translation by T. Wislawsky, annotated by S. H. Bergmann and N. Rotenstreich, introduction by S. Ucko, epilogue by I. ben-Shlomoh, was published in Jerusalem by Mossad Bialik, 1971. In a lecture delivered by Ernst Cassirer on "Hermann Cohen's Philosophy in its Relation to Judaism" before the Franz Rosenzweig Memorial Foundation in April 12, 1931 (Verene cat. no. 207/a, b, e), the original, first title is surprisingly still used. Verene says that it was "apparently not published." Since it is unknown, I want to give a summary of it here. It consists of forty-four manuscript pages, in English and for an English audience. The lecture may be said to consist of four parts: 1–9, a long, beautiful, and very personal introduction about Cohen; 9–15, about Cohen's Kant interpretation; 15–23, about religion in general in Cohen's systematic works (22–25 about "idealized religion"); and 23–44, about Judaism as universal ethics, by way of Cohen's Maimonides interpretation. Two small points strike the attention of a Cohen expert: Cassirer quotes Cohen's posthumous work by its first and false title: "Die (!) Religion der Vernunft . . ." (9, 43), and he uses the notion of "mind" in a rather un-Cohennian, psychologistic, quasi-Natorpian way. Comp. Verene catalog no. 78, also designated as "apparently not published," undated, which handles exactly the same subject more briefly, soberly, and technically,

in German. For the problem of the horrible condition of the text of the first edition, cf. Bruno Strauss's epilogue in the 2d ed., 6:3–29. (Re Bruno Strauss, cf. his entry in *International Biographical Dictionary of Central European Emigrés* 1933–1945 [Munich: K.G. Saur, 1983], 2, pt. 2:1137. What does not come out in this article is how closely knit the world of the German-Jewish intelligentsia was: Bruno Strauss's father was a close friend of Cohen's when the former was a Jewish teacher in Marburg, and Bruno's brother married Ilse Hahn, sister of Edith, who in turn was Franz Rosenzweig's wife [Edith Hahn Rosenzweig Scheinmann]; in other words, Bruno Strauss was also *me'chuttan* to Rosenzweig (Bruno Strauss lectured on Cohen in Rosenzweig's *Lehrhaus* in the 1923–1924 semester).

2. Franz Rosenzweig quotes Robert Fritzsche as reporting Cohen's refrain: "Das Philologische muss immer in Ordnung sein": "Vertauschte Fronten," in *F . Rosenzweig—Der Mensch und sein Werk—Gesammelte Schriften*, vol. 3, ed. R. and A. Mayer (Dordrecht: Martinus M. Nijhoff, 1984), 235. (Rosenzweig's essay, in which this sentence occurs, is the centerpiece of my forthcoming study "Heidegger and Rosenzweig: The German and the Jewish Turn to Ethnicism" The Heidegger connection is the most interesting aspect of this last essay of Rosenzweig's, but actually it is a renewed discussion of Cohen's *Religion of Reason*.)

3. Cf. Cohen, *Ethik des reinen Willens* (*Werke*, vol. 7) (Hildesheim/ New York: Olms, 1981).

4. Cohen, *Jüdische Schriften*, (Berlin, 1924), 1:249; cf. also 33, 120, 175f.

5. *Religion of Reason*, 278, 291 [engl. 238, 249f.]. M.M. Findley puts forward the same thesis: cf. *History and Theory* 4/3 (1965): 294.

6. *Religion der Vernunft*, 535–543. Leo Rosenzweig is an unfortunately neglected figure in modern Jewish intellectual history. Born and educated in the talmudic Judaism of Lithuania, he studied with Cohen, earned his PhD with *La Restauration de l'a priori Kantien par Hermann Cohen* (Paris, 1927), and ended his life, unappreciated, as a teacher of midrash in the Jewish Theological Seminary of America in New York. To me he was a teacher and a friend.

7. Cf. Cohen's *Logik der reinen Erkenntnis*, (Logic of Pure Cognition), 1:8 and 2:2, on "the logic" and "the judgment of origin" (Cohen, *Werke*, vol. 6).

8. Cf. *Religion der Vernunft*, p. 83 [engl. 71]: "cause" in the sense of "prerequisite/condition" ("Vorbedingung").

9. Cf. Cohen's *Das Princip der Inifinitesimal-Methode und seine Geschichte* (The Principle of the Infinitesimal Method and Its History—a Chapter in the Foundation of the Critique of Cognition), Berlin 1883

(reprint in Cohen, *Werke*, vol. 10); *Logik*, 2d ed., 32, 79ff. (reprint in *Werke*, vol. 6); *Religion of Reason*, paras. 9, 14, 15, and p. 76. (In order to "logicize" the still partially mythological notion of "beginning," Cohen prefers to speak not of *creatio ex nihilo* but of *creatio ab nihilo* [*Logik*, 84].)

10. *Religion der Vernunft*, 517 [engl. 448].

11. Ibid., 284 [engl. 243].

12. Cf. Benzion Kellermann, "Die philosophische Begründung des Judentums," in *Judaica, Festschrift zu Hermann Cohens siebzigsten Geburtstage* (Berlin, 1912, 94: Judaism as "the originating concept" of ethics).

13. For "idealization" cf. S. Schwarzschild, "'Germanism and Judaism': Hermann Cohen's Normative Paradigm of the German-Jewish Symbiosis," in *Jews and Germans from 1860 to 1933: The Problematic Symbiosis*, ed. David Bronsen (Heidelberg Carl Winter, 1979), 142–154. In this volume, pp. 93–118.

14. *Religion der Vernunft*, 39f. [engl. 34], the end of the "Introduction," *Jüdische Schriften*, 168.

15. Cohen, "Dem 50-jährigen Doctor medicinae Herrn Sanitaetsrath Dr. S. Neumann ein Festgruss," *Allgemeine Zeitung des Judentums* (September 16, 1882), 447f. (Cf. Marx's famous and notorious statement in "On the Jewish Question" that Christianity is practical Judaism!)

16. Cohen, *Jüdische Schriften*, 2:308f., and in "Religiöse Bewegungen der Gegenwart," *Jüdische Schriften* 1:64, and *Der Begriff der Religion im System der Philosophie* (The Concept of Religion within the System of Philosophy) (1915), 120 (reprint Cohen, *Werke*, vol. 10). Rosenzweig, then, in *The Star of Redemption*, assigned precisely this role to Judaism—to keep Christianity on the straight and narrow, as it were! (Cf. *The Star of Redemption*, trans. W.W. Hallo [New York: Holt, Rinehart 8: Winston, 1970]), 399–402.

17. Cf., for example, *Neue jüdische Monatshefte*, 1:106–111, 135–138 (on Gunkel); 1:509–514 (on Wilhelm Herrmann); 1:652–654 (on Troeltsch); 2:45–49 (on Luther); 2:178–181 (on Wellhausen), and so on. (My copy of *Neue jüdische Monatshefte* was given me, with his extensive marginalia, by Leo Rosenzweig.) Cf. Walter Jacobs, "Hermann Cohen on Christianity," *C.C.A.R. Journal* (January 1970), 61–69 (also published as *Christianity through Jewish Eyes: The Quest for Common Ground*. Hebrew Union College Press, 1974], chap. 9). (Cohen's personal library, now in the National Library in Israel, comprised a large number of books on Christianity and Bible criticism.)

18. For Herrmann, cf., for example, *Schriften zur Grundlegung der Theologie Wilhelm Herrmanns*, Theologische Bücherei, vol. 36 (Munich: Chr. Kaiser, 1965). Cohen's discussions with Paul Natorp, which are implicitly also a Jewish-Christian polemic and which centered on Natorp's *Religion innerhalb der Grenzen der Humanität* (Religion within the Bounds of Humanity) (1894), 2nd 1908 ed. with a new epilogue that addresses Cohen, are analyzed in greater depth in the second section of my introduction to *Religion of Reason*. Some people never learn: Christoph v. Wolzagen, "Schöpferische Vernunft. Der Philosoph Paul Natorp und das Ende des Neukantianismus" (!), *Frankfurter Allgemeine Zeitung* (March 17, 1984), no. 66, apostrophizes the Natorp-Heidegger line at the expense of Cohen.

19. Cf. Schwarzschild, "Germanism and Judaism," 145f., in this volume pp. 112–113.

20. For Cohen's argument against Tröltsch, cf. n. 17 earlier. Cohen's close disciple and friend, Benzion Kellermann, the radical Reform rabbi, wrote a whole monograph in this sense, *Der ethische Monotheismus der Propheten und seine soziologische Würdigung* (*The Ethical Monotheism of the Prophets and Its Sociological Evaluation*), but it was turned down by the journal *Logos* in the same spirit in which the Kant-Studien published Bruno Bauch's racist doctrine of a "German Kant" vs. a "Jewish Kant" at the time, so that Kellermann had to publish it separately (Berlin: Schwetschke, 1917). Cf. H. Liebeschütz, *Von Georg Simmel zu Franz Rosenzweig* (Tübingen: Mohr Siebeck, 1970), 198f.; and cf. Wendell Dietrich, *Cohen and Tröltsch: Ethical Monotheistic Religion and Theory of Culture*, Brown University Judaic Studies (Providence, 1985), chap. entitled "Hermann Cohen's Objections to E. Tröltsch's Interpretation of the Prophetic Ethos" (Comp. *Jüdische Schriften*, 2:481) .

21. Cf. Grimm's *Wörterbuch*, the etymology of "mere" (Latin merus) in relationship to *purus* ("pure"). ("Blösse" = "naked") ideas require phenomenal garb, "naked virtue," "chaste."

22. One has to keep in mind, of course, that, unlike the *Critiques*, Kant's *Religion within the Limits of Reason Alone* was not originally composed as one continuous work; it is a compendium of several essays. Under these circumstances a degree of imprecision is understandable. The textual misfortune that befell Cohen's last work, as we have noted, may then be regarded as another partial analogue.

23. Cf. Nathan Rotenstreich, "Religion Within the Limits of Reason Alone and Religion of Reason," *Leo Baeck Institute Year Book* 17 (1972); 187—for the rest, a misinterpretation.

24. Cf., however, Schwarzschild, "Franz Rosenzweig's Anecdotes about Hermann Cohen," in: *Gegenwart im Rückblick—Festgabe f. d. Jüdische Gemeinde zu Berlin*, ed. H. A. Strauss and R. K. Grossmann (Heidelberg: L. Siehm, 1970), p. 35–42 of this volume.

25. Cf. Hugo S. Bergmann, *Faith and Reason* (Washington, DC: B'nai B'rith, 1961), chap. 2; Paul Gruenewald, *Hermann Cohen*, Schriftenreihe der Landeszentrale für politische Bildung (Hannover, 1968), 32, 35, 48; Nathan Rotenstreich, *Jewish Philosophy in Modern Times* (New York: Holt Rinehart 8: Winston, 1968), 64; Eugen Rosenstock-Huessy, *Judaism Despite Christianity* (University: University of Alabama Press, 1969), 40; Karl Loewith, "Philosophie der Vernunft und Religion der Offenbarung," *Sitzungsberichte d. Heidelberger Akademie d. Wissenschaften, Philosophisch-Historische Klasse* (1968), 7. Abhandlung; Joseph Klein, *Die Grundlegung der Ethik in der Philosophie Hermann Cohens u. Paul Natorps—eine Kritik d. Neukantianismus* (Göttingen, Vandenhoeck & Ruprecht, 1976), 8, 23, 137f., 146, and so on, which has to be used with the greatest wariness: cf. Schwarzschild, "Germanism and Judaism," 208, n. 36; even Henning Günther, *Philosophie des Fortschritts: Hermann Cohens Rechtfertigung der bürgerlichen Gesellschaft* (Munich: W. Goldmann, 1972), 5, 80ff., 110.

26. Cf. on Ferdinand Toennies, "Ethik und Sozialismus," *Archiv f. Sozialwissenschaft v. Sozialpolitik* 25 (1909): 895–930, and the Cohen-Toennies correspondence, 1893–1918, in the Cohen-Archives of the University of Marburg, nos. 127–179, 1109; Günther, 44–46, 95f., 111, 116, "Geschichte und Dialektikverweigerung." (Joachim Kahl writes stupid bolshevik attacks on the Marburg School: "Joseph Dietzgen und der Neukantianismus," in *"Unser Philosoph" J. Dietzgen*, ed. H. D. Strusing [Frankfurt Marxistische Blätter, 1980], 146–160, and "F. A Lange und Hermann Cohen—Begründer der Marburger Schule des Neukantianismus und philosophische Wegbereiter des Revisionismus," *Universität und demokratische Bewegung-Ein Lesebuch zur 450-Jahrfeier der Philipps-Universität*, ed. D. Kramer and C. Varija (Marburg: Verlag Arbeiterbewegung und Gesellschaftswissenschaft, 1977), 123–147.

27. Cf. H. Holzhey, *Kants Erfahrungsbegriff* (Basel, 1970), 13, 199–244. Basically this historical line can be described by the names Ortega y Gasset—Natorp—Nikolai Hartmann—Heinz Heimsoeth (cf. Heinrich Knittermeyer, "Zu H. Heimsoeths Kantdeutung," *Kant-Studien* 49 [1957–58]; 193f.)-Knittermeyer himself—Husserl—Heidegger—Bultmann—Barth, and so on. (An important post–World War II link in this chain is also Hans Wagner, *Philosophie und Reflexion* [Munich

Basel: Ernst Reinhart, 1957]; cf. his p. 50, 60, 124f., and so on for Wagner's self-defined genealogy.)

28. Cf. Guenter, 116, and so on: Hans Ludwig Ollig, *Religion und Freiheitsglaube—Zur Problematik von Hermann Cohens später Religionsphilosophie*, Monographien zur philosophischen Forschung, no. 179 (Königstein: Forum Academicum, 1979), for example, 4f., 106f., 163, 171f., 354.

29. For example, Martin Buber, "The Love of God and the Idea of Deity," in *Eclipse of God* (New York: Harper, 1952)—though Buber admits that Cohen never changed his mind on the ideal character of "God" (cp. also Buber's famous attack on Cohen's anti-Zionism, "Concept and Reality" [*Der Jude*, 1:281–289, and "Zion, the State, and Mankind . . ." [ibid., 425–433]); ben-Schlomoh's ideological attack on Ucko's insistence on "the God-idea," 15ff., 20f., 489ff., 508; Eliezer Schweid, "The Foundations of Hermann Cohen's Religious Philosophy" (Hebrew), *Jerusalem Studies in Jewish Thought*, vol 2, no. 2 (1982–83), which rightly, if in a pedestrian fashion, arrives at basically the same conclusions as do we here and yet, at the end (306), extrapolates Cohen via Rosenzweig and Buber to a "Land of Israel" lesson. Cf. also Mordecai Kaplan, *The Meaning of God in Modern Jewish Religion* (New York Jewish Reconstructionist Foundation, 1937), 44: "For God must not merely be held as an idea, He must be felt as a presence, if we want not only to know about God but to know God"; Emil Fackenheim, *Encounters between Judaism and Modern Philosophy—a Preface to Future Jewish Thought* (New York: Basic Books, 1973), 131ff., 248; and *Hermann Cohen—after 50 Years*, Leo Baeck Memorial Lecture, no. 12 (New York: Leo Baeck Institute, 1969), 5, 10ff., et al.

30. "Hermann Cohens Begriff der Korrelation," in *In Zwei Welten—Bishnay Olamot*: On S. Moser's 75th Birthday (Tel-Aviv, 1962), 397; cf. also Schwarzschild "Truth: The Connection between Logic and Ethics," in *Judaism* 15 (Fall 1969): 466 (in this volume p. 29–31); and "The Tenability of Hermann Cohen's Construction of the Self," *Journal of the History of Philosophy* 13 (July 1975): 368, n. 30, 371, n. 39 (in this volume p. 69–92); Sinai Ucko, "Compassion: Notes on Hermann Cohen's Philosophy of Religion" (Hebrew), Iyyun 20 (January 1969): 24 (Ucko was an editor of the 2nd ed.: cf. n. 1 earlier, and, for his treatment of Cohen, cf. ibid., 7–30).

31. Cf. Cohen, Begriff der Religion, 103f. (reprint Cohen, *Werke*, vol. 10).

32. *Religion of Reason*, chap. 7: and "Der heilige Geist," *Jüdische Schriften*, 3:176–196.

33. Cohen, *Jüdische Schriften*, 1:265f.

34. Cohen *Kants Begründung der Ethik*, 74f.: we should say: "only a phenomenon," not "only an idea" (reprinted in Cohen, *Werke*, vol. 2).

35. *Religion der Vernunft*, 480 [engl. 414]. Cp. Maimonides' Code, "Book of Knowledge," 2:10, and his *Guide for the Perplexed*, 1, chaps. 53, 68.

36. Cohen, *Jüdische Schriften*, 3:135. If anything, Cohen wrote to his disciple and intimate Benzion Kellermann to the contrary, on February 16, 1908: "For me the ontological valence ('Seinswert') of God does not coincide with the ideal of eternity. Therefore, I can ethically demand the adoration of the idea of God in addition to moral action. Thus I affirm cult. And thus also the bulk of ritual. Why do we always think of the dietary laws when we speak of ritual and not rather of holy communion?" (A private letter in the possession of the Kellermann family. It contains also Hebrew notes by Cohen in script.)

37. Cf. Cohen, *Ethik*, 528f. "(The prophets) religion is morality" (*Werke*, vol. 7).

38. Strauss, 625.

39. Cf. my introduction, Olms ed., VIIIf, p. 120 of this volume.

40. Compare the table of virtues in the last third of Cohen's *Ethik* and *Religion of Reason*, chaps. 18–22, to Alasdair MacIntyre, *After Virtue* (University of Notre Dame Press, 1981), and W.F. Frankena, *Ethics*, 2nd ed. (Englewood Cliffs, NJ: Prentice-Hall, 1973), 62–70. Cf. H. Holzhey, "Hermann Cohens Weggang aus Marburg," *Neue Zürcher Zeitung* (March 21, 1971), 49f., which describes Cohen's moving farewell lecture at Marburg University in 1912, again devoted to the virtues; and Leo Strauss, "Introduction" to Kaplan's English trans. of *Religion of Reason*, XXIV, XXXVI, K. Loewith, 9, Wilhelm Kluback, *Hermann Cohen—The Challenge of a Religion of Reason*, Brown Judaic Studies 53, Chico, CA: Scholars Press, 1984, devotes itself entirely to Kant's and Cohen's treatments of the virtues. Unfortunately, he comes to the wrong conclusion—in line with the Rosenzweigian thesis discussed above. (Cf. my review in *Idealistic Studies*, pp. 202–203 of this volume.)

41. On creation, see *Religion of Reason*, chap. 3, especially paras. 7ff., and chap. 5: "The Creation of Man in Reason." For cross-reference, see, for example, *Religion of Reason*, 73.

42. Cohen, *Begriff der Religion*, 1915 (Cohen, *Werke*, vol. 10, Hildesheim, 2002).

43. Cf. Schwarzschild, "Germanism and Judaism," 130f., p. 94f. of this volume.

44. Cf. Schwarzschild, "Franz Rosenzweig's Anecdotes about Hermann Cohen," 213f., in this volume, p. 40.

45. Cp. Mrs. Cohen's original introduction, para. 2. Jews usually refer to their fathers in Hebrew as "my father and my teacher."

46. The epigraph is missing in the 3rd ed. Cf. Lev. 16:30, Yoma 85b. (Cohen preferred to quote the *gemara ad locum*, rather than its text in the *mishnah*.)

47. On the reversal of the two questions, cf. Strauss, 625; cp. also L. Rosenzweig's correct Hebrew text, ibid., 539, *ad locum*.

48. *Religion der Vernunft*, 260f. [engl. 223–224]. On 260 he includes pantheism in this.

49. Cp. Julius Guttmann, *Die Philosophie des Judentums* (Munich, 1933), 361f. (the end of the book).

50. David Silverman, in his English translation of Guttmann's chapter on Cohen in *History of Jewish Philosophies*, 260ff., misses the point entirely by mistranslating the mishnah, Guttmann, and Cohen!

51. Cp. Maimonides, Code, "Law of Repentance," 2:2, and so on, and Schwarzschild, "On Jewish Eschatology," in *Human Nature in Jewish and Christian Faith*, ed. F. Greenspahn (New York: Ktav, 1985), 26. Notice, in particular, *Code*, "Laws of Ritual Baths," 11:12 (the climax not only of this section but of the entire "Order of Laws of Purity") where (1) a Hebrew pun on "mikveh" ("hope") and "mikvah" ("bath") is operative throughout, (2) Ezek. 36:25 is silently collocated with Lev. 16:30, and (3), while the laws of ritual baths are designated as divine fiat (*khok*), they are then daringly interpreted as "the waters of pure reason" (*dahat hatahor*)! Hermann Cohen picked up this pun: cf. *Jüdische Schriften*, 21:1ii.

52. Cf. Loewith, 6.

Chapter 13. History of the *Religion of Reason*

1. Hermann Cohen, *Das Prinzip der Infinitesimal-Methode und seine Geschichte*, Berlin 1883 (reprinted in Cohen, *Werke*, vol. 5, Hildesheim, 2012).

2. Helmut Holzhey, "Vor und nach dem Krieg–Zur Revision unseres Bildes vom Neukantianismus," in *Neue Zürcher Zeitung*, October 18–19, 1980.

3. Cohen, "Dem 50 jährigen Doctor medicinae Hrn. Sanitätsrath Dr. Salomon Neumann ein Festgruß," *Allgemeine Zeitung d. Judentums*, September 16, 1892, 447–448.

4. Cohen, *Jüdische Schriften*, vol. 3, 197f., 202 (1916).

5. Cf. Franz Rosenzweig, "Atheistische Theologie," in *Kleinere Schriften*, 278–290, in English: Franz Rosenzweig, "Atheistic Theology: From the Old to the New Way of Thinking" (trans. Robert G. Goldy and H. Frederick Holch), in: *Canadian Journal of Theology* 14.2 (April 1968): 79–88.

6. Paul Natorp, *Religion innerhalb der Grenzen der Humanitat: ein Kapitel zur Grundlegung der Sozialpadagogik*, Tübingen, 1908.

7. Ibid., 86ff.

8. Ibid., 90.

9. Ibid., 117.

10. Ibid., 121–124.

11. Cf. Th. Mahlmann, "Das Axiom des Erlebnisses bei Wilhelm Herrmann," in *Neue Zeitschrift für systematische Theologie*, 4, 1962, 11–18, and Peter Fischer-Appelt, *Metaphysik im Horizont der Theologie Wilhelm Herrmanns*, Munich, 1965.

12. Cf. Wilhem Herrmann, *Schriften zur Grundlegung der Theologie*, Part II, Munich 1965, 55ff., 158ff., "Die Auffassung der Religion der Religion in Cohens and Natorps Ethik" (1090), 208ff, 215, 222, and "Der Begriff der Theologie nach Hermann Cohen" (1916), especially 318–323.

13. Holzhey, diss., XCIII–XCVI, 109, 97–104.

14. Ibid., 99.

15. Cf. Cohen, *Begriff der Religion*, 32f. (reprint: Cohen, *Werke*, vol. 10).

16. Holzhey, 100.

17. Ibid., 101. Cf. Cohen, *Begriff der Religion*, 66: "Christ partakes of the ambivalence of pantheism . . .," and *Religion of Reason*, 30f. on Spinoza, pantheism and Christianity.

18. Cohen, *Begriff der Religion*, 85–107.

19. Cohen, *Religion der Vernunft*, 23ff. [engl. 21–23].

20. Paul Celan, *Gedichte*, Frankfurt 1975, vol. 1, 280.

21. Cohen, *Religion der Vernunft*, 131–207 [engl. 113–177].

22. Cohen, "Charakteristik der Ethik Maimunis," in Bacher (ed. et al.), *Moses ben Maimon*, vol. I, Berlin 1908, 63–134, new edition in Cohen, *Werke*, vol. 15, Hildesheim 2009, 161–269, English trans. and commentary Almuth Bruckstein, *Ethics of Maimonides*, Madison 2003.

23. Cohen, *Charakteristik*, 120. *Werke*, vol. 15, 248.

24. The street in Tel Aviv named after Cohen bears on one side street signs with his German name and on the other signs with this Hebrew name of his.

25. Cohen, *Religion der Vernunft*, 25, 219–229 [engl. 22, 187–196].
26. Ibid., chap. 6, "Attributes of Action," 109–115 [engl. 94–99].
27. Cohen, *Jüdische Schriften*, vol. 1, 92ff.
28. Ibid., 134–139.
29. Cf. Steven Schwarzschild, "Law-Noachite," in *Encyclopedia Judaica*, and Cohen, Religion of Reason, 124.
30. Cohen, *Religion of Reason*, 152–156.
31. Cf. Cohen, *Religion und Sittlichkeit*, Berlin 1907, new edition: Cohen, *Werke*, vol. 15. Again, the total identity of this philosophical theology with Cohen's earlier systematic philosophy is easily demonstrated. All of the argument here extracted from his last writings is embodied in the expert testimony he gave in 1888 before a court in Marburg, cf., with various changes, introduced into later editions, "Der Nächste," Berlin, 1935 (ed. Buber). Compare also his treatment of Lev 19:18 ("you shall act lovingly toward your neighbor, for he is like you") in *Religion der Vernunft*, 137ff. [engl. 120f.], and in "Der Nächste" (op. cit.).
32. Cohen, *Begriff der Religion*, 137 (reprinted in *Werke*, vol., 10).
33. Schwarzschild, "Franz Rosenzweig's Anecdotes about Hermann Cohen," pp. 37–38 of this volume.
34. *Jüdische Schriften* and so on.
35. Cohen, *Der Nächste*, Berlin 1935 (ed. Buber).
36. *Der Jude*, vol. 1, 1916, no. 5, "Einige Worte über Hermann Cohen," 316–319.
37. Ibid., 281–89.
38. Ibid., no. 7, p. 425–33, "Zion, der Staat und die Menschheit."
39. Cf. Davke, (Yiddish), vol. 8, no. 32, Buenos Aires, 1957, Aron Steinberg, "Incidental Conversations in Hermann Cohen's School," and Chief-Rabbi Jacob Maze of Moscow, "Perspectives," who, while hailing him as "the Cohen (= priest) of science" and ethics, argues with him in favor of Zionism: "Oh, our teacher and rabbi, we love your name for your great teachings, we and our children, till the end of time. But we want to add one doctrine, which is also prophetic: we want to return to our land."
40. My own copy of *Neue Jüdische Monatshefte* I/II has extensive marginalia by Leo Rosenzweig.
41. Cf., for example, *Neue Jüdische Monatshefte*, 1/2, October 25, 1916, 50–52, *Der Jude*, I, 1916/17, 149–156. Cohen here mentions in passing his parents' regular hospitality to Jews from Poland, his trip to Russia in 1914, his hope to go there again, and he constructs an "ideal" of

German-Jewish/Polish-Jewish synthesis. On p. 155 here Buber stipulates their disagreement on Zionism together with their full agreement on the immigration question.

42. Cf. Holzhey, Cohen und Natorp–Ein Beitrag zur Geschichte des Neukantianismus - Texte, Briefe, Interpretation, Zurich, 1974, p. CCIVff.

43. Cf. *Neue Jüdische Monatshefte*, I/1, 19–22, on the Jewish New Year, I/3, November 10, 1916, 79–82, on "faith(fulness) to God," I/4, November 25, 106–111, I/5, December 10, 135–138, on messianism (with reference to Gunkel's Bible-Critical work), I/6, December 25, 166–169, on religion and ethics, and many more.

44. Verlag der *Neuen Jüdische Monatshefte*, 1917, 2nd ed. 1918.

45. "Hermann Cohen," dated May 17, 1920, in *Korrespondenzblatt des Vereins zur Gründung und Erhaltung einer Akademie für die Wissenschaft des Judentums I*, Frankfurt: Kauffmann, 1920, 1–10.

46. Cf. Heimsoeth's and N. Hartmann's correspondence with one another during the war, while away from Marburg University.

47. Cohen, *Ethik des reinen Willens*, 1st ed., 602ff. (reprinted in Cohen, *Werke*, vol. 7).

48. Ibid., 417.

49. Cohen, *Ästhetik des reinen Gefühls*, 432 (reprinted in Cohen, *Werke*, vol. 8).

50. Cohen insisted on a lot of italics in his publications. Apart from the widespread German orthographic practice to this effect at the time, one suspects that this is an attempt on his part to reproduce in writing his oral rhethoric, which is universally lauded by those who heard him.

51. The list of university courses that Cohen taught, in the Hermann Cohen—Archives of the University of Zurich, shows that he offered "Psychology" in 1877/78, winter, 1879, summer, 1882, summer, "Psychology in Relation to Pedagogy" in 1885, summer, 1888, summer, 1890, summer, with an accompanying seminar, and, under sometimes slightly changed titles, "Psychology as Encyclopedia of Philosophy" in 1893, summer, 1896, summer, 1899, summer, 1902, summer, 1905/06, 1908/09, together with a companion seminar, 1916, summer.

52. Cf. P. Grünwald, *Hermann Cohen*, Schriftenreihe der Landeszentrale für politische Bildung, Hannover, 1968, 27, 44f., and even Ucko, loc. cit., 23.

53. This is behind the title "Psychology as Encyclopedia of Philosophy."

54. It is a great pity that Cohen's writings and lectures toward such a comprehensive philosophy of culture by way of psychology do not seem

to have been preserved. His personal library, now kept in bulk in the Israeli National Archives, contains a very large proportion of books and journals concerned with psychology.

55. Paul Natorp, *Einleitung in die Psychologie nach Kritischer Methode*, Freiburg, 1888.

56. Three vols., Berlin, 1916/1923; English: Yale University Press, 1953; vol. 1, 80: "Thus the critique of reason becomes the critique of culture." Comp. Marx's famous dictum about the critique of religion becoming the critique of society.

57. Cf. H. Holzhey, Cohen und Natorp–Ein Beitrag zur Geschichte des Neukantianismus - Texte, Briefe, Interpretation, diss., University of Zurich, 1974, L; Paul Natorp, *Allgemeine Psychologie nach kritischer Methode*, 1912, and *Allgemeine Psychologie in Leitsätzen*, Marburg, 1910. Wenrich de Schmidt's *Psychologie und Transzendentalphilosophie - Zur Psychologie-Rezeption bei Hermann Cohen und Paul Natorp*, Bonn, 1976, is a thoroughly inadequate treatment of this subject.

58. Library of the University of Marburg, Handschriften-Standardkatalog II–MS 697/839.

59. Hs 8331

60. Holzhey, CLXXIV.

61. Ibid., CLXXXV, CXCVIII, CCXI

62. Ibid., CCXV, CCXXV.

63. Bruno Strauss in Cohen, *Religion of Reason*, 624.

64. Ibid., 623, 627

65. Ibid., 623f.

66. See the eulogies in: *Neue Jüdische Monatshefte*, No. 15–16, 1918, p. 347–357.

67. The editors were Benzion Kellermann (an intimate disciple of Cohen's, one of the editors of "the Cassirer edition" of Kant's *Collected Writings*, and a Reform rabbi), Prof. Nathan Porges, Rabbi Nehemiah Nobel himself, Leo Rosenzweig, and Bruno Strauss: cf. Mrs. Cohen's preface to the first edition.

68. Bruno Strauss's father, a Jewish teacher, had been a personal friend of Cohen's in Marburg. Bruno Strauss' brother married Ilse Hahn, sister of Edith (Hahn) Rosenzweig (Scheinmann). Thus, Franz Rosenzweig and Bruno Strauss were *mechutannim*.

69. End of *Religion of Reason*, 1929, 623–29.

70. Cf. his "Die philosophische Begründung des Judentums," in: *Judaica - Festschrift zu Hermann Cohens siebzigstem Geburtstage*, Berlin, 1912, 75ff.

71. Cf. his "Compassion: Remarks on Hermann Cohen's Philosophy of Religion," (Hebrew), *Iyyun* XX/1-4, January–October 1969, 23–28, 312–314.

72. Though no disciple of Cohen's, Trude Weiss-Rosmarin understands him well (*The Jewish Spectator*, XXXI/5, May 1966, 6).

73. Cohen talks about Rosenzweig in his very last published letter, Holzhey, op. cit., CCXXV.

74. For Rosenzweig's revisionist attitude toward his teacher Cohen cf., for example, J. Fleischman, "Two Eternities - Franz Rosenzweig on Judaism and Christianity" (Hebrew), *Iyyun* V/1, 64–71.

75. Cf. Guttmann, *Philosophie des Judentums*, 360–366. Though on p. 358 he himself stipulates some reservation regarding his interpretation; my own "The Democratic Socialism of Hermann Cohen," last page (p. 21 of this volume), still follows this line.

76. Cf. Martin Buber, "Die Tränen - Zum 10. Todestag Hermann Cohens" (1928), in *Kampf um Israel—Reden und Schriften* 1921-1932), Berlin: 1933, pp. 180ff., and "Philon und Cohen- ein Fragment" (1928), ibid., 183ff., though in "The Love of God and the Idea of Deity" in *Eclipse of God*, he admits that Cohen himself would have disapproved of this revision of his thought; Mordecai Kaplan, *The Meaning of God*; who, despite his own Deweyite pragmatism, or perhaps because of it, says (244): "For God must not merely be held as an idea; He must be felt as a presence, if we want not only to know about God but to know God"; Sacher, *Modern Jewish History*, Delta, 1958, who, nonphilosopher that he is but even factually full of mistakes (411f.), says of Cohen (409) that he is "purely cerebral ... quite arid."

77. *Religion of Reason* (Hebrew), Jerusalem 1971, 481–511.

78. Ibid., 482ff.

79. Ibid., 491ff., 505.

80. Ibid., 501, 508–511.

81. Cf., for example, the almost hagiographic and mystical, indeed, "chassidic" description of Cohen at prayer in Geneva, before the war, by M. ben-Ami, "With Hermann Cohen on New Year's Day" (Hebrew), *Sefer haMo'adim*, vol. 1, 139–142, and in Poland on "The Day of Atonement" in *In Zwei Welten*, op. cit., by Shai Agnon, 17 (Hebrew).

82. See Dimitri Gawronski (a favorite disciple of Cohen's and close friend of Cassirer) "Ernst Cassier–Leben und Werk," in Paul Schilpp (ed.), *Ernst Cassirer*, Stuttgart 1966, p. 11 on the emotional power of Cohen's practical reason.

83. Frankfurter Israelitisches Gemeindeblatt (VIII/9, May 1930), 357–359.

84. Ibid., 359–361.
85. Fedor Stepun, *Vergangenes und Unvergängliches aus meinem Leben* (1184–1914), München 1947, p. 110, on Marburgian influence in Moscow and throughout Russia.
86. David Singer and Moshe Sokol report that Soloveitchik "had hoped to prepare a dissertation on a very different subject: Plato and Maimonides. The project never materialized because no one of the philosophical faculty of the University of Berlin qualified to supervise it." In fact for Kant himself and for Cohen and his Jewish disciples the two subjects are not really so very different ("Josef Soloveitchik–Lonely Man of Faith," in *Modern Judaism*, 1982, 268, n. 24).
87. Soloveitchik, *On Repentance* (Hebrew), ed. p.H. Peli, Jerusalem, 1975.

Chapter 14. The Theologico-Political Basis of Liberal Christian-Jewish Relations in Modernity

1. Ronald Rotunda, "The 'Liberal' Label: Roosevelt's Capture of a Symbol," in *Public Policy*, vol. 17, 1968, 378.
2. Rotunda, *The Politics of Language—Liberalism as Word and Symbol*, University of Iowa Press 1986; also Stanley Aronowitz, "The Decline of American Liberalism," in *New Politics*, vol. 1, 1, 1986, 54: "It is important to note that what Europeans call liberalism is generally called conservatism in the U.S., and both major wings of American liberalism are roughly parallel to what is sometimes designated as right-wing social democracy in Europe."
3. Arthur Liebert, *Der Liberalismus als Forschung, Gesinnung und Weltanschauung*, Zurich, 1938, 85: "Die Partei der Freiheit und des Liberalismus hat nicht nur die Aufgabe und die Pflicht, sondern sie vor allem besitzt auch die einzigartige Möglichkeit, eine vernunftmäßig einleuchtende und eine moralisch überzeugende Verbindung zwischen den Polen herzustellen, die sonst in ihrer Auswirkung in katastrophaler Weise entweder allzu sehr nach rechts oder allzu sehr nach links hinstreben und hingeraten."
4. See Schwarzschild, "'Germanism and Judaism'—Hermann Cohen's normative paradigm of the German-Jewish Symbiosis," in *Jews and Germans from 1860 to 1930: The Problematic Symbiosis*, ed. D. Bronsen, Heidelberg, 1979, 162. In this volume, p. 99.
5. Marjorie Lamberti, *Jewish Activism in Imperial Germany—The Struggle for Civil Equality*, Yale University Press 1978, chap. 3, 41.

6. Ibid., 51 and chap. 3 and 4. Her thesis, that official German Jewry was a self-respecting and honorable echelon, not the craven "assimilationists" that they are commonly represented as, is, however, fully convincing.

7. Klaus E. Pollmann, "Der Nationalliberale Rudolf von Bennigsen," in *Der Nationalliberalismus in seiner Epoche*, Baden-Baden, 1981, 3: "Am Ende dieses Abschnitts ist der Liberalismus unter der Führung Bennigsens soweit nach rechts gerückt, daß es fraglich erscheint, ob er überhaupt noch seine Parteibezeichnung liberal zu Recht trägt."

8. James J. Sheehan, *German Liberalism in the 19th Century*, University of Chicago Press, 1978, especially the last chapter, "The Wilhelmine Age 1890–1914" and particularly p. 244, 250, 258, 267f.

9. The present-day Free Democratic Party in the Federal Republic naturally likes to boast of Jews in its ranks in the past; R. Sassin, *Widerstand, Verfolgung and Emigration Liberaler* 1933–1945, Bonn, 1983, the largest bulk of whose political biographies deals with Jews. But (1) the earlier liberals-cum-Jews were typically Left Liberals; (2) almost all of the Jews were thoroughly de-Judaized, totally assimilated and Germanized, if not actually baptized Jews; and (3) especially the later Jewish Liberals, Rathenau, for example, were, of course, members of high finance and high capital. Still, nowadays it is as popular and respectable to discover one's Jewish greatgrandfather as it was fifty years ago to lose him.

10. The following is taken from my "Modern Jewish Philosophy" in *A Handbook of Jewish Theology*, ed. A.A. Cohen, P. Mendes-Flohr, New York, 1986, 628ff.

11. In *Salo W. Baron Jubilee Volume*, English section, vol. 2, Jerusalem, 1974, 919–938. Compare P. Ettinger, *The Critique of Judaism in the Teachings of the Young Hegelians as One of the Roots of Modern Antisemitism* (Hebr.), Israel Academy of Sciences, 1968.

12. Georg G. Iggers, *The German Conception of History—The National Tradition of Historical Thought from Herder to the Present*, Middletown, CO: Wesleyan University Press, 1968.

13. Iggers, ibid., 169, on Weber. Compare Uriel Tal, "Theologische Debatte um das 'Wesen' des Judentums," in *Juden im Wilhelminischen Deutschland* (ed., E. Mosse et al.), Tübingen, 1976, quoting Greive on the growth of "sacral nationalism" and of the "folkish"-proto-racist conception of nationhood in Germany in the second half of the nineteenth century.

14. Iggers, 207.

15. Ibid., 288, the end of this chapter in Iggers: even after World War II Meinecke "ascribes a significant share of the responsibility for this

process (of modernization) to the negative and disintegrating influence of the Jews"; ibid., 355, n. 228: "The positive elements of Hitlerism"(!).

16. Trans. R. Kimber, Princeton University Press, 1970. To me the most outrageous part of the book is the very first footnote (p. 10), "On the natural (!) foundations of the nation (i.e., blood and soil), Bauch, "Vom Begriff der Nation, 1916." For the role of this potboiler of Bauch's see note 30 in this section.

17. For all this, compare also George A. Kelly, *Idealism, Politics and History - Sources of Hegelian Thought*, Cambridge University Press, 1969, 21ff.

18. Sheehan, 234: "Jurisprudence, for example, became dominated by a legal positivism which deemphasized the political implications of the law, removed the critical impulse from the concept of the *Rechtsstaat*, and turned legal theory into an uncritical defense of the status quo." Compare note 53 below on philosophy of law in the context of our problematique.

19. Compare Wendell S. Dietrich, "Loisy and the Liberal Protestants," *Sciences religieuses/Studies in Religion* 14 (1985): 303–311, where it becomes quite clear that what I shall be arguing below, namely that German Protestant Liberals wanted to collapse philosophico-theological normativity into an historical reality, also applies to the liberal Roman—Catholics and that the only point on which any of them quarreled was which historical facts also constituted normative and ultimate values.

20. Uriel Tal, *Christians and Jews in the Second Reich 1870–1914—A study in the Rise of German Totalitarianism* (Hebr.), Jerusalem, 1969, 33–36 on Theodor Mommsen's identification of Christianity with Germany. The ultimate radicalization of this notion was perpetrated by the "German (-Nazi) Christians," against whom the Confessional Church had to rise. Ibidem, 246 and U. Tal, "On Modern Lutheranism and the Jews," in *Leo Baeck Institute Year Book*, vol. 30, 1985, 203–213.

21. In *American Historical Review*, vol. 91, 3, 1986.

22. Ibid., 573ff.

23. Ibid., 574.

24. See Schwarzschild, "Germanism and Judaism," pp. 93–118 of this volume.

25. Werner T. Angress, "The German Army's Judenzählung of 1916," in *Leo Baeck Institute Year Book*, vol. 23, 1978, 117–137.

26. Helmut Holzhey, *Cohen und Natorp*, Basel & Stuttgart, 1986.

27. Schwarzschild, "The Lure of Immanence—The crisis in Contemporary Religious Thought," in *Tradition*, 1967, 78f. (again in *The Pursuit of the Ideal*, ed. M. Kellner, p. 61–81)

28. Dühring, *Der Ersatz der Religion durch Vollkommeneres und die Ausscheidung alles Judentums durch den modernen Völkergeist*, Karlsruhe, 1883.

29. Chamberlain, *Immanuel Kant—Die Persönlichkeit als Einführung in sein Werk*, München, 1905.

30. Note 16 earlier.

31. I use primarily: Tal, *Theologische Debatte*, 599-632, and his canonical *Christians and Jews*, especially chap. 4, "Protestantism and Judaism in Liberal Perspective," 121-171. I have not used the English translation of this book, *Christians and Jews in Germany - Politics and Ideology in the Second Reich 1870-1914*, Ithaca, 1975. Also, the only recently rediscovered "Das Wesen des Judentums," in Franz Rosenzweig, *Zweistromland, Gesammelte Schriften*, Bd 3, ed. R.A. Mayer, Dordrecht 1984, 521ff.

32. Sheehan, 255.

33. Tal, *Theologische Debatte*, 623, describes the situation pithily: "Zu Ende des 19. und zu Beginn des 20. Jahrhunderts fanden sich die beiden liberalen Lager gleichmäßig von der befreienden und erlösenden Kraft der Vernunft, der Aufklärung und vielleicht sogar des Intellekts enttäuscht. Beiden war das Gefühl gemein, daß die Systeme des Rationalismus und Liberalismus keine ausreichende Antwort auf die Fragen der Zeit boten. Können Judentum oder Christentum das Herz und den Verstand des modernen Menschen ansprechen im Zeitalter der Technologie und der Herrschaft des Empirismus, Pragmatismus und der positiven Wissenschaft?"

34. Kelly, *Idealism*, 316.

35. Iggers, 273 (compare also p. 147), where he goes on to delineate the typical dichotomy that was then stipulated between this German spirit and simplicistic "Western" (Anglo-French) "civilization," the "is"/"ought" distinction (as though David Hume had not been justified on this score by Kant).

36. Iggers, 174.

37. Wendell Dietrich, *Cohen and Troeltsch - Ethical Monotheistic Religion and Theory of Culture*, Brown University Judaica Series 1986. Ernst Troeltsch, "Der historische Entwicklungsbegriff in der modernen Geistes - und Lebensphilosophie. II. Die Marburger Schule, die südwestdeutsche Schule, Simmel," in *Historische Zeitschrift*, vol. 124, 1921, 389-395; Troeltsch, *Was heißt Wesen des Christentums*? Gesammelte Schriften, vol. 2, 386-451.

38. Vol. 4/5, columns 57-62.

39. Freed, 573: "German historiography has always had a tendency to be zeitbedingt:(!) . . . German historians may not have been Nazis themselves, but their conservative nationalistic views had much in common with Nazi ideology."

40. Cohen, *Neue jüdische Monatshefte*, vol. l, 652–654.

41. *Neue jüdische Monatshefte*, 1916–1917, Heft 8 (25.1.1917), 227.

42. It was published in a series that revolved about the war. Several monographs in the series were concerned with the relationship of Jews and Judaism toward Germans and Germany. *Logos* rejected Kellermann's study exactly as at the time the *Kant-Studien* rejected Ernst Cassirer's reply to Bruno Bauch's Teutonization of Kant, see note 16, 30 earlier.

43. In an article, "The Philosophy of the Bible," also written in 1917 but published posthumously in *Jüdisch-liberale Zeitung* vom 27, Juni 1924, Kellermann put this point formulaically: "The absoluteness of the prophetic Weltanschauung prohibits the absolutization of all non-prophetic goals of culture and life."

44. Kellermann, *Der ethische Monotheismus*, 635.

45. Ibid., 24.

46. Cohen publicly identified himself with Kellermann's reply to Troeltsch. Rabbi J. Galliner, in a letter of condolences to Mrs. Kellermann on her husband's death (26 September, 1924—the sons of B. Kellermann have kindly let me have copies of these and other documents), quotes Cohen: "Kellermann replied to (Troeltsch's) harshest attack that an alleged science in this age of antisemitism has brought upon us. His reply comes from the full depth and clarity of philosophical methodology, from comprehensive mastery ot the Bible-Critical material, and from an illuminating treatment of the relevant questions . . ." (a full monograph Benzion Kellermann is long overdue).

47. At this point the Marburgers tend to make the same mistake that the German-Protestant liberals make, namely they identify, inconsistently with either their progressive evolutionism or with their infinitely futuristic theories, a past occurrence with rational, regulative values. Kellermann should have argued that the Prophets ought to be read as he reads them, not that they said and meant what he himself wishes to say.

48. An interesting and little-known example of this attitude is Moritz Lazarus, *Unser Standpunkt, Zwei Reden an seine Religionsgenossen am 1. und 16. Dezember 1880*, Berlin, 1881. It turns, of course, on the Treitschke Affair, which was then at its height. For present purposes I cull from it only the point that . . . "my colleague Treitschke" (22) is, rightly, said to

assert that it is at best with "difficulty," if at all possible, to be civilized without being Christian. However, "for us there is something still higher, namely that which is one and the same in Christianity and Judaism ... and which will in the future unify them" (36).

49. Leo Baeck, *Judaism and Christianity*, trans. Walter Kaufmann, Philadelphia 1958, "Romantic Religion." Compare Walter Jacob, "Leo Baeck on Christianity," in *Jewish Quarterly Review*, vol. 56, 2, 1962, 158–172 (Jacob, *Christianity through Jewish Eyes—The Quest for Common Ground*, Hebrew Union College Press, 1974, chap. 13).

50. It has rightly been pointed out that in Baeck's last major work, *The People Israel: The Meaning of Jewish Existence*, New York, 1965, the place of Judaism "has been taken by this people Israel," and the place of "essence" has been taken by "existence." In other words, the very partial concretization of Judaism in his first major book has been greatly expanded. On the other hand, this should not be exaggerated into a total metamorphosis, as Albert Friedlander rightly shows in: *Leo Baeck—Leben und Lehre*, Stuttgart, 1973, 209ff. (Also, Baeck remained throughout his long and much-tried life the, if anything excessive, gentleman: as in *The Essence of Judaism* the name of von Harnack never occurs in the text, although he is the chief target, so in *This People Israel* Israel is always modestly referred to as "this people.")

51. Pace's talk about "the religious genius of the Jewish people" (*Jüdische Zeitung*, Jg. 3, No. 63) (compare Max Wiener, *Jüdische Religion im Zeitalter der Emanzipation*, Berlin, 1933, 55, etc.) and Leo Baeck's talk about "Israel as a particular type of religious personality among the nations, endowed with religious creativity: this is the core of Baeck's thinking" (Friedlander, op. cit. p. 79, 85, 101: "The counter-piece to Harnack's Golgatha is Baeck's People of Israel").

52. Joachim Doron, "Rassenbewußtsein und naturwissenschaftliches Denken im deutschen Zionismus während der wilhelminischen Ära," in *Jahrbuch des Instituts für deutsche Geschichte*, Bd. 9, 1980, 421: (Max Brod) "Wir streichelten die Höllenhunde, die an ihren Ketten zerrten."

53. Per contra note 18 earlier.

54. My introduction to Cohens *Ethik des reinen Willens*, Hildesheim and New York, 1981, p. 17f. (in this volume, p. 127-128).

55. My former student and friend Henricus van der Linden, *Kant's Ethics and Socialism*, Indianapolis, 1987.

56. Joseph Mali, "Ernst Cassirer's Interpretation of Judaism and its Function in modern Political Culture," in *Jahrbuch des Instituts für deutsche Geschichte*, Beiheft 10, 1986.

57. Helmut Holzhey, "Vor und nach dem Krieg—Zur Revision unseres Bildes vom Neukantianismus," in *Neue Züricher Zeitung* vom. 18–19. Okt. 1980.

58. Cohen, "Dem 50jährigen Doctor medicinae Herrn Sanitätsrath Dr. S. Neumann," in *Allgemeine Zeitung des Judentums*, September 1882, 447f.

59. Cohen, *Jüdische Schriften*, vol. 3, 1916, 197f., 202.

60. Paul Natorp, *Religion innerhalb der Grenzen der Humanität: Ein Kapitel zur Grundlegung der Sozialpädagogik*, Tübingen, 1908 (see the Nachwort).

61. Holzhey, *Cohen und Natorp*, vol. 2, 424

62. Natorp, *Religion*, 1908, 86ff.

63. Natorp, *Religion*, 90.

64. See Schwarzschild, "The Religious Stake in Modem Philosophy of Infinity," in *Daat*, Bar-Ilan University, Spring 1987, p. 185–196 of this volume.

65. Natorp, *Religion*, 1908, 117.

66. Ibid., 121–124.

67. Wilhelm Herrmann, *Schriften zur Grundlegung der Theologie*, vol. 2, München, 1965, 885. Theologische Bücherei, vol. 36. Compare also Herrmann, *Die Auffassung der Religion in Cohens und Natorps Ethik*, 1909, vol. 2, 208, 215ff., 222, and Herrmann, *Der Begriff der Theologie nach Hermann Cohen*, 1916, 318–323.

68. Holzhey, *Cohen und Natorp*, 99–102.

69. Ibid., 99.

70. Compare Cohen's *Begriff der Religion*, 32ff. (reprint in Cohen, *Werke*, vol. 10).

71. Holzhey, 100.

72. Ibid., 101. Compare also *Begriff der Religion*, 66: "Christ partakes of the ambivalency of pantheism ... ," and *Religion der Vernunft*, 52 [engl. 44–45] on Spinoza, pantheism, and Christianity.

73. Cohen, *Ethik des reinen Willens*, 1904, 235; *Religion der Vernunft*, 25 [engl. 22]: "And now the question of thou and I (Die Frage von Du und Ich) can begin anew," and 245 [engl. 209]: "All dialogue with God, by Abraham as by Moses. . . ." A note of Natorp's, dated June 3,1923, A.4.C. in his posthumous papers at the University of Marburg, reads: "Vermittlung mit Bubers Ich und Du."

74. See Schwarzschild, "The Tenability of Cohen's Construction of the Self," in *Journal of the History of Philosophy*, vol. 13, 1975, no. 3, 368, note 29 (p. 239 of this volume) about Karl Loewith's *Das Individuum in der Rolle des Mitmenschen*, München, 1928.

75. Karl Löwith, *Philosophie der Vernunft und Religion der Offenbarung in Hermann Cohens Religionsphilosophie*, Heidelberg, 1968, 14, 23 (originally a lecture at the University of Marburg on the fiftieth anniversary of Cohen's death); compare also his *Religion der Vernunft und Religion der Offenbarung*—Hermann Cohen, dem deutschen Juden zum Gedächtnis, in *Neue Rundschau*, Heft 4, 1968, 644–660.

76. Löwith, *Philosophie der Vernunft*, 43.

77. Albert Görland, *Die Grundweisen des Menschseins*, Hamburg, 1954; published posthumously.

78. Ibid., 103.

79. Ibid., 60.

80. Natorp. *Platons Ideenlehre*, Leipzig, 1921.

81. Joseph Klein, "Nikolai Hartmann und die Marburger Schule," in "N. Hartmann—Der Denker und sein Werk," Göttingen, 1950, and I. Vuillemin, "La dialectique negative dans la connaissance et l'existence" (Note sur l'épistemologie et la metaphysique de N. Hartmann et de J.-P. Sartre), in *Dialectica*, vol. 4, 1950, 22–31.

82. The very title of his *Studien zur Philosophie Immanuel Kant—Metaphysische Ursprünge und ontologische Grundlagen*, Köln, 1956. Hinrich Knittermeyer, who had himself taken his philosophical direction, then even claims, on his own as well as on Heimsoeth's behalf, that the later stages of Cohen's very neo-Kantianism, not to speak of his commitment to Jewish philosophy, that is, his Logic, and so on, were "on the way to metaphysics and ontology. ("Zu Heimsoeths Kantdeutung," in *Kant-Studien*, Bd 49, 3, 1957–58, 293ff.).

83. C.M. Arroyo, *El sistema de Ortega y Gasset*, Madrid, 1968, 53–90, 399f.; Julian Marias, *Ortega. I. Circunstancia y vocación*, Madrid, 1960, 209–217; N.R. Orringer, "Simmel's Goethe in the Thought of Ortega y Gasset," in *Modern Language Notes*, vol. 92, 1977, 300–304.

84. Roger A. Johnson, *The Origins of Demythologization—Philosophy and Historiography in the Theology of Rudolf Bultmann*, Leiden, 1974.

85. Ibid., 38ff.

86. Compare H.W. van der Vaart Smith, "Die Schule Karl Barths und die Marburger Philosophie," in *Kant-Studien*, vol. 34, 1929, 333–350. (It is amusing to watch K. Loewith—note 74 cite on the same page Cohen's perennial polemic against immanentist Christology and his influence on Barth, op. cit. 12, note 22.) Also H. Herrigel, "Die Theologie Wilhelm Herrmanns," in *Zwischen den Zeiten*, Bd. 5, München, 344, about Barth's alleged attempt "to rescue Herrmann from the danger of liberalism" (by

what might be called "Buberianizing," "dialogicizing" him). Herrigel argues that Herrmann cannot so be saved.

87. Johnson, *Demythologization*, 41, 59, and so on.
88. Ibid., 58.
89. For Gadamer on Natorp and Cohen his introduction to Natorp, *Philosophische Systematik*, Hamburg, 1958, xi–xvi.
90. Johnson, *Demythologizatio*, 79.
91. Hans-G. Gadamer, "Heidegger und die Marburger Theologie," in *Philosophical Hermeneutics*, University of California Press, 1976; (where "Marburg theology," ironically, has nothing to do anymore with Cohen and the Jews that surrounded him but refers to Natorp, Herrmann, Bultmann, etc.).
92. For Cohen and Gadamer, see Steven Schwarzschild, "Authority and Reason," in *Studies in Jewish Philosophy*, vol. 2: "Reason and Revelation as Authority in Judaism," Melrose Park, Academy for Jewish Philosophy 1982, 45–63 and for Habermas' misunderstanding of Gadamer as a "Marburger," ibid., 59, note 21.
93. H.R. Niebuhr, *Faith and Ethics*, P. Ramsey (ed.), New York, 1957, 47f. on Barth's: personalization and hypostatization of Cohen's concept of "origin."
94. In *Abhandlungen der Akademie der Wissenschaften in Göttingen*—Philosophisch-Historische Klasse, Folge 3, No. 100.
95. Klein, 7f.
96. Ibid., 7, and so on. Compare also J. Klein, *N. Hartmann*, 111.
97. Klein, *Grundlegung der Ethik*, 13, and so on.
98. Ibid., 8, and so on.
99. Ibid., 112, and so on, and compare Toni Cassirer, *Mein Leben mit Ernst Cassirer*, Hildesheim, 1981, 144–146, 200, 260ff., for Görland's atrocious behavior under the Nazis.
100. Klein, 138.
101. Ibid., 20, and so on.
102. Ibid., chap. 4, where, 259, 283, the connections to Heidegger und Gadamer are intimated, and 20, 36–40, and so on.
103. Ibid., 277f., 291f.
104. Ibid., p. 295.
105. Compare Klein, 111f.
106. Sheehan, 280ff.
107. Sheehan, 283.
108. My introduction to *Religion of Reason*, p. 141–149 of this volume.

109. Joseph M. Bochenski, *Contemporary European Philosophy*, Berkeley, Los Angeles 1957, 89.
110. Cohen, *Schriften zur Philosophie und Zeitgeschichte*, Berlin, 1919.
111. Knittermeyer, 293.
112. Friedrich Niewöhner, "Primat der Ethik oder Erkenntnistheoretische Begründung der Ethik? Thesen zur Kant-Rezeption in der jüdischen Philosophie," in *Judentum im Zeitalter der Aufklärung*, Bremen u. Wolfenbüttel 1977, 119–161. Wolfenbütteler Studien zur Aufklärung, Bd. 4.
113. Ibid., 125ff., 132ff.
114. In *Monographien zur Philosophischen Forschung*, no. 179, Königstein i. Ts., 1979, 105f. (I abstain here from a critique of this academic dissertation as a whole.)
115. Ollig, 4, 171f., 353f., 361.
116. Mechthild Dreyer, *Die Idee Gottes im Werk Herrmann Cohens*, Königstein i. Ts., 1985. Monographien zur Philosophischen Forschung, no. 230. My review of this in *International Studies in Philosophy*, p. 204–207 of this volume.
117. New York, 1983.
118. *Religion of Reason*, Hebrew trans. T. Wislawsky, Jerusalem 1971, epilogue by ben-Shlomoh, 489ff., 508.
119. See Schwarzschild, "An Agenda for Jewish Philosophy in the 1980's," in *Studies in Jewish Philosophy*. 1.: "Jewish Philosophy in the 1980's," ed. N. Samuelson, Melrose Park, 1981, 55–71.
120. Leo Loewenthal, "The Integrity of the Intellectual: In Memory of Walter Benjamin," in *The Philosophical Forum*, vol. 15, 1–2, 1983–84, 150: "The Jewish assimilation to Philosophical liberalism (with or without socialist coloring) was all the more hopeless, since spiritual liberalism in Germany had always remained something foreign." (Compare ibidem, p. 155—the essay is translated into awful English.)
121. Quoted as a motto to Peter Viereck's *Metapolitics: From Romantics to Hitler*, New York, 1941.
122. Viereck, 575.

Chapter 15. The Religious Stake in Modern Philosophy of Infinity

1. Cf. J.N. Findlay, *Hegel: A Re-Examination*, New York, 1962, 163, 173ff., 181; Hegel's *Phänomenalogie des Geistes*, Stuttgart, 1951, 465, 473ff.

2. For Herbert Marcuse's summary of this distinction in "The Jena System" cf. his *Reason and Revolution: Hegel and the Rise of Social Theory*, Boston, 1964, 68ff.

3. Cf. *Grundlinien der Philosophie des Rechts* (German), Stuttgart, 1952, para. 184. This, too, is directed against Kant: an "ought"-comp. *Science of Logic*, I, 155, quoted from William H. Werkmeister, "Hegel's Phenomenology of Mind as a Development of Kant's Basic Ontology," in Darrel E. Christensen, ed., *Hegel and the Philosophy of Religion*, The Hague, 1970, 100. Cf. also Findlay, 219, 240–269.

4. This is the only "actual infinite" that Aristotle and the Greeks generally allowed: *Physics* III/4–8, especially 265–267. *Metaphysics* II/2, XI/10. *Nich. Ethics*, chapter 2: "In Pythagorean terminology evil is a form of the Unlimited, good of the Limited." Cf. also O.J. Baendel, *Symbolism of the Sphere—A Contribution to the History of Earlier Greek Philosophy*, Leiden: Brill, 1977. In Greek *peros* is "limit," and *aperon* is "infinite = no-limit."

5. Cf. Findlay, *Hegel*, 173, 219.

6. Carl Friedrich, *The Philosophy of Hegel*, the Modern Library, 1954, 39, 164, 380, 463 (Phenomenology).

7. Findlay, 164; *Large Logic*, 87, W 49.

8. Hegel, *Phänomenologie*, 481; Findlay, 162–164, 173f., 180 (Science of Logic). I think too little attention has been paid to the fact that the whole Hegelian/Marxist/Sartrean business of "in-and-for-itself" is an elephantine ordinary-language pun. No later than by Kant the noumenon was designated in German as das Ding-an-sich, "the thing in itself." Now, for the ordinary English phrase "in itself" or "in and of itself" (or *per se*) the Germans say *an-und-für-sich*. Hegel just expanded the Kantian *terminus technicus* and built a whole metaphysic on it!

9. "Intensive magnitude" is, of course, an important *topos* in Kant. To put it most summarily, by means of this conceptualization Kant made it possible to mathematize what has been and is usually considered to be the scientifically, mathematically, inaccessible experience of "quality," qualitative predicates, and so on. Science in a large number of fields has since Kant profited greatly from this Kantian analysis. It would be another large topic to study Kant's logic of "nothing" cf. his marvelous categorialization of nothing in the *First Critique* and Cohen's *Kant's Theorie der Erfahrung*, 2nd ed., 1885, for example, 435 on the function of the *nihil privativum*. Hermann Cohen greatly deepened it and expanded its serviceability. (Cf. below). This whole Hegelian discussion has to be put in its historical context—between Leibniz' relationless, noumenal

monads, Kant's phenomenal categories of relations, Hegel's interpretation of Leibniz and Kant, L.A. Feuerbach's full-volume treatment of an Hegelianized Leibniz, and Marx's use of Leibniz, Kant, and Hegel (cf. e.g., Bertell Ollman, *Alienation: Marx's Conception of Man in Capitalist Society*, Cambridge, 1976), and so on—Marburg neo-Kantianism took up the Kantian logic of "infinite judgments" (cf. G.R.G. Mure, *A Study of Hegel': Logic*, Oxford, 1950, 179) and especially of negative infinite judgments: (1) A is not B (negative judgment); (2) A is non-B (infinite judgment); (3) A is not non-B (negative infinite judgment), (Cf. Jakob Gordin, *Untersuchungen zur Theorie des unendlichen Urteils*, Berlin, 1929; Zwi Diesendruck, "Maimonides' Theory of the Negation of Privation," *PAAJR*, VI, 1934–1935, 139–151 and the literature there adduced. Gordin's whole book is really a confrontation of Hegel and Hermann Cohen on the present issue and on its full implications for their respective philosophical enterprises.) Hegel, to the contrary, prefers negations of negations, that is, "determinate negations" to negative infinite judgments as the source of infinity (which is thus also "determinate") (cf. Q. Lauer, *The Triumph of Subjectivity—An Introduction to Transcendental Phenomenology*, 450; Gordon, 18–28). Gordin, 164, n. 23 then trenchantly formulates the basically religious issue that underlies this logical and mathematical debate like this: "The difference between Hegel's 'negation of negation' and the method of infinite judgment (comp. Hermann Cohen, *Das Prinzip der Infinitesimal-Methode und seine Geschichte*, intr. Werner Flach, Frankfurt, 1968) becomes acute in a particularly clear way in the religious problematic, specifically in the doctrine of the attributes. (Comp. Diesendruck, loc. cit., and Hermann Cohen, *Religion of Reason out of the Sources of Judaism*, Frankfurt, 1929, chapter 6. "Attributes of Action," especially 131–134, 464–467). Hegel's doctrine of the negation of negation aims at the "representation of the self-determination of God toward Being" (*Logic*, II, 356) and represents (even apart from pantheistic motifs) the method of "perfectionist" theology, the theology of the *ens perfectissimum*. On the other hand, the adequate expression of the method of infinite judgment is the doctrine of "negative attributes" (Maimonides and others). The systematic core of this doctrine consists of the negation of negative attributes, which leads not to the affirmation of positive attributes with respect to God, their predication of him, but to their affirmation in themselves, for themselves, as principles and foundings of the order of mankind and the world."

10. Findlay, *Hegel*, 164, 204. Comp. Josef Klein, *Die Grundlegung der Ethik in der Philosophie Hermann Cohens und Paul Natorps—eine Kritik*

des Neukantianisrnus, Göttingen 1976 (an extremely dubious book with a very dubious history), 213, 235: the infinite takes up residence in the finite and thus becomes history and the individual.

11. Cf. Friedrich. 463, 487 (Phenomenology). This then becomes the Hegelian version of the noumenal self: cf. *Philosophy of Right*, ibid., 238.

12. lbid., 50ff. (*Philosophy of History*). *Vorlesungen über die Philosophie der Religion*, Hegel, *Werke*, vol. 17, eds. M. Moldenhauer and K.M. Michel, Frankfurt a/M 1969 "The Religion of Sublimity [Jewish]," 46–96, 83: "The Jewish God is only for thought."

13. Ibid., 273.

14. The "awful weariness" (Friedrich, 174), "the infinite anguish" (Findlay, 35) of "this bad infinity is the same in itself as the ever-recurring ought … the self-repeating monotony" (*Science of Logic*, I. 155, 164; *Phänomenologie*, 443). Comp. S.-F. Lyotard, *Le Différent*, Editions de Minuit, 1983, 168 on Hegel's Judaism as "mechanical abstractness."

15. *Phänomenologie*, ibid.,B)II).

16. Findlay. *Hegel*, 39–42; J.M.E. McTaggart, *A Commentary on Hegel's Logic*, Cambridge, 1910, 202f. (For a discussion of this cf. also M. Rubinstein, "Die logischen Grundlagen des Hegelschen Systems und das Ende der Geschichte," in *Kant-Studien* XI, 1906, 84ff. It is worth noting that Rubinstein tries to argue that Hegel contradicted himself, on his own terms, in insisting on the completed infinity (ibid., 96ff.), but it can be shown that he is mistaken on this score). The history of the idea of "tasting God" is extended and interesting: cf. *Psalms* 34: 8; R. Yehudah HaLevy, *Kuzari*, IV/17 in its context; the Yiddish *geshmackt* = "tasty/*es schmeckt aweg* = "in very good taste" (usually the precise contradictory of ordinary German *abgeschmackt*); in Hegel's *Phänomenologie*, B(l). The derogatory chapter on "culture," 443, even the expression *geschmeckt gesehen* = "seen tastily" occurs. The Kant-disciple, of a sort, Salomon Maimon, for Kantian as well as Jewish reasons, called the "metonomy" of thinking that we could "taste God" an "insipid synaesthesia … in need of metaphysical fumigation" (N.J. Jacobs, "Maimon's Theory of the Imagination," *Scripta Hierosomolytana*, VI, 264).

17. *First Critique*, "Dialectics," book 2, section 2, chap. 8, and following. Kant actually discusses at one point the Hegelian notion of good and bad infinities, without using such silly terminology: "The End of All Things," Cassirer ed., vol., 6, 418ff.: even in "practice," in Kant's sense of this term as well as in the ordinary sense, he affirms that continuous growth, even in some projected state of eternal bliss (cf. Schwarzschild, "On Jewish Eschatology," in *The Human Condition in the Jewish and*

Christian Traditions, ed. F. Greenspahn, New York, 1987) is preferable to a completed state of perfection.

18. Ibid., appendix, "Of the Ultimate Purpose." Comp. "Es gibt kein *quantum assignabile infinitum et infinitum parvum*" (quoted by Hermann Cohen, "Zur Orientierung in den losen Blättern aus Kants Nachlass," *Schriften zur Philosophie und Zeitgeschichte*, eds, A. Görland and E. Cassirer, Berlin, 1928, vol. I, 461). Cf. also Lucien Goldmann, *La communauté humaine et l'univers chez Kant*, Paris, 1948, especially 8 on Kant's "problematic" versus Hegel's "real" totality. (On "as-if" = Hebrew *kivyachol/ke'ilu* cf. Schwarzschild, "An Introduction to the Thought of R. Isaac Hutner," *Modern Judaism*, October 1985, 273. n. 154.)

19. In the Third *Critique* "the beautiful" is finite, "the sublime" (*erhaben* = *unaufgehoben!*) infinite.

20. Akademie-Ausgabe, vol. XVIII, 377f., N 5893. Cf. Lyotard, 293f., on Kant's beautiful apostrophe to Jewish iconoclasm versus Christian *Schwärmerei*—the former resulting in the ethical "presentation or the infinite," the latter in crazy "intuition beyond sensibility." (Comp. Schwarzschild, "The Jewish Kant," unpublished manuscript)

21. The broad historical line from Spinoza to Hegel and beyond should here, like elsewhere, he kept in mind. Spinoza's God = *sive natura* is, of course, infinite, but he is also "actual," if only because he is also extended = material. The direct line from here to the "actual infinity" of the British Spinozist/Hegelians is brought out in F.H. Hallet, *Aeternitas—A Spinozistic Study*, Oxford, 1930. "Excursus V: The Actual Infinite," 160-163 (and Hallet's concern with Bradley presumably sets the background to Bertrand Russell's interest in this question later: cf. nn. 37, 43, 84ff. below). The convergence of Spinoza, Hegel, Marx, and U.S.S.R. academic philosophy is then also illustrated on this score in, for example, A.M. Deborin, "Spinoza's World View" (1927), in G.L. Kline, *Spinoza in Soviet Philosophy*..., New York, 1952. 110, n. 2: "Spinoza makes a very important distinction between what is infinite by virtue of its essence or its own nature and what is infinite by virtue of its cause. This distinction is the same as Hegel's doctrine of good and bad infinities."

22. *Science of Logic*, I, 392f.
23. Friedrich, 59, 80 (*Philosophy of History*).
24. Findlay, 164; Marcuse, 139f.
25. Friedrich, 142 (*Philosophy of History*).
26. Ibid., 509-515. Cf. n. 16 above.

27. Cf. Findlay, 180f. *Science of Logic*, I, 392f., 464. I cannot here take the space to show how Hegel's rehabilitation, against Kant, of "the ontological proof" (cf. e.g. *Philosophie der Religion*, chaps. 5, 9, 10, insertions) and his argument against "negative theology" is part of his entire project.

28. A good overview of all this is given in the dissertation by Joseph Bloch, *Die Entwicklung des Unendlichkeitsbegriffes von Kant bis Cohen*, Berlin,1907.

29. Georg Cantor, *Gesammelte Abhandlungen*, ed. E. Zermelo. 1932, 470. Abraham Fraenkel in the biographical appendix.

30. Cantor, *Abhandlungen*, "Über die verschiedenen Standpunkte in Bezug auf das Unendliche," ibid., 372ff. "Grundlagen einer allgemeinen Mannigfaltigkeitslehre," ibid., 181, "Mitteilungen zur Lehre von Transfiniten," ibid., 378, and Joseph W. Dauben, "Georg Cantor and Pope Leo XIII - Mathematics, Theology and the Infinite," *Journal of the History of Ideas*, XXXVIII/1, January–March 1977, 92, 103.

31. Cantor, *Abhandlungen*, 76, 374, 400. Cantor's checkered religious biography, a father born a Jew and baptized a Protestant (Dauben's article, loc. cit., is a very useful study, but the author, while discussing the religious strain in Cantor's life and work very instructively, is totally unaware of his Jewish background. So is Lewis S. Feuer, despite his pervasive and perverse Jewish ideology, in "America's First Jewish Professor: James Joseph Sylvester at the University of Virginia," *American Jewish Archives* XXXVI/2, November 1984, 192, where he speculates that Cantor used the Hebrew alphabet for some transfinite numbers only because he got them from the Jew Sylvester)—Roman-Catholic mother, himself raised a Protestant, with, however, frequent and strong Roman-Catholic proclivities (Cantor, 482, and his letter to Cardinal Franzelin, 399ff. Fraenkel, in his biographical sketch, ibid., 458ff., says that it was "kein blosser Zufall, dass Cantor gerade auch bei den Scholastikern in die Schule gegangen ist," ibid., 478. For Fraenkel himself as professor at the Hebrew University, cf. his foreword to W. M. Feldman, *Rabbinical Mathematics and Astronomy*, London, 1931) may be seen as psychologically and even logically connected with his scientific, mathematical breakthroughs. One might also think that Cantor's assertion of the "givenness" of infinities can be understood sociologically in terms of the attitude of the "civil servant" in the Prusso-German empire, especially, perhaps, the super-assimilationist Jewish civil servant, who deals with "realities," not with fancy intellectual abstractions. Thus Cantor, who was, of course, a civil servant as a professor, first repeats Newton's *hypotheses non fingo* and then adds—talking about transfinite numbers: *Ich bin nur ein Berichterstatter*

und Beamter (Cantor, 480). It is difficult to judge whether one prefers such a sociological explanation of the last-quoted sentence or a psycho-pathological explanation, or both together—for Cantor also came to believe that God revealed his mathematical truths to him, while he himself merely transmitted them. Also otherwise Cantor suffered from serious and frequent mental breakdowns. (Cf. Dauben, loc. cit., 105f.)

32. Cantor, 399f. ("firm convictions" about "probably"?). Cf. also the quotation in Bloch, *Entwicklung*, 47. n. 108, in which Cantor's concerns with God, physical infinity, and mathematical transfiniteness are all merged.

33. Cantor, 206, 376, 391. Dauben's study, unlike Bloch's, avoids discussing the dimensions of philosophical prehistory to Cantor's theory. Cantor made the distinction between "absolute infinity" and "actual infinities" in order to side-step the Roman-Catholic accusation leveled at him of pantheism, and he succeeded with this ploy: cf. Dauben, loc. cit., 102f.: the former is *naturae naturans*, the latter *natura naturata*.

34. Cantor, 207, 375, and Bloch, op. cit. 46. n. 107.

35. Ibid., Mannigfaltigkeitslehre, 172.

36. Ibid., 165ff., *et pass*.

37. Cf. Bertrand Russell, *The Principles of Mathematics*, London, 1956, 330.

38. Original German: Theodor W. Adorno, *Jargon der Eigentlichkeit* Frankfurt 1964, english edition: *The Jargon of Authenticity*, Evanston 1973.

39. Cantor, 204f., 402f.; Dauben, loc. cit., 102: "This was a strong form of Platonism, but one to which Cantor repeatedly turned for support."

40. Indeed, Cantor acquired his degree at the university of Halle (Cantor, 474) for the same reason that Hermann Cohen went there. Cf. Rudolf Odebrecht, *Hermann Cohens Philosophie der Mathematik*, Berlin, 1906 (a dissertation in Erlangen, 1906) (generally a subject on which much work needs to be done), and Geissler, *Die Grundsätze und das Wesen des Unendlichen in der Mathematik und Philosophie*, Leipzig, 1902. In Hermann Cohen's private library, which is by-and-large preserved in the National Library in Israel, a large number of mathematical works testify to his scholarship also in this field. (I am indebted to the Deutsche Forschungsgemeinschaft for having helped me to survey Cohen's personal library in 1975/76). There is, for example, Husserl's *Philosophy of Arithmetic*, 1891, a good deal of Helmholtz, Darwin, Einstein, and so on. Even here Cohen's mind can perhaps be read more subtly: he had a lot of Markus Herz, Lazarus Bendavid (*Versuch einer logischen Auseinandersetzung des mathematischen Unendlichen*, Berlin, 1796, with

a full set of Cohen's typical markings), Moses Ensheim = Moses Brisac of Metz, *Recherches sur les calculs differentiels et integrals*, Paris, 1799, of course, Moses Mendelssohn and Solomon Maimon, and so on. I think he clearly thought there was a real "Jewish Stake" in the philosophical foundations of the mathematics of infinity.

41. Cohen, *Das Princip der Inifinitesimal-Methode und seine Geschichte*, republished in: *Schriften zur Philosophie und Zeitgeschichte*, Berlin, 1928, vol. 2, 137; cf. New edition by Werner Flach, Frankfurt 1968, 194 (reprint of the original editon from 1883 in Cohen, *Werke*, vol. 5, Hildesheim 200) and Max Simon, *Über Mathematik*: *Erweiterung der Einleitung in die Didaktik*, Gießen, 1908, 4 (see note 52 later).

42. *Deutsche Literaturzeitung*, 5, 1884. cols. 266–268.

43. Russell, *Principles of Mathematics*, 338–345. Cf. also Nelson, *Göttingische gelehrte Anzeigen*, 167 (1905), 610–630; Hessenberg, *Vierteljahrsschrift für wissenschaftliche Philosophie* 32 (1908), 405f.; Kantorowicz, in a particularly offensive review of the second ed. of Cohen's *Ethik*, *Archiv für Sozialwissenschaft & Sozialpolitik* XXXI (1910), 603, n. 2. For the a revival of the logic of "the infinitesimal" cf. the work of Abraham Robinson and its applications: *Non-Standard Analysis*, Amsterdam, 1966.

44. Cf. Simon, p. 27: "The infinitely large and the infinitely small are twin-concepts. They result from the same process. . . ." (Comp. on this also Bloch, loc. cit.) For its prehistory comp. Pascal on "the two infinities" (infinity and the infinitesimal) in *Of the Geometric Spirit*.

45. Paul Natorp, *Die logischen Grundlagen der exakten Wissenschaften*, Leipzig/Berlin 1910; here, too, the "Marburg"-reply to Cantor's critique is to be found; ibid., 222f., note 1.

46. Natorp, 163–170, 193–200. Cf. also Cohen, *Inifinitesimal-Methode* (in *Schriften zur Philosophie und Zeitgeschichte*, vol. 2) 153f. = paragr. 101 on different orders of infinity, and paragr. 53 on the (mathematically) "ontic status" of all numbers, not excluding infinity.

47. Cantor, 479.

48. Ibid., 377, 439.

49. Natorp, *Grundlagen*, second revised ed., Marburg, 1910, 36ff. (my translation).

50. For Veronese cf. Bloch, 49. n. 112.

51. Compare on this, systematically and brilliantly, Ernst Cassirer, "Kant und die moderne Mathematik (Mit Bezug auf Bertrant Russells and Louis Coutourats Werke über die Prinzipien der Mathematik)," *Kant-Studien* XII (1907), 25f. (Nothing less than Freudian blocks can explain

that the editors of the *Kant-Studien* cannot get Hermann Cohen's first-name initial right: 31, 38.)

52. Cf. Cassirer, 35–42. on "syntheticity"= scientific, "transcendental" applicability. Comp. also Max Simon, *Über Mathematik* (=*Philosophische Arbeiten*, eds. H. Cohen and Paul Natorp, vol. II/I), Giessen: A. Toepelmann, 1908, which, throughout, demonstrates the assiduous work that was being done in and near the Marburg School on the philosophy of mathematics in general and the close attention that was being paid, from the Cohen/Natorp viewpoint to Cantor's set-theory, Simon refers to Cantor as his childhood-friend (21) but more polemically than Natorp and contrary to Bloch argues the limit-method against set-theory. (Further on Simon [1844–1918] cf. Max Simon, *Nichteuklidische Geometrie*, [*Beihefte zur Zeitschrift für mathematischen und Naturwissenschaftlichen Unterricht*, no. 10], Leipzig/Berlin 1925, with a biography of the author that is also instructive as a German-Jewish exemplar. Simon's role in mathematics, especially non-Euclidian geometry, here comes out and §36 is a short neo-Kantian statement on the function of non-Euclidianism. The present author will, perhaps, be forgiven for one quotation, p. 94: "But that a non-Euclidian geometry is useful for conditions in the cosmos [beyond our solar system] the work of Schwarzschild and Einstein has made very probable.")

53. It appears from his dissertation that Bloch studied neither at Marburg nor with any "Marburgians." Despite this, he identifies himself fully, though not uncritically, with Cohen's philosophy: cf. chap. 5/3, and 63.

54. Bloch, 68; Cassirer, 15, 27, 30f.

55. Cf. Cassirer, loc. cit., 19 and 21, note 1, where he promises to answer Russell on the question of infinitesimals.

56. Bloch, 65, note 147.

57. Cohen, *Religion und Sittlichkeit—eine Betrachtung zur Grundlegung der Religionsphilosophie*, Berlin, 1907, *Jüdische Schriften* III, 98–168, new editon: Cohen, *Werke*, vol. 15, Hildesheim, 2009, 3–101.

58. The classic Jewish philosophical (in this instance Aristotelian) rejection of actual infinities in favor of God are Maimonides' "principles 1–3" in the Introduction to Part 2 of the *Guide*.

59. Paul Natorp, *Religion innerhalb der Grenzen der Humanität: ein Kapitel zur Grundlegung der Sozialpädagogik*, Tübingen, 1908, 96–99, 117–126.

60. Natorp, *Religion*, 101.

61. Ibid., 104.

62. Cf. Natorp, *Platons Ideenlehre*, 2nd ed., Leipzig, 1921.
63. Natorp, *Religion*, 121–124.
64. Cf. Wilhelm Hermann, *Schriften zur Grundlegung der Theologie* (Theologische Bücherei, vol. 36), Munich, 1965; Peter Fischer-Appelt, *Metaphysik im Horizont der Theologie Wilhelm Hermanns*, Munich, 1965.
65. Natorp, *Religion*, 111–117. Cf. also his draft-letter to Cohen of December 31, 1915 (Helmut Holzhey, *Cohen und Natorp, Der Marburger Neu-Kantianismus in Quellen*, vol. 2. Basel, 1986, 97ff., 444ff.), which completely turns on this question.
66. For other subsequent examples of Christian, ontologistic detections within "Marburg" cf. Heinrich Knittermeyer, "Zu Heinz Heimsoeths Kantdeutung," *Kant-Studien*, 49/3, 1957–1958, especially 299, 307 et al. on "actual infinity," and Albert Görland, *Die Grundweisen des Menschseins*, Hamburg 1954 (written in 1947), pp. 103, 160, about *"unendlich"* (indefinite) vs. *"ohnendlich"* ("actual infinity"), for Görland's dubious behavior under the Nazis cf. Toni Cassirer, *Mein Leben mit Ernst Cassirer*, Hildesheim, 1981, 144–146, 200, 260ff.
67. Cf. the list of derogatory terms compiled in W. de Schmidt, *Psychologie and Tranzendentalphilosophie–zur Psychologierezeption bei Hermann Cohen und Paul Natorp*, Bonn, 1976, 177: "subjectivism, subject-purism, logicism, theoreticism, mathematicism, scientism, positivism, problematicism, pan-methodism, rationalism, relationalism, etc."
68. Rosenzweig, "Das neue Denken," in *Kleinere Schriften*, Berlin, 1937, 298. For *cognoscenti* of the history of modern Jewish philosophy it may here be worth referring to Hugo Bergmann's *Das Unendliche und die Zahl*, Halle(!), 1913, which is "self-advertised" in *Kant-Studien*, VIII, 1913, 526f. and which, deriving itself from Bolzano, opposes both Cantor and Hermann Cohen.
69. Buber, "The Love of God and the Idea of Deity," in *Eclipse of God*, New York, 1952. This debate was renewed in the Hebrew translation of Cohen's *Religion of Reason*, trans. T. Wislawsky, Jerusalem, 1971, between Sinai Ukko in his introduction pp. 15ff., 20f. and Ben-Shlomoh in his epilogue, 489ff., 508.
70. On the Buber-Levinas relationship cf. Levinas' own writings on Buber, for example, "La pensée de M. Buber et le judaïsme contemporain," in *M. Buber, l'homme et le philosophe*, Brussels, 1968, 43–58, and so on, and some secondary literature, for example, P.N. Lawton Jr., "Love and Justice - Levinas' Reading of Buber," in *Philosophy Today* 20, 1976, 77–83.

71. Cf. Schwarzschild, "Jenseits von Sein und Zeit... (review)," *International Studies in Philosophy* XIV/1, 1981, 102–104.

72. Levinas, *Totality and Infinity*, Duquesne University Press, 1969.

73. Ibid., 196.

74. Ibid., 197, cf. also 204, 211, and so on. For philosophical discussions in the wake of Levinas, cf. Alphonso Lingis, "The Origin of Infinity," *Research in Phenomenology*, vol. VI, 1976, 27–45, Edith Wyschogrod, "Is Man Infinite? A Phenomenological Perspective," in *Infinity: Proceedings of the American Catholic Philosophical Association*, vol. 55, 1981, 108–117.

75. Cp. n. 71 above.

76. In *L'écriture u la différence*, Paris, 1967, 117–228.

77. Levinas, *Totality*, 158.

78. Ibid., 173.

79. Ibid., 172.

80. Ibid., 176f.

81. Ibid., 177f.; comp. 142f. note 2: "Perhaps one regrets that no systematic and patient confrontation particularly with Kant has occurred. To our knowledge a mere allusion, barely in passing, is made in an article ('L'ontologie est-elle fondamentale?,' *Revue de métaphysique et de morale*, 1951) to Kantian echoes and to Kant's practical philosophy, to which we feel particularly close."

82. Ibid. Cf. also S. Strasser, *Jenseits von Sein und Zeit–ein Einführung in E. Levinas' Philosophie*, Hague, 1978, para. 92, and my review of it—cf. note 71.

83. *L'écriture*, op. cit., "E. Jabes," 108.

84. In chap. 17.

85. Russell, *Our Knowledge of the External World as a Field for Scientific Method in Philosophy*, Chicago/London 1914.

86. Russell, *Our Knowledge*, 159. J. Thomson, "Infinity in Mathematics and Logic," *Encyclopedia of Philosophy*, vol. 4. 186ff.: even logicists, here Russell, hold that the algorithm ("the defining concept") that generates an infinite series is "given," and in this sense, therefore, also the transfinite series, which it can ("potentially") produce, is given, but they also have to admit that "the applicability of the notion of infinity or the conditions of its applicability," or "a physical exemplification" is, as Russell once expressed it, "medically impossible" (here: "cannot be reached by successive enumeration").

87. Russell, *Our Knowledge*, op. cit. 182.

88. Ibid., 208.

89. Schwayder, "Wittgenstein on Mathematics," in *Studies in the Philosophy of Wittgenstein*, ed. Peter Winch, London, 1969, 69–100.
90. Ibid., 72, 33. 86f.
91. Ibid., 89.
92. In *Philosophical Review*, 1959, 324–348.
93. Oxford: Clarendon Press, 1978.
94. Dummet, *Elements of Intuitionism*, 376, 389.
95. Ibid., 60, 401.
96. Ibid., 32.
97. Ibid., 6.
98. Ibid., 32.
99. Ibid., 55. Comp. ibid, 3.1: "The Notion of Infinity," 55–65.
100. I am indebted to my colleague Prof. Robert Barrett for conversations; on the subject of this paragraph.
101. Nelson Goodman and Willard V. Quine, "Steps Toward a Constructive Nominalism," in Nelson Goodman, *Problems and Projects*, Indianapolis, 1972, 173f. (with cross-reference to *The Structure of Appearance*). Cf. also *Roots of Reference*.
102. Willard V. Quine "On What There Is" (1948), in *From a Logical Point of View*, Harvard, 1980, 13.
103. Ibid., 14f.
104. Comp. also Richard S. Rudner. "What Do Symbols Symbolize? Nominalism." In *The Delaware Seminar: Philosophy of Science*, vol. 1, ed. B. Baumrin, 1963.
105. Quine, "On What There Is," 15–18. Here as elsewhere it would be worthwhile to show the important, though unconscious, convergences of as well as the important divergences between Quinean and, indeed, Goodmanite constructionalism and Marburg neo-Kantianism, but this take would take us too far afield. Comp. A. Robinson, para. 10:3 on set-theory: "Future generations of mathematicians, while accepting the formal results of Set Theory, may reject the platonistic claims commonly associated with it."
106. Cf. particularly *Set Theory and its Logic*, Harvard, 1970, especially 145, 282ff. and §30.
107. Cf. for this also Cassirer, *Kant und die moderne Mathematik*.
108. Steven Körner, *The Philosophy of Mathematics*, London 1960.
109. Körner, *The Philosophy of Mathematics*, 111; comp. his refutation of naive logicists, 62–66.
110. Ibid., 114; comp. 30f.

111. Ibid., 115.

112. Ibid., chap. 4. Comp. also Wolfgang Marx, *Transzendentale Logik als Wissenschaftstheorie—Systematisch-kritische Untersuchungen zur philosophischen Grundlegungsproblematik in Cohens 'Logik der reinen Erkenntnis'*, Frankfurt, 1977, 107f., 122f.

113. Dimitrios Markis, *Protophilosophy—Toward the Reconstruction of Philosophical Language* (German), Frankfurt, 1980, 235, says: "An understanding that thinks intuitively, i.e., that cognizes the actual infinite theoretically, or that cognizes theoretically the highest good as the ultimate purpose, or that cognitively grasps the teleology of nature in the way in which it grasps mechanism—such an understanding is for Kant unintelligible, untranslatable. When opponents claim such intuitive understanding or intellectual intuition—then they are, to be sure, infinite and 'holy' beings, but the *Critique of Pure Reason* was not written for them. . . . Such a [Kantian] metacritique is possible only at the price of humility, the limitation of our reason, i.e. its total and ultimate criticizability." Comp. ibid., 244: "The empirical infinity of understanding can never be supplemented by the actual infinity of reason."

114. *Meta-Mathematik*, Mannheim: Bibliographisches Institut, 1962, 9–13, and "Das Aktual-Unendliche in der Mathematik," in *Methodisches Denken*, Frankfurt, 1968, 94–101.

115. "Das Aktual-Unendliche," ibid.

116. For another and important dimension of this problematic one ought consider all the implications of the vulgarly scientific arguments of Eugen Dühring (cf. Bloch, 28ff.), well known as the enemy of Marx and Engels but less well-known as notorious antisemite: *Die Juden als Rassen-, Sitten- und Kulturfrage*, Leipzig, 1881, and *Der Ersatz der Religion durch Vollkommeneres und die Ausscheidung alles Judäerthums durch den modernen Völkergeist*, 1883. (Comp. J.A. Petrov, *Logische Probleme der Realisierbarkeits- und Unendlichkeitsprobleme*, Berlin-East, 1981.)

Chapter 16. Book Reviews

1. To read Maimon along with John Wild's classic *George Berkeley: A Study of His Life and Philosophy* (Cambridge: Harvard University Press, 1936) is to see striking parallels. Cf. also J. Solowiejczyk, *Das reine Denken und die Seinskonstituierung bei Hermann Cohen* (Berlin, 1932), 109f.: "The epistemological idealism of Cohen could conceivably pass

into a metaphysical spiritualism. The conclusions could be drawn from it which Berkeley once drew with complete radicalism, namely that Being is spiritual since it is identical with *percipi*. Though such a turn would be of a different character in Cohen, it would, in any case, be a consistent conclusion. (It is recognized that Natorp's philosophy, in his last period, became a metaphysical idealism.) Cohen was conscious of this danger and with all the means at his disposal guarded against a metaphysical interpretation of his system and against a spiritualistic transformation of his concepts. And he in fact succeeded in removing epistemological idealism as far as possible from metaphysical idealism."

Index of Names

Adorno, Theodor W., 188
Anselm of Canterbury, 192
Atlas, Samuel, vii, 16, 162, 170, 177, 197–201, 249n,

Baeck, Leo, 171, 175, 286n
Barth, Karl, 180, 181, 212, 272n, 288n, 289n
Bauch, Bruno, 97, 99, 170, 173, 231n, 250n, 251–252n, 254n, 262n, 271n
Bendavid, Lazarus, 50, 228n, 296n
Bernstein, Eduard, 104, 121, 134, 177, 210
Bismarck, Otto von, 1–2, 98, 135, 166, 168, 184
Boehme, Jacob, 54, 229n
Bradley, F.H., 83–84, 244n, 294n
Buber, Martin, xiii, xiv, xv, xxv, 23–24, 26, 44, 46, 47, 113, 132, 138, 156, 158–159, 176, 179, 192, 198, 212, 223n, 224n, 235n, 241n, 250n, 254n, 257n, 260n, 273n, 278n, 280n, 289n, 299n
Bultmann, Rudolf, 180–181, 212, 272n, 289n

Cantor, Georg, 56, 187–188, 190, 193, 195, 196

Carnot, Lazare Nicolas Marguerite, 52
Cassirer, Ernst, vii, 47, 59, 82–83, 97, 100, 110, 159, 160, 162, 170, 171, 177, 182, 190, 198, 204, 210, 213, 225n, 231n, 232n, 251–252n, 256n, 268n, 280n
Celan, Paul, 155
Chamberlain, Stewart Houston, 97, 170, 251n
Cohen, Gerson, 94, 148
Cohen, Martha (nee Lewandowski), 40, 94, 162, 209

Derrida, Jacques, 192–193, 218n
Descartes, Rene, 91–92, 110, 192, 246n
Diesendruck, Zvi, 110, 162
Dilthey, Wilhelm, 97, 168, 174
Dubnow, Simon, 101, 171

Ebbinghaus, Julius, 158, 205–206
Eisner, Kurt, 104, 121, 177, 210
Erikson, Erik, 79–82

Falk, Adalbert, 98, 101
Fichte, Johann Gottlieb, 70, 95, 197
Fischer, Kuno, 96, 99, 206, 254n
Frege, Gottlob, 193

Index of Names

Fromm, Erich, 47

Gadamer, Hans-Georg, 180–181, 289n
Galileo Galilei, 190
Gawronsky, Dimitri, 100, 104,
Goldmann, Nachum, 99, 254n
Goodman, Nelson, 83, 194, 195
Görland, Albert, 126, 128, 177, 180, 181, 182, 289n

Halevy, Yehuda, 37, 122, 225n, 293n
Harnack, Adolf von, 171, 172, 174, 175, 286n
Hartmann, Nicolai, 153, 180, 181, 213
Hegel, Georg Wilhelm Friedrich, 5–8, 23, 27, 46, 55, 84, 95–97, 103, 108, 113, 117, 134, 142, 167–169, 170, 172, 180, 185, 186, 187, 188, 192, 197, 212, 231n, 240n, 244n, 259n, 291n–295n
Heidegger, Martin, ix, xxv, 42, 45, 133, 153, 180, 181, 192, 218n, 225n, 239n, 247n, 256n, 269n, 271n, 272n, 289n
Heimsoeth, Heinz, 153, 180, 183, 272n, 278n, 288n
Helmholtz, Hermann von, 56, 66, 232n, 296n
Herrmann, Wilhelm, 133, 137, 144, 154, 172, 173, 179, 180, 191, 212, 267n, 270n, 288n, 289n
Herz, Marcus, 50, 52, 228n, 296n
Hirsch, Samson Raphael, 93
Husik, Isaac, 110
Husserl, Edmund, 56, 90–92, 153, 180, 192, 193, 247n, 248n, 272n
Hutner, Isaac, 149, 164, 212

James, William, 26, 223n, 237n
Jänsch, Erich F., 158, 256n

Kant, Immanuel, vii, xix, xx, xxi, xxiv, xxv, 2, 6, 15, 21, 23, 26, 27, 34, 37, 38, 41, 44–46, 50–52, 54–58, 62, 64– 67, 72, 73, 77–79, 82–87, 89–91, 95, 96, 99, 103, 106–110, 112, 114, 115, 119–124, 126, 127, 130, 132, 134, 144, 146, 147, 151, 152, 157, 158, 160, 167, 168, 170, 173, 176, 180, 182, 184–188, 190, 193, 195, 197, 198, 200, 202–204, 207, 209, 210, 211, 225n, 231n, 235n, 236n, 237n, 242n, 243n, 245n, 246n, 247n, 251n, 257n, 259n, 262n, 266n, 271n, 274n, 281n, 284n, 285n, 291n–295n, 300n, 302n
Karpeles, Gustav, 255n
Kellermann, Benzion, xv, 100, 110, 136, 138, 162, 173, 174, 215n, 232n, 256n, 257n, 271n, 274n, 279n, 285n
Kelsen, Hans, 128, 138, 176, 266n
Kierkegaard, Sören, 23
Klatzkin, Jakob, xv, 44, 99, 113, 138, 212, 254n
Krochmal, Nachman, viii, 8, 26, 112, 114, 174, 262n

Landauer, Gustav, 254n, 260n
Lange, Friedrich Albert, 40, 98, 101, 104, 139, 209, 231n
Lazarus, Moritz, 209, 285–86n
Leibniz, Gottfried Wilhelm, 51, 54, 55, 82, 110, 144, 190, 197, 230n, 245n, 291n, 292n

Index of Names | 307

Levinas, Emmanuel, 192, 193, 299n, 300n
Lewandowski, Louis, 158, 250n
Liebmann, Otto, 96, 170
Löwith, Karl, xviii, 180, 288n

Maimon, Salomon, 24, 26, 50, 197–201, 228, 242n, 293n, 302n
Maimonides, Moses, xvii, xviii, xx, xxi, xxiv, 3, 38, 39, 41, 45, 52, 53, 55, 106, 110, 147, 156, 203, 207, 211, 218n, 263n, 268n, 281n, 292n, 298n
Mann, Thomas, 97, 171
Marr, Wilhelm, 99
Marx, Karl, 4, 6, 7, 9, 11, 12, 15, 16, 97, 108, 237n, 270n, 279n, 292n, 294n, 302n
Meinecke, Friedrich, 97, 168, 171, 212, 251n, 263n, 282n
Mendelssohn, Moses, 50–52, 57, 66, 175, 297n

Napoleon (Bonaparte), 37, 52, 95, 98, 168, 229n
Natorp, Paul, 82, 90, 92, 96, 99, 100, 102, 106, 110, 111, 117, 126–128, 133, 136, 137, 139, 153, 154, 159–163, 170–173, 177–181, 183, 188, 191, 210, 212, 213, 228n, 232n, 243n, 244n, 247n, 251n, 267n, 271n, 272n, 287n, 289n, 298n, 303n
Naumann, Friedrich, 166, 168
Newton, Isaac, 52, 54, 55, 107, 190, 230n, 231n
Nietzsche, Friedrich, 84, 113, 171, 176, 192, 262n

Nobel, Nehemia, 138, 149, 162, 250n, 279n

Ortega y Gasset, José, 107, 158, 180, 213, 244n, 272n
Otto, Rudolf, 154, 178, 203

Paine, Thomas, 98
Planck, Max, 56
Plato, xx, xxiv, 14, 27, 44, 106, 110, 188, 195, 201, 211, 259n, 281n

Quine, Willard Van Orman, 194, 195, 301n

Reuchlin, Johannes, 53, 55
Rosenzweig, Franz, ix, xiii–xv, xvii–xix, xxv, 23–26, 29, 30, 33, 34, 36–39, 41, 46, 59, 113, 132, 133, 138, 142, 145, 159, 162–164, 176, 177, 181–183, 192, 202, 210, 212, 217n, 219n, 223n–225n, 260n, 263n, 269n, 270n, 273n, 279n, 280n
Rosenzweig, Leo, 44, 142, 161, 164, 177, 249n, 269n, 270n, 277n, 279n
Russell, Bertrand, 188, 193, 194, 294n, 298n, 300n

Sartre, Jean Paul, 90–92, 245n, 247n, 248n
Schelling, Friedrich Wilhelm, 55, 95, 197
Schiller, Friedrich von, xxiv, 73, 106, 112, 176, 237n
Schleiermacher, Friedrich, 137, 154, 178
Seligmann, Raphael, 158
Sellars, Wilfred, 89, 216n, 246n
Shoemaker, Sidney, 88, 89, 216n

Index of Names

Soloveitchik, Joseph, 24, 47, 149, 164
Spinoza, Baruch, 5, 23, 27, 192, 244n, 294n
Stammler, Rudolf, 126–128, 138, 176, 265n, 266n
Steinthal, Heymann, 160, 209
Strauss, Bruno, 162, 224n, 269n, 279n
Strauss, Leo, 38, 115, 218n, 225n, 263n, 268n
Strawson, F.P., 84–89, 216n, 241n, 245n

Tillich, Paul, 179
Tönnies, Ferdinand, 139, 172, 241n, 265n

Treitschke, Heinrich von, xxiii, 39, 97, 99, 166, 168, 175, 253n, 285n
Troeltsch, Ernst, 168, 171–174, 203, 270n, 285n

Veronese, Guiseppe, 189
Vico, Giambattista, 55
Vorländer, Karl, 104, 121, 127, 128, 177, 263n

Weber, Max, 105, 128, 132, 138, 168, 172, 174, 176, 268n
Wellhausen, Julius, xiv, 112, 144, 173, 174, 212, 270n
Wittgenstein, Ludwig, 83, 85, 88, 193, 194

www.ingramcontent.com/pod-product-compliance
Lightning Source LLC
Chambersburg PA
CBHW030128240426
43672CB00005B/63